Introduction to Japanese Politics

FIFTH EDITION

Louis D. Hayes

An East Gate Book

M.E.Sharpe
Armonk, New York
London, England

An East Gate Book

Library of Congress Cataloging-in-Publication Data

Hayes, Louis D.
Introduction to Japanese politics / by Louis D. Hayes. — 5th ed.
    p. cm.
"An East Gate Book."
Includes bibliographical references and index.
ISBN 978-0-7656-2278-5 (cloth: alk. paper)—ISBN 978-0-7656-2279-2 (pbk.: alk. paper)
1. Japan—Politics and government—1945– I. Title.

DS889.H394 2008
952.04—dc22   2008018084

Printed in the United States of America

BM (c)   10   9   8   7   6   5   4   3   2   1
BM (p)   10   9   8   7   6   5   4   3   2   1

Contents

Part VI. Conclusions

Preface

During the 1980s, it became popular in the West, and especially in the United States, to look upon Japan with a mixture of admiration and suspicion. Admiration was born of the fact that Japan had made enormous economic progress in a short time, allowing it to all but capture certain world markets, such as those of cameras and consumer electronics. This success produced suspicion that Japan somehow posed a threat—that it was devious and did not play fair. The ambivalence of this view is due in part to the character of Japanese behavior but derives as well from a lack of knowledge among outsiders of Japan's history, culture, and distinctive approach to politics and economics.

Since the 1990s, the popular perception of Japan has changed. Japan is now seen by many as a spent force, at least in economic terms. After the Japanese people's sense of well-being was assaulted by the combined disasters of the Kobe earthquake and the Tokyo subway gas attack in 1995 and the economy became mired in the doldrums, the Japanese began to lose confidence in their national purpose.

It would be a mistake to go too far and dismiss Japan as a significant player in world affairs, however. The Japanese have met serious challenges before and impressively overcame them. There is too great a tendency to prejudge Japanese institutions and actions and to presume that, because they differ from those in the West, they must be inferior. Both the education and employment systems, for example, are dismissed by many in the West and by some Japanese as perverse. In this view, Japanese students pay a high price, including psychological damage, to achieve the status of world leaders in math and science. Economic success comes about because workers are oppressed and exploited. But the Japanese are not a nation of neurotics driven by some strange need to be number one. Although they may work harder than some other people, they also enjoy the pleasures of life. This is not to say that Japan has invented the perfect society. It has many problems, some of which are discussed in the pages that follow.

There is much to be learned from the Japanese, but doing so requires an open mind. Politically, Japan is a bridge between the experiences of the West and those of Asia. The institutional structure has been intentionally patterned after that of Europe and the United States, while the political culture upon which this structure rests is distinctly Asian in character. Apart from its own intrinsic merits as a political system, therefore, the Japanese polity affords the student an opportunity to study the processes of interaction between Western-style political development and a non-Western social and cultural tradition.

The book is divided into six parts. Part I is introductory and, in addition to describing the physical character of Japan, briefly surveys historical background before World War II. The U.S. occupation after the war, an experience that had considerable impact on the development of Japan's political institutions, is also covered in this section.

Part II describes the operation of the political process. This process is viewed from three perspectives: the formal structure of government, the political party system, and political behavior and participation.

Political processes do not exist independent of other aspects of society but interact with and upon them. These are the subjects of Part III, which is concerned in particular with how society is made up and how it organizes itself. Also of concern, especially to outsiders, is the operation of the economy, which is neither monolithic nor as decisively important as is widely believed.

Part IV provides a close look at three areas of public policy and the workings of government: education, health care, and public safety. Japan has few peers in the academic achievement of its students; it also has an effective and efficient health-care system and, to the envy of Americans, a low crime rate. Japan's distinctive approaches to these predominant areas of public concern are explored.

The focus of Part V is Japan's role in contemporary international politics. Two key elements of this role are Japan's relationship with the United States and international economic issues.

Part VI offers a general assessment of Japan's strengths and weaknesses, successes and failures, potentials and limits. For a while it was popular in the West to assign to the Japanese and their ways qualities that made them superior to others. Today there is a tendency to look for weaknesses and inconsistency. The approach taken here is that neither of these points of view is completely accurate or fair. As with most everything else in the world, the truth lies somewhere in between.

Part I

Modern Japan: Background

Introduction

When measured against the usual standards of political and economic development, Japan has come a long way in a very short time. Beginning in the middle of the nineteenth century, Japan took but a few decades to transform itself from a provincial backwater to a modern state and a major international power. In keeping with the foreign policy practices established by Western nations and effectively employed by them, Japan chose to exercise this new-found power by defining its relationship with its neighbors largely in military terms. As a result, much of Asia was subjected to the consequences of Japanese conquest and domination. But Japan's entry into empire building came when the process had just about run its course and was becoming impractical. New forces affecting both international and domestic political orders began to make themselves felt toward the end of the century. The decline of colonialism accelerated rapidly after World War I, frustrating Japan's efforts to achieve the kind of long-lasting imperial results that rewarded European conquests. By the turn of the twentieth century, national self-awareness had replaced docile acceptance of foreign colonial rule in many areas of the world. Moreover, the destructive capacity of military force in its unlimited application had come to exceed its practical utility, become too great, and was too widely shared for armed conquest to be an affordable instrument of foreign policy for most nations. Learning this lesson ultimately proved very costly to Japan.

But military disaster dimmed Japan's prospects for international greatness only temporarily. In a short time, barely two decades, not only were its cities and industries rebuilt and its political institutions transformed but Japan came to assert itself again on the world stage and to occupy a prominent position among the world's major powers. This time Japan's status is defined mainly in economic terms, although it also possesses greater military capacity than is generally assumed. From being unable to feed its own population immediately after the conclusion of World War II, Japan has since amassed such an enormous fortune that it has assumed the role of the number one creditor nation. Because more money is owed to it than to any other country in the world, Japan exerts important influence in international relations.

The economic conditions of the United States and Japan have seesawed back and forth. While Japan ascended, the United States appeared to be going in the opposite direction in the 1970s and 1980s. In the first few decades after World War II, the United States was both militarily and economically the most powerful nation on earth. Then, after the Vietnam debacle, the United States turned away from using military power to shape international developments (the Vietnam syndrome) and American economic influence declined. The United States has the largest economy but it also has the largest balance-of-payments deficit. Americans buy more from other countries than they sell, producing a deficit that is financed, in part, by the Japanese. In the late 1980s, the Japanese upward trajectory experienced a serious reversal as the "bubble economy" collapsed. At the same time, the United States got its economic house in order and embarked on a record-setting period of economic growth, especially in areas of advanced technology. The bursting of the "dot-com" bubble and the shock of 9/11 led to recession in the United States while Japan's economy remained stagnant. However, by mid-decade both the United States and Japan seemed to be on the road to recovery until 2008 when a financial crisis in the United States reverberated globally. The trouble was a result of a mortgage loan crisis, a negative savings rate, and the cost of wars in Afghanistan and Iraq. The dollar briefly fell below 100 yen and the price of petroleum skyrocketed.

The Japanese had accomplished their postwar reconstruction without the usual foundations of national power. In terms of natural resources, Japan is not a richly endowed country, nor is it a large one, and much of the land is mountainous. Hence, minerals, energy sources, and foodstuffs must be imported in significant quantities. Japan's present-day success is not attributable to the beneficence of nature, but is the result of a combination of favorable circumstances, national commitment, and efficiency.

Japan shares with Britain a degree of national success out of proportion to its size. This success is due in no small part to one thing they have in common: both are island nations. One advantage of being an island is that the surrounding ocean serves as a protective moat. The country is secure from all but the most enterprising invaders. From the Norman conquest in 1066 onward, the British have been spared defeat on their own soil at the hands of a foreign enemy. The English Channel kept at bay numerous conquerors, the most notable being Napoleon and Hitler. The Japanese did nearly as well, suffering defeat and occupation only once, in 1945. But, perhaps more significantly, an island is fairly safe from another kind of invasion, that of population migration. This isolation, no doubt, played a key part in shaping the national development of both countries.

The Japanese archipelago consists of the four principal islands of Hokkaido, Honshu, Shikoku, and Kyushu, plus many smaller islands. The total area of the country is 145,730 square miles and extends for a length of 2,360 miles. Japan is approximately one-twentieth the size of the United States and is half the size of the United Kingdom. Located in the temperate zone, it has abundant vegetation, which, together with its rugged terrain, creates a landscape of considerable beauty.

The physical makeup of the country presents conditions of both adversity and advantage. The terrain is approximately 80 percent mountainous, and there are over 580 peaks that are more than 2,000 meters high. The tallest of them all is the famous Mt. Fuji, which rises to 3,776 meters. These mountains are the product of the extreme instability of the earth's crust in this area of the planet. This instability has confronted the Japanese with numerous hazards. Volcanic activity has produced mountains, of which Mt. Fuji is the finest and most famous example. More serious and immediate dangers come from frequent earthquakes. The weather can also be a threat. Japan is in that part of Asia that is regularly visited by typhoons, tropical storms that often wreak considerable damage. Many lives have been lost and much property destroyed as heavy rains are followed by mudslides that sweep away houses, together with their occupants. However, typhoons have also been a blessing, as in 1281, when a storm destroyed the Mongol invasion fleet as it was approaching the Japanese coast.

There are many rivers, but they are short and generally not navigable. This is not a serious problem, however, as the country is very narrow and any point is relatively close to the sea. The highly irregular coastline provides many natural harbors, an advantage of immeasurable significance for the economy as it reduces the cost of transportation.

The climate is varied, ranging from hot summers to cold winters. There are four regular and distinct seasons, and the changes in these seasons tend to be more dramatic than in other areas of the temperate zone. The country experiences considerable rainfall—a boon to agriculture—as well as heavy snowfall. The resulting runoff allows for extensive hydroelectric development.

As substantial as Japan's economic development has been, it is not built on a very firm foundation. Japan is poorly endowed with those mineral resources necessary to sustain a modern industrial structure.[1] Oil, iron ore, coking coal, and nonferrous metal ores, such as copper, nickel, and bauxite, used in the manufacture of aluminum, plus a host of others, must be imported. Only a fraction of electrical power needs are produced from domestic resources. Most electricity is generated either by imported oil or imported coal. There has been an attempt to exploit the relatively more fuel efficient nuclear power industry. But that development too depends on outside suppliers for fuel and some of the equipment that goes into reactor construction.

Not only are there few minerals but the agricultural resource base is limited. The fact that the countryside is mountainous means that only about 16 percent of the land is arable, with another 3 percent for pastures and meadows. To scratch a living from this environment, farmers have been faced with a difficult task. These efforts come at considerable cost, however, as food prices are among the highest in the world. While agricultural productivity has increased, the percentage of the population engaged in farming has declined. Part of the increasing productivity is the result of land reform measures introduced during the U.S. occupation after World War II. As Japan has experienced an improvement in its overall economic well-being, there has been an increase in the consumption of foodstuffs, such as beef, that Japan cannot produce in sufficient supply to meet demand. This has resulted in a substantial increase in imports. But the politically privileged position of the farmer has kept the volume of imports well below the level of potential demand. Moreover, consumers are willing to pay high prices in order to protect Japan's domestically produced food sources. The failure of Japan to open its markets to other countries is not just a matter of protectionism. It reflects the peculiar nature of the Japanese marketplace and the attitudes of consumers. The trade situation is, moreover, a continuing international problem.

Japan's accomplishments in achieving major influence in world affairs in such a short time are made even more remarkable by the fact that its total recorded history has itself been extraordinarily brief. This is all the more striking when compared to the ancient origins and immense cultural accomplishments of China. Japan remained underdeveloped by all standard measures of civilization until the past few centuries.

Although the prehistory of Japan is not certain, it is clear from archeological evidence that the ancestors of the present-day inhabitants of the islands came from East Asia and the South Pacific. These people, called the Yamato, asserted themselves over other warring tribes and clans during the first three or four centuries of the Christian era and became the dominant group. Since then, there has been very little infusion of other ethnic groups, resulting in a contemporary population that is fundamentally homogeneous. For this, the Japanese can thank their geographical isolation.

The population of Japan was estimated on September 1, 2006, at 127,700,000. The growth rate continues to slow, and the median age of the population continues to rise. The share of the population up to age fourteen was 13.6 percent. The share between fifteen and sixty-four was 65.7 percent, sixty-five and above was 20.6 percent, and those seventy-five and above was 9.4 percent. By contrast, the proportion of people age sixty-five or above in 2003 was 18.8 percent.

As is true everywhere in the world, where people live and how they live is a function of the physical environment. For the Japanese, one of the most important aspects of this environment is the limited amount of land available. This means that the people must necessarily live, work, and play in dense concentrations. About 70 percent of the population live in cities, and of this urban population, almost 60 percent are crowded into the four main metropolitan areas of Tokyo, Osaka, Nagoya, and Kitakyushu. This has not always been the case, however. Before World War II, a substantial percentage of the population lived in rural settings. Today, the pattern of migration from rural areas to cities, especially among younger people, seems to be changing. In keeping with a phenomenon visible in some other countries experiencing postindustrial change, many Japanese are opting for the simpler and less hectic lifestyle of smaller cities.

The concentration of people in urban areas has considerable social and political significance. In urban areas, traditional social connections, and particularly extended family ties, tend to weaken over time.[2] There is also a greater demand for public services in cities, since people cannot provide most basic needs for themselves. Urban populations are also more frequently politicized and easier to mobilize than are rural people.

One of the most important characteristics of the contemporary Japanese population is the increase in the median age. As mentioned above, the share of the population that is over age sixty-five was about a fifth of the population as of 2006, and that percentage is expected to reach 26 percent by 2015. Because of the increase in older people and the decrease in younger people as a share of the population, social priorities change. Among older people, probably the greatest demand for social services is in the area of health care. For young people, the emphasis is on education. Young adults are mainly concerned about employment and housing. An aging population also means fewer wage earners, particularly industrial workers, and expanding requirements in service industries.

Another important development is the changing social role of women. Although they do not enjoy full equality with men, they are much better off than before the war. Women are entering the labor force in growing numbers and constitute almost 40 percent of all workers. There has also been a dramatic increase in the numbers of women participating in higher education.[3] Women are also increasingly active politically and independent in their thinking about public issues. More women vote than men, and they are putting themselves forward as candidates in increasing numbers. The scandals that have beset political parties, especially the Liberal Democratic Party, have galvanized women voters as never before.

The waters surrounding Japan are abundant in sea life and seafood is an important part of the Japanese diet. Problems with industrial pollution and increased consumption have in some places despoiled the environment and the quality of life. Progress has been made in correcting this situation by policies requiring a cleanup of industry. But another way in which the Japanese have addressed pollution and environmental degradation is by exporting it. Many polluting "smokestack" industries have been transferred to other countries, where costs are lower and sensitivity toward pollution less of a factor. Japan's impact on the global environment is extensive. Japanese fishermen have been forced to venture farther from home in order to meet consumer demand, contributing to the depletion of the world's fisheries. Japan has imported large quantities of timber, exacerbating the loss of rain forests in Southeast Asia and South America.

Dependence on outside sources of raw materials and foodstuffs means that Japan is heavily dependent on an uninterrupted flow of international trade. The advancement and protection of this trade is the cornerstone of the country's foreign policy. Japan's growing economic power will contribute significantly to its ability to ensure its economic welfare. But with the problems of homelessness and starvation in many parts of the world, the Japanese are called on to contribute more and benefit less.

Much has been made of Japan's extraordinary economic development and political resiliency since its defeat in World War II. Many books have been published describing this phenomenon in superlatives, such as "Japan as Number One." Various explanations are offered to account for this meteoric rise. Many attribute Japan's success to one factor—national character. The Japanese themselves seem preoccupied with self-examination and are inclined to stress their distinctiveness as a nation.[4] This distinctiveness is predicated on the belief that the Japanese character is the product of a deeply rooted tradition. Some scholars contend that this tradition is a fairly recent invention. "Over the past several decades Japanese have shown a vast capacity to create an idealized past."[5] To outside observers, the Japanese are perceived as possessing a unity of purpose that derives from their value system. A particularly strong aspect of this system is a submissiveness to authority; those who possess authority by virtue of their sex, family status, social position, or political office command deference. Contrariwise, those who have authority have obligations to exercise it on behalf of the general community. But this authority is not based on some body of abstract principles or "fundamental truths." Instead, authority derives from the context of interpersonal relationships. Nor is authority narrowly defined. To a much greater extent than would be tolerated in the West, superiors actively involve themselves in the personal affairs of subordinates.

The traditional view, prevalent as recently as the prewar period, and still widely shared, elevates the status of officials and lowers that of ordinary people. Society manifests a definite hierarchical ordering, and there is limited mobility between strata. Most people, it seems, approve of, or at least tolerate, this arrangement. A practice that is hardly unique to the Japanese is that which holds the individual subordinate to the group. But there are increasing signs that this is beginning to change as new generations become further and further removed from the prewar value system.

The Japanese are ethnocentric, but the basis is not simply race or even, as with the Chinese, culture, but, rather, it is seen as natural for the strong to dominate the weak. They see themselves as more able and efficient. It is "natural" for them to be a dominant economic force because they are better at it.

The Japanese are tribal; they "have a sense of mutual obligation and loyalty to colleagues and compatriots based on emotion rather than contracts."[6] They fear that adoption of Western ways will undermine this tribal system. This attitude inhibits significant opening of society to the outside. Their ideology is of a rather peculiar sort. Capitalism is held in low esteem, but socialism and the like are not. Thus Japanese capitalism has a strong "social" consciousness.[7] Likewise, a modern type of nationalism linking the masses at the base of society with the sociopolitical elites and institutions at the top has not developed. Instead, Japan has had "a pre-modern nationalism, compounded of traditional local loyalties, paternalistic sentiment and quasi-religious national myths."[8]

Although the Japanese are committed to democratic values, their view of how democracy should operate in a functional sense is rather different from that common in the West. They seek to avoid contention and antagonism. The Hegelian process of the interplay between conflicting views that are synthesized into a qualitatively higher and superior decision is not an approach much valued in Japan. There is an aversion to partisanship and little attraction to the idea of majority rule. Perhaps this is a result of the acute awareness that majority rule always carries with it the problem of minority consent. In small groups, where people know each other, "it troubles people to see the group divide into a majority and a minority and to witness the defeat of the minority before one's own eyes."[9] Hence, the Japanese favor their traditional method of arriving at decisions through consensus. This does not mean that everyone ultimately agrees with a decision, but it does mean that everyone has been involved in the decision-making process in some significant way, at least for them, and they share in the decision and accept it.[10] This may make for a slow decision-making process, but once a decision has been made, it is quickly and effectively implemented.

Many commentaries on Japan remark upon the strong group orientation of its people. From this perspective, everything in society involves identity with a collectivity and consensus decision-making is universal. Workers prefer to work in a genial environment, defined as a harmonious group, as opposed to employment under less felicitous conditions but with higher pay.[11] The same approach exists in education. Students display a strong commitment to the learning enterprise in order to avoid calling attention to themselves by falling below the group standard. Japan is one of the most socially and culturally homogeneous countries in the world, which is one of the main reasons for its development from a technological backwater in the middle of the nineteenth century to an industrial power in but a few decades. It also helps explain Japan's rapid recovery from the devastation of World War II.

What this homogeneity means is the absence of costly and debilitating conflicts within society. Energy is not dissipated in ethnic or linguistic quarrels. Organized religion plays only a limited role, thus virtually eliminating the possibility of friction from that quarter. This is not to say that the Japanese lack spiritual values. The society is steeped in Confucian tradition and Christianity is likewise an important ethical influence, but very few people are active in Christian churches. Shinto and Buddhism "are for most people more a matter of custom and convention than of meaningful beliefs."[12]

All these factors and more are expressed in the political system, a system that differs in many essential respects from those found in other countries. Japan is a democracy, but it lacks many of the attributes that distinguish democracies in other parts of the world. For instance, there has been little real competition among political parties. One party, the Liberal Democratic Party, ruled without interruption from the mid-1950s to 1993. The constitution contains a long list of civil liberties and real freedoms exist, although many people do not enjoy them. Japan has achieved great economic success, yet the masses of the people have not received a proportionate share of it. Enormous political power rests in the hands of a bureaucratic elite. Gaining access to elite status is extremely difficult, yet that fact seem to engender little frustration. Japan has renounced the use of armed force in the conduct of its foreign policy, while military spending levels exceed those of all but a handful of countries. These are but a few of the contradictions and paradoxes of modern Japan.

1
General History

Asia has played host to not only the world's oldest but the richest and most complex civilizations. China, India, and Southeast Asia were highly sophisticated at the time of the Roman empire and before. But Japan did not share in or contribute to this ancient tradition. Comparatively speaking, the recorded history of Japan not only is short but has neither the political legacy nor the record of substantial intellectual achievement that is characteristic of other parts of Asia. There is nothing like the intellectual and cultural accomplishments of the subcontinent of India, for example, where both Hinduism and Buddhism originated. Japan's historical record contains little that would compare to China's rich history. In fact, very little is known about Japan before the seventh century c.e. A written language did not exist until the fifth or sixth century. Human activities and institutions prior to that time are shrouded in mystery. The historical record was kept orally and only later written down.[1]

In the absence of powerful indigenous forces, Japan's historical evolution has frequently reflected developments that have their origins elsewhere. For instance, language, literature, politics, and philosophy were significantly influenced by China and Korea. The result is an amalgam of foreign influences mixed in with native traditions. Historically, the Japanese have sought to preserve their cultural identity within a larger, universally valid social philosophy that was developed in China—Confucianism.[2] Political institutions were shaped between the sixth to eighth centuries based on the model of Tang China. The Japanese imperial institution was predicated on Chinese doctrine.[3]

For the first 600 years of its recorded history, Japan was composed of a loose collection of local political units nominally held together by a monarchy. During these years the development of political institutions, economic growth, or cultural achievement, were modest. Moreover, during much of this period, the country suffered from chronic instability and conflict.

In the twelfth century, some semblance of political integration occurred. In 1192, after a prolonged period of brutal civil wars, unification was achieved at the hands of a military dictatorship. The monarchical form of government had not proved vigorous enough to hold all the warring factions together in one unit. The result was a system called the shogunate or *bakufu*. In theory, the shogun's official capacity was that of commander in chief of the imperial army. Sovereign political authority remained with the emperor to whom the shogun paid allegiance. The power of the government, however, was in the hands of the shogun, but only so long as he was able to retain military supremacy. "Legitimacy lay with the Court, where the sovereign linked the present with the semihistorical past. . . . Matters of governance, however, were the province of the *shogun*, who, as supreme hegemon and head of the military houses, delegated responsibility to his vassals."[4] For nearly seven centuries, this arrangement prevailed, with the emperor having little more than ceremonial significance and often existing under conditions approaching house arrest. While this isolation prevented the emperor "from having the slightest influence over public affairs," it also "increased the mystery and awe with which the contemporary society invested the persons of the Court and their works."[5]

Although the emperors did not rule, they did reign, which is a matter of considerable constitutional significance. The imperial institution legitimized the state and the authoritative relationships within it. This made the philosophy of government, the obligations of rulers, and the duties of citizens clear and understandable, if not always agreeable, to all. There were, of course, interminable struggles and not a few battles waged over how political power would be exercised and by whom; but at least the rules of the game were reasonably well defined. The sovereignty of the emperor remained a vital part of Japanese political philosophy until after World War II, when it was replaced with the doctrine of popular sovereignty.

There were, in all, three shogunates, each involving the political dominance of a particular clan. In all three, political power was seized, after intense war, on the strength of the military ability of the leader. The first of these three military houses—the Minamoto—lasted for 200 years. After a successful challenge from another clan—the Ashikaga—the second shogunate came into existence, lasting from 1392 to 1573. But from 1467 to 1568, the country was plagued by almost continual warfare. Devastation extended from the emperor and his courtiers, who "barely survived by begging alms from individual lords" to the commoners, who perished by the thousands from famine and disease.[6] Central control of political affairs dissolved and governing power was in the hands of local petty rulers. The most important institution was the small feudal state dominated by the local lord and his band of warriors. The lord's power was based on his military strength that in turn derived from a system of personal loyalties. There was little if any formal development of political institutions. The high social status of military men, interestingly, is the reverse of the Chinese experience where the soldier was placed near the bottom of the social hierarchy.

The wars finally came to an end, and political unity was restored through the efforts of three *daimyō,* or feudal barons. They were able to persuade other lords to join together and form a powerful coalition that ultimately defeated the opposition and unified the country. These daimyō were Oda Nobunaga (1534–1582), his chief vassal (feudal retainer) Toyotomi Hideyoshi (1536–1598), and his vassal Tokugawa Ieyasu (1542–1616). Hideyoshi employed two very effective strategies to consolidate his political position. First, he was able to gain greater administrative control over the land than had existed before that time and thereby controlled the peasants who worked on it. In the 1580s, he ordered a resurvey of land in order to determine its productivity and to identify who was responsible for payment of taxes. By clarifying this responsibility, the government was more successful in raising revenue and, more importantly, in keeping track of politically ambitious local lords.[7] The Tokugawa also placed additional restrictions on the emperor, when, by 1615, they has established "systematic control of the imperial institution."[8]

Hideyoshi's second measure was to prohibit the possession of swords by anyone other than his own soldiers. To achieve this end, he conducted a sword hunt and confiscated all weapons in the hands of civilians that were then melted down and used in the construction of a Great Buddha monument.[9] This absence of weaponry in private hands made it nearly impossible to raise popular rebellion against the government. Hideyoshi's efforts led to the emergence of a professional warrior class called *samurai.*[10]

The third and most famous shogunate was the Tokugawa which lasted from 1603, when Ieyasu assumed the title of shogun, until 1868. In order to maintain control over the unwieldy feudal coalition that was the Japanese political system, the Tokugawa established a complicated system of governance. One of the most important devices was the reassignment of control over land to different feudal lords, depending on their reliability. In this way, those suspected of disloyalty or of harboring troublesome political ambitions could be kept under close check. Their lands could either be on the fringes of the empire, where they could do little mischief, or close to the seat of government, where they could be kept under surveillance.

A second technique used to discourage political opposition was the alternate residence system, whereby the lords were required to maintain a home in the capital as well as the one on their lands. When back at their fiefs, the barons were required to leave their heirs behind as security for their loyalty. The practice of holding hostage the relatives of their followers in order to guarantee loyalty had been used by Japanese rulers for some time. The alternate residence system was a financial drain on the feudal barons that diminished their military potential.[11]

A third device was seclusion. Both China and Japan feared that Western influences would prove socially and politically disruptive. Perceiving Westerners, and especially Catholic missionaries, as intent on extending European colonial control over Japan, the bakufu prohibited trade and cultural contacts. Actually, Christianity had been banned by Hideyoshi in 1597, but the ban was not vigorously enforced. Another ban in 1612 issued by the Tokugawa led to the expulsion of missionaries and the persecution of Christian converts.[12]

Japan's insularity, reinforced by 250 years of isolation from the rest of the world, promoted a semimystical nationalism. This nationalism was reinforced by state-supported indoctrination, resulting in "a religious or semi-religious belief that the country is the centre of the world." The policy of seclusion required not only isolation from the West but from Asia as well, which, ironically was the source of Japan's culture. "Here the Chinese doctrine of China as 'the Middle Kingdom' was adopted to make Japan the centre of the world, and the stress was laid on 'Japanism' and the natural purity which existed before it was corrupted by a heavy coating of Chinese culture." The doctrine of cultural purity led, inevitably, to racism "with the Indians in particular being regarded as an inferior species. It should be stressed that the main targets of these racial teachings were not Europeans but other Asians."[13]

The policy intended to exclude other cultures and promote "Japanism" worked successfully until the middle of the nineteenth century, when a more determined effort to open Japan to commercial and diplomatic contact was encountered. The Japanese intention had not been to be a hermit kingdom seeking complete isolation, but only to avoid corrosive cultural influences. Political and economic relations with other Asian countries were maintained by the Japanese, on a limited basis and on their own terms, for some time.[14]

War often serves to disrupt the intended course of national development. Countries that have frequently fallen victim to invasion and defeat reflect these experiences in their cultures and institutions. Contrariwise, countries that have been spared such experiences are just as strongly influenced. Japan is in the latter category. Apart from its defeat in World War II, Japan has never been successfully invaded by a foreign power. The only serious threat occurred in the thirteenth century, when attempted Mongol invasions in 1274 and 1281 were foiled, the second due largely to the timely intervention of a typhoon.

It may very well be true that the absence of foreign contacts slowed evolution of Japanese social and political institutions. But it is also likely that since the Japanese were not forced, by invasion and occupation, to deal with such influences, they could ultimately do so at a more leisurely pace and on their own terms. The Chinese, Indians, and a host of other peoples, had Westernization forced on them. Moreover, the Japan of the mid-nineteenth century was in a good position to respond creatively to new challenges. Indeed, in many respects, Japan was in a better position to meet the challenges of "Westernization" than the West itself had been at a similar stage of development.

The character of Japanese feudalism was such as to provide the elements of a successful response to modernization once it came. Compared to the West, which had a legalistic type of feudalism, the Japanese system was ethical. Political arrangements based on law can be formally changed only by competent authority, and disputes as to what constitutes "competent authority" can lead to the complete breakdown of political order. Ethical structures, by contrast, are more adaptable, and loyalties can be transferred without undermining the integrity of the system. Ethically defined political order is more adaptable in a structural sense than order that is defined in objective legal terms.

Comparing Japanese and Western feudalism, both involved bodies of armed men obligated to render aid and service. The peasants were bound to the land and committed to support the lord. But there the similarities end. The emperor was more developed as a political institution in Japan than was his Western counterpart, and the role of an institutionalized religion similar to that of the Roman Catholic Church was missing in Japan. This would prove an advantage in easing the process of building secular political institutions. The burdens on the Japanese peasants were lighter, as they were not expected to perform as many tasks (e.g., participation in foreign wars and corvée or unpaid labor for the lord) as were the common people in Europe. A potential source of internal political opposition was thus missing in Japan.[15]

Japan and the West

For 200 years before the visit of a U.S. naval force under Commodore Matthew C. Perry, Japan had been largely successful in keeping itself isolated from the Western world. Part of this success can be attributed to the fact that Japan was on the margins of the area of most intense Western imperial interest. Isolation was abetted by the Dutch, who successfully kept other Europeans away from the few trade or other commercial opportunities made available by the Japanese. Until the mid-nineteenth century, Western nations were mainly interested in South and Southeast Asia and China. But sooner or later, Japan would have to come to terms with the expanding network of international activity.

Russia was the first to challenge the Dutch monopoly of foreign trade, when in 1792 it received permission to trade on a temporary basis. England and finally the United States followed with attempts to open Japan to trade and diplomacy. Most Japanese regarded the West as barbarian and corrupt, but a few saw the need to promote the study of Western ways, and especially Western learning in science and technology. It was fortunate for the Japanese that the political integrity of the shogunate was declining at the same time that pressure from the outside world was increasing. Had the political system under its military rulers been stronger, it might have been able to resist modernization more effectively, perhaps with unfortunate consequences. The weakness of the government made the exclusion policy politically easier to overcome. The growing number of Japanese who saw the twin need for external accommodation and internal modernization confronted a political leadership that was becoming weak and irresolute and increasingly unable to maintain a united front against outsiders.

In a treaty signed in 1854, the Japanese opened two minor ports to the Russians. Another, negotiated in 1855, included the practice of extraterritoriality or extrality, which is a concession by the host country exempting a foreign power from some aspects of domestic law. In the contemporary world, the practice of diplomatic privilege in which accredited diplomats and their families are not subject to prosecution for criminal offenses in the country where they serve is an example. U.S. Consul Townsend Harris was able to persuade the Japanese to open trade with the United States, arguing that if they failed to do so, Europeans would use force to extract even more onerous concessions. The provisions of this agreement were included in a treaty of 1858, which contained many of the concessions to Western demands that China had already made. Even though the treaty was opposed by many conservative daimyō, it was accepted by the emperor, thus making criticism of it impolitic.[16]

As it turned out, the advocates of the policy of exclusion were right: contact with the West would prove disruptive. They were especially concerned about the ability of Christianity "to lead the people's minds astray."[17] Opposition to Christianity was abetted by leading Buddhists, who, quite naturally, found the new religion a threat to their influence.[18] In the final analysis, however, the Japanese really had little choice; they could either accommodate themselves to outside influences or, as the Chinese, be overcome by them.

Trouble was first felt in the economy. The sudden intrusion of Western commerce produced severe inflation. The political discontent that followed created added problems for the government and hastened the process of political restructuring.

The physical presence of many Westerners was a source of strain in a society unaccustomed to linguistic and ethnic differences. The arrogance and peculiar behavior of the foreigners encouraged self-examination among the Japanese, which contributed to the reinforcement of an already strong sense of national identity and a desire to compete with foreign nations on their own terms. The Japanese did not suffer from the cultural superiority complex that inhibited Chinese development and were thus in a better position to accept the necessity of change.

Japan was politically unsettled during the 1850s and 1860s. Somehow the government had to meet the mounting challenges to its authority by either accommodating the demands for change or suppressing them. Adhering to its traditional biases, the shogunate attempted to strengthen itself by suppressing dissention. Reform factions came to realize that little could be accomplished within the existing political setup. The advocates of modernization did not call for revolution but, rather, restoration. The emperor served as the rallying point for the progressive movement, which advocated the return of governing authority to the emperor. In so doing, of course, they intended to create new and more effective political institutions, not simply substitute an absolute monarch for the military dictatorship of the shogun.

In 1863 the government attempted to set the clock back by expelling the Western "barbarians," but the effort failed; it was too late for that. Many progressive Japanese were particularly impressed with Western military superiority. The bakufu initiated a program of modernization and reform of the military in 1866, but many of its troops still employed swords and pikes, while others lacked motivation. In the final battles against the imperial forces, the shogun's armies were deficient in modern organization and technology. They were also often poorly led and suffered from morale problems. This led to the defeat of the shogun's forces, the liquidation of his regime and the "restoration" of the imperial structure.[19]

Those who took part in the rebellion against the military dictatorship were young and talented men who did not have a vested interest in the established elite structure since they were not members of it. Hence they were relatively free of the constraints of cultural tradition and personal loyalties. Because innovations did not threaten their prestige or status, they were in a good position to make changes, something the traditional elite could not bring itself to do.

The Restoration

Discontent with the status quo permeated society. Among those contributing their weight to the effort to bring about political change were intellectuals who questioned the integrity and legitimacy of the shogun's regime. There was widespread discontent in the imperial court over the deteriorating political condition of the country. Economic changes contributed to the progressive weakening of feudal connections. Of course, an important influence was the penetration of Japan, despite its efforts to keep them out, by Westerners particularly after Perry's visit in 1853.

Nominally, the end of the shogunate meant the full restoration of imperial powers. While it originated in the fifth century c.e., throughout most of its history the monarchy exercised only ceremonial functions and was little known and largely irrelevant to most people.[20] The political importance of the imperial office did not change significantly after 1868. The emperor reigned as little more than a figurehead, although his popular role as symbol of national sovereignty was substantially enhanced. Governing powers were in the hands of a small elite. Nevertheless, the institution of the emperor provided national focus and served as the embodiment of political authority. The emperor was transformed from an ethereal and largely functionless component of the feudal system into a necessary ideological and institutional element of the modern Japanese state.[21] "In Japan's modern ideology, long and thoroughly disseminated by techniques of education and control, the emperor was viewed with great awe as the more-than-human father of the island family of Japan, with roots deep in Japan's mythical and historical past. The emperor was above and beyond politics, and worthy of the total sacrifice of each of his subjects."[22]

The forty-five-year period from 1868 until 1912, known as the Meiji era, was one in which Japan experienced political and economic transformation that was truly breathtaking in scope. On April 8, 1868, the emperor Mutsuhito, at the initiative of the new governing elite, issued a declaration that was known as the Charter Oath. The oath contained the following important provisions: (1) Deliberative assemblies shall be widely convoked and all matters shall be decided by public discussion; (2) Upper and lower social orders shall unite in active conduct of the affairs of state; (3) Men of all classes, including the nobility and the military, shall each pursue his calling so that there shall be no stagnation of spirit; (4) Evil customs of the past shall be broken off and everything shall be based upon the universal law; (5) Knowledge shall be sought throughout the world in order to strengthen the foundations of the imperial rule.[23]

The declaration reflected a clear commitment to social change and political modernization. The ambitious agenda outlined in the Charter Oath was not matched by institutional capabilities, however. It is always easier to overthrow a decrepit and poorly functioning political system than it is to fabricate a new one and, even more so, to make it work. Political change relied not just on the introduction of new procedures but on new people with a commitment to new ideas. After some trial and error, an effective, centralized political apparatus was developed. This centralization ultimately proved the most important political consequence of the Meiji reforms.

Dismantling of the obsolete feudal system included the social groups that had made feudalism function. The most important of these was the warrior class. Men of samurai background, many of whom were unable to find professional military employment in the new order, were a principal source of political leadership and economic manpower. Some went into government service, while others found occupations in such unfamiliar fields as agriculture and commerce. Others were unable to adjust to the new conditions and fell into poverty.[24] The samurai were more than simply warriors but also possessed erudition and cultural attainment. While not all professional soldiers were learned, many were. Moreover, their personal code called *bushidō* contributed a wealth of lore and legend that would have a major impact on the political culture for decades to come. Recognizing the need to "rehabilitate" the 1.8 million or so samurai in order to make them productive members of society, the government embarked on a program designed to facilitate their entry into agricultural, industrial, and commercial activities.[25] The samurai, together with a growing merchant class, many of whom were themselves samurai, provided the manpower resources that propelled the country politically and economically forward. One of the more significant and ultimately portentous steps taken during this period was the introduction in January 1873 of universal male conscription. For nearly three centuries before the restoration, commoners had been kept apart from military activities and were not even allowed to keep weapons in their possession. This new step thus represented a radical break with the past practice of maintaining a class distinction based on the functional difference between commoners and the warrior class. Now, not only would the masses be the foundation of the military system, but ultimately the state would rest on a broader popular base. A conscripted military provided strong encouragement for the development of modern nationalism. Changes in the military system had other implications as well. By the mid-1870s, the samurai were disappearing as a class through the reduction of their stipends. Many of the feudal lords, who no longer needed the services of military retainers, entered the ranks of the bourgeoisie.

Not everyone was enthusiastic about the process of modernization. Many saw, and rightly so, that change would come at the expense of their traditional privileges and social position. Those who would not themselves change and seek new opportunities in the transforming political and economic environment, tried to halt the development process. After the restoration of the monarchy, there were frequent acts of violence by those seeking to preserve their traditional privileges and arrest the process of change. These outbreaks culminated in the great Satsuma Revolt of 1877. But these forces of reaction were ultimately defeated, significantly by an army composed of commoners, thus dispelling the notion that only samurai possessed martial ability. By the end of the century, having established itself as a modern state, Japan entered the ranks of the world's influential nations.

Modernization

Economic and political development proceeded at a faster pace than did that during the corresponding period of development in Europe. As a late modernizer, Japan was able to build on the experience of others and to avoid some of their mistakes. To catch up in all fields of knowledge and to exploit this knowledge for social development, a major emphasis was placed on education. Impressive results in educational achievement meant not only a literate population but one with the skills necessary for economic and political growth. Public officials were not allowed to waste resources or to use them for their own advantage, resulting in substantial efficiency in government. There was considerable emphasis on innovation and initiative, especially in the rural areas, which accelerated entrepreneurship.

The robust agricultural economy was a major factor in promoting industrial development. Agricultural production doubled in the last quarter of the nineteenth century. As a result, Japan developed not only the capacity to feed its population but surplus capital for investment and expansion.

Motivated by the desire to resist what was perceived to be the Western menace, the government committed itself to the promotion of industrialization. This policy focused on those industries that would have the greatest impact on overall economic strength and in particular on those industries on which modern military power depended.

To achieve its ends, the government initiated industrial projects on its own using public money. These basic industries were eventually acquired by private investors at relatively low cost, and they usually turned a handsome profit.[26] Since only the most powerful economic interests were in a position to invest such substantial amounts of money, this industrial policy contributed to the concentration of industry in few hands. Powerful economic combines emerged, which were later known as *zaibatsu*. The pattern of industrial development that had been common in Western Europe, in which light consumer industries developed first, in turn generating the need for heavy capital goods, was reversed in Japan. They began with heavy industry, which allowed light industry to follow quickly. This "top–down" approach has not always been successful, however, as the experience of the Soviet Union illustrates.

The radical transformation of Japan during the last decades of the nineteenth century went beyond the economic. During the 1880s, copying of Western social customs was widespread.[27] In popular culture, many Japanese adopted Western fashion. Western music and dancing enjoyed considerable popularity in the cities. The military was especially affected by Western-inspired technical and social innovations. The military also led the way in organizational change, a process that would ultimately touch all aspects of society.[28]

Politically, it was a time of mobilization and institutional development, manifesting, in particular, the influence of French organizational models. One of the most significant achievements was the transformation of local government administration. In the 1870s, many groups formed to press for representative government. In response, popular assemblies were created in

1878 at the prefectural level, which were the first popularly elected political organs in the non-Western world. There was also concern for civil liberties leading to a "people's rights" movement, in which former samurai played an important part. This movement pressed its demands with such enthusiasm that agitation sometimes led to violence.[29] There was also considerable rural unrest brought about by high land rents, dispossession of small landowners, and government policy that favored industry over agriculture. Rapid urbanization also created unrest. But, overall, economic growth meant more money for common people, ameliorating, to some extent, the difficulties of daily life.[30] In 1885 a Cabinet system of government was introduced based on up-to-date Western models. A less felicitous development was the centralization of police power that ultimately would become an instrument of social repression and authoritarianism. In 1887 an exam was established for recruitment to the public service. A revised legal code based on German precedents went into effect in 1896.

In 1889 a major step in the process of political modernization was taken with the introduction of a constitution that defined the emperor as sovereign not only in the symbolic sense of legitimacy but in the legal sense of the supreme authority. Exclusive authority to amend the constitution was reserved to the emperor from whom it had been presented to the country as a "gift." It was in fact never amended. Had the emperor chosen to exercise that authority, the significance of the constitution would have been diminished. But while the emperor reigned, he did not rule. His role was passive; the real power of government was in the hands of an oligarchy of influential leaders who had emerged during the Meiji restoration movement.

Under the constitution, a bicameral legislature (the Diet) patterned after the parliamentary bodies of Europe was created. The upper house (House of Peers) was made up of nobility and imperial appointees who were usually distinguished scholars. Members of the lower house (House of Representatives) were chosen by an electorate limited to tax-paying males twenty-five years old and over. The right to vote was thus limited to about 5 percent of the male population. In 1925, the suffrage was expanded to include all adult males, but it was not until after World War II and the introduction of reforms under the U.S. occupation that the right to vote was extended to women.

The legislature suffered from severe limitations not only in the extent to which it functioned as a representative body but in its ability to enact public policy. One limitation lay in the fact that the parliament did not control its own legislative agenda. Legislation could be introduced in either house, but to do so required the approval of a government minister. This requirement handicapped efforts to initiate political reforms through the legislature, as for many years most Cabinet posts were held by members of the conservative oligarchy. Even though political parties began to appear at this time, their significance as electoral and legislative vehicles was limited. The emperor made ministerial appointments and Cabinets were responsible to him rather than to the parliament. Parliamentary influence was limited by additional constraints in budgetary matters. If the legislature refused to enact a new budget, the previous year's automatically was continued.

The bureaucracy, which was becoming increasingly centralized and influential, was nominally under the direction of the emperor but he invariably acted on the advice of the *Genrō*. The term *Genrō*, which originally referred to seven restoration leaders, later came to mean senior statesmen. These influential individuals often acted through the Privy Council that advised the emperor on matters of constitutional interpretation, emergency decrees, martial law, treaties, and international law.

Under the 1889 constitution, many civil rights were guaranteed, although these were hedged by language that qualified them severely. Although the citizenry theoretically were guaranteed freedom and liberty, the constitution allowed them to be circumscribed by the government. The practical effect of these constitutional guarantees on the lives of citizens was limited, but a precedent was established that at least had symbolic importance. The Japanese, on the basis of this experience, were familiar with civil liberties when the issue came up again in the 1947 constitution.

Military leaders reported directly to the emperor and were drawn from the active officer corps. Later, during the period 1915–36, the top military leadership was drawn from retired officers. This gave them a considerable measure of independence from government direction and reduced the level of civilian control over the military. The growing importance of the military would end only with defeat in World War II.

Under the new constitutional system, tension developed between the Diet and the Cabinet. Parliamentary politicians, many of whom were active in party politics, were inclined to favor continued political modernization. The Cabinet was made up of the traditional elite, that is, the oligarchs who had been behind the 1868 Meiji restoration. Now in power, however, they were inclined to slow the process of change. Progressives and conservatives were in agreement about one thing, however, and that was the goal of enhancing security and achieving equality with the West by promoting national unity.[31]

The development of the modern state proceeded rapidly. But the energy generated by this process was not effectively channeled into a broad pattern of democratic institutionalization. Instead, efforts were directed outward, toward imperialism, and toward those national institutions that supported it.[32]

In promoting its international stature, Japan looked first to Korea. Historically, Korea has had considerable influence on the culture of Japan. But in terms of direct and continuous official relations, the two countries were not close. One of the most important events in Japan's relations with Korea occurred in the sixteenth century, when a Japanese military expedition was launched. The effort did not last long, but the long-term consequences were significant. In the 1870s and 1880s, Japan's Korea policy resulted in an inevitable confrontation with China, which asserted a historical claim of suzerainty over Korea as a tributary state. Out of this confrontation resulted the Sino–Japanese war of 1894–95, in which the Chinese suffered a major defeat. As a result it was forced to cede Taiwan, the Pescadore islands, and Kwantung peninsula in southern Manchuria. China was also forced to formally acknowledge the independence of Korea.

Japan's reputation and influence grew rapidly following the Sino–Japanese war. Japan's participation along with Western powers in the suppression of the Boxer Rebellion in China in 1900 further enhanced its international stature. Concern about Russian intentions in Asia led Britain to form an alliance with Japan in 1902. The Russo–Japanese war of 1904–5 resulted from the clash of Russian and Japanese interests over Manchuria and Korea. The humiliating Russian defeat had enormous implications. It contributed to the disintegration of the tsarist regime in Russia, and it showed that European nations were not militarily invincible vis-à-vis non-Europeans, a lesson not lost on many colonial peoples. Victory catapulted Japan to the status of a significant military power. Adding to its string of successes, Japan annexed Korea in 1910. In 1911, extraterritorial concessions made earlier in treaties with Europeans were ended. From the Japanese point of view, equality with the West was achieved by the end of World War I, when Japan sat with the victors at Versailles, although it had played only a minor role in the war. China, by contrast, continued to be treated very differently. Nevertheless, despite its growing might, Japan was regarded by the West as essentially a regional power and not to be taken too seriously in global matters.

Japan had to pay a price for its increasing power, however. Modernization was not an unmixed blessing. Population growth added to the pressure for economic development, resulting in growing dependence on foreign imports and markets. The pursuit of an ambitious foreign policy agenda and especially the emphasis on the military, led to international rivalries. The unity of thought that had existed for centuries gave way to diversity and complexity. Urbanization brought with it rural anxiety and the growth of proletarian unrest. Leadership tension between military elites and political/economic elites would eventually result in a military dictatorship. Demands for greater popular participation were politically destabilizing and difficult to satisfy, especially given the tendency to regard political opposition as subversion.[33]

Sensitive to these and other divisive consequences of modernization, the governing elite stressed the importance of an ideological bond to hold society together. The development of such an ideology became one of the highest priorities of the state. "It was not enough that the polity be centralized, the economy developed, social classes rearranged, international recognition striven for—the people must also be 'influenced,' their minds and hearts made one."[34] To guard against political deviation, the police "came to see themselves as responsible for surveillance of all thought that might disturb the national polity."[35] An important milestone in this process was the issuance of the Peace Preservation Ordinance of 1887, which not only prohibited secret organizations and meetings but also gave the police considerable authority to interfere in political activities.[36] The government went even further in 1890 with the Public Meeting and Political Association Law, which effectively banned national political organizations. Women, foreigners, and underage men were barred from political meetings and from membership in political organizations.[37]

The Imperial System

From the 1890s, when the emperor-centered system crystallized, until 1945, Japan's formal constitutional framework was representative in character. But, because it lacked a commitment to the spirit of democracy, it is not surprising that it eventually failed to function in a democratic fashion. Indeed, the political elites of both right and left had given little support to civil liberties, and there was a lack of concern among the general public.[38] Politics was dominated by small groups, including army and navy service chiefs, whose direct responsibility to the emperor gave them much independence; the leadership of the civil bureaucracy; a select group of people who had the confidence of and access to the emperor, especially former prime ministers; and the heads of the zaibatsu. The lower house of the Diet, given its control over permanent laws and budget, was also a center of power, but this power diminished with the drift toward authoritarianism.[39]

In the early part of the twentieth century, there were some abortive moves toward democratization. The efforts of political parties to gain an increased share of political power initially met with success. In the aftermath of World War I, a social movement emerged that advocated a variety of democratic reforms. This broad-based movement consisted of political groups ranging from labor unions to student organizations. But the liberalization of the regime began to lose its momentum by the end of the 1920s, as the conservatives successfully extended their control over the apparatus of government.

Among the more significant restrictions on democratic politics were the Public Peace Police Law, enacted in 1900, and the establishment of the

Special Higher Police in 1911. The former was aimed at any group deemed antigovernment. Such groups were required to register, and their meetings were frequently disrupted by police. Labor organizations were regarded as disturbing the peace, and strikes were illegal, provisions that seriously weakened the labor movement.[40] The Special Higher Police came to be known as the "thought police" and was charged with controlling social movements and with suppressing the spread of dangerous foreign ideologies.[41] The provision making strikes illegal was soon repealed, however.[42] These measures were followed by the enactment of the Peace Preservation Law in 1925 that defined permissible ideological limits for individuals and groups. It prohibited advocating change in the basic political nature of Japan and criticism of private property.[43] Displaying anything other than orthodox ideas was dangerous, and "by July 1928, there was hardly a liberal professor left in any high school or college in Japan."[44]

Democratic politics was perverted by more than restraints on civil liberties. Corruption and bribery grew to epidemic proportions. Charges and countercharges became a principal medium of political discourse. "Indeed, during the era of party government, politicians engaged in an orgy of mutual vilification, with opposition politicians who schemed to destroy a Cabinet trying to discredit Cabinet officers and their Diet supporters by charging them with indictable offenses."[45]

Japan's eager entry into world politics as an imperial power and its embrace of authoritarian-fascist politics were due in part to internal political and social dynamics. Another factor was the outside world and the opportunities and challenges presented by it. "Ever since Commodore Perry's visit to Japan in 1853, international politics have been decisive in the development of Japan's legal and political institutions."[46] Some scholars have argued that, had there been no external influence, Japan might have continued its slow evolution toward full parliamentary government.[47] In the event, however, these influences upset the elite balance in favor of the military and an emperor-based political cult.[48]

From the time of the restoration in 1868 to the 1930s, Japan's development was conditioned by a sense of insecurity, both physical and cultural. This insecurity led to an exaggerated ambition for national power, respect, and equality. These motives, intertwined and often inseparable, made up the distinctive nationalism that impelled Japan's historical evolution. Japanese nationalism, unlike that in Europe, lacked strong mass support but possessed a dynamism represented by the bureaucracy, the military, and powerful economic interests.[49] This nationalism, moreover, was fed by international developments. World War I upset the balance of power among European nations in East Asia. Japan, which was not a combatant in the war but did have an alliance with Britain, was allowed to seize German holdings in Shandong province, China, and German-held islands in the South Pacific: the Caroline, Mariana, Marshall, Palau, and Yap islands, names that would become familiar to Americans during World War II.

In January 1915, Japan made twenty-one demands of China, furthering a process of encroachment on the sovereignty of China that began with the 1894–95 war. The Japanese demanded control of Shandong, Manchuria, Inner Mongolia, the southeastern coast of China, and the Yangtze river valley. Another demand, "the most sinister of all, required employment of Japanese advisers in Chinese political, financial, military, and police administrations, as well as purchase of at least 50 percent of China's munitions from Japan."[50] This move by Japan was particularly significant for two reasons. It was a departure from the understanding developed among world powers over the preceding decades not to act unilaterally with respect to China. It also exacerbated the growing estrangement between Japan and the United States, which had become the main protector of the Chinese republic, newly established in 1911.[51] Another factor contributing to estrangement between the United States and Japan concerned the issue of race. In 1905 the California legislature passed a resolution calling for a ban on immigration, and Congress passed the Japanese Exclusion Act in 1924, which understandably rankled the Japanese.[52]

In the late 1920s, while relations with China worsened, conservatives adhered to the view that Japan's international security was being compromised by the activities of political groups operating within the country. This argument was used to justify the massive arrests of leftists in 1928–29. Conservative anxiety about Japan's political integrity was further stimulated by economic problems that made left-wing politics and socialist ideologies more attractive among the lower classes.

In the decade leading up to World War II, the Great Depression unsettled the politics of many countries. Fearful for their own survival, governments showed increasing preference for authoritarian political methods. Japan did not escape the crushing effects of the worldwide economic collapse of the 1930s. The economy, already weakened in the previous decade, encountered severe problems.[53] Workers and peasants, who were particularly hard hit, were eager to find relief from their plight, and a political climate prevailed in which the public wanted to find someone to blame for the state of affairs. A scapegoat was found in political parties. The question became who should rule—the civilian elites, who many felt were responsible for the country's difficulties, or the military, whose reputation was as yet unsullied.

Political interests favoring the rightward drift of politics were able to exploit patriotic enthusiasm when the Japanese position in Manchuria appeared to be at risk. After the first war with China, Japan did not annex Manchuria but maintained the facade of Chinese sovereignty. But the Japanese viewed with suspicion the success of General Chiang Kai-shek's efforts to unify China during the period 1926–28 and the ensuing rise of Chinese nationalism.[54] For China to put its political house in order was not in Japan's interest.[55]

Many Japanese saw Manchuria as a vital economic asset that they could ill-afford to surrender. Faced with a crumbling situation, the army contrived a bomb incident on September 18, 1931, which was used as justification for a full-scale attack on Chinese troops. The civilian government in Tokyo wanted an end to hostilities and ordered the army to stop, but the advance continued anyway. This became known as the Manchurian (or Mukden) Incident, and it spurred rightist revolutionary activity in Japan during 1931–36, including the Young Officers Rebellion of February 26, 1936. The latter led to a purging of the military and the suppression of the left and liberal political factions, all in the name of patriotism. Patriotic zealots assassinated leading generals and politicians, including one prime minister. Their hostility toward the ruling elite came in part from the widespread corruption of Japanese politics.[56] In subsequent trials, the killers were treated as heroes. Most received light sentences and were freed after a few years.[57]

The success of European fascism attracted the attention of the Japanese right and served as an appealing political model. Indeed Japan's increasing restlessness and international ambitions made it ripe for a pattern of development like that occurring in Germany and Italy. The government had used education, the media, and various grassroots organizations to encourage chauvinistic nationalist sentiment in support of industrialization and international stature. Now the government was caught in a trap of its own making and reaped the whirlwind. "Such was the success of Japanese society in marrying an ancient, premodern, undemocratic structure with modern machine civilization."[58]

> Army officers who had built a centralized, planned economy in Manchukuo (i.e. the name given to Manchuria by the Japanese) wanted to do the same for Japan. They wanted to do away with the stale ideas of political parties competing for power and private corporations competing for money. If all Japan could be united in a common goal, Japan could unite all of East Asia. The resulting bloc—the resulting Japanese empire—could withstand any challenge, military or economic. Then, and only then, would the final goals of the Meiji Restoration be realized. To these officers, this was the path to true independence and security. It turned out to be the road to disaster.[59]

The growing military confrontation with China over Japan's continental empire strengthened the hands of the militarists and jingoist bureaucrats. From

1932 to 1936, Japan was governed by Cabinets twice headed by admirals. While there was considerable sentiment for a more pacific approach, these voices were drowned in the cheers that accompanied military success. The Japanese also found little to discourage them in the broader international context. Their imperial inclinations were stimulated by the West's weak response to Japanese aggression in China.[60]

The second Sino-Japanese war began in 1937. Japanese of all persuasions regarded their country's involvement in China as sanctioned by economic need. They considered it their destiny to create a new order in Asia that would expel Western influence and establish a new structure based on Asian concepts of justice and humanity.[61] Of course, the Japanese would take the lead in defining and implementing these concepts.

Japan's defeat in World War II can be attributed to a combination of factors. Tokyo seriously underestimated the capacity of the United States in both material and psychological terms. The Japanese high command also lacked a clear vision of what it was doing. Economic colonization of China was one thing, but imperial activities in other parts of Asia lacked a clear purpose. One serious tactical error was Japan's failure to exploit the anticolonial sentiment among the peoples of Asia. Instead, the Japanese acted in ways often more abusive than the Europeans.[62]

Japan's defeat in World War II should not be construed to mean that the intellectual and political legacies of the prewar years have been totally discredited and forgotten. Authoritarianism may not travel well in the contemporary world of Japanese prosperity and growing world influence, but liberal-democratic values are continually under assault, even in those countries where they have been long established. In Japan, the roots of these values do not go very deep.[63]

The failing health of Emperor Hirohito in 1988 led many Japanese to a reassessment of their traditional values in the context of the modern world. The new emperor—Akihito—undertook to diminish the symbolic significance of the imperial institution.[64] But for many Japanese, the emperor stands for the fundamental essence of the state and is not to be trifled with.[65] It is likely that beneath the surface, there is still considerable reverence for the past and the real or imagined values implied by it. With the right combination of circumstances, traditional values could once again assert themselves. This does not mean that the Japanese might seriously entertain the notion that international influence can be obtained by the exercise of military power. It does mean that the Japanese want to attain an important position in world affairs, but on their own terms. They do not wish to join the West in any psychological sense or become like it. The way in which Japan sorts through the issues of self-identity and awareness will have considerable significance for the rest of the world.

2

The Occupation

Defeated in World War II, Japan, like its erstwhile ally Germany, was forced to accept the humiliation of occupation by foreign troops. But for Japan there was an important difference. While the occupation was theoretically an "allied" affair acting through the eleven-member Far Eastern Commission (FEC), in actuality it was almost exclusively American.[1] The country would not be partitioned into communist and non-communist sectors, and there would be no zones of occupation, each controlled by troops from one or another of the victorious allies. Not only were the military elements of the occupation from the United States, but the determination of policy was kept as a closely guarded American prerogative. "In the event of differences of opinion among the allies," the operating principle, as stated in the presidential directive on the occupation, was "the policies of the U.S. will govern." General Douglas MacArthur, who held the designation Supreme Commander Allied Powers (SCAP), tolerated no interference with his efforts, especially those intended to eradicate all vestiges of the emperor-centered political system. He intended to accomplish this mission in his own way by democratizing all aspects of Japanese society and instilling Christian values. While the former effort to build democratic institutions was largely successful, the latter objective reflected the personality of MacArthur and proved of less-enduring significance.[2]

The allies, especially the Soviet Union, wanted a hand in the reformation of Japan, but the United States consistently and effectively resisted their efforts. The Soviet Union wanted a zone of occupation for itself on the northernmost of the main islands of Japan—Hokkaido. The United States, in no mood to add Japanese territory to the Soviet empire, firmly rejected the request, leaving the Soviet Union with little more than the opportunity to fulminate against U.S. policies in an essentially powerless commission—the Allied Council for Japan. This Council was intended to advise the SCAP and consisted of the Soviet Union, the United States, Great Britain, and China.[3] The Soviet Union was invited to contribute troops to the occupation and place them under U.S. command. They at first refused, proposing instead a joint military operation with shared Soviet-American command. When they later agreed to a limited military presence, MacArthur withdrew the offer.[4]

The occupation was driven by a sense of urgency. The old order had to be dismantled, a new constitution written, and the "free-will of the Japanese people expressed legitimizing the whole effort. Taking too much time would allow for closer scrutiny of the entire process and opposition to develop, especially in the FEC which was strongly opposed to MacArthur's style. Hence, an election was called for April 1946 that served both as an expression of democracy and a referendum on the constitution. While democratic in form, the election was a weak referendum given that the public had little time to inform itself about the new constitution."[5] The significance of MacArthur's operational style rivaled that of the policies he introduced.[6] He held himself in almost Olympian detachment from the daily routine of business, although many important initiatives were taken solely on his own authority. Although there was an elaborate planning process, MacArthur and his close associates often preferred to act on their own.[7] As a consequence of his high-handed approach, MacArthur was frequently in conflict with his own government.[8] His penchant for independent action, which had been made evident during World War II, ultimately led President Harry Truman to dismiss him from command during the Korean War. After he retired from the army, MacArthur came to be associated with conservative political causes in the United States and was briefly considered a possible candidate for the presidency. During his service in Japan, however, his sympathies were with the moderate left.

MacArthur was an able military man, although he, like most of his colleagues, made serious mistakes.[9] His reputation among the American public was probably unrivaled by any other military leader, something he took every opportunity to cultivate. Although his hunger for publicity and frequent grandstanding tarnished his reputation, he must be given substantial credit for the effectiveness and long-term success of the occupation.

The style of the U.S. occupation was distinguished in another way. It was run by people with little, if any, experiential or academic understanding of Japan. In fact, those who possessed language skills or expertise of other kinds were excluded from important positions. Top advisers were typically China experts with little knowledge of, and even less sympathy for, Japan and the Japanese.[10]

The Goals of the Occupation

In 1945, Japan was faced with two contradictory political traditions. On the one hand, there was the democratic-parliamentary tradition that was neither very extensive nor very substantial. The stronger and certainly more recent tradition was the legacy of authoritarianism. American leaders viewed the latter tradition of authoritarianism as an aberration and the democratic-parliamentary tradition as the normal trajectory for Japan.[11] Given these circumstances, it is no doubt fortunate that the occupation was American. "Had Japan been occupied by the Soviet Union, Japanese capabilities for national planning and collective endeavor would doubtless have made it a model Communist state."[12] The occupation, which originally was expected to last for about two years,[13] actually took seven. During this time, especially until early 1948, the occupation authorities undertook with missionary enthusiasm the task of eradicating authoritarianism and building up liberal democracy through the complete transformation of Japanese society. It was an article of faith that Japan's institutions should be remade in the image of American and European patterns. The occupation's efforts were not only extensive in scope but unique in character. "Before World War II, however, in no modern case did the postwar planners conceive their mission as requiring the total restructuring of the defeated nation's values, behavior, and political, economic, and social institutions with the goal of eventually restoring to that nation a status of independence and equality in the international community."[14] For some Japanese, these efforts were not only unwelcome but tantamount to disaster. This group perceived democratization as misguided, serving the purposes of left-leaning members of the occupation in league with Japanese communists.[15] For most Japanese, however, the changes brought on by the occupation were simply endured as a consequence of defeat.

There was a general absence of conflict between the occupiers and the local population, the latter being pleasantly surprised when the Americans failed to live up to expectations for rape and pillage. Nevertheless, in an operation this large, difficulties were bound to occur, especially given the zeal with which some Americans pursued their occupation duties. At the official level, there were inevitable misunderstandings and disagreements with the Japanese, who were trying to preserve as much of the old order as possible, and the Americans, who were seeking to change it. Considering the viciousness and length of the war, the Japanese got on surprisingly well with the Americans. A spirit of cooperation prevailed despite the wide disparity between the two in culture and personal standards of behavior.[16] But for many Japanese the occupation was a time of severe trial. Many did not have enough to eat and were forced to give up their possessions piece by piece, a situation exacerbated by the initial American indifference to the economic situation in the country.[17] A burgeoning sex industry sprang up to accommodate the occupiers. Some Japanese grew rich in a vigorous black market while others barely survived.[18]

The direction of occupation policy, in broad outline, had been set forth in the Potsdam Declaration issued in July 1945 by the United States, Britain, and

China. The declaration called for the removal of those responsible for the war and the punishment of war criminals. The structure of the economy would be transformed to prevent rearmament and allow for the payment of reparations. Democratic values would be instilled and imperialist ways abolished. Japan would lose its overseas possessions, limiting its sovereignty to the four main islands plus some minor ones.[19]

After the occupation was in place, the first objective, and the most immediate, was the demobilization of the Japanese armed forces. This meant bringing approximately 6.5 million soldiers and other personnel back from the many battlegrounds, disposing of their weapons, and, most important of all, finding some sort of employment for them and reintegrating them into society. This task was largely completed by 1948, although Japanese who found themselves in Soviet hands often waited years to be repatriated. In May 1949, the Soviet Union ended repatriation, with some 375,000 Japanese unaccounted for.[20] The Soviet forces subjected Japanese prisoners of war to intense indoctrination, apparently with the intention of their supporting the Japan Communist Party upon their return home.[21] Related to the repatriation and demobilization of troops was the dismantling of the organizational structure of the military, which formed the basis of government and politics. For the most part, this process went smoothly, although the returning soldiers were not always welcomed by their countrymen.

To ensure that Japan's authoritarian and imperial past would not be repeated, a greater concern for civil liberties and human values was to be instilled in the population. Further, procedures were to be found to promote such an attitude in everyday practice, a goal closely tied to reforms in education.

Conversion from war production to a peacetime economy occasioned policy disputes among the authorities and hardship for the people. Munitions industries were dismantled or converted. In many cases, rebuilding was necessary as a result of wartime destruction and American assistance was of critical importance in this endeavor. The ultimate success of the effort can be seen in Japan's contemporary economic power. It is ironic that Japan, like Germany, came out of the war economically stronger, in the long run at least, than did many of their former adversaries.

In their economic reforms, the occupation authorities were mindful of the lessons of the depression of the 1930s. The economic model favored by the New Deal reformers determined on restructuring Japan was essentially the same as that embraced by the ultranationalist military officers who participated in the failed coup of February 26, 1936. The only difference between the two groups was the American emphasis on democracy and the officers' commitment to the imperial system.[22]

Japan had acquired overseas possessions through military conquest, beginning with the first Sino-Japanese War of 1894–95. Now this empire was to be dismembered and the conquered territories given their independence or put under the jurisdiction of other powers. Taiwan and Manchuria were returned to China, Korea regained its independence, France re-established its claim to Indochina, and the United States found itself in charge of a vast array of Pacific islands administered under a United Nations trusteeship arrangement.

On the social and political agenda were the emancipation of women, educational reform, and economic liberalization. Interestingly, the initiative behind the reforms in women's rights did not come from ideological commitments or the practical efforts of American or Japanese leaders, but from "a policy alliance between a group of low-ranking American women serving in the Occupation and a core of Japanese women leaders who worked closely with them to formulate and advocate women's rights policies."[23] The leadership was soon convinced, however, of the intrinsic merit of these policies, and they were also seen as contributing to the expansion of the popular political base and to the democratization of the economy. Liberalization of education was seen as a vehicle for increasing social and economic opportunity and ending the adoration of the emperor. Education was also expected to promote concern for civil liberties and to encourage social change. Economic reforms, always with an eye toward democratization, were intended to broaden income distribution, expand land ownership, and enhance political competition.

It is ironic that the Americans sought to achieve democratic ends by authoritarian means. "The contradictions of the democratic revolution from above were clear for all to see: while the victors preached democracy, they ruled by fiat; while they espoused equality, they themselves constituted an inviolate privileged caste."[24] During the first phase of the occupation, from 1945 to 1947, the reforms, which were often pursued with zealotry, achieved considerable success.[25] This success was due to the timeliness of the reforms, cooperation on the part of the Japanese, and a willingness by the occupation authorities to be flexible. The more obvious elements of the Japanese military establishment were expeditiously eliminated. Although some Japanese conservatives considered these measures excessive, the military found little support among the general population. The empire was quickly dismembered and Japanese troops returned home from abroad, although a few holdouts remained in hiding in the jungles of Asia for years afterward. The demobilization of the military created a serious problem of unemployment and added to the worsening economic situation.

Ultranationalist and paramilitary groups were formally disbanded, although many simply changed their names to something less objectionable to the occupation. For example, the National Essence Mass Party became the National League of Working People.[26] In the Shinto Directive, issued in

December 1945, state sponsorship of religion was abolished and the people were relieved of the obligation to support religious institutions financially. The teaching of Shinto doctrines in schools was prohibited.[27] Commitment to Shinto was widespread among the Japanese and the occupation authorities viewed it as one of the institutions most supportive of the old imperial system. The Home Ministry (police and local government) was abolished in an effort to weaken the power of the central government. Its replacement, the Local Autonomy Board, eventually became the Ministry of Home Affairs. The police were decentralized and their powers curtailed. Political prisoners, mostly communists and others holding left-wing views, were released.[28]

Top Japanese government officials held responsible for the war and for crimes against humanity were tried by the International Military Tribunal for the Far East. Seven of those found guilty were hanged, and sixteen were sentenced to life in prison. Two others received lesser sentences, two died while the trial was in progress, and one went insane. Several thousand lower-ranking personnel also confronted postwar justice and nearly a thousand were executed.[29]

Japanese war crimes drew much less international attention than did the Nuremburg Tribunal, which tried Nazi war criminals. Nor has there been any continuing effort or even interest, at least in the West, in seeking out and punishing Japanese guilty of atrocities during the war, of which there was no shortage in the Asian theater. The enduring significance in the West of the genocide inflicted by Nazi Germany on European peoples and seeming indifference to war victims in Asia is much resented, particularly by the Chinese.

In addition to those accused of war crimes, a second group of people to be purged from government service was identified. A list of 220,000 persons to be removed from office and barred from holding any future position, of whom 180,000 were military officers, was prepared.[30] Many of the former top officials in the previous government escaped this process, however. Despite strong opposition from several quarters, the emperor was retained albeit with diminished importance. The issue of the future of the emperor system was controversial. Many believed that Hirohito, while not personally to blame for atrocities or the war in general, bore some responsibility and was at least a symbol representing the evils of prewar Japan.[31] Others, such as U.S. Ambassador Joseph Grew, defended the throne.[32] Resisting the call from those who wanted to inflict the fullest measure of retribution on Japan, the Americans acknowledged the symbolic value of the emperor for Japanese pride as well as the need to gain their cooperation. Accordingly, the emperor was retained as constitutional head of state but with no political power. Not only was the emperor absolved of responsibility for the war, but so were all members of the imperial family, some of whom had played important military roles.[33] For his part, Emperor Hirohito made every effort to cooperate with the occupation (a practice that was not universal among Japanese political leaders), which made the occupation easier all around. Hardliners opposed the retention of the emperor, maintaining the Japanese would never understand and practice democracy so long as any vestige of the emperor-based system remained.

The occupation declared its intention to democratize and reform the bureaucracy. But this effort was constrained by, among other things, the inability of the American forces to govern Japan relying exclusively with their own resources. As a practical matter, it was necessary to work through the existing Japanese bureaucracy. In fact, even before the end of the war, MacArthur had envisaged "maximum utilization of existing Japanese governmental agencies and organizations."[34] This dependence proved to be a major barrier to a complete and effective purge of right-wing elements in the government and economy. Removing from positions of influence all persons who shared in the responsibility for the war became even more difficult when the "reverse course" policy was introduced in 1947. When concern about the threat from the political left replaced worries over revived militarism, the old conservative elite was rehabilitated and wartime sins forgotten. Ultimately, the occupation failed to reduce the power of the bureaucracy or to make it more politically responsible.[35] Aldous goes even further: "The Japanese political system appeared to have assumed democratic credentials, but in reality it operated in much the same way as before."[36]

The occupation's reliance on local resources was exploited by the Japanese, who were careful to maintain good relations with the Americans. The Japanese soon discovered that the Americans had a "weakness for entertainment" and plied them with food and drink at every opportunity.[37]

Phase 2 of the occupation, or the "reverse course" period, lasted from 1947 until 1952. This policy reversal was driven by a reinterpretation of the postwar world situation, mainly the changing role of the Soviet Union, the communist revolution in China, and real and potential threats to the security of the Middle East and Asia.[38] From the Japanese point of view, the Korean War greatly altered the situation in Asia.[39] American interest in enhancing Japanese economic strength began to take precedence over the desire for retribution and even over the commitment to achieve reforms. Indeed, enthusiasm for experiments in social and political engineering had begun to wane as early as 1947, when most of the reforms were either completed or shelved. Since the end of the war, political alignments had come full circle. The United States and its severest critics, conservative Japanese, were now in close alliance. The former harmony of interest between the United States and Japanese reformers had turned into antagonism.[40] As occupation policy turned in new directions, the influence of SCAP declined. A formal settlement of the war in the form of a peace treaty did not occur until 1952. Symptomatic of the emerging problems of the time, neither the Soviet Union nor China signed the treaty.

Initiative for the reverse course came from the United States, especially from conservative businessmen, and it fit in neatly with the views of Japanese leaders, such as Shigeru Yoshida.[41] Although the initial approach to postwar Japan had been seen in the context of Japan's wartime activities, by 1947, U.S. policymakers were viewing with favor Japan's potential role in Asian economic expansion.[42] The Dodge Plan, introduced in 1948, called for deflationary measures intended to make Japan economically self-sufficient by 1953. Government expenditures were reduced, the size of the bureaucracy was curtailed, and credit was tightened. Big business was back in favor because of the advantages of "economies of scale." To promote economic expansion, the Ministry of International Trade and Industry was created in 1949.[43] The austerity measures contained in this approach hit small business very hard and had Japan sliding into depression by 1949. But the program eventually produced a thorough shakeout of the economy and provided the basis for later growth. One distinctive advantage in the economic recovery stemmed from the fact that Japanese economic resources did not flee the country when it became clear that the war was lost. Nor did the Japanese engage in organized efforts to hide their assets from the occupation authorities.[44]

Labor

In the 1920s and 1930s, opposition to the developing pattern of authoritarian politics had come from labor organizations and some political parties. They fought for democratic institutions and practices, but their efforts met with little success. When the right wing came to dominate the political scene, labor rapidly lost influence and fell into a state of political and economic ineffectiveness. As a result of this experience, labor had little stake in the preservation of the old prewar value system and readily embraced, perhaps too enthusiastically, the democratic goals of the occupation.

Occupation encouragement of a strong labor movement and especially unionization reflected the ideology of the Americans. The desirability of a politically and economically vigorous labor movement, an article of faith among New Dealers, was seen as a way of broadening the popular base of the system. Unionization was also seen as a part of the process of eliminating barriers to the exercise of civil liberties. On October 5, 1945, SCAP issued a directive on Removal of Restrictions on Political, Civil, and Religious Liberties. This directive abrogated laws, ordinances, and other restrictions on labor and other groups in their exercise of freedom of speech, press, and organization. The Thought Police, which had been a key agency in promoting philosophical orthodoxy, was disbanded, and its members declared ineligible for other public office. Responsibility for labor issues was transferred from the Home Ministry to the Ministry of Welfare.

On October 11, 1945, MacArthur stated publicly that he expected action to "encourage unionization of labor." This was followed in 1946 by the Trade Union Act and the Labor Relations Act. The Labor Standards Act was promulgated in 1947. Collectively, these measures gave workers the rights to organize, to bargain collectively, and to strike. Employers who refused to deal with unions were penalized and mechanisms were established to deal with labor disputes.[45]

The success of these efforts would prove their undoing. The growing political militancy of the labor movement prompted a reassessment of labor policy. Both the occupation authorities and Japanese leaders feared the growing strength of the political left. Unionization of the workforce seemed to be having the undesirable effect of promoting the leftward political drift of the labor movement.[46] To prevent labor-related political instability from spreading, the labor movement was weakened by discouraging industry-wide unions. The resulting fragmentation of labor in time led to the development of enterprise unions and to a permanent state of political weakness in the labor movement. Although labor possessed the formal right to strike, bargain, and organize, in actual practice, this part of the occupation reform agenda was heavily retrenched.

The retrenchment had enduring consequences, not only for organized labor but for areas of public policy, such as education. Concern for "the Red Menace" during the occupation resulted in a polarization between conservatives and progressives that affects education to this day. Conservatives saw that even the American advocates of democracy could compromise their principles. For their part, the progressives saw little alternative but to radicalize their approach.[47]

By 1952, the occupation had made a complete about-face in its crusade against undesirable elements in the Japanese body politic. At first, the right wing was viewed as the biggest problem, presenting the danger of a renewal of militarism. But within five years of the end of the war, left-wing, especially communist, influences were the subjects of occupation purges.[48] In this, labor was a principal target. The beneficiaries of this new orientation were individuals previously purged for their association with Japan's militaristic past. Now these people were rehabilitated and allowed to return to public activity.[49]

Land Reform

In contrast to efforts addressed to labor, "perhaps the most successful reform measure implemented by SCAP" was land reform.[50] Credit for this success, however, should not be assigned exclusively to American initiative. Land reform was a program whose time had come in Japan irrespective of the war and the occupation. The Japanese themselves saw the need for changes, and, in this area at least, they and the Americans happened to be largely of the same mind.[51]

Before the war, 46 percent of the land had been cultivated by tenant farmers who paid 75 percent of their rent in kind. The proportion of farmers who owned no land was 28 percent. Under the reform program, farmers could keep 7.5 acres to farm, plus another 2.5 acres that they did not have to cultivate. The government purchased the rest and sold it to former tenants, who were to pay for it over a thirty-year period at 3.2 percent interest.[52] As a result of this program, by 1950, 90 percent of all farmers were landowners. Only 10 percent of the land was cultivated by tenants. Rents were controlled at half or less of prewar levels and were to be paid in cash, rather than a share of the crop.[53] Land reform was not so revolutionary in scope that the traditional landed elites were politically and economically crushed. Eventually, they would be handsomely compensated for their losses by the Japanese government. Nor were the benefits of the reform evenly distributed, since more prosperous tenants working larger plots of land tended to gain more than those on tiny plots.[54] Because of this favorable treatment, the agricultural community remained a loyal supporter of Liberal Democratic Party (LDP) governments and enjoyed influence out of proportion to its numbers.

Education

Before the war, Japanese schoolchildren were confronted by an educational system that was rigorously selective. The type of study program a student would follow and his advancement in it were based on aptitude and ability. There were three basic tracks: technical, vocational, and university. Students with the weakest academic potential entered technical or vocational schools, while those showing greater promise went to the universities. Such a system was not unique to Japan, of course, as the same approach was common in Europe. The elite nature of this educational philosophy, however, ran counter to the democratic values of the occupation authorities. Given the importance of education for attaining its reform agenda, the occupation assigned a high priority to restructuring the educational system and changing the philosophy on which it rested.[55] To this end, two laws were enacted by the Japanese government in March 1947. The first was the Basic Law on Education, which defined the new philosophy under which education would henceforth operate. The second measure was the School Education Law, which delineated the new organizational structure of the system.

The postwar reforms were intended to make education less rigid and to afford greater opportunities for larger numbers of people, an undertaking that received widespread support from the Japanese.[56] An attempt was made to introduce educational methodologies like those used in the United States, which stress the "development" of the individual based on interests as well as ability. Greater emphasis was placed on analysis and interpretation as teaching methods, as opposed to the traditional system of rote learning and indoctrination. The inculcation of authoritarian political values, especially Shinto, was prohibited. Support in this effort came from the Japan Teachers' Union (JTU), which criticized the prewar role of teachers as too subject to state control.[57] Indeed, teachers as a group had been among the most devoted supporters of the imperial system, being "one of the most militaristic groups of people in Japanese society, perhaps next only to the military itself."[58]

In its dissatisfaction with the prewar role of the teaching profession, the JTU placed much of the blame on centralized authority over education, a view that the JTU shared with occupation authorities. Efforts to decentralize education, however, ran counter to the interests of the Ministry of Education (MOE). Thus when they departed, the Americans left behind a politically polarized educational system pitting the JTU against the MOE. This conflict, among other things, jeopardized the long-term effectiveness of the occupation reforms.[59]

Another problem diminishing the reform's impact was the fact that the new education philosophy was alien to Japanese culture, which values orderliness and predictability over individual initiative and freedom of choice. Conservatives opposed the reforms on the grounds that they resulted in a loss of commitment to the teaching of social values and citizenship.[60] In time, "progressive education" yielded to more familiar methods, including rote learning. Occupation reforms and the resulting educational system are discussed further in Chapter 11.

To broaden opportunities for higher education, 226 universities of various types were established by 1952. These were not new institutions but enhancements of schools that had existed before the war. Enrollment in these institutions increased dramatically, but their performance was substandard given the lack of educational resources.[61] The sudden appearance of institutions of higher education that were necessarily of marginal quality enhanced the prestige of the older schools and increased competition to gain entry into them.[62] The high status of a handful of schools is a phenomenon that continues today.

The *Zaibatsu*

During the later stages of the war, as it was becoming increasingly clear that military defeat was unavoidable, the business community took measures to protect itself from blame for starting the war and for losing it. Records were destroyed and personnel reassigned. Large stocks of equipment were obtained by industrial interests during the war, which were hidden for later disposal.

These farsighted efforts bore considerable fruit after the war. The political and economic power enjoyed by the large cartels, called *zaibatsu,* made them likely targets for reformers. President Truman moved to break up the zaibatsu as he viewed them as a source and major supporter of militarism. But in this as in most everything else, it was necessary to rely on Japanese cooperation. The government and the business community resisted and delayed. It was only the power of MacArthur's position that forced any action at all.

Several plans were developed to deal with the zaibatsu issue. One was the Yasuda Plan, in which the zaibatsu themselves had a substantial input. It called for the breakup of the four largest clan-dominated combines. The families would give up their shares in the holding companies that controlled hundreds of subsidiary firms. The subsidiaries themselves, however, would remain intact.[63] This was largely a cosmetic gesture intended to screen smaller companies from scrutiny by occupation authorities. Another, the Pauley Plan, was offered by the United States and called for sweeping action, including the transfer of Japanese industry to the countries ravaged by the war. Half of machine-tool capacity, all shipyard facilities (except that needed for repairs of equipment deemed "essential to the occupation"), all magnesium and aluminum production capacity, and half of all thermal-generating plants would have been removed under this plan.[64]

The breakup of the zaibatsu was essentially a failure for two reasons. First, the move was unpopular among the Japanese. There was considerable resistance and foot-dragging by the government and the business community, which were more comfortable with a hierarchically structured system of industrial organization than with "industrial democracy."[65] The purge of those involved in the war was not complete; many of the old political and economic elites not only survived but continued to hold important positions. Second, by the late 1940s, opposition to the idea of crushing the zaibatsu was growing in the United States among business leaders. In April 1948, the United States announced that it was abandoning most of the anti-zaibatsu program.[66] International events, especially the advent of the cold war, were responsible for a change in attitude and a new perception that Japan needed a strong economy rather than a weak one. After the occupation ended, the practices of cross-ownership of stock and interlocking directorates were revived. The zaibatsu, which were family-based holding companies, were replaced by *keiretsu,* networks of companies held together by common linkages to banks and trading companies.[67]

The 1947 Constitution

Although there has been considerable controversy over the appropriateness of many occupation reforms, all things considered, American efforts to rebuild and reform Japan, especially the establishment of a new constitution, constitute one of the greater success stories in the history of U.S. foreign policy.[68] This remains true despite the fact that the constitution was an American invention that was not well received by all Japanese. It is perhaps surprising that the constitution has endured, given the gap between American and Japanese political philosophies. "The adoption of the postwar constitution proceeded through a maze of mutual misunderstanding attributable to deep-rooted differences in legal culture."[69] The most plausible explanation for the initial acceptance of the constitution and its subsequent durability lies in the fact that it was presented to the Japanese people in its Japanese-language version as a logical continuation of the Meiji constitution.[70] Nevertheless, as the past nearly half-century has revealed, long-term results of this approach have certainly been more felicitous than those produced by the approach to the defeated countries following World War I.

The new constitution reflected much of American political philosophy and especially that of the New Deal, a philosophy that at the time was widely held even among conservative Republicans like Douglas MacArthur.[71] The genesis of the constitution was ticklish, and some issues had to be addressed carefully in fear of serious popular opposition. The Japanese, as might be expected, wanted to retain as much of their old system as possible. Given the central importance of the emperor, not only as a political institution but as a central ingredient in Japanese political philosophy, there was great concern that he be retained. The U.S. government saw the need to keep the emperor as a unifying force but with his importance much reduced. The Japanese communists, the Soviet Union, and some American allies, such as Australia, wanted all the old ways to be scrapped, in particular the emperor, whom they regarded as a war criminal.[72]

The diminished role of the emperor is one of the main differences between the constitutions of 1889 and 1947. Not only had the emperor been the source and location of all authority, but he had been accorded religious importance. The emperor-based state concept was replaced in the new document by the doctrine of popular sovereignty. This idea, a distinctly Western notion, was essentially imposed on the Japanese, since it was not part of their historical and philosophical tradition and it is fairly evident that they were not altogether clear about its meaning.[73] The fact that they have found it a genial idea and accepted it as part of their value system is a rather remarkable development. Many other countries have tried popular constitutional government at their own initiative and have failed. The Japanese had it forced on them by an occupying army and have made it work. Part of this is due to a vigorous educational effort to inculcate the population with the values of the constitution, an enterprise in which teachers were largely sympathetic and enthusiastic.[74]

Several parts of the constitution are, for the Japanese at least, highly innovative. In Chapter I, Article 1, the new status of the emperor is defined by the words: "The emperor shall be the symbol of the state and of the unity of the people, deriving his position from the will of the people with whom resides sovereign power." At one point in the drafting process, Prime Minister Kijuro Shidehara substituted the word "supreme" for "sovereign." Four months later, the U.S. authorities noticed the change and reinstated "sovereign."[75]

Another critical innovation in the constitution is in Chapter II, Article 9. An objective of victorious powers in any war is to prevent the defeated from waging war again. After the conclusion of World War I, the victorious allies, especially the French, wanted to impose penalties and reparations on the Germans so that they could never again be a military threat. On General MacArthur's initiative, a different approach was taken to Japan. Article 9 of the constitution called for the permanent renunciation of war.

> Aspiring sincerely to an international peace based on justice and order, the Japanese people forever renounce war as a sovereign right of the nation and the threat or use of force as a means of settling international disputes.
>
> In order to accomplish the aim of the preceding paragraph, land, sea, and air force, as well as other war potential, will never by maintained. The right of belligerency of the state will not be recognized.

In addition to the obvious effect of curtailing Japan's war-making potential, this measure was intended to mollify the allies, especially Australia and the Soviet Union, which had wanted the emperor to be tried as a war criminal.[76] Many U.S. officials in the State and War Departments saw a link between the institution of the emperor and Japanese militarism. This view was largely shared by the American public.[77]

In an effort to promote civil liberties and ensure their survival, Chapter III contains a lengthy enumeration of the rights and duties of the people.[78] Interestingly, while the Japanese are serious-minded about their rights and freedoms, there has been less controversy and political friction over them than has occurred in the United States where the very notion of "natural rights" is the basis of the republic. This may be due in no small measure to the novelty of the concept of rights. "As of 1945, neither judges nor citizenry were accustomed to the notion of a constitutional right—to free speech for example—that was legally binding in and on a court of law."[79]

Despite the fact that the constitution is a document crafted largely by Americans, it does not establish a government employing the "separation of powers" doctrine. There is no provision, for example, for the direct election of the chief executive.[80] Instead, "the basic model here was the classic British version of parliamentary government, commonly identified as the Westminster model." This approach was thought to be consistent with Japanese constitutional experience and scholarship that equates democracy with a popularly elected legislature.[81]

Chapter IV describes the legislative branch of the government, the Diet. It is to be a bicameral body (the Americans at first favored a unicameral legislature), although the lower house is the more powerful. Members of the lower house, the House of Representatives, are elected for four-year terms or less if the house is dissolved. The upper house, the House of Councillors, is elected for a six-year term and is not subject to dissolution. In the event that the upper house does not concur with the lower, the latter may override the wishes of the former by a two-thirds vote of the members present. The House of Councillors must act within sixty days of receiving a bill from the lower house. Failure to act within this time limit may be taken to mean rejection of the bill. On budget matters, initiative rests with the House of Representatives. In the event of irreconcilable differences with the House of Councillors or if the latter fails to act within thirty days, the decision of the House of Representatives is final. The same applies to treaties. Finally, ministers are required under the constitution to appear in the Diet to answer questions.

Chapter V describes the Cabinet. All ministers must be civilians, another effort to keep the military out of government. All ministers are collectively responsible to the Diet. The prime minister is chosen from the Diet, and he in turn appoints other ministers, but the majority must come from the Diet. That is, some ministers in the Cabinet may not be members of the Diet but in practice almost all of them have been.

Chapter VI details the judiciary. Judges are appointed by the Cabinet, while the chief justice is appointed by the emperor on recommendation of the Cabinet. To give a measure of popular control over the judiciary, there is a requirement that judges be reviewed by the voters at the first election following their appointment and every ten years thereafter. This is not significant in practice, however, as no judge has yet been removed. In Article 81, the Supreme Court is given the explicit authority to review the constitutionality of any government act, but this authority has been used sparingly.

Chapter VIII, Article 92, concerns privileges of local government and was designed to strengthen local government as a further protection against a return to authoritarianism. The spirit of this constitutional provision was modified during the reverse-course period, and, as a result, local government has since enjoyed little autonomy.

Chapter IX enumerates the process for amending the constitution. Amendments are proposed by two-thirds of the Diet and ratified by a majority of the voters. The constitution has yet to be amended.

Postwar Japan offers one of history's happier examples of defeat, occupation, and reconstruction. It was so regarded by the Japanese themselves: "Criticism of Americans is a right accorded even to Americans. But in the enumeration of their faults we cannot include their Occupation of Japan."[82] On balance, the "American interlude" must be judged a success, although there is considerable room for reasonable dissent over specifics. This is especially true regarding the proposition that Japan's brand of economic development, nurtured by the occupation, constitutes an ideal type. But by most conventional standards—stability, civil liberties, literacy, prosperity—Japan has done well.[83]

Part II

The Political Process

3

The Structure of Government

The politics of democracy is an exercise in balancing the need for efficiency in the conduct of the business of government with protection against the arbitrary and abusive exercise of power. Historically, there have been few successful attempts to achieve and maintain such a balance. For most political systems, the power that government exercises over the people is checked in only the most limited way, if at all. The ruler is accountable only to God if he is unable to claim successfully to be a God himself. The intervention of God in the political affairs of man is infrequent, at least in knowable form.[1] Apart from appeals to divine intervention, formulas for controlling political power take a variety of forms, usually consisting of political institutions arranged in different combinations. Constitutions, which themselves act as a bulwark against tyranny by placing the source of governing authority outside government itself, are employed to define such institutional combinations. Among the many institutions that play a part in guarding against tyranny, three have proved most important. The first is a system of popular elections to make the government in some way accountable to the people. (The Japanese electoral system is discussed in Chapter 7.) The second institution is a judiciary that is capable of making independent judgments, free of coercion from other branches of government. The third is a legislative process that draws its authority from and is ultimately responsible to the citizenry. In the most immediate sense, the integrity of democracy in any country is determined by the condition and vigor of its legislature.

The Legislative Process

Legislatures typically operate in a slow, cumbersome, and contentious manner. They contribute little to the expeditious conduct of the business of government, a circumstance for which they are often criticized. But by virtue of this very dilatory manner, legislatures are an important element in promoting the cause of democracy in government. Legislative deliberations are usually less decisive and more prolonged in proportion to the complexity or controversial nature of an issue. But this is as it should be. Those charged with the management of political affairs are tempted to place in jeopardy the broader, and enduring, public interest in order to achieve immediate results. The legislative branch, more than the other branches, carries the burden of measuring the need for timely action against public interests as they are now or will be in the future. Never have the virtues of democracy been preserved, for long at any rate, when the government has been the exclusive province of executive authority. The existence of a legislature whose members owe their position to the voters rather than to the executive is an effective, although by no means infallible, protector of democratic interests. In Japan, as elsewhere, the legislature's function is to identify and put in focus the public interest while, at the same time, acting as a check on the executive. How effective is the Japanese legislature, the Diet, in meeting this challenge?

Legislatures differ significantly in their composition and operation. Although Japan's has much in common with counterparts elsewhere in the world, it also has some distinctive qualities. Members of the Diet do not collectively see themselves as the supreme power of the state, as is typical in parliamentary systems, in particular, the British Parliament.[2] The Diet does not have the kind of independence that characterizes many legislatures, especially the U.S. Congress. The system of "checks and balances," so familiar to Americans, does not exist in Japan. Power is shared among the legislature, the "government" (i.e., the Cabinet), and the bureaucracy. The Diet does not play a decisive role in the initiation and refinement of public policy; for all practical purposes it is limited to "rubber-stamping" decisions made elsewhere. Nevertheless, the legislative process is of considerable political significance, especially in its role as a focal point of public discussion and opinion formation and in maintaining popular support for the overall governing process.[3]

Legislatures are delicate things. They are easy to create, but making them work effectively is another matter. The list of successful legislatures throughout history is short. One important factor is longevity and the ability to build on experience. All too frequently legislatures are dismissed by authoritarian rulers, usually under the excuse of preserving order, thus preventing the legislative process from achieving maturity. The Japanese are not unfamiliar with legislatures; the legislative system established under the constitution of 1947 was not a radical innovation. Experience with legislative bodies goes back at least as far as the 1889 constitution, and the present arrangement is basically a refinement of practices developed in the 1920s.

The Diet is bicameral, and, in common with the great majority of the world's democracies, most power resides in the lower house. It is a parliamentary system in the pattern of the Westminster model in Britain. The upper house is weaker than the lower, but it is not essentially irrelevant to the legislative process, as is the British House of Lords. Although its organization and operation resemble those of the British Parliament, the Diet does have a few things in common with the U.S. Congress, such as a significant committee structure. In addition, some of the rules of procedure are like those used by American legislators.[4]

Membership in the Diet is broadly based, at least in theory. There are no narrow qualifications for membership, such as property, religion, or political affiliation. Any person who is twenty-five years old and a qualified voter is eligible to run for the Diet. Many candidates run, and some are elected, as independents. Typically, however, winning a seat in the Diet is a function of party affiliation. Members of the Diet are not legally required to be residents of the district that they represent. In actual practice, however, close personal ties exist between politicians and voters. No one would run in a district in which he or she was totally unknown.

The role of party identity in the electoral and legislative processes is somewhat paradoxical. The party is the single most important variable governing election to the Diet, but as a general rule, party loyalty among voters is fairly weak. Most voters do not have a strong psychological attachment to a particular party, even though they might vote for it regularly. This does not mean, however, that there is a lack of discipline or internal cohesion among parties in the parliament. It is not common for members of the Diet to vote against their party's position and rarer still for them to "cross the floor," that is, change their party affiliation. This has been less true in recent years as several new parties have come into existence made up of members of older parties.

There is a distinct commonality in the social background of members of the Diet. The experience of most members, outside politics, has been in the world of business. Following at a considerable distance in terms of numbers are representatives formerly employed by bureaucracy with organized labor, the third most common background. Unlike the U.S. Congress, most of whose members are lawyers, the Diet has very few members with legal credentials. "This phenomenon may be accounted for by the decline in prestige of lawyers in general and the fact that detailed legal knowledge is not a critical qualification or a condition required of a Diet member. It should also be noted that lawyers are not in the best position for collecting votes."[5]

Another important factor governing electoral success among Diet candidates appears to be family. Nearly 40 percent of the Liberal Democratic Party (LDP) candidates in the 1990 lower house election were children of Diet members.[6] This phenomenon is, however, a product of the growing influence of support groups (kōenkai) in selecting candidates. Those candidates who have the stamp of approval of the local kōenkai are more likely than are others to win a seat in the Diet. There is also a distinct tendency for kōenkai to choose relatives of the previous occupant of the seat.[7] This is probably because relatives of the incumbent become known to members of the kōenkai during the course of ongoing political activities. Thus relatives have an advantage, not because they are relatives, but because they are well positioned to establish important contacts.

Organization

The upper house, called the House of Councillors, is the successor to the prewar House of Peers, a body that had been made up mainly of the hereditary nobility. After the abolition of the aristocracy, a system of elections was introduced as a method of legislative recruitment. These elections now produce 242 members of the upper house, who serve six-year terms. Of these, 146 are elected from the forty-seven prefectures. In addition, 96 run at large on party lists, that is, they are chosen by all voters nationally. Half the seats in the House of Councillors are contested in elections held at fixed three-year intervals.

The visibility of the upper house, together with the fact that part of its membership is chosen from a national or at-large constituency, has attracted a considerable number of celebrities who are able to exploit their name recognition with the public. As in the lower house, the LDP has enjoyed a long history of success in House of Councillor elections. Candidates who have the backing of large groups, such as unions, also do well.[8]

Beginning with the 1983 election, councillors from the national constituency have been selected by a process in which voters cast their ballots for a party, rather than for an individual candidate. It was initially thought that the new system would diminish the "popularity contest" aspect of upper house elections. This has not proved to be the case, however, as parties, especially the LDP, have recruited well-known figures to run under their banners. Small parties have been less successful in attracting famous people to run and are affected by the proportional representation system; seats are allocated on the basis of the size of the total party vote. To attract enough votes, small parties are sometimes forced to form coalitions, a practice that can add to voter confusion.[9]

The lower house, called the House of Representatives, underwent major changes in the 1990s. The old arrangement in which 512 members were elected from multiple member districts was replaced with one in which 300 members are now chosen from single-member districts and 180 under a party-list system of proportional representation. The term of office remains four years. The time between elections can be shortened at the discretion of the prime minister, who can dissolve the House and call elections. Elections are also normally held if the government loses a vote of confidence. The members of the House themselves can also call an election.

Each chamber of the Diet chooses its own presiding officers: the speaker and vice speaker in the lower house and the president and vice president in the upper house. When the LDP has been in power, these leaders have usually been selected from the ranks of senior members of the party, a practice that compromises their independence and neutrality.[10] Nominally the presiding officers have broad formal powers, including, for example, that of making committee assignments. In practice, however, such assignments are handled by party leaders.

The Diet meets annually for a normal session of 150 days, and it can be extended once. Under the constitution, extraordinary sessions may be called, and there are usually two or three of these each year since the Diet does not complete its work during the regular session. There are also special sessions that deal with such matters as the selection of a new prime minister.

Like the U.S. Congress, the Diet employs committees to expedite legislative business. In the United States, this practice tends to fragment power and weakens the effectiveness of the legislature as a collective entity. The effect is attenuated in the Japanese Diet by the fact that the committees are considerably less powerful than their American counterparts. The committees generally parallel the various ministries. In addition, two other committees—Audit and Budget—are theoretically very important. The Audit Committee is supposed to review past government practice and performance but has not been very effective. The Budget Committee deals with the all-important matter of public expenditures. The Budget Committee has had little opportunity to act independently on the budget since the committee has been controlled by the same party (the LDP) that has controlled the Ministry of Finance and other important executive agencies. The LDP's loss of control over the Diet (see Chapter 4) has meant greater autonomy for the ministries. In committee sessions, members query ministers on all manner of topics, whether or not related to the budget.[11] Questioning government officials during Budget Committee sessions affords opposition party members one of the few opportunities available to them to call government officials and their policies to account.[12]

Each member of the Diet can expect at least one committee assignment. Typically assignments are made, by the LDP at any rate, by reverse seniority. Junior members are given choice committee assignments in order to enhance their relationship with their constituents. Senior members, who already have strong organizations, take the less politically rewarding committees, such as foreign affairs.[13]

Committees have little opportunity to shape the character of legislation that is eventually approved by the Diet. Nevertheless, the fact that they can hold hearings serves as something of a check on the government's ability to enact any law that it wants. On balance, "the standing (subject-matter) committee system is probably the least successful postwar innovation in the internal organization of the Diet."[14]

According to the rules, committee chairmen are elected in each house from among members of the committee but, in practice, they are appointed by the speaker in consultation with the parties. Chairmen have extensive formal powers governing the procedural operation of the committees.[15] They do not, however, have the power of life and death over legislation that committee chairmen have in the U.S. Congress.

Members of the Diet are provided with a staff of two secretaries, although influential members frequently hire more at their own expense. It is also typical for members to have someone working for them in their districts. One of the most important functions of secretaries is maintaining good relations with constituents, who have come to expect favors from their Diet representative.[16]

The Diet maintains a substantial support bureaucracy that provides research and legal assistance to the members. Each chamber has a secretariat headed by a director general. The work of the secretariat is mainly to aid members of the opposition parties, since the LDP can draw on the ministries and other government agencies for support services as well as an elaborate party bureaucracy.[17]

Procedure

All legislatures have their own distinctive formal and informal styles of operation. The British House of Commons has been known historically for its dignity and the quality of debate. In the U.S. Congress, important decisions are made in committees or in informal gatherings of a few key representatives, senators, or even staff personnel. In Japan, the dominance of the LDP throughout most of the postwar period has worked to define the legislative process.

Even though it has controlled the Diet, the LDP has not always been able to get its way simply because it has a majority of the votes. The opposition can even prevent enactment of legislation if it is unified and has public support, but that confluence of factors does not often occur. Sometimes, the LDP failed repeatedly to pass legislation, but usually got its way in the end. This was true of the consumption tax, for example, which took ten years to enact.[18] The LDP did not thoroughly dominate the Diet because minority parties have had tactics available to them that accorded influence exceeding mere numbers. These tactics include a pattern of legislative behavior that occasionally has lacked the orderliness and decorum that might be expected from a people who generally conduct themselves in a disciplined and mannerly way. Dignified proceedings are sometimes absent in the legislative process when controversies reach high levels of intensity. This rarely happens, however, since compromise is usually reached through intensive and prolonged bargaining. Disorder occurs over an issue that is too volatile for compromise or when someone, particularly in the opposition, wants to make a highly visible public statement. On occasion the government has locked out the opposition, such as occurred in 1960, when rancorous debate prevented a vote on the renewal of the Mutual Security Treaty.

Perhaps due to finding itself perpetually in the minority, the opposition has resorted to disruptive tactics. Since it has been excluded from the process of drafting the government's legislation and its own proposals stand no chance of success, the opposition tries to force concessions by methods that can include obstructionism.[19] Opposition members talk or debate at length to tie up legislative business, a tactic called a filibuster. They can engage in an "ox walk," a procedure in which members take an inordinate amount of time to walk a short distance to cast their ballots. This tactic was used in the successful effort to defeat Prime Minister Yasuhiro Nakasone's plan to introduce a 5 percent tax in 1987. The plan was opposed by many Diet members, including several in the LDP, not only because of its unpopularity with the public, but also because it was poorly designed.[20] The "ox walk" tactic was used again in 1988 in an unsuccessful attempt to block the Noburu Takeshita government's tax reform bill, which included a revised 3 percent version of the sales tax.[21] General hostility toward the tax was one of the reasons for the unraveling of LDP control of the parliament, beginning with the loss of the upper house in 1989.

The conduct of business can be interrupted by members blocking the doors and the corridors of the Diet. Near-riots have occurred in the chambers when tempers have been pushed too far. Although only one-third of the members are needed for a quorum, a boycott of the proceedings by the opposition has been effective; not having the opposition present looks bad politically and embarrasses the government. The more extreme forms of disruption, while rather common in the past, have been seen less frequently in recent years.

Differences between the two chambers over the content of legislation can be worked out through a formal reconciliation process. But this process has not been used since the 1950s, reflecting the penchant for resolving disputes behind the scenes. In each session of the Diet, the upper house can be expected to reject two or three bills coming from the lower house. The House of Representatives can make the necessary changes or, if it chooses, override the House of Councillors by a two-thirds vote. On treaty and budget matters, the concurrence of the upper house is not required if the bill is approved at least one month before the end of the legislative session.

In a practice common among parliamentary systems, Cabinet members are required under the constitution to answer questions put to them by members of the Diet. This is supposed to give the opposition an opportunity to subject government officials and their policies to public scrutiny. Such public examination is largely missing from the routine legislative process, since it is under the control and direction of the majority party, that is, the government. It is the government's interest to move legislation through the parliament with a minimum of controversy, which means without argument and debate. The question-and-answer sessions create an environment in which issues of general public concern can be openly discussed. A similar situation exists in legislative committees where questions can also be put to ministers.

In actual practice, the question-and-answer procedure serves the worthy goals of democratic discussion rather poorly. Instead a ritual process takes place in which a minister does not answer himself but defers to a top bureaucrat from his own ministry. The questions are generally known in advance, so prepared answers are given. The system is not without cost in that senior bureaucrats must spend a large part of their time "backing up" their ministers in the Diet, rather than doing their administrative jobs. Because opposition politicians do not have access to the inner workings of the government, they are not informed about policy matters to the point that they can regularly ask penetrating questions.

The parliament itself has little opportunity to develop an independent identity because the legislative process is dominated by the government. Most important legislation is introduced by the prime minister representing or on behalf of the Cabinet. For the most part, the content of these bills, which are drafted by the bureaucracy, is based on a carefully crafted consensus among party leaders, bureaucrats, and relevant private groups, such as business. An important part of this process is the Policy Affairs Research Council (PARC), which consists of leaders of the LDP. The numerous division directors of the PARC enjoy more power and prestige than do committee chairmen in the Diet.[22] The PARC has been the most important party element in the bureaucracy-party-interest group network in relation particularly to the budgetary process.[23] It is in the context of the PARC that Diet members who have close links to interest groups are particularly effective.[24]

Long service in the Diet makes it possible for some members, especially in the LDP, to develop influence based on policy expertise. Some of these Diet members have knowledge of their own preferred area of policy that rivals that of the most senior bureaucrats from the relevant ministry. This expertise can lead to committee assignments in the Diet and to important positions in the PARC. These "policy-specialized cliques" are called *zoku* and are another important element in the linkage among the public, the legislature, and the ministries.[25]

In particular, the ties between zoku representatives and government bureaucracies are strong and have become increasingly institutionalized. Early in their careers, politicians elected to the House specialize in the affairs of one ministry or another and become members of the Diet committee and LDP policy research committee related to that ministry. Throughout their careers, these representatives cultivate their relationship with the ministry. Because many representatives act as the Tokyo treasury officer or lobbyist for municipal bodies or public works in their constituencies, a good relationship with the ministry is essential.[26]

The legislative process is, for the most part, a ratification of policies that have been formulated outside the Diet. Individual members of the Diet have the opportunity to introduce their own bills, but these usually represent a response to a special interest appeal or a request from a constituent, and few are ever passed. In order to be considered, bills introduced by individual members require the support of twenty members of the lower house or ten members of the upper house. If it is a budget-related bill, this requirement increases to fifty and twenty, respectively.[27]

The Cabinet

In a parliamentary system, the legislative and executive branches of government are fused. That is, the chief executive (the prime minister), is also leader of the legislative branch, more specifically the lower house. The prime minister and all ministers of state must be civilians. Ministers, a majority of whom must be chosen from among members of the Diet, are appointed and removed by the prime minister. Japanese prime ministers normally do not remain in office as long as their Western counterparts do. Since the 1970s, there has been turnover in the office of prime minister about every two years. After the election victory of a multiparty coalition in 1993, there were three prime ministers in one twelve-month period. Changes in the various ministerial assignments are even more frequent. From 1964 to 1987, the average term of office for a Cabinet minister was less than a year.[28] The frequent change in Cabinet ministers means that they lack sufficient time to gain full control over their ministries. A minister is not likely to have much personal influence, deferring instead to his subordinate officials because "he might be on hand barely long enough to find his way around the building."[29]

According to the Cabinet Law (Article 2), the Cabinet is limited to twenty ministers of state. This restriction is circumvented by creating ministries without portfolio and by ministers of state heading more than one agency. Apart from the administrative structure of the various ministries, there is a bureaucracy associated with the executive branch, that is, the Cabinet itself. There is the Cabinet Secretariat, which provides staff assistance to the ministers primarily in their dealings with the Diet. There is also the prime minister's Secretariat, which provides staff assistance to the chief executive. Sometimes these two Secretariats overlap. Under the Cabinet are the Cabinet Legislative Bureau, which aids in the drafting of legislation; the National Defense Council, which provides the top civilian control link to the Self Defense Force; and the National Personnel Authority (NPA). The latter nominally develops policy on personnel matters, but these issues are jealously guarded by the various ministries, thus reducing the significance of the NPA.

A Cabinet post is the principal way by which party loyalty and influence are recognized. During the long tenure of the LDP, there was a considerable need for rotation at the top to create room for rewarding more people. Being selected prime minister does not carry with it a mandate to implement a policy agenda, a factor that significantly weakens the leadership capacity of the prime minister.[30] In forming a Cabinet, prime ministers from the LDP gave careful consideration to balancing the factions of their party by distributing the twenty Cabinet posts in proportion to faction size, with a bonus going to those that supported his bid for the party presidency. Important posts go to House of Representatives members, while House of Councillors members can expect to receive only the less significant Cabinet positions.[31] There is also a need to have a balance between veterans and newcomers, although the latter are not exactly neophytes, since rarely does a ministerial appointment go to anyone with fewer than seven terms in the House of Representatives.[32] Veterans are selected for their wide-ranging knowledge and experience rather than expertise. For newcomers, a Cabinet post is a reward for party (and faction) loyalty and service.[33]

Unlike most democracies, Japan produces few political leaders who are colorful or charismatic, exceptions being Yasuhiro Nakasone and Junichiro Koizumi. Top government leaders tend to possess the same kinds of personal qualities and attainments as business leaders.[34] They are men of ability in the management and organizational sense, but as public figures, they are rather bland.[35] Achieving the prime ministership or a major Cabinet position may be the capstone of one's political career, but these positions carry with them more status than influence. "The Japanese prime minister has less real power than any head of government in the Western world, or in most countries of Asia."[36]

Bureaucracy

For a democracy, Japan is perhaps a bit unusual in that its political process operates largely out of public view. The broad airing of important public issues in the media, debate over alternatives in the legislature, and general consideration of matters of national import in election campaigns are considerably less a feature of the political process than is true in most democracies. Decisions are made through an extensive, and time-consuming, process of consultations and negotiations among government agencies and relevant interest groups.[37] On the few occasions when the political dialogue has become public, the openness is due to the fact that the process of consensus building has failed to work properly. In these instances, debate can become rancorous and may involve public demonstrations and occasionally violence.

> Instead of the enlightened debate that one hopes for in parliaments, there is more brute confrontation over issues that have not been resolved through negotiations and consensus. The part of the public's participation in the process that is most visible is not the endless informal consultations that go on with pressure groups or the ultimate sanction of the voter but demonstrations in the streets over still unresolved matters.[38]

In recent years, such "brute confrontations" have occurred with diminishing frequency due in part to the fact that radical political energies seem to have been largely spent. There is little "enlightened debate" either. Instead, decisions are made within the context of bureaucratic authority and among officials who probably have close personal ties to one another and always a high degree of mutual trust.[39] By the time legislative proposals reach the Diet, basic decisions have been made and compromises reached by a process involving appropriate ministries, influential party politicians, members of the Diet, and interests outside the government but with access to it.[40]

Japan is not unique in the power of its bureaucracy. A distinguishing feature of parliamentary systems is the influence typically exercised by bureaucracy in shaping public policy, compared to other institutions, such as parties or the legislature. In Japan, the power of the bureaucracy, at least in the minds of some observers, is extraordinary. "For what it is worth, Japanese bureaucrats are frequently more influential than bureaucrats in dictatorships."[41] Whatever the exact extent of this power, it derives from a variety of sources. Public agencies actively cultivate clientele groups that in turn support the agencies' existence and activities. Bureaucracy is strong relative to the weakness of parties and the legislature.[42] The rapid turnover at the ministerial level allows bureaucrats to build organizational strength. An important source of bureaucratic power comes from the issuance of ordinances and ministerial communications. Although these are technically clarifications and interpretations of the law, they can be so significant as to revise the original intent of the law.[43] As Chalmers Johnson has observed: "The politicians reign and the bureaucrats rule."[44]

J. Mark Ramseyer and Frances McCall Rosenbluth contend that the power of the bureaucracy is overstated. The reason that the legislature rubberstamps bills submitted by the bureaucracy is that the bureaucracy prepares bills designed to please the legislature, that is, the LDP. "The image of a largely autonomous bureaucracy that promotes its own distinctive vision of the Japanese commonweal may be no more than a mirage. Real Japanese bureaucrats, the evidence suggests, administer in the shadow of the LDP."[45]

The power of the bureaucracy is not a new development in Japanese politics but the product of long-standing political style and traditions. The bureaucracy was an important element of the political modernization process during the second half of the nineteenth century. Moreover, the bureaucracy as an institution was basically unaffected by World War II and the subsequent occupation. "The historical record shows that little direct effort at bureaucratic reform was ever considered by the United States."[46] But despite its significance in the political system, the bureaucracy is smaller and costs much less than the administrative structures in other countries.

Recruitment into government service is based on a system of competitive examinations or by personal evaluation. Taking public employment as a whole, evaluation is the most common form of recruitment. But this includes large numbers of health-care and education professionals. Excluding such personnel, most civil servants are recruited by competitive exam. There are three types of exams corresponding to levels of education: college graduates, junior college graduates, and high school graduates. Although these exams correspond to levels of educational attainment, there is no formal degree requirement to take an exam.[47] At each level there are several tests, beginning with a general exam and one on a specialty chosen by the applicant. Those who pass at this level (usually 10 percent or less) go on to take further tests.[48]

Japan differs little in comparison to Western countries in the role and status of women in the bureaucracy. Women are underrepresented at all levels, especially among higher civil servants. Not only are the number of women taking the higher civil service exam a fraction of that of men, the passing rate is also lower.[49]

Because of the prestige accorded to it, admission to government service is highly sought after by college graduates. The higher civil service is a thoroughly professional and elite group made up of the top graduates of the best educational institutions in the country, especially Tokyo and Kyoto universities, which together provide about half the candidates who pass the Higher Civil Service Examinations.[50] Two-thirds of Japan's students attend private universities, yet only about 7 percent pass the Higher Civil Service Exam.[51] This narrow base of recruitment creates a tendency toward parochialism and "old boy" ties among bureaucrats. Almost three-fourths of the upper levels of the administrative machinery are dominated by men with a common academic specialization: law. Of these, almost two-thirds are graduates of Tokyo University law faculty.[52] This involves training in what would be political science and business administration in an American university.[53] Below them are the countless officials of the national and local governmental agencies who do the routine work of the modern state. In one interesting practice, national government bureaucrats are "lent" to local governments (*shukkō*). This provides a learning experience for bureaucrats, specialized help for local governments, and a linkage between the two levels of government.

Employment in a government ministry is a high-status occupation in Japan. Among the various ministries, there is a rank ordering of prestige, with the Ministry of Economy, Trade, and Industry and the Ministry of Finance at the top. Because these ministries are the most influential, they harbor the most coveted appointments. Within the latter ministry, service in the Budget Bureau is the key to success for officials intent on rising to the top in career terms.[54] Other ministries also have their own internal status divisions. Throughout the bureaucracy the most significant factor in the promotion process is university background.[55]

Important interpersonal connections are maintained by the practice of officials rotating among bureaucracy, business, and politics. A similar practice, called the "revolving door," draws frequent criticism in the United States, where retired public officials, such as military officers, obtain jobs with private industry, often those with which they had dealt in their public capacities. Far from being condemned, this is a normal aspect of administrative life in Japan, which is generally viewed with favor, as the term for it—"descent from heaven" (*amakudari*)—would imply.[56] Many retirees from public service, some at an early age, join private industry or in some cases "special legal entities" such as public corporations.[57] Agencies such as the Ministry of Construction operate as veritable employment agencies for retiring bureaucrats seeking jobs in industry.[58] Some go into party politics, especially in the LDP, and for them the most promising avenue to elected office is the House of Councillor's national constituency where a broad organizational base is an advantage.[59]

The practice of leaving public service to pursue a second career in business or politics is not only condoned but expected. For one reason, this practice contributes to the effective operation of the political process. Personal contacts, the more extensive the better, are the medium through which negotiation and consensus decision-making are achieved.

Like workers in the private sector, public-service employees can receive in addition to their basic salaries a variety of allowances for such things as family, housing, and "diligence." Basic salaries are also augmented by a bonus called the "end-of-the-term allowance," which is paid in three installments and amounts to 380 percent of regular salary.[60]

Most employees at the municipal and prefectural levels (about 60 percent) belong to a union (*Jichiro*), which has had strong links with the Japan Socialist Party and with the large labor federation *Sōhyō*. Some union locals have had ties with the Japan Communist Party.[61] Some public employees, such as teachers, have been very active politically. Although there are public-service unions, the right to collective bargaining is limited.[62] Together, political activism and union participation have not significantly benefited public employees as a group.

The efficiency of the bureaucracy is one of the reasons that Japan enjoyed its long run of political stability and economic success. The bureaucracy was able to deliver the services demanded of it by the public until the economic difficulties of the 1990s. Then the bureaucracy, especially the Ministry of Finance, lost much of its luster. The decline of the bureaucracy, among other things, enhanced the role of the LDP in the policy-making process.[63] In addition, there are other potential problems. Job opportunities in the public service are few, and advancement is slow. Less than 5 percent of those taking the higher civil service exam pass it in any given year, and, once there, civil servants must wait at least twenty years before attaining the level of bureau chief.[64] Competition among candidates for employment is fierce and is getting more so because efforts to keep public expenditures down mean limited expansion of personnel opportunities.[65] If and when the public begins expecting more and better services, the demands on the bureaucracy will intensify.

Local Government

The Local Autonomy Act of 1947 was intended to insulate local government from excessive interference by the central government. In addition to furthering the democratic constitutional principle that government is best when it is closest to the people, this measure was also designed to help prevent a return of the authoritarian concentration of power at the center. As seen in Chapter 2, the policy of decentralization of political authority was impractical in the Japanese context and did not survive the occupation.[66] Controversy over the concentration of authority has continued, however, particularly in two areas: education and the police. In 1956 the central government changed the system of selection of school boards from elective to appointive in an effort to overcome the growing political strength of left-wing parties. In 1954 the Diet passed a law establishing a unified police system in each prefecture.

Today the authority of local government is closely prescribed by the central government. It has control of the entire tax structure, allowing local governments to collect themselves only about 30 percent of their revenue needs. The remainder of local government budgets is made up of various transfers from the national government. Both local and national governments have been forced to engage in deficit financing due to the implacable hostility of the public toward tax increases.[67]

Even though local governments operate within rules set down at the national level, local government is not unimportant. Local governments can, in theory at least, do anything not specifically prohibited by law.[68] While they do not take advantage of this opportunity, local governments are responsible for the implementation of most public policy, something that is achieved, incidentally, with considerable efficiency. The uniformity imposed on policy by national requirements, however, does not allow for much local variation, despite the existence of social and economic differences among local communities. The central government has become increasingly involved in local government affairs amid the continuing demands of local government and citizens' movements favoring greater local autonomy.[69]

For many students of democracy, popular participation in government is most effective at the local level. There is, no doubt, a closer connection between voters and elected officials at the local level of the political process. It is as true in Japan as anywhere else that popular sentiment is most clearly and readily expressed in the elections and the give and take between citizens and government officials at the local level. However, local politics in Japan have little impact on policy. Local assemblymen are less concerned about policy matters than about ensuring that their constituents receive their share of government benefits.[70] The political dialogue at the local level does not have the effect of "refining and enlarging public opinion" but reflects much narrower specialized interests.

Sometimes local governments take independent action in the form of "illegal" local ordinances enacted to address some problem that the central government has been unable or unwilling to resolve. In these cases, the usual practice is for the central government to rewrite the regulations incorporating the local ordinance thus making it legal and a matter of general government policy. The first initiatives in the development of public policies for pollution control occurred in this way.[71] One advantage of this approach is that when the central government "catches up" with innovative local governments and makes their actions a matter of national policy, all local governments are then brought up to the same performance level.[72]

There are several different levels of local government: prefectures, cities, towns, and villages. The prefectures, important administrative units created to replace the feudal structure after the Restoration, mainly exercise the function of coordinating the activities of other units of local government.[73] The larger metropolitan areas are further divided into wards. Representatives sent to these local bodies are chosen by the voters in elections normally held every four years.

The Legal System

The origins of the Japanese judicial system can be traced back to the Tokugawa period (1615–1867). The legal system as it exists today is patterned after that of continental Europe. The French court system was introduced in 1875, and German influence was pronounced after the adoption of the Meiji constitution in 1868. The Anglo-American legal tradition was added after World War II.[74] The substance of the law is also similar to that in Europe except as pertains to family matters, where the tradition of Confucian ethics prevails. Neither the adversarial system nor jury trials are used. Legal precedent is not binding in subsequent cases, as it is in the United States, where the doctrine of *stare decisis* is used. Japanese courts, while not totally indifferent to precedent, are likely to decide on the basis of "the prevalent sociopolitical climate of a given moment."[75] In the inquisitorial system employed in Japan, judges are not passive referees but take an active part in seeking out the facts. In the absence of juries, they also render verdicts. The role of lawyers is generally limited to that of adviser to their clients rather than their champions. The absence of jury trials suggests the Japanese have little anxiety about receiving justice at the hands of state-run courts.

Until the modernization of the Meiji period, judicial activities were intertwined with the administrative structure associated with the feudal system. Europeans considered this unsatisfactory and imposed extraterritoriality on Japan. This encroachment on their sovereignty encouraged the Japanese to introduce modern judicial practices.[76] Even with institutional development and democratization, the idea of judicial independence has not taken hold. The court system, as it exists today, is unified and simple. The plethora of courts familiar to Americans is missing in Japan. There are no administrative courts, for example, nor are there municipal courts, police courts, or small claims courts. All criminal matters and civil issues that require litigation, and most do not, are handled by the regular court system.

Many changes were made in the legal code during the occupation. Especially in the area of civil rights, a whole new field of law was created, enshrined in a lengthy section of the constitution. Despite these obvious American influences, Japanese law is nowhere near as vast or as complex as that in the United States. A compendium of laws is published in one lengthy book, which is available to everyone. The law is not the exclusive privilege of judges and lawyers, as it all too often appears to be in the United States. The judiciary is a career service, and those who aspire to become judges must serve an apprenticeship of ten years as an assistant judge before becoming eligible for the bench.[77]

Before World War II, the courts were not independent of the executive, a tradition that continues to contribute to the judiciary's lack of assertiveness. The courts do not take an activist role with regard to public policy. The Supreme Court has the constitutional authority of judicial review, but it has been disinclined to use it.

Although judges are appointed by the executive branch, there is a procedure in which the voters can express their opinions on the way the courts are functioning. The constitution subjects Supreme Court justices to review by the voters every ten years after their appointment. But the justices attract so little attention and, accordingly, are so little known that they never provoke any substantial opposition. The largest negative vote ever received by an individual justice was 15.2 percent.[78]

The constitution invests the Supreme Court with all judicial power but also authorizes the establishment of lower courts. The result is a judicial system that is arranged hierarchically. The Supreme Court consists of fifteen judges, fourteen of whom are appointed by the Cabinet from a list provided by the court itself. The Chief Justice is normally influential in the process of selecting the other justices.[79] The Chief Justice is appointed by the emperor, on recommendation by the Cabinet, a procedure that is presumed to give the job more prestige. The court sits as the Grand Bench, involving all fifteen justices to hear cases of special importance, especially constitutional issues. More often, the work of the court is conducted by the petty benches composed of five justices who consider routine cases submitted for review.

Thousands of cases are appealed to the Supreme Court, and all are placed on the docket; none are screened out on procedural grounds. But only a few cases are actually considered by the court; the rest are summarily dismissed.[80] Cases are first referred to petty benches and then are assigned to individual justices. The justices are assisted in screening their cases by one of the court's twenty-nine "research officers," who are themselves experienced judges of lower courts. Twelve of these researchers are assigned to criminal cases, twelve to civil cases, and four to administrative cases. The chief research officer has no specific assignment. Unlike American law clerks, these research officers are not assigned to specific justices. No more than about 20 percent of civil cases and 10 percent of criminal cases are considered to have sufficient legal merit to be considered by the Supreme Court. After serving for about five years, these officers return to their judicial duties on the lower courts.[81]

The Supreme Court typically does not hold public hearings in which opposing attorneys argue their cases and answer questions from the justices. Hearings are held in criminal cases when the court is likely to reverse a lower court judgment, in capital punishment cases and in reviewing public security incidents.[82]

Until American influence was felt, the Supreme Court published only the majority opinion, as in the European tradition. But not all cases have the decision published, only those considered significant.[83] Now concurring and dissenting opinions are published. Lower courts publish only majority opinions.[84]

In federal systems, it is customary for the Supreme Court to have original jurisdiction on such matters as disputes between states. Since Japan is a unitary state, there is no such need and, accordingly, there is no mention of original jurisdiction in the constitution. The Supreme Court's role is to oversee the judicial system by determining the rules of procedure and practice and to hear cases on appeal from the lower courts. In addition to Japanese law, the Supreme Court sometimes refers to European courts' decisions in its judgments.[85] The second level consists of eight High Courts corresponding to geographic regions. Next, are district courts (roughly one per prefecture, with the exception of Hokkaido, which has four) with more than 200 branches. At the lowest level are summary courts, with three judges each, which handle minor criminal and civil cases. Summary courts are distinct from the courts at higher levels in that the justices of summary courts are not career judges but, rather, are like American justices of the peace. Decisions of summary courts can be appealed only as far as the High Court.[86] Another system is that of the family courts, which structurally parallel the district courts. Family courts adjudicate domestic complaints, such as inheritance, divorce, and juvenile matters.

The court system has a slightly different organization depending on whether the issue is criminal or civil. There are three levels for criminal proceedings: (1) family court, summary court, and district court; (2) High Court; and (3) Supreme Court. There are four levels for civil proceedings: (1) summary court; (2) district court and family court; (3) High Court; and (4) Supreme Court. The High Courts hear appeals from the district and family courts. The High Courts have jurisdiction over administrative actions.[87]

Compared to the U.S. Supreme Court, the Japanese Supreme Court is very conservative and not disposed to taking an "activist" role of judicial decision-making. The court is reluctant to reverse established judicial policy so there is a tendency to avoid establishing such policies. It is also rare for the court to render decisions that are inconsistent with changes in public policy enacted by political branches of government. When decisions are handed down that are inconsistent with existing policy, it usually means that the replacement of judges has not kept pace with changes in the political environment. On occasion the court will act in advance of political branches by making progressive decisions.[88] In general, judicial decisions have corresponded closely to the preferences of the LDP.[89]

The Legal Profession

The Japanese prefer to resolve disputes through mediation and compromise, rather than litigation.[90] Informal, less visible approaches to conflict resolution are preferred because of the embarrassment associated with a public airing of controversy. "There is abundant evidence that in the conduct of their daily lives, the Japanese are at pains to avoid contention and confrontation."[91] To retain the services of a lawyer is an admission that the usual and proper way of dealing with a problem has failed.[92] Hence the legal profession is nowhere near as large nor as prestigious as in the United States. There is one lawyer for every 5,518 people in Japan, compared with one for every 285 in the United States. The size of the legal profession is not limited only by demand for legal services. The government, as a matter of policy, puts restrictions on the numbers of lawyers available. In 1999, only 1,000 applicants passed the bar exam. The government increased this number to 2,099 in 2007, and plans on 3,000 by 2010. There are also more women in the legal profession, with the number increasing by 50 percent over the past decade. Limiting the number of attorneys means that there are few opportunities to become judges and government lawyers, called procurators. The number of judges has not increased since the turn of the century, although the case load would suggest the need for more. There are around 2,000 government lawyers in Japan, compared with 400 in the Los Angeles County District Attorney's office alone.[93]

In 2003, the Ministry of Education approved the establishment of U.S.-style law schools, of which there are now seventy-four. This new approach to legal education is intended to increase the number of legal practitioners with more practical legal training, compared to the technical approach that had previously existed. Until these reforms, there were no postgraduate law schools as such and almost all licensed lawyers received their training from the Supreme Court's Legal Training and Research Institute.[94] Gaining admission to the Institute has been extremely difficult. In the past, as few as 2 percent of those taking the exam passed.[95] Many legal functions requiring a lawyer in the United States, such as drawing up contracts, have been handled in Japan by nonlicensed lawyers, who have received an undergraduate level of education from a faculty of law at one of the universities. The new legal training system will produce more lawyers and make legal services more broadly available.

There are three career tracks open to graduates of the Legal Training and Research Institute. Most decide to go into private practice, where the opportunities for making money have increased in recent years owing to the importance of law in commercial activities. Some decide to become judges, which, until recently, attracted the top performers. In the third group are those who become prosecutors.

During the two-year training program at the Institute, candidates choose from among three options. They can seek to be judges or prosecutors or go into private practice. Those who choose to be judges receive intensive training and are expected to possess a high degree of professionalism and a concern for the public interest.[96] Missing from the Japanese legal scene is the philosophy of "judicial activism."[97] In the twentieth century, American courts have been increasingly inclined to make basic policy decisions affecting all areas of life, including the most sensitive. Moreover, American courts show no reluctance to involve themselves in the most rancorous and divisive issues. By contrast, the Supreme Court in Japan has gone to great lengths to avoid involvement in politically controversial areas. In general, the court has been inclined to support the government and has overturned lower court decisions that have gone against the government's position.[98] In 1983 the court held that a distortion in the ratio of voters per parliamentary seat of as much as five to one was insufficient grounds to declare the election void. The court has, however, been less cautious in its rulings in the area of civil rights. Following a decade of progressively worsening industrial pollution, the court established in 1983 the principle that the polluter is legally responsible and must pay damages to individuals. Great strides have since been made in cleaning up the environment.

The growing complexity of industrial society has encouraged increased use of formal legal procedures to resolve disputes. This does not alter the fact that, generally speaking, there is a reluctance to employ the adversarial procedures that such methods imply. Among the reasons for this is the Japanese tendency to see conflicts in shades of gray rather than in black–white, right–wrong terms. All participants in a dispute share some responsibility. Moreover, resorting to legal processes is not rewarding in the sense of receiving large sums of money for damages. Settlements are likely to be modest. Overall, the system is weighted in favor of the government. "When sued, the Japanese government always wins."[99] Legal confrontation also disrupts the sense of community solidarity and causes personal embarrassment by making conflicts open and public. The Japanese go to extraordinary length to disguise conflicts by, among other things, the use of elaborate rituals. Another approach is citizen participation in the process of conflict resolution through lay commissions. These commissions, set up by courts, act as conciliators and arbitrators.[100]

How well does the Japanese political system meet the test of democracy? Definitions of democracy abound, differing from one another in details and points of emphasis. For some, democracy is procedural; it involves a process like majority rule. For others it is substantive; it is a condition of freedom and liberty. Whatever the definition, there is agreement on the need for safeguards and protections against the abuse of power. At its root, democracy requires the *real* opportunity to change the government. Japanese voters displayed extraordinary patience and forbearance as the governing process dominated by the LDP became more corrupt and less capable of managing the affairs of the country. But this patience finally wore out. In the 1993 election, the voters ended, at least temporarily, the LDP's long reign and opened the way for political reform and restructuring.[101]

4

Political Parties—I

Political parties are a relatively recent addition to the mechanics of government. Many countries today have had only limited experience with them, and
in only a few do parties compete in an open, democratic environment. The
advent of political parties followed the development of the territorial state in
Europe in the seventeenth century. Precursors emerged in the parliamentary
experience of England, but the first true political parties appeared in the
United States. As the modern state grew in complexity and sophistication,
organizational mechanisms had to be devised to make it work. Among the
more important of these were political parties that served to link the citizenry
with the institutions of government, particularly legislatures. Political parties grew out of the mobilizational style of politics that developed during
the eighteenth and nineteenth centuries, in which political power under the
control of hereditary aristocracies and landed elites yielded to demands for
broader popular participation. Expansion of popular involvement in government necessarily meant voting. During the Jacksonian period in the United
States, political parties became fully developed as links between voters and
the institutions of government.[1] It has only been in the past century, or even
less, that most countries outside Europe and North America have confronted
the need for vehicles to channel popular political energies.

The Japanese Party System

In Japan, political parties appeared during the period of rapid political transformation beginning with the Meiji Restoration in 1868. In 1874, the Liberty
and Popular Rights Movement (Jiyu minken undo) published a demand for
a constitution and an elected assembly. This was followed by the creation of
the Patriotic League (Aikokusha), which became the Liberal Party (Jiyūtō)
in 1881 and changed its name to Seiyūkai in 1900. After World War II it was
revived as the Liberal Party. In 1882 the Constitutional Progressive Party (Rikken kaishinto) and the Constitutional Imperial Party (Rikken teiseito) were
founded. Another party, known as the Minseitō (Popular Government Party)
after 1927, was revived after the war as the Progressive Party (Shinpotō) but
soon changed its name to the Democratic Party (Minshutō).[2]

The character of Japanese political parties, like those everywhere, is shaped by the kind of environment in which they operate. This environment consists of several aspects, such as social values and myths, customs and traditions, and the ways in which people identify themselves in the social order. Another factor is formal political structure, which in Japan's case is the parliamentary/ cabinet form of government. In the parliamentary model, the legislative and executive branches are combined in that the prime minister and the Cabinet provide leadership for the legislature and the bureaucracy. A third factor is the type of system used to elect people to the legislature. There are many such systems, ranging from single-member districts, where election requires only a plurality of votes, to proportional representation systems, where seats are apportioned on the basis of the percentage of votes received by each political party. Two of the most important aspects of political parties are organization and ideology.[3] Possibilities range from large and vigorous grassroots organizations, and the membership takes an active part in party affairs. Other parties are loosely organized, and leadership has not only considerable power but a great deal of independence, a characteristic of most conservative parties. A second variable is the degree to which there is a psychological bond between the party and its adherents based on shared ideology. In the model of mass membership parties, voters' political and sometimes even social activities are encompassed by party organizations and programs. Some of the opposition parties in Japan, such as the Socialists and the Clean Government Party (Kōmeitō), emphasize membership and ideology. The organization of the dominant party, the Liberal Democratic Party (LDP), is loosely based on individual politicians, and there is considerable division and factionalism within the party. The importance of ideology for the LDP and its backers is minimal. All Japanese political parties have national organizations, with the first subdivision occurring at the prefect level. Generally, these prefectural units "implement national party directives, coordinate activities of lower party units, formulate party policies on problems specific to a prefecture, supervise the work of party-endorsed assemblymen and recommend the endorsement of Diet candidates to the national parties."[4]

Although there have been several parties in the Japanese system, one party—the LDP—has been in a commanding position most of the time since 1955. The LDP has formed coalitions with other parties when it lacked a majority of votes in the parliament or when it needed to bolster its margin. But coalition formation is not a dominant feature of Japanese parliamentary politics, in contrast to other multiparty systems, where coalition government is standard practice. In addition, in multiparty systems, it is fairly common for governments to fall when the coalitions on which they are based come apart, which they often do. In 1993, the LDP lost its commanding position in the political system, and there followed a period of unstable coalition govern-ments. But until that time, government stability had been the rule.

Partisan identity is weak among Japanese voters. Steven Reed observes that between 40 and 55 percent of voters have no partisan identity. Even the LDP has consistently commanded only 30 percent of voter support.[5] Some of these votes come from groups that, although opposed to LDP policies, will vote for it in order to have some influence with the government.[6] Absence of voter identification holds even for those parties in which ideology is an important source of identity, such as the Japan Communist Party.[7] Votes cast for parties with distinctive ideologies cannot be construed, necessarily, to indicate philosophical support for that ideology. Some voters cast ballots for opposition parties less out of empathy with the party than as an expression of general dissatisfaction with the political order. The socialist parties have relied on labor unions for support, but this has had little to do with socialist policies. Other opposition parties, such as the Kōmeitō, draw strength from the socially marginalized. The plethora of new parties that emerged in the 1990s reflected a desire for political reform and especially to bring corrup-tion under control.

The success of the LDP is attributable to its favorable record in promoting economic prosperity.[8] Good economic times play well in all democracies; bad times spell trouble for the party in power. The LDP's continuing good fortune is also due to the absence of viable competition. The opposition parties have not been equipped individually or collectively to challenge the LDP for power. The LDP does not mobilize voter support on the basis of its ideology or policy preferences; rather, its prosperity is linked to a close personal bond maintained between voters and local political organizations called *kōenkai*. These organizations, whose purpose is to generate and sustain popular back-ing for individual politicians, are not party mechanisms but are directly as-sociated with the individual Diet member. The Diet member and his kōenkai serve as a link between the voter and party factions. This linkage relies not on formal party structure but, rather, on personal connections.[9] Kōenkai serve as focal points to bring together the common interests of the many diverse groups making up the electorate. Strong groups, such as trade associations, can come to dominate the Diet member's support group.[10] What emerges in this kōenkai-dominated system, therefore, is a candidate-oriented pattern of voting behavior in which the voter votes *in* the party, rather like the American primary election system, rather than *for* the party.[11] Despite the introduction of a new electoral system, the kōenkai remains an important link between the candidate and the voter and, if anything, has grown even stronger.[12] Even though ideology has little to do with voting behavior, parties are distinguish-able from one another by their philosophical orientation. The LDP embraces a generally conservative philosophy although it is far from doctrinaire. Some opposition parties, by contrast, have staked out fairly distinctive ideological territory. Moreover, opposition parties have tended to be ideologically consistent in their views to the point of rigidity, showing little inclination to adapt their thinking to changing conditions or voter preferences. Thus their ability to broaden their appeal to the electorate has suffered from self-imposed limits. A specific ideological position may be attractive to voters who share those ideas but has little appeal and may, in fact, be offensive to others. Ideological parties have difficulty attracting new voters, which means that their strength will remain relatively constant unless conditions change making their particular philosophy more enticing. Alternatively, if the party's philosophy begins to lose its appeal, as occurred with the Japan Socialist Party during the 1980s, it must either reinvent itself or face extinction. Socialist efforts to develop a new image proved unsuccessful.

Another characteristic of the party system is the weak connection between parties and sociocultural divisions in society. The formation of party and voter coalitions based on such divisions is largely missing from Japanese electoral politics. There is nothing like the Hispanic vote or Jewish vote in the United States. The absence of these factors also means that an important source of political competition is missing. Class identity is not a powerful influence on voting behavior either.[13] Age has not consistently correlated with voting preferences. In years past, younger voters tended to favor progressive parties, although they were less likely to vote. Moreover, women tended in the past to be more conservative than men.[14] There is little reason to assume that sociocultural factors will become any more important in the future.

Party election campaigns have not been characterized by efforts to mobilize voters through an appeal to their expectations. Information manipulation and access to voters, especially by means of television, is constrained by law. Parties reach voters through support groups or other organizations, such as labor unions. Overall, voting behavior is influenced more by friends, family, and coworkers campaigning.

In 1994 the parliament approved legislation that changed the electoral system for the lower house of the Diet. A combination of single-member districts and proportional representation replaced the multiple-member district arrangement. These changes were expected to foster the coalescence of fewer but stronger and more competitive national parties.[15] The results may be judged from the tabular data in Appendix B.

Parties that were resurrected after the war had a strong conservative political orientation. This conservatism favored parties on the right but, at the same time, confronted them with a dilemma. The public mood, while essentially conservative, was tempered by the trauma of military defeat, which was attributed to the misguided policies of the government. The conservative parties, which had been closely identified with wartime policies, were faced with the need to overcome the legacy of the imperial past, yet remain true to their fundamental principles while developing new approaches to achieving national grandeur.

The parties on the left also faced a dilemma but of a different sort. Their opposition to Japan's imperial policies had been vindicated by the results of the war. Thus they renewed their commitment to the socialist agenda and added to it a vigorous crusade against rearmament. However, this approach failed to generate much popular enthusiasm, and the Socialists eventually abandoned it.

The experience of militarism and war meant that nationalism, at least in terms of intense loyalty to the state, has been muted. The expression of nationalism in flags, parades, and other symbols was missing for two decades after the surrender. The emperor-state orthodoxy had been discredited. In his diminished constitutional capacity, the emperor was left with no real power, yet he continues to command considerable personal and symbolic respect. National anthem singing and flag displays have returned, at least in schools, as Japanese leaders seek to promote patriotism.

Defeat in war does not always mean a disintegration of collective identity. In fact, the opposite is frequently the case, where defeat generates a renewed sense of purpose. Certainly for the Japanese the sense of "we-ness" remains very strong. This social solidarity is seen by many non-Japanese, and not unjustifiably so, as a smugness or arrogance. Japanese aloofness is interpreted by outsiders, whether rightly or wrongly, as a manifestation of this attitude of superiority. Foreigners can live for years in Japan and never become culturally integrated or fully accepted in the society. When living abroad, Japanese have tended to keep to themselves although the demands of economic interaction in today's world have eroded this practice. The tightly knit and, in many respects, closed society is giving way to a more outwardly oriented, cosmopolitan approach to dealing with other people and their cultures. Certainly this is reflected in the evolution of contemporary Japanese political philosophy and, even more so, in popular culture. Political parties, as much if not more than other institutions, combine continuity with past traditions together with newly emerging approaches to coping with political reality.

The Liberal Democratic Party

Officially organized in 1955, the LDP can trace its lineage as far back as the 1870s.[16] The mainstream of major Japanese political parties, in which the LDP squarely fits, has been in the moderate to conservative part of the political spectrum. The party system has traditionally displayed less of a competitive relationship among left, center, and right parties than rivalry among or within conservative parties. The LDP has inherited this tradition as one observer has noted:

> As the case stands now, it may not necessarily be an exaggeration to say that LDP's factions seem to have more of party-ness than opposition parties: They have their own leaders, policies, political funds and organizational setup, conduct campaigns on their own and try hard to come to power installing their leader in the premiership. For this reason, the LDP's factions could be more appropriately called "parties" and the opposition parties "quasi-parties."[17]

The immediate circumstances leading to union between the Liberal and Democratic parties included concern on the part of the business community for good relations with Washington, the challenge posed by the Japan Socialist Party (JSP), and intensifying demands from labor. In the late 1950s, the LDP received covert financial support from the American CIA, so great was the concern in the United States over the JSP's prospects.[18] In this environment it was thought that unity among conservatives was necessary in order to promote stable government.[19]

Conservative parties in the West generally stress limited government and private initiative. The philosophy of the LDP is rather vague, but most politicians who belong to it favor a centralized and efficient government that exercises an important role in the economy. This is to be achieved by a management approach to public policy that closely approximates that employed in business. The LDP does not favor strong local initiative, a favorite American conservative theme. It endorses Keynesian approaches to economic policy and a paternalistic free-enterprise system. Its foreign policy has been pro-Western and anticommunist, but the party has been in favor of trade with the erstwhile Soviet Union and China.

The ideology of the LDP substitutes an economic definition of national security for a military one. The party has enjoyed success in promoting the re-establishment of Japan's importance in the world arena and has done so almost entirely by economic means. The LDP can justifiably claim a substantial measure of credit for promoting Japan's economic development, but it has been less responsive to the consequences of that development. The party has not dealt constructively with the by-products of modern industrial society. The needs of the burgeoning urban middle class only lately came to occupy a major place on the government's agenda.

The LDP's commitment to economic development has generally received broad public support. This support has softened, however, in certain instances, such as when industrial growth has produced pollution and public health risks. Another area where the public views the costs of development to outweigh the benefits is the nuclear power industry. Legal efforts to stop nuclear power have failed in the courts, and the need for electrical power has blunted political opposition. In addition to public anxiety, the nuclear power issue presents the government with another complication. Japan's efforts to develop nuclear power pose a conflict with long-standing American policy that opposes nuclear weapons proliferation. Although the Japanese are not interested in nuclear weapons, the development of nuclear technology affords them the capability to acquire them.

The LDP maintains close ties to business, especially larger corporations, and the bureaucracy. "The bureaucracy . . . staffs the LDP with its own cadres to insure that the party does what the bureaucracy thinks is good for the country as a whole, and guides the business community toward developmental goals. The business community, in turn, supplies massive amounts of funds to keep the LDP in power."[20]

This relationship has led to the development of an effective national economic policy but has also encouraged corruption. Japan's substantial economic growth under the tutelage of the LDP has helped insulate the party from accountability by the voters. The LDP passes up few chances to turn the opportunities of power to its own advantage. "[I]t is clear that the aggregate of many small favors delivered to many areas over the years had helped maintain LDP strength."[21]

The Role of Factions

The LDP divided into factions immediately upon its formation in 1955. There were as many as eight factions in the late 1950s, but typically the number has been five although they vary considerably in size. There were usually five factions because with electoral districts having from three to five seats, each faction could contest and win seats in the larger districts without necessarily creating losers or drawing too many votes away from other factions' candidates.[22] Factions keep membership lists, which are a matter of public record, although the exact size of any given faction is not completely clear because included in the membership are politicians who are temporarily out of office.[23] Factions hold regularly scheduled meetings, have leadership positions that mirror those of the LDP itself and publish their own newspapers.[24]

The importance of factions within the LDP and in politics in general contrasts with the fact that they have generally been viewed negatively by the public. Even within the LDP, there have been attempts to control or even abolish the faction system as occurred in the early 1960s. But this was like "defying Newton's law of gravity," and factions were soon back in business, more robust than ever.[25]

Factions consist of members of the Diet who commit themselves to the leadership of a senior party figure. To attain such a leadership position requires influential connections with the business community and the bureaucracy and the ability to raise money. This has become more difficult because of changes in the law governing money in politics. But money from the faction leader is still important for those just entering parliamentary politics and for those elected to the Diet for the first time.[26] An effective leader must also be involved in the personal lives of the members of the faction, looking after their needs.[27] Membership in a faction is necessary not only for support in getting elected but as a channel for political advancement. Factions are also decisive in the process of selecting the party leadership, especially the party president. Top party posts are usually shared among factions in proportion to their strength. Factions fill the strong psychological requirement among all Japanese for participation in a group.[28]

By and large, factions have little direct relevance to the making of policy. Factions are not identified with alternative policy approaches, nor are they distinguished from each other by ideological divisions. They do, however, sometimes gain influence in specific areas of government activity, such as the Tanaka faction, which was closely involved in the construction industry. The Nakasone faction was involved in telecommunications.[29] They have very little impact on routine policy-making processes, but from time to time factions have played a role in some areas of foreign policy.[30] The importance of factions lies in their role in party and legislative operations and, perhaps most important, kept the LDP from fragmenting into separate conservative parties.[31]

Membership in factions tends to be stable. Japanese parliamentarians from all parties do not broker their votes or sell their support to the highest bidder. Moreover, changing factions means loss of seniority, which is determined by the number of times an individual has been elected to the Diet as a member of a given faction.[32] Those who change factions find themselves in the company of others with junior standing and little influence. Opportunity to add members to a faction is found among those running for office for the first time. After factional loyalties have been established, there is little electoral competition, since factions do not often support more than one candidate in the same district.[33] The battle for political influence is fought out in raising funds, establishing connections in the economic world, placing people in the bureaucracy and in shaping the character of public policy.

Factions within the LDP are not rigid, and membership in them does not preclude interaction with members of other factions. The fluidity of relations between members of different factions is an important source of opposition and competition within the political elite.[34] The oppositional role of factions looms even larger given the general weakness of interparty competition.

The new electoral system accelerated the decline of factions as younger members of the Diet are displaying less loyalty to faction leaders. As prime minister, Junichiro Koizumi owed less to faction support than to popularity among the voters. The introduction of single-member districts encouraged the LDP to find a better method of selecting party nominees than through the faction process, which often allowed rejected nominees to run under the LDP banner or as independents. A more prominent role for local party organizations has led to an increase in the number of seats passing from father to son or daughter. "Japan has the highest percentage of inherited seats in the industrialized world."[35] Kakuei Tanaka's daughter inherited his seat, as did the daughter of Keizo Obuchi.[36] Prime Minister Taro Aso is a grandson of Shigero Yoshida.

LDP Party Politics

By aligning themselves with big business and the bureaucracy, members of the LDP formed an alliance that not only controlled the public policy process but served as a conduit for the transfer of large sums of money and other favors. The laws governing this aspect of politics proved to be weak and indifferently administered. Bribery and corruption were the normal way of doing business, attracting little attention except when the practice took on extraordinary proportions.

One such case involved Kakuei Tanaka. Tanaka was a master of Japanese politics who rose to the top of the power structure and remained a player even after he was forced from office. Unlike most of his colleagues in the political elite, who in effect were born there, Tanaka worked his way to the top by perseverance and an extraordinary display of political talent.

In 1974 Tanaka was forced to resign the prime ministership following published charges that he had been involved in questionable real estate and financial dealings. On August 16, 1976, Tanaka was indicted on charges of accepting $2.1 million in bribes to influence the purchase of Lockheed Tristar aircraft by All Nippon Airways. The repercussions of the Lockheed affair were felt immediately by the LDP, and its tribulations caused voter support to erode. In addition to Tanaka, other top party people were touched by the Lockheed scandal, which also exacerbated friction among the factions within the party. The Lockheed affair was one of the contributing factors leading six LDP members of the Diet to leave the party and form the New Liberal Club.

Choosing the Party Leader

J. Mark Ramseyer and Frances McCall Rosenbluth identify several leadership roles within the LDP. First, "they protect the party's brand-name capital by formulating the party's stance on public goods and maintaining a ceiling on the private goods that backbenchers dispense." They also broker interests within factions as they relate to elections and policy choices. They are also important in fundraising and maintaining party discipline.[37]

Leadership selection in the LDP has traditionally involved a process of factional bargaining. As a result of difficulties experienced during the 1970s, the LDP changed the rules for electing the party president. As early as 1974, the then–newly elected LDP leader, Takeo Miki, decried the unsatisfactory method for selecting party leadership. The party was in "its greatest crisis" and needed "drastic reform."[38] In January 1977, his proposal for a primary election system involving a two-stage process was introduced.[39] All members of the party who paid 1,500 yen and party friends who paid 10,000 yen to party-funded organizations would be eligible to vote in a primary. The two highest vote getters (later the top three) would face each other in a runoff, with only the LDP members of the Diet participating. In order to run in the primary, a candidate needed endorsements from at least fifty Diet members, later reduced to twenty.[40] Should there be fewer than four candidates, the Diet alone would do the selecting. In 1978 the new approach resulted in the upset of incumbent Takeo Fukuda by Masayoshi Ohira.[41]

Ohira's tenure was rocky from the beginning. Bickering broke out over appointments to other party positions.[42] Factional bitterness continued for some time, weakening Ohira's effectiveness. In May 1980, the government lost a vote of confidence, but Ohira stubbornly refused to resign despite growing opposition both in and out of the LDP.

The succession issue was further complicated on October 12, 1983, when Tanaka was found guilty of accepting the bribe from the Lockheed Corporation. Despite considerable pressure from across the political spectrum, Tanaka refused to resign his parliamentary seat. He headed the largest faction in the parliament and controlled the best vote-getting machine in the country. He resigned from the LDP and continued to serve as an independent. He also retained control over his own faction due to his personal magnetism, his fund-raising ability, and the size of his political machine, which was itself virtually a party.[43]

The guilty verdict touched off a political storm ultimately forcing Prime Minister Yasuhiro Nakasone to dissolve the lower house and hold new elections. In the 1983 elections, the LDP was down, if not out. It failed to win an absolute majority in the lower house and had to rely on conservative independents and coalitions with small parties.[44] Eventually, however, the LDP regained its hold over the Diet and Nakasone's own popularity increased.

The LDP entered into a coalition with the Kōmeitō in 1983 and with the New Liberal Club in February of the following year. Formation of coalitions was in the interest of both the LDP and the smaller parties. The former had been unable to capture an outright majority of the House of Representatives and needed partners in order to enhance its capacity to rule. For the latter, coalition gave them additional political influence, greater than their numbers allowed. These unions also indicate the limited substantive ideological or policy differences between the LDP and some of the smaller parties.

The usual pattern of leadership succession required two developments. Room would have to be made at the top of the party hierarchy for younger men, as none of the old guard could expect to recapture the office. Moreover, one of the aspirants would have to rally sufficient support to succeed Nakasone. But in a radical departure from tradition, there was talk of Nakasone staying on for a third term as party president, an eventuality made possible by his commanding victory in 1986.

In March 1985, the sixty-six-year-old Tanaka suffered a stroke. This did not end his political career, however. Although his influence began to erode, he nevertheless remained quite powerful behind the scenes.[45] But his failing health eventually meant that Tanaka had to pass control of his faction to the next generation of political leaders.

The Nakasone Era

In 1986 it appeared that Nakasone was losing his grip over the LDP and the electorate. But by the end of May he had won approval to hold elections for both houses of the Diet, although the legality of the move was somewhat dubious.[46] Nakasone also won approval from the party leadership for a supplementary budget calling for considerably more expenditure on public works projects than was envisioned in the budget developed by the Finance Ministry. To some extent, this represented a test of strength between Nakasone and the party, on the one hand, and the bureaucrats in the most powerful ministry, on the other.[47]

Nakasone chose as the centerpiece of the election campaign the breakup of the Japanese National Railways (JNR) into twenty-four private companies. This measure was conceived as a way of saving vast amounts of public revenue from a heavily subsidized system. Costs would be reduced considerably by cutting the labor force. The new arrangement called for the retention of less than two-thirds of the JNR employees. The Japan Socialist Party and the largest railroad union, the National Railway Workers' Union, opposed the measure and, as a result, were weakened by the partition and privatization. In their view, the system's problems were not the result of overcompensation of workers and featherbedding. Rather, financial losses were due to politicians running unprofitable lines into their constituencies.[48] The Kōmeitō and the Democratic Socialist Party favored privatization and some other railroad unions were induced to support the move by government promises of benefits favoring their members.

A potentially divisive issue—Japan's participation in Ronald Reagan's Strategic Defense Initiative (SDI)—was played down by concentrating on the JNR. This was an effective electoral strategy because public debate on the sensitive issue of weapons development might prove embarrassing. The public generally favors industrial expansion and exports, which could, in time, include Japanese participation in the international weapons market, something then prohibited.[49] Japan joined in SDI research out of fear of falling behind other countries in the developing new fields of technology and the promise of valuable industrial spin-offs.

The July 6 election results surprised everyone, including probably Nakasone himself. The LDP gained an unprecedented 300 seats in the lower house. The number was later raised to 304, when four independents joined the LDP. In the upper house it gained 142 seats out of 252, six more than in the 1983 election. By holding elections to both houses at the same time, Nakasone had hoped that the higher turnout would work to the advantage of the LDP. The strategy was clearly successful. One effective tactic used by the LDP was to limit the number of those contesting the election so that LDP candidates did not take votes away from one another. Those who did not earn the right to run as LDP candidates were discouraged from running as independents.

Although the LDP victory was sweeping, the measure of the defeat for two of the four opposition parties was perhaps of greater significance. The JSP efforts to put distance between itself and Soviet and East European–style socialism did not catch on with the public. It won only 86 seats, compared with its previous total of 111. The result reflected the declining appeal of socialist philosophy and the diminishing strength of unions in Japanese politics. Union membership had dropped more than 5 percent since 1975.[50]

As is often the case in democratic elections, the voters did not necessarily endorse the winner with the measure of enthusiasm that it rejected the losers. The voters did not see the opposition parties, especially the Socialists, as providing an acceptable alternative. The dual election worked to the advantage of the LDP because it allowed the party to maximize the effectiveness of its candidate support system. Nakasone's strong leadership image was also a factor. The LDP enjoyed a reputation for sound government management, and it had a more effective campaign organization than did the other parties.[51]

The stigma of the Lockheed scandal had disappeared, and there seemed to be little concern over corruption. This translated into a big loss for the New Liberal Club.

The LDP was not able to enjoy its renewed electoral success for very long, however. In 1987, local elections produced a reversal of Liberal Democratic fortunes. This was followed by the Recruit scandal (see Chapter 6), which cost Prime Minister Noboru Takeshita his job. But the power of money in Japanese politics is so strong that the scandal was not limited to the power brokers in the LDP. The Kōmeitō and the Socialists were also implicated. In all fourteen businesspeople and bureaucrats were indicted, and forty-five politicians resigned. Both Prime Minister Takeshita and Finance Minister Kiichi Miyazawa resigned, and former prime minister Nakasone left the LDP for a few years.[52]

The LDP rewarded Nakasone for leading the party to its resounding victory by extending his term of office by one year, beginning October 30, 1986. One of his first efforts was a move to strengthen the powers of the prime minister's office vis-à-vis the bureaucracy and LDP party organization. He created six new sections in the Cabinet Office out of the previous four and expanded the powers of three of them. Basically the idea was to develop a speedier and more effective decision-making system. If successful these measures would centralize power in the prime minister to a much greater extent than heretofore.[53]

Nakasone's flamboyant political style was a combination of a fresh and engaging personality with superior public relations skills.[54] More than any other postwar Japanese politician up to that time, he exploited the media, particularly television, to generate a positive public reaction. He also used foreign relations more effectively than did his predecessors. He was successful in winning a favorable response from the public and news media in the United States, something that had rarely happened in the past. However, his inclination to agree with the American emphasis on military preparation ran counter to the strong Japanese peace orientation.[55] His candor and straightforward presentations of issues to the public had also won him support.[56]

However, Nakasone's style was a temporary departure from the norm, rather than the beginning of a new pattern of national political leadership. Those individuals lined up in the wings seeking the prime ministership and other top political jobs were in the mold of blandness characteristic of prime ministers and party leaders since the end of the war. This was certainly true of Noboru Takeshita, Sousuke Uno, and Kiichi Miyazawa. This type of leadership style appears to be in keeping with the preferences of the electorate, which has demonstrated time and again a desire for solid managers rather than dynamic politicians with an orientation toward making significant policy initiatives.[57]

Takeshita had not been in office long when the LDP was struck by another scandal, this time involving insider stock trading. One of the first casualties was finance minister and faction leader Kiichi Miyazawa, who resigned in early December 1988. He was followed by the chairman of the Nippon Telegraph and Telephone Corporation and the justice minister, who ironically had been charged with the investigation of the scandal. Insider trading was an accepted practice in the Japanese stock market until the Diet passed a Revised Securities and Exchange Law in May 1988.

The New Liberal Club

In the 1970s there was mounting dissatisfaction within the LDP, especially among younger members, over the faction system and the domination of the party by very senior members. In 1976, six members of the party left and formed their own party, called the New Liberal Club (NLC). The shock of this event was considerable since it called into question the very essence of the LDP structure.[58] The NLC enjoyed some immediate success as its numbers grew to eight in the Diet, and in the 1976 election it won seventeen seats. Due to election losses, the ranks of the LDP in the House of Representatives shrank to the point that it no longer had a majority, thus affording the New Liberal Club the opportunity to join the governing coalition and take up ministerial posts. In the 1979 election, the NLC dropped to four seats, but the following year it was back up to twelve seats, and in 1983 it won eight seats. Although the party was seen as a possible moderate alternative to the LDP, the appeal of the NLC had all but disappeared within a decade of its founding. After the loss of two seats in the 1986 election, the party disbanded and its remaining members returned to the LDP.

Decline and Fall

In the late 1980s, the LDP was beset by scandal touching many top party officials, some of whom were forced out of office, at least temporarily. Faction leaders Shinzo Abe and Kiichi Miyazawa resigned their ministerial posts and Takeshita was replaced as prime minister by Sousuke Uno, whose brief tenure was also marked by scandal. Uno accepted blame for the LDP's electoral loses in the July 1989 elections and was succeeded by Toshiki Kaifu, whose efforts to reform the electoral system resulted in his early departure from office.

The troubles, which began when the LDP lost heavily in Tokyo municipal elections, prompted the minister of international trade and industry to suggest that the LDP government resign in order to reform itself.[59] The idea was not taken seriously. The LDP platform contained an apology for the scandal as well as a pledge to reexamine the unpopular consumption or sales tax.[60] As the Diet elections approached, the JSP campaigned vigorously against the LDP, rather than on socialist doctrine. The strategy was especially effective among women, who voted in larger numbers than men and elected twelve of thirteen JSP female candidates to municipal assembly seats.[61] The bloc vote from women carried over into the House of Councillors election, where the strategy of running women candidates paid off.[62]

Strangely, perhaps, the problems dogging the steps of the top LDP politicians did not produce dramatic changes in either the size or the leadership of factions. Although there was no shortage of younger members eager to take over from leaders compromised by the scandal, the latter were in no hurry to move aside. These senior party officials had waited a long time for their turn at the top of the party hierarchy, and they were not inclined to descend into obscurity. This made the choice of successors to Takeshita and Uno all the more difficult.

In the years that followed, the LDP began to lose its grip on the Japanese political system. Beset, on the one hand, by unrelenting pressure from the United States to ease the trade deficit and, on the other, by domestic problems brought on by the collapse of the "bubble economy," the government was confronted by mounting public dissatisfaction with financial corruption.

Morihiro Hosokawa formed the Japan New Party in May 1992. Hosokawa, a very popular figure, and his party were well positioned to exploit the disintegration of the LDP the following year. After the elections of 1993, Hosokawa headed a nine-party coalition government that enjoyed an unprecedented 71.9 percent public approval rating. But his government lasted only eight months, and Hosokawa himself fell from grace after disclosure of personal financial irregularities.[63] The party did not survive because "the JNP was a personal vehicle for Hosokawa and never established an image of its own independent of its leader."[64]

Opposition parties coalesced into the New Frontier Party (NFP; Shinshintō) in late 1994. The new government headed by Tsutomu Hata soon ran into trouble because of the NFP's tactics in the Diet, the irreconcilability among its factional divisions, and the bulldozing style of the party's leader, Ichiro Ozawa, who was even unpopular with his own party colleagues.[65]

Despite the changes in the electoral system, the political process remained much as it had been before. Ronald Hrebenar notes four areas of continuity. First, while parties have come and gone with almost breathtaking speed, the LDP remains in command of the political landscape. Second, the character of political leadership is the same. "[T]he LDP continues to recycle one weak prime minister after another as though they were faceless cogs in a perpetual machine."[66] Third, factions have resisted all efforts to eliminate them and they continue to determine party organization and leadership. Fourth, the opposition remains fragmented and has failed to offer a clear alternative to the LDP.

Rebuilding

In 1993, the LDP was removed from power and replaced by a seven-party coalition, a government that lasted until June 1994. A new coalition composed of the LDP, the JSP, and Harbinger Party (Sakigake) established a government headed by the JSP's Tomiichi Murayama, but his party did poorly in the July 1995 upper house elections. The JSP changed its name to the Social Democratic Party of Japan (SDPJ) and the realigned government was headed by the LDP's Hashimoto. On September 27, 1996, Prime Minister Ryutaro Hashimoto called for new elections to the lower house. The campaign lasted from October 8 to 19, and the election was held on October 20. This was the first lower house election test of the 1994 Public Office Election Law.

For the Socialists to enter a coalition with the LDP seems odd, given the strong ideological position long held by the JSP. But by this time, the party's pacifist philosophy had lost momentum. As the JSP tried to redefine itself, it may have appeared that this would prove to be one last chance to hold power, at least nominally. The LDP's alliance with the Socialists is probably easier to explain. For one thing, "the LDP has few, if any, inviolable principles."[67] Since compromising on policy matters did not pose a problem, the LDP could do whatever was necessary to get back into power.

Many SDPJ and Sakigake members expected that the new electoral system would have negative consequences for smaller parties. In July 1996, sixteen junior members of the SDP formed a group in the hope of attracting enough liberal support in the Diet to counter the strength of the larger conservative parties, the LDP and Shinshintō. Eventually, twenty-two more SDP members and fourteen Sakigake members joined the group, to form the Democratic Party of Japan (DPJ) on September 17. This new party claimed to be citizen oriented and called for an end to government corruption and a loosening of the bureaucracy's control over economic and other policy matters. The DPJ rejected the prospect of joining the governing coalition on the grounds that it would weaken the party's commitment to reform.

Other parties added their voices to the call for bureaucratic reform. Shinshintō leader Ichiro Ozawa attacked the ruling coalition government for failing to enact significant reforms. He put forth a plan to halve the bureaucracy and reduce administrative regulations. The Japan Communist Party (JCP) called for an end to the close relationship between government and business. SDP leader Takako Doi suggested taking the bill introduction function away from ministries and have Diet members assume greater responsibility for drafting and submitting legislation. She also called for an end to the practice of "descent from heaven" (*amakudari*). (This practice, by which government bureaucrats go to work for businesses that they had regulated while in government service, fosters collusion between business and bureaucrats. Given the close personal relationships that develop in Japanese organizations, retired government officials are in a good position to lobby their former colleagues.)

The LDP joined the crusade to reform the bureaucracy by suggesting that the number of ministries be cut in half. The government called for immediate action and chose as its first target the Ministry of Finance, which was unpopular with the public because it had failed to deal effectively with Japan's economic problems.

Another volatile issue was the tax system, especially the unpopular consumption tax, which had been increased from 3 percent to 5 percent. Because of the government's dire financial situation (Japan ran significant deficits) parties tended to agree that the tax increase was necessary. They tried to deflect public criticism by calling for help for those with lower income and stressing the need to eliminate government waste.

Voter participation reached an all-time low on October 20 when only 59 percent of the electorate cast ballots. The LDP emerged as the big winner, capturing 169 of the 288 seats that they contested in the single-member districts, and did so with only 38.6 percent of the vote. The new system had not eliminated the LDP's ability to capture a higher proportion of Diet seats than the percentage of the popular vote. The LDP's seventy seats in the proportional representation districts more closely corresponded to the percentage of the vote. Party leaders effectively exploited the dual nature of the electoral system by running in both single-member and proportional districts. Should they lose their bid for a single-member seat, they stood a good chance of winning a proportional representation seat. In the proportional elections contests, candidates were listed according to their rank in the party, but voters cast their ballots for a party. The LDP fell short of a majority, but its twenty-eight-seat gain made it the dominant factor in the new coalition.

Sakigake and the SDP lost badly in the election. The former, already weakened by defections to the DPJ, won only two seats. The SDP suffered its worst showing in its fifty-one-year history, winning only four single-member seats and eleven proportional seats. Shinshintō did reasonably well, losing only four seats, and it lost several close contests to the LDP in single-member districts. The DJP retained fifty-two seats in the Diet. Surprisingly the JCP garnered 13.08 percent of the vote, its largest ever. But it won only two seats, a result it blamed on the new system.

No formal coalition emerged from the elections, but various parties agreed to cooperate. The LDP, the SDP, and Sakigake formed an alliance in which they would join forces on policy matters, while the Cabinet was exclusively LDP. The DPJ agreed to cooperate on reform implementation but was not part of budget strategy. The LDP also agreed to work with some non-LDP conservative legislators who called themselves the Twenty-first Century group. Hashimoto returned as prime minister and announced his Cabinet on November 5. It consisted of senior LDP members, most of whom came from traditionally powerful political families.

Keizo Obuchi assumed the office of prime minister in July 1998. At the time of his accession he had the lowest public approval rating of any prime minister since the end of the war, 25 percent. As a result of promising economic developments through 1999, Obuchi's once-dismal prospects of staying in office more than a few months improved. In September 1999, he was able to retain both the party presidency and the prime ministership. His Cabinet balanced factional strength and included one minister from each of the two non-LDP parties that supported his government, the Kōmeitō and the Liberal Party.[68] But on April 2, 2000, the prime minister suffered a stroke, leaving him in a coma. He was succeeded by Yoshiro Mori, who, shortly after assuming office, called for new elections. These elections were held on June 25, resulting in significant losses for the LDP and its ruling partners, the New Kōmeitō and the New Conservative Party (NCP) (see Chapter 5). Nonetheless, Mori remained prime minister, and the ruling parties captured enough seats to retain control of the House of Representatives. The prospects for the House of Councillors election were not so bright, however. Accordingly, the selection of the new party president was opened to include party members outside the Diet. The forty-seven prefectures were allowed three votes each based on a primary election. Junichiro Koizumi won 123 out of 141 of these seats, allowing him to best Ryutaro Hashimoto, who controlled the largest faction but could not muster enough votes from LDP members of the Diet to overcome Koizumi's lead.[69]

By 2000, most of the new parties had either merged or simply gone out of existence. The Japan New Party and the Shinseitō joined the Shinshintō, which, together with the Sakigake, had disappeared in 1998. Two new parties came into being, the Democratic Party (Minshutō) and the Liberal Party (Jiyūtō), the latter joining a coalition with the LDP in 1999. In the 2000 election, the LDP was once more back on top, winning 239 seats.

Koizumi assumed the office of prime minister in April 2001 and served until September 2006. In September 2003, Koizumi was reelected head of the LDP and continued as prime minister. The following month he dissolved the House of Representatives and called for elections, which were held on November 9. There were 1,159 candidates competing for the 480 seats in the House. Voters chose 300 from single-member districts and 180 from the proportional representation lists in eleven regional constituencies. Voter turnout was 59.73 percent, which was down 3 percent from the June 2000 election. The LDP captured 237 seats, down from 246 before the election. To this number were added the four seats won by the NCP, giving the LDP a one-seat majority. The NCP had been the smallest of the LDP's coalition partners. The NCP formerly had nine seats and, after it lost five of them, the party leadership decided to merge with the LDP.

In the July 2004 upper house election, the LDP retained control. But in the July 2007 election, the LDP relinquished control to the Democratic Party and its allies. In the September 2007 lower house election, the LDP captured a large majority. Koizumi was succeeded by Shinzo Abe, who rapidly lost popular support and suddenly resigned in late 2007. He was succeeded by Yasuo Fukuda, son of former prime minister Takeo Fukuda. In August 2008 Fukuda appointed a rival, Taro Aso, as secretary-general of the LDP, and a month later announced his own resignation from the premiership. In short order Aso won election to the presidency of the LDP and was chosen by the Diet as the new prime minister on September 24. The Emperor formally appointed him to the position that same night.

5

Political Parties—II

Political parties first appeared in Japan in the late nineteenth century. The most successful of them have always been of a conservative political persuasion. Parties on the left have tended to fare poorly at the polls and have never attained majority status with the voters. In fact they have often been suppressed; the Japan Communist Party was banned in 1924, for example. The authoritarian politics of the 1920s and 1930s culminating in World War II changed the fortunes of leftist parties, at least temporarily. The experience with militarism during the 1930s and 1940s compromised the reputation of conservative parties and partially exonerated that of progressive parties. This did not mean, however, that after the war progressive parties were swept forward on a wave of popularity. Their philosophies did not resonate with the public any more after the war than they had before, and their politicians were certainly no more skillful. If the ideologies and programs of the left encountered only measured hospitality in postwar Japan, at least they did not bear the burden of responsibility for the disasters of recent decades. The conservatives managed to avoid calling attention to their own background and were soon forgiven by the voters. Among the parties created or revived after the war were the Progressive Party and the Cooperative Party, which, despite their progressive sounding names, held conservative views.[1]

The Japan Socialist Party

In the years immediately after the war, the political environment favored parties that were philosophically left of center.[2] One factor working in favor of the left was the New Deal liberalism of the U.S. occupation, which tended to favor groups advocating change. Progressive political groups also benefited from a purge undertaken in January 1946, which focused on the conservatives because of their association with wartime activities. The purge was devastating to the Progressive Party and had the effect of dividing the leadership of all conservative parties as politicians fought for control over their fragmented organizations.[3] More than 70 percent of the politicians who had been members of the Diet before 1945 were removed from politics by the purge.[4]

The Socialists took courage from the tribulations of the conservatives and increased the number of Diet seats they contested, but their success was modest. Prewar indoctrination of political ideas and values had been so effective that loyalty to the conservative cause remained strong. Many powerful conservative figures escaped the purge by the subterfuge of replacing themselves with their subordinates during the latter days of the war. The scheme worked because the occupation authorities did not have the time or indeed the desire to probe too deeply. Moreover, occupation efforts to decentralize authority, which would have favored the Socialists because of their strength at the local level, were soon rolled back. To a very large extent, the prewar ruling political elite emerged from the occupation period with its powers largely intact.

The first postwar political party, established in October 1945, was called the Japan Socialist Party in Japanese but the Social Democratic Party in English in hopes of not provoking the occupation authorities, who, despite their democratic leanings, became increasingly suspicious of political groups on the left. The Socialists were the first on the scene because the conservatives "were still suffering from the shock of defeat" and communist leaders had not yet been released from jail.[5]

The Socialists' electoral fortunes peaked in 1947 when they won 143 seats, giving them a plurality in the lower house of the legislature. But the margin was thin; the Liberals won 132 seats and the Democrats won 126. By virtue of this newly gained parliamentary strength, the Socialists were in a position to augment their power by placing their people in important positions in the bureaucracy. But they were unable to take full advantage of this fleeting opportunity as they dissipated their strength quarreling among themselves. The left wing of the party opposed participation in a coalition government made necessary by the fact that the party lacked a majority in the Diet. For the left wing of the Socialist Party, involvement in a coalition would compromise the party's principles, which was unacceptable. To form a coalition, the Socialists needed the support of the Liberals or the Democrats, both of which, despite their names, were conservative. Moreover, the combined strength of these two opposition parties was greater than that of the Socialists.

In addition to their distaste for participation in a coalition for ideological reasons, left-wing members of the JSP considered it unwise for the party to form a government given the conditions then existing in the country. Prospects were not encouraging for any government because of the difficult and indeed worsening economic situation. Not only would the conservative opposition be able to obstruct and frustrate Socialist efforts at every turn, but the future of the JSP would not be bright, should it form a government and fail to govern effectively. But the right wing of the JSP favored taking advantage of the opportunity to exercise political power and in due course a government under Katayama Tetsu was assembled with the Socialists working in coalition with the Democratic Party. The Socialists were forced to pay a high price in return for conservative cooperation, however. They had to agree to exclude left-wing elements of their own party from cabinet posts.

The Socialists were clearly not prepared to govern. They had serious philosophical and organizational problems, the party had only been in existence a short time, and they had little understanding of the operation of the parliament.[6] In addition, they took over a government faced with an almost insurmountable crisis: wages and prices were rising rapidly, labor was becoming increasingly militant, and there was a food shortage. Because of their weak command of governing power, the Socialists were unable to enact their agenda. The only socialist measure they were able to get through the Diet was a watered-down program calling for state control of coal mining that passed in November 1947. Actually, it only meant modernization of machinery at taxpayers' expense while the mines themselves were soon returned to private hands.

A second Socialist attempt to establish a government was a revised coalition put together under Ashida Hitoshi but it fell apart after only eight months in office. It failed to curb inflation or make any appreciable gain toward economic recovery. It was saved from an onslaught of labor protests only by the intervention of the occupation authorities. From this time onward, the labor movement and left-wing parties experienced almost continuous decline in their influence. All in all, the experience of the Socialist government was disastrous for the party, although its brief tenure did advance the cause of democracy and enhance a sensitivity for civil liberties.[7]

In 1950, the persistent philosophical differences between the left and right factions in the JSP resulted in each forming its own youth group. The two factions differed in their attitude toward the occupation and on the proper approach to the peace treaty. As a result of this division of opinion, the party's effectiveness in putting forward its program and attracting voters to it was substantially reduced. When the treaty was voted on in 1951, the JSP split into two parties. The left opposed the treaty, the provisions of the mutual security pact with the United States, and Japanese rearmament. The right favored the peace treaty but was divided on security matters.[8]

Throughout the 1950s the Socialists found themselves and their ideas under conservative assault. In 1952 an important legislative battle was fought over the Subversive Activities Prevention Bill. This measure was nominally directed against communists but the Socialists feared it was a potential threat to anyone with left-wing political views. Despite the fact that the bill provoked extensive public demonstrations and violence, it was eventually passed.

For a brief period in 1953, the Socialists made gains at the expense of conservative parties, which had fallen to bickering among themselves. But in 1954 the left and right factions of the JSP divided further when controversy developed among labor unions over aspects of the party platform. In October 1955, the two Socialist parties reunited but only after much wrangling and discontent over the new party platform. In response to the reunification of the Socialist party, the Liberal and Democratic parties joined in November 1955 forming the Liberal Democratic Party (LDP). The Socialists seemed to be content to avoid formal political power, preferring instead to assert themselves from the position of a perpetual opposition party. In this they seemed to believe, naively as it turned out, that they could remain a vigorous party with substantial voter support.[9]

In 1956, the conservatives made another attempt to weaken the political left. This time their strategy was to change the electoral district system. Their scheme involved the creation of small, badly gerrymandered single-member districts that would have been clearly to the disadvantage of the Socialists. The conservatives failed in this effort but the imbalance among districts in favor of rural areas has consistently been an electoral asset of the LDP. For all its defects, the electoral system remained fundamentally unchanged until the reforms of 1994.

The conservatives mounted an attack against one of the most important bases of Socialist strength—the teachers' union. The confrontation between the union and the LDP-controlled Ministry of Education began in 1952 over school board elections. Later the government moved to make school board members subject to appointment by heads of local bodies rather than by election. The executive heads of local bodies were usually conservative; elections often returned Socialists. A change in method of choice would also have the effect of reducing the ability of the Japan Teachers' Union (JTU) to exert pressure on school boards. The Diet approved the change in June 1956 "despite JTU-led Socialist opposition of riotous proportions."[10] The violence proved costly for the union, however, as its membership dropped by as many as 80,000 teachers and 15,000 principals. It was also costly to teachers, thousands of whom were demoted, reprimanded, or suffered pay cuts.[11] In 1958 the LDP succeeded in introducing a teacher-rating system intended to further weaken the JTU. But teacher noncooperation rendered the system ineffective.[12]

As if they did not have enough trouble with conservative plots to undermine their strength, the Socialists suffered from other handicaps. One of these was intransigent union pressures, which weakened their popular appeal and even alienated some moderate elements within the party. The split between the Soviet Union and China, which burst into the open in 1962, created ideological confusion. The JSP's neutral posture vis-à-vis the excesses of the Cultural Revolution in China in the late 1960s, a matter of considerable interest to the Japanese public, cost the party additional support. Its attack on the evils of capitalism, an essential ingredient of socialist doctrine, was politically untimely given the significant rate of economic growth that was widely beneficial to Japanese society. As a result of these and other factors, the chances of the Socialists by themselves or in league with other parties replacing the LDP declined.

During the second half of the 1950s, there was great tension within the JSP brought on by the retrenchment of occupation reforms. This tension, which reached a climax in 1960 with the confrontation over renewal of the Security Treaty with the United States, quickly declined in the 1960s. This changing climate was due in part to the emergence of a new political generation that had not been involved in prewar struggles hence they were less concerned with past battles and power disputes. Moreover, the shakeout and adjustments concerning occupation reforms had been largely concluded. But perhaps the most important factor was the magnitude of economic success, which dampened protest ideology. By the 1970s the goal of a workers' paradise based on Marxist-Leninist models of the Soviet Union, Eastern Europe, and China had become unattractive. As a result of these developments, the appeal of the Socialists lessened and they settled into a permanent opposition.[13]

By 1960, the JSP was confronted again with a split in its ranks. Many members of the party, especially younger ones, did not have ties and loyalties dating back to the prewar era. Nor did they have the unshakable faith in doctrinaire socialist principles that characterized their older colleagues. They also opposed the extremes of union pressure. Moreover, left-wing socialist ideas and policies were becoming less popular among voters in general. These factors combined to provoke a rebellion leading moderate Socialist elements to leave the JSP and form the Democratic Socialist Party (DSP). The DSP modeled itself on brand of socialism found in Western Europe. It held out little attraction to the radical left but neither did its mild socialism capture the imagination of the public. As a result, it had only limited success.

During the 1970s, the fortunes of political parties on the left were on the rise. Many politically progressive chief executives were chosen in local elections. They governed localities that encompassed almost half the population. Thus encouraged, progressive parties looked forward to the further expansion of their influence to the national level of government. But for a variety of reasons, the progressive challenge to LDP dominance had begun to recede by 1980.[14]

One factor contributing to the declining fortunes of progressives was the oil shock of 1973, which put considerable strain on the economy and diminished interest in experimenting with economic changes. The progressives were also the victims of their own success. The lavish spending on social programs that they had introduced at the local level was becoming an embarrassment as the public was unwilling to bear the mounting costs. Another reason was the ability of the LDP to form coalitions with other parties, thus enabling it to retain and even strengthen its overall control of the government. The LDP was also adroit in co-opting those aspects of the progressive's program that had popular support and taking credit for enacting them into law.[15]

In the 1983 lower house election, the LDP appeared to be in serious trouble. It failed to gain an absolute majority, but continued to rule through a coalition. The JSP expanded its lower house strength by 11 seats to bring its total to 112. The most important development, however, was the growing recognition in the party that it would have to undertake substantial changes if it were to achieve greater popularity among the voters.

The process of redesigning the party began in earnest and in January 1986, the JSP adopted a program that explicitly renounced Soviet and East European–style socialism in favor of a "social democratic philosophy." Instead of references to Marxism-Leninism, the term scientific socialism was employed. Dictatorship of the proletariat was dropped in favor of workers' power.[16] At its fifty-fifth regular party convention in 1990, the party dropped from the party rules language advocating "socialist revolution" in favor of "social democracy."[17] In a major retreat, the party backed away from its long-held position favoring unarmed neutrality as the basis of Japan's foreign policy. Although this was a clear attempt to improve the party's vote-getting ability, it masked deep philosophical divisions within party ranks. A more moderate posture, the JSP hoped, would improve its chances of forming a coalition with other small parties, like the Kōmeitō or the Democratic Socialists. But there was little likelihood of a coalition government.[18] One problem was the JSP's position on nuclear power; although it accepted existing plants, it opposed new ones, a position not shared by potential coalition partners. They also did not share JSP opposition to the U.S.–Japan security agreement. The Self Defense Force was a major bone of contention within the JSP with the left wing opposing it and the rest of the party taking a more moderate view. The JSP faced a dilemma: to move closer to the center of the political spectrum and try to become a more effective electoral force seemed to compromise its principles and alienate or even drive out the left wing of the party.[19]

The strategy of redefining the party's ideology was not immediately effective, as it turned out, at least not in the 1986 elections as the JSP lost ground. It is doubtful that its attempts at moderation were perceived or appreciated by the voters.[20] Having become accustomed to the JSP's doctrinaire position for so many years, the electorate did not readily adapt to the "new" Socialist Party.

The JSP and the other opposition parties had their best opportunity to date to unseat the LDP in 1990. The LDP was racked by scandal, the party leadership was in turmoil, voters were unhappy with a new sales tax, and farmers were protesting agricultural imports. Since the LDP had already lost control of the upper house the previous year, it appeared a coalition government might be a real possibility. The JSP added substantially to its numbers in the House of Representatives, but these gains came largely at the expense of other opposition parties, not the LDP. The margin of the LDP was only slightly reduced but for the Japan Communist Party and the Democratic Socialists, the result was devastating. Their numbers shrank to such an extent that they could no longer introduce legislation in the lower house.[21]

Following the collapse of the Hata government in 1994, parties once again scrambled to form new alliances. As an indication of just how far the JSP had moved away from its ideological foundations, the Socialists entered into a coalition with their arch rivals, the LDP. The prime minister was the Socialist leader Tomiichi Murayama. Under his leadership, the party abandoned its long-standing opposition to the Self Defense Force and the Mutual Security Treaty with the United States. All of these developments were unavailing, however, as the Socialists' strength continued to dwindle in subsequent elections. Murayama resigned as prime minister in January 1996 and was succeeded by Ryutaro Hashimoto from the LDP.

Before the political realignments of the 1990s, the JSP was the largest opposition party in Japan, yet it never came close to capturing a majority in the Diet. The party's inability to challenge the LDP for power may be attributed to two fundamental weaknesses: ideology and organization. First, until recently, the ideology of the JSP was a disparate collection of various left-wing beliefs that, although strongly held, did not fit comfortably together under the same party roof. Historically, Socialist ideology has run the gamut from revolutionary Maoism to more moderate emphasis upon evolutionary reform. In 1945, the JSP rejected an offer from the communists to form a popular front, not on the grounds of ideological incompatibility between the two parties, but because the parties were not sufficiently well-established.[22] By 1947, the differences between the two parties precluded cooperation.[23]

The JSP was divided into factions reflecting the different ideological divisions within the party. On the far left were Marxist revolutionaries generally sympathetic to the Chinese model, who talked about a class-based party and argued among themselves over whether the greatest enemy of Japan was American imperialism or Japanese monopoly capitalism. On the right were reformers who are committed to parliamentary government and the welfare state.[24]

A particularly serious problem facing parties on the left is the weak sense of class consciousness on the part of the Japanese people. Marxist exhortations to attain political ends in the name of class conflicts have little voter appeal. Many of those voting for the Socialist or Communist parties do so in protest against something the LDP did or failed to do or because of some broader public concern. But even important and enduring issues such as air and water pollution, the energy crisis, and the threat of war have not translated into expanded support for the opposition. Paradoxically, some of the vote received by opposition parties is predicated on the expectation that they cannot win. If voters perceived that these parties stood a real chance of taking power, their enthusiasm might diminish.[25]

The JSP was unable to put together an organizational structure that would enhance its electoral effectiveness.[26] The Socialists relied heavily on labor unions for support and financial assistance. The JSP had particularly close ties to the Sōhyō Federation in which the public-sector unions dominate. The union connection is not an unmixed blessing, however. Japanese unions themselves are relatively weak since many of them in the industrial sector are enterprise unions. Those in the public sector are politically more aggressive but no more effective. Moreover, the percentage of workers represented by unions has been declining. Many JSP candidates have been former union officials, which tied the party closely to union issues and tended to discourage support among the general public.

Throughout most of its postwar history, the position of the JSP on international security relations was closer to that of the Soviet Union than to that of the United States. In the JSP view, the threat to Japan came not from the Soviet military presence in Asia but from the U.S.–Japan Security treaty, which could cause a war. To avoid entanglement in such a war, the proper policy for Japan should be that of unarmed neutrality.[27] In the first place there was no reason to assume that there existed a threat of invasion from any quarter, hence there is no need for defense existed. As to the vulnerability of the sea-lanes on which Japan's economic lifeblood depends, the facts of life are that they are simply cannot be defended. Japan is better off, therefore, not to make the effort. Thus, the JSP adopted in 1949 a foreign policy of "permanent neutrality" to which it would adhere throughout most of its existence. To this principle would be added two others—one favoring a peace treaty with all belligerent powers involved in World War II and another opposing military bases in Japan for any foreign power.[28]

The downward spiral of the party's fortunes continued into the 1996 election. Shortly before the election a group from the SDP split off and formed the Democratic Party of Japan (DPJ). Its support came mainly from labor unions. The DPJ won fifty-two seats in the 1996 election while the Social Democrats gained only fifteen. Since then the fortunes of the old Socialist Party have continued to sink.

The Clean Government Party

The Clean Government Party (Kōmeitō) is the only party in postwar Japan with links to a religious organization. Its sponsor, the Value Creation Society (Sōka

Gakkai), is the layman's affiliate of the Nichiren Shoshu sect of Buddhism. Sōka Gakkai was founded November 18, 1930, by Tsunesaburo Makiguchi, who sought to reform education as a means of improving society. The greatest impact on the movement came at the hands of Makiguchi's protégé and successor, Josei Toda, who assumed the presidency of the group in 1951.[29] Toda defined the themes of the group, including relief from misery, the importance of social belonging, and prosperity. It directed its appeal "to the down and out, the economically deprived and the socially disoriented."[30] Sōka Gakkai first entered politics in 1955 when its cultural department put up fifty-three candidates in local elections and all but one were victorious. In 1956 it did well in upper house elections, where the national constituency permitted the party to concentrate its scattered support and two of its four candidates won. The same year, all seventy-six of its candidates for Tokyo ward assemblies were elected. Elsewhere in the country, 264 out of 287 candidates were elected.[31] In an effort to put some distance between Sōka Gakkai's religious and political activities, Kōmeitō was formed in 1964 but it did not take part in lower house elections until 1967. In the political shakeup of the 1990s, the lower house members of the Kōmeitō joined the New Frontier Party (Shinshintō). It later reappeared as the New Kōmeitō and aligned itself with the LDP.

The Kōmeitō claims to represent all people.[32] It contends other parties represented parochial interests: the LDP has a rural and business appeal and the Socialists' connection with unions constitutes a class orientation. Moreover, the government, run by corrupt politicians, can be corrected by the election of members of the Kōmeitō. In fact, however, the Kōmeitō has not been broadly representative of the population but reflects its parent organization's emphasis on the socially marginalized. This target population includes people alienated from society and those holding negative views of government.[33] The party appeals especially to women, younger people, unskilled workers, and those with comparatively less education.[34] Leaders of Sōka Gakkai are committed to the goal of fusing Buddhism with politics. The Kōmeitō works toward the realization of this goal by seeking "the structural changes in society that will produce a social, economic and political environment in which Nichiren Shoshu can be fully accepted."[35] This has necessitated a claim by Kōmeitō of its independence from direction by the leadership of Sōka Gakkai.

Basically conservative in its orientation, the Kōmeitō argues contemporary problems are the result of a lack of commitment to fundamental values. Western democracy stresses individual freedom to such an extent that those without talent or money are social castoffs and are thrown into poverty. Marxist democracy, however, enslaves the people at the altar of materialism.[36] The Kōmeitō's policy agenda includes measures to enhance social welfare.[37]

The Kōmeitō's success at the polls has been due to its effective system of local organization.[38] However, its techniques have not always been as scrupulous as the name "Clean Government Party" would imply. Sōka Gakkai's style of religious proselytizing has involved pressure and intimidation.[39] The Kōmeitō was touched by the scandals that rocked the country in 1988–89. In one instance there was suspicion that large sums of Sōka Gakkai money were being used improperly to influence politics.

During the 1960s, the Kōmeitō, and the Communists as well, expanded their popularity among the voters. They achieved this by effectively organizing in urban areas and appealing to the electorate by promoting such issues as social welfare and antipollution. In contrast, the JSP and the DSP lost ground because they attached their fortunes to labor unions which were of diminishing importance in elections.[40]

In the 1983 election, the Kōmeitō nearly doubled its numbers in the lower house, jumping from thirty-four to fifty-eight seats. These gains came at the expense of the LDP, which was facing serious problems due mainly to the conviction of former prime minister Tanaka on bribery charges. But the Kōmeitō could not build on this success; in 1986 it lost one seat. Its fortunes have fluctuated in subsequent elections and as of the last election in 2007 he held thirty-one seats in the lower house.

In 1990 the Kōmeitō abandoned its traditional policy of seeking a coalition with the JSP. The chairman of the Kōmeitō stated that in twenty years the JSP had "never responded in any meaningful way to our approach for a coalition."[41] This opened the way for a possible link with the Liberal Democrats. But the Kōmeitō set three conditions before a coalition would be possible. The LDP must reform itself, consumers, rather than business, must be given the highest priority and the LDP must be defeated in a national election thus necessitating a coalition.[42] But, rather than join with the LDP as the parties realigned following the 1993 election, the Kōmeitō merged with the Ozawa-Hata group, the Japan New Party, and the DSP to form the New Frontier Party. When this arrangement fell apart, the party reappeared as the New Kōmeitō. The party continues to draw strength from its ties to Sōka Gakkai.

The Japan Communist Party

The Japan Communist Party (JCP) was founded July 15, 1922, with the encouragement and financial support of the Soviet Union. Throughout most of its history, the party has had close ideological connections with and taken its lead from Moscow.[43] The party has always been handicapped by its inability to identify itself with nationalistic goals and symbols. The monopoly on nationalism held by an emperor-centered ideology denied the Communists a share in this important political force.[44] Although the Chinese Communist revolution of 1949 influenced the JCP's development, during the 1980s and 1990s the party moved closer to the model of Euro-communism. This meant a political line largely independent of both Moscow and Beijing and a strong effort to identify itself with nationalist ideals.

After World War II, the U.S. occupation authorities freed imprisoned political leaders including the Communists, and encouraged political activity by groups of liberal and progressive persuasion. The JCP was initially committed to a united front, common cause strategy with the Socialists. But this was a most improbable union as the Socialists stood for much that the Communists found objectionable.[45] The successes and exuberance of the political left were too much for the authorities and as a result it was reined in. Since then, the JCP has had its ups and downs but always remaining a distinct minority. The Korean War and the advent of Communist China created a new situation for the JCP and changed its orientation. Encouragement of political violence cost the Communists popular support, and the JCP did not win a single seat in the 1952 House of Representatives elections. Its greatest successes came in the 1979 election when it won forty-one seats.

The JCP is divided between those who favor peaceful coexistence and advocates of violent revolution. A majority of the party has tended toward the former view and present day Communists are almost exclusively concerned with peace issues. The party has had little ideological appeal among the general public. Instead it focuses on controversial issues, such as the alliance with the United States. It also takes the strongest position of all Japanese parties on the Northern Territories issue (see Chapter 12). The JCP demands the return to Japan of all the Kurile island chain, all the way up to the Kamchatka peninsula. But this may have been little more than a gimmick to show its independence from Moscow.[46]

The party contests more seats than it expects to win because of its consciousness-raising role, particularly with reference to groups that are dissatisfied with the existing order. These groups include the lower elements of the industrial working class, some farmers, ethnic minorities, and women. Communism has been popular among students and intellectuals, especially those drawn to the peace movement.[47] It appears that the limit of the JCP's electoral support is around 10 percent of the vote. All in all the future does not look promising for the political left. Possible coalition partners for the JCP are themselves growing weaker or are moving to the right. In 1980, the Socialists formed an alliance with the Kōmeitō in which it agreed to support both the Mutual Security Treaty with the United States and the Self Defense Force. It also agreed to exclude the Communists from any future coalition.[48] The 1993 coalition government headed by Morihiro Hosokawa included all opposition parties except the Communists.

As a party committed to an ideological position, the JCP suffers even more than other opposition parties from the ideological neutrality of the Japanese voter. Any effort to mute its Marxist orientation would bring into question its very raison d'être. Moreover, membership in the international communist movement is a liability. The JCP's link with the Soviet Union made it, in the view of many Japanese, a tool of a foreign power and a highly objectionable one at that. The excesses of the Cultural Revolution and the 1989 Tiananmen incident discredited the Chinese brand of communism and diminishing its appeal as a model for the JCP.

Even though it attempted to distance itself from both Soviet and Chinese models of communism and pattern its ideology along the nationalist lines of European communist parties, especially the Italian, it has not been able to expand its electoral base; in fact its support has continued to erode. As countries in central Europe, as well as parts of the former Soviet Union, repudiated Marxist-Leninist ideology and organizational methods, communist parties such as that in Japan could not help but feel the shock waves.

In June 2003, a proposal was submitted to the Central Committee Plenum of the JCP calling for extensive revisions in the party's manifesto. The changes were significant including the substitution of "democratic reform" for the party's goal of "socialist revolution." Phrases such as "U.S. imperialism," which appears in the old document thirty-two times, now appears only once. "Japanese monopoly capital," used twenty times in the old manifesto, has been dropped altogether.[49]

The Democratic Socialist Party

The DSP was formed in 1960 when the right wing of the JSP broke away. At issue was the continued adherence to the goals and tactics of Marxism by the party's left-oriented faction. Like the JSP, the DSP maintained ties to labor, in particular with the federation called Dōmei that includes a variety of industrial and trade workers.

Philosophically the party was close to the LDP and, despite its name, had little enthusiasm for doctrinaire socialism. It saw itself mainly as a coalition partner and frequently joined with other centrist parties, such as the Kōmeitō, in electoral alliances. It differed most specifically with the JSP over the issue of defense where it supported the Self Defense Force.

In several elections, the DSP functioned as an alternative to the LDP for many voters; LDP losses translated into DSP gains and vice versa. In 1983, when LDP strength dropped to the point that it no longer had a majority of seats in the lower house, the DSP added seven seats, for a total of thirty-eight. But in the 1986 election, the DSP lost eleven seats, from thirty-seven to twenty-six with the LDP gaining a proportional amount. In the 1990 election, in contrast, both the DSP and the LDP lost seats, with the former going from twenty-six to fourteen. In 1993 it captured nineteen seats and then disbanded when it joined the New Frontier Party. After the collapse of the New Frontier Party in 1998, the DSP joined the Democratic Party.

Other Parties

The Japan New Party (JNP, or Nihon Shintō) was founded by Morihiro Hosokawa, former governor of Kumamoto prefecture, with the stated purpose of ending LDP control of the government. The Japan New Party was formed in May 1992 although some of its people had been elected in 1989 to the upper house. The Japan New Party drew support from the new middle class, women, and urban salarymen. It took advantage of the tribulations of the Miyazawa government. Racked by scandal, unable to enact political reforms despite solemn promises to do so, and forced to accept embarrassing compromises in its quest for legislative authorization for Japanese participation in peace-keeping operations, the LDP also faced internal rebellion. Hosokawa was soon himself implicated in scandal, thus weakening the JNP which united with the Japan Renewal Party.

In 1993, eleven junior members of the lower house left the LDP and formed the Harbinger Party (Sakigake) and immediately aligned themselves with Hosokawa's group. The competition for the party presidency resulted in a split when a group headed by Ichiro Ozawa, protégé of former LDP kingmaker Shin Kanemaru, and Tsutomu Hata, former minister of finance, left the party and formed the Japan Renewal Party (Shinseitō) on June 22, 1993.

On July 18 a general election was held that ended the LDP's control of the parliament. The LDP did reasonably well, considering the magnitude of the recent defections; it won 223 seats later raised to 227 as individuals elected as independents aligned themselves with parties. The Socialists were devastated, dropping to only seventy seats to which were later added six independents. The Shinseitō wound up with sixty seats, the Kōmeitō fifty-two, Sakigake-JNP alliance fifty-two, DSP nineteen, Communists fifteen, and ten independents.

A seven-party coalition established a government after the LDP failed to attract enough support to form a coalition government of its own. The new government was headed by Morihiro Hosokawa who moved ahead with political reforms and restructuring the electoral system, an accomplishment that ultimately worked to the advantage of the LDP.[50] The task was not easy and early defeat in the upper house forced the government to make concessions.[51] Hosokawa's Japan New Party linked up with the Sakigake, which was led by

Masayoshi Takemura, another defector from the LDP. Hosokawa was soon caught up in a scandal of his own, when it was revealed he had accepted money for personal use. He was forced to resign and was succeeded by Tsutomu Hata, who survived in office for only a short while. A new coalition government was then formed combining the LDP, its former arch rival the Socialist Party, and the Sakigake. The new prime minister was Tomiichi Murayama, leader of the JSP. Most of the ministries went to the LDP.

The October 1996 election was the first test of the 1994 reformed system. The new system was confusing to voters, whose interest in politics was not renewed by confronting a different way to elect members of parliament. The campaign did not generate interest in policy matters as candidates said much the same thing or little at all. When the votes were counted, the LDP and the Communists gained seats; all other parties joined the new parliament with their numbers diminished.

The new government was pretty much like old times for the LDP. Although it lacked a majority, other parties were reluctant to join in a coalition opposing the LDP because their previous experience suggested that coalitions were a recipe for going out of business. Cabinet positions were all held by LDP members and were distributed according to faction strength. Six of the twenty portfolios went to the Obuchi faction and its leader soon became prime minister.[52]

In the months that followed, political parties underwent elaborate reshuffling. Tsutomu Hata left the New Frontier Party in December 1996 and formed the Sun Party (Taiyōtō), which united with the Democratic Party in April 1998. The NFP dissolved in December 1997. In January 1998, Ichiro Ozawa established the Liberal Party. In November 1998, the New Peace Party (Shintō Heiwa), composed of House of Representative members who were formerly members of Kōmeitō, and the remaining members of Kōmeitō in the House of Councillors formed the New Kōmeitō (Shin Kōmeitō). In October 1999, the LDP, the Liberal Party and the Shin Kōmeitō formed a coalition government. The parties agreed to a joint policy position and to cooperate in adjusting their candidacies in the next general election.

The frequent change of party names and shifting affiliation by their members created a confusing situation for voters. Only the LDP and the JCP retained their names during this period of party transformation.[53]

The 2003 election brought about party consolidation and exhibited signs of an emerging two-party system. The DJP won 177 seats up from 137, well short of a majority, but the best showing of an opposition party since the demise of the JSP. With the exception of the Shin Kōmeitō, which added three seats to its margin of thirty-one, smaller parties did poorly. The JCP dropped from twenty seats to nine. The Democratic Socialist Party won only six seats and its president, Takako Doi, lost her bid for a single-member district seat but remained in the Diet through the proportional-representation system. The New Conservative Party, one of the LDP's coalition partners along with the Shin Kōmeitō, dropped from nine seats to four.

Political Parties and Democracy in Japan

An active legislature, an independent judiciary and competitive political parties are the institutions mainly responsibly for the operation and protection of democratic governance. Of these, political parties are the engines of democracy. Without them, it is difficult to imagine popular government working beyond the local, town hall level. As with many other things, the party system in Japan differs from most other democracies. So far, there has been only one party capable of gaining a majority in the Diet—the LDP. One scholar observed in 1969 that "the present Liberal Democratic Party seems fairly certain to rule for some time to come."[54] Despite its recent setbacks, there is little reason to doubt the continued validity of this statement. The assessment remains valid more than two decades later. Second, opposition parties have only been able to gather up the bits and pieces of voting groups not attracted to the LDP.[55] Lacking the will to strive to majority power status, they rely on "radicalized posturing," rather than purposeful efforts to win voters away from the LDP.[56] They have also suffered from inadequate leadership. "For the leaders of the opposition parties, their priority was not to challenge the LDP but to ensure the survival of their organizations and their place within them."[57] The claim that opposition parties have been dismal failures may be overstated. They have shared governing power through coalitions and thereby influenced policy. During the 1970s and 1980s they pushed the LDP to the edge of fragmentation.[58] That the LDP survived the challenge may be due in no small measure to the fact that the opposition frequently chose to compete with itself rather than with the LDP.[59] Third, there is little emotional bond between voters and parties. This is indicated by weak party identification among voters and limited opportunity for voter participation in party activities. All this results in a party system that is not a decisive factor in the political process. Finally, citizens' movements, which formerly had been a source of politicization, are increasingly de-linked from partisan politics. Although these citizens' movements continue to exist, they deal with consumer and environmental or other types of issues that have not been captured by political parties.[60]

6

Political Corruption and
Political Reform

Political bribery has been a fixture of Japan's politics since the beginning of recorded history. Referring to the period before World War II, Richard Mitchell notes: "The evidence, then, is overwhelming: political bribery was a common affair."[1] Since then, the advent of democracy has not improved the situation. The tendency of politicians, irrespective of party, to become involved in financial scandals seems to be one of the more enduring characteristics of postwar Japanese politics. "Since the rebirth of democracy after the war, money's corrupting influence has been a recurring plague."[2] It may even be said to have become a legitimate aspect of the political process.[3] In 1948, the Shōwa Denkō scandal resulted in the demise of the Cabinet. Government officials had taken bribes from the company in return for which they made sure the company received low-interest loans. In 1954, more officials were caught accepting bribes, this time from shipbuilding companies in return for government business. But none of these was of the magnitude of the Lockheed scandal, which burst upon the scene in the 1970s. The Lockheed affair was followed in the 1980s by the Recruit scandal in which politicians received bribes in the form of company stock. This controversy was not yet over when an even bigger storm broke, involving the Sagawa Kyūbin Company's channeling of large sums of money into the hands of important politicians.

The magnitude and persistence of money scandals in Japanese politics raises several questions. First, what factors account for the tendency toward financial irregularities especially involving the Liberal Democratic Party (LDP)? Second, why has the public displayed such a high level of tolerance for political misbehavior? Third, what is the relationship between political scandal and political reform?

The Politics of Corruption

The Japanese people have been more than indulgent in allowing political corruption and have coined a saying describing the phenomenon: *tokage no shippo kiri* (cutting the tail of the lizard). Nature has increased the lizard's chances of avoiding capture by its enemies by equipping it with a detachable tail. When a predator seizes a fleeing lizard by the tail, it breaks off and the lizard escapes. But this loss is not permanent because the lizard can regenerate this portion of its anatomy. This metaphor alludes to the capacity of Japanese political groups to lose leadership as a result of scandals and then, like the lizard, regenerate themselves without suffering permanent damage.[4]

Japan's political lizards have lost their "tails" several times in the postwar period. Politicians caught engaging in improper behavior can usually redeem themselves by performing an obligatory ritual of apology and contrition. Some have stepped down from their leadership positions and assumed roles of comparative obscurity (although not necessarily lacking power). Formal responsibilities of those who have fallen from grace are assumed by other party members, politics goes on as if nothing has happened, and, for the most part, nothing much has. Rarely has scandal cost a politician elective office. Some endure neither disgrace nor permanent exclusion from important jobs. For them comes rapid rehabilitation and higher political office. Kiichi Miyazawa, for example, was implicated in the Recruit scandal and resigned as minister of finance, but soon thereafter became prime minister. Although the immediate effectiveness of government may be diminished during these episodes, neither the formal structure of the political process nor the electoral fortunes of political parties were permanently or significantly altered. "In the Japanese system, the person nominally in charge at the outbreak of a scandal is expected to assume ritual responsibility. That involves bowing deeply, looking contrite, and making heartfelt public apologies. Provided that the minister, executive, or senior bureaucrat in question performs his part with a suitable show of sincerity, his 'apology' is accepted and the scandal ends there."[5]

It is, perhaps, surprising given the magnitude and frequency of political scandals that little political change has occurred. Scandals have weakened but have not interrupted, much less ended, the LDP's domination of politics. The failure of the LDP to retain its parliamentary majority in the 1993 election can be attributed, in part, to voter dissatisfaction over official corruption. A more important factor was the paralysis of the government, which was incapable of acting on a range of issues, including, especially, economic stagnation. But it is unlikely that the issue of corruption alone will inaugurate a voter-initiated process of political change of such magnitude as to end the importance, even preeminence of the LDP.

Despite much talk on the subject, political parties, even those among the opposition, have displayed little real enthusiasm for reforms that would effectively constrain the tendency toward political corruption.[6] Laws have been enacted over the years purporting to clean up political practices but they have been full of loopholes and ineffectively administered. The efforts of Prime

Minister Toshiki Kaifu to change the rules governing political activities earned him early retirement. But things began to change in 1993, when the government of Kiichi Miyazawa lost a vote of confidence after it failed to fulfill its promise to enact political reform. In the election that followed, the LDP lost its majority, but the big loser was the largest opposition party—the Social Democratic Party of Japan (SDPJ).

The Lockheed Scandal

Kakuei Tanaka assembled the largest faction within the LDP and had few peers as a political manipulator. On August 16, 1976, Tanaka was charged with accepting a bribe from the Lockheed Corporation to buy their airplanes. The case ground on for years. Finally a guilty verdict was returned on October 12, 1983, and Tanaka was sentenced to four years in prison and a fine equal to the amount of the bribe he had accepted from Lockheed. Despite the conviction, Tanaka did not resign his parliamentary seat, but he did leave the LDP, continuing to serve as an independent. His stock with the voters was undiminished as he took very good care of his own constituency. Voters in his prefecture—Niigata—were the beneficiaries of more government largess than any other prefecture. For every yen in taxes sent to Tokyo, they received three in return. Included among the public works obtained by Tanaka was an extension of the *shinkansen* (bullet train), built at a cost of $6.3 billion but that served relatively few passengers.

In 1992, the Tanaka case was still before the Supreme Court. The matter had been referred to the Grand Bench from the Petty Bench over the issue of depositions taken in the United States and used in the original trial. The court had to decide the admissibility of such evidence.

In 1985, ill health began to erode Tanaka's influence although he continued to be an important figure behind the scenes.[7] He was eventually forced to relinquish formal control of his faction to others who would themselves soon become embroiled in scandal. He died in December 1993.

The Recruit Scandal

Tanaka's successor as faction leader, Noboru Takeshita, assumed the prime ministership but he was not in office long when another scandal struck, this time involving insider stock deals. Many top LDP officials were affected, including the ministers of finance and justice. As the scandal broadened, it claimed as its victims the top leadership of the party. Shintaro Abe and Kiichi Miyazawa were forced from their leadership positions and Prime Minister Takeshita resigned on April 25, 1989, offering to assume personal responsibility for the scandal.[8] But perhaps the greatest damage was suffered by the bureaucracy which, until this point, enjoyed an unsullied reputation. That elected politicians are basically corrupt is a view widely accepted by the public, but the honesty of the bureaucracy had been taken almost as an article of faith. This faith was shattered when it was revealed that top officials in the Ministries of Education and Labor had taken bribes from the Recruit Company.[9]

Takeshita's successor as prime minister, Sousuke Uno, was soon embroiled in a scandal of another sort, this time over having paid a Tokyo geisha for sexual favors. The story was first reported by a weekly magazine and probably would not have received widespread attention had it not been the subject of a *Washington Post* story.[10] The net result of all the bad publicity was a disaster at the polls. In the July 1989 elections to the upper house, the LDP lost control for the first time in thirty-five years. Uno accepted blame for the debacle and resigned. His successor, Toshiki Kaifu, within a matter of days, was confronted by the revelation that his chief cabinet secretary had a long affair with a bar hostess. Kaifu filled the position of cabinet secretary with Mrs. Mayumi Moriyama, obviously hoping to blunt the growing alienation toward his party of Japanese women. The sex scandal was also exploited by the female head of the Japan Socialist Party (JSP), Takako Doi.

The troubles led the LDP to place in its platform an apology for the Recruit scandal and a pledge to reexamine the unpopular consumption or sales tax.[11] As the elections approached, the Socialists campaigned vigorously against the LDP corruption, rather than on socialist doctrine, as was their custom. The strategy was especially effective among women, who voted in larger numbers than men and elected twelve of thirteen JSP female candidates to municipal assembly seats.[12] The bloc vote from women carried over into the House of Councillors election, where the strategy of having female candidates paid off.[13]

The LDP was not the only party touched by scandal. The chairman of the DSP resigned because he had received 5,000 shares of stock in the Recruit Company.[14] The Clean Government Party (Kōmeitō) also fell under a cloud when a safe full of money was discovered at a waste dump. It was suspected that the money, perhaps raised by questionable means by the party's parent organization Value Creation Society (Sōka Gakkai), was intended to support political causes.[15] Takako Doi became entangled in the growing web of controversy when it was reported she had accepted campaign money from the pachinko industry. Doi and other JSP members were accused in a press report of accepting donations from the pachinko industry in return for help in blocking legislation that would have made it easier to monitor the finances of pachinko parlors.[16] More than half of these popular Japanese gaming facilities are owned by Koreans. Although the contributions to the JSP were not illegal and certainly not unusual, the affair exacerbated the common popular view that Koreans are involved in unsavory activities.[17]

In the July 1989 House of Councillors election, LDP candidates won only thirty-six seats, compared to forty-six for the JSP. The LDP's poor showing was the product of voter antagonism brought on by three factors: political scandal; the widely unpopular 3 percent sales tax; and the opening of Japanese markets to agricultural products from abroad which produced a hostile reaction among farmers, one of the most loyal LDP constituencies.

The trials and tribulations of the LDP and its leadership had relatively little effect on the operation of the political process, and the outpouring of public concern was brief. The frequent changes in the prime ministership and leadership problems in general did not send tremors of uncertainty through the economy. It was more or less business as usual in the financial and stock markets, which displayed little anxiety over the unstable political situation. This apparent calmness suggests both public tolerance of scandal and a substantial institutional insularity that effectively resists the effects of turmoil at the top of the political system.[18] This disconnect between economic practice and the political process accounts in part for the collapse of the bubble economy in the 1990s.

As it turned out, the LDP need not have been overly concerned about a prolonged voter rebellion. In the February 1990 elections to the lower house, the LDP retained its majority. Although it did fall from the high of 300 seats captured in the 1986 election to 275, this was a comfortable margin. Prime Minister Kaifu was rewarded with eighteen months more in office. But his job was not to be an easy one. Within the LDP, Kaifu provoked substantial discontent when he excluded the Abe and the Michio Watanabe factions from participation in the Cabinet on the grounds that they were tainted by scandal.[19]

Among top party leaders, some of whom—like Nakasone—had been fearful of losing their parliamentary seats, there was not a single casualty. Abe, Miyazawa, and the others all survived to continue the contest for influence within the party. In fact, only one of the fourteen members of the Diet implicated in the Recruit scandal failed to win re-election. One victor had even been under indictment on bribery charges.[20] Secure in the victory of his party, Prime Minister Kaifu saw no further need for the largely symbolic gestures that had been made to win voter support. Among these was the appointment of two women to the cabinet. Both were replaced by men.[21]

In 1991, the Kaifu government responded to the calls for political reform by introducing three bills including one that would have changed the electoral system. The bills were rejected as was the cabinet of Prime Minister Kaifu. It is clear that the political establishment thought that the issue would blow over, and they might have been right had it not been for a succession of even bigger scandals to explode on the political scene.[22]

The Sagawa Kyūbin Scandal

The Sagawa Kyūbin Co., a Tokyo parcel delivery firm, had made substantial contributions to the political coffers of the Takeshita faction leader Shin Kanemaru. This faction had been assembled by Noburo Takeshita from a majority of the old Kakuei Tanaka faction. Kanemaru took over the faction, the largest in the LDP, after Takeshita became implicated in the Recruit scandal. Hiroyasu Watanabe, president of Sagawa Kyubin, provided 500 million yen to Kanemaru who supposedly distributed it to sixty of his faction followers. This transaction was illegal, and when prosecutors made a case against him, Kanemaru agreed to pay a fine of 200,000 yen. He resigned as LDP vice president on August 27, 1992. Efforts by prosecutors to trace the money to its recipients was frustrated by the lack of records.

Kanemaru's attempted return to his duties as faction leader failed due to negative public reaction to the small size of the fine and general discontent with the "business as usual" attitude of politicians. Growing opposition to the status quo came to include some elements of the LDP itself. As a consequence, on October 14, Kanemaru resigned from the parliament and as faction leader. That in turn brought about a leadership crisis within the faction. After days of wrangling, Keizo Obuchi, a former LDP secretary general, was nominated as leader. He was supported by, among others, Transport Minister Ryutaro Hashimoto. In opposition to Obuchi's candidacy was Ichiro Ozawa, protégé of Kanemaru and acting faction chairman who was himself unpopular with many because of his tendency to be abrasive in his interpersonal relations. His group, consisting of thirty-six members in the lower house, nominated Finance Minister Tsutomu Hata. In the end Obuchi prevailed and his warm reception from other faction leaders seemed to certify the arrangement. But Ozawa and his group were not willing to go along and they ultimately split, forming their own faction, which other "reform-minded" members of the party were invited to join. This group, which joined the opposition and voted for the no confidence motion in 1993, formed a new party called the Japan Renewal Party (Shinseitō).

Kanemaru was not charged with bribery because of the very narrow limits placed on such crimes under the law. As interpreted by the government, Kanemaru was acting as a party official when he accepted the money, not as a member of the Diet. Official duties are limited to action on the floor of the Diet or when acting as a cabinet minister.[23]

Meanwhile the situation took on an added dimension when it was alleged that Noburo Takeshita had links to organized crime. Takeshita, who was being frustrated in his efforts to assume the post of prime minister by public ridicule from a right-wing political group, had reportedly called upon organized crime figures to help rid him of the embarrassing attacks. On October 24, 1992, Takeshita agreed to appear before the Diet to explain these charges but he succeeded only in provoking more controversy. Despite demands that he resign from the parliament, he steadfastly refused to do so.

All this proved only preliminary to the major bombshell dropped on March 13, 1993. Several million dollars in bank debentures, cash, and gold ingots were discovered at Kanemaru's office. He was charged with evading taxes for 1987 and arrested, ironically on the day before the statute of limitations ran out. His former aide Masahisa Haibara was also arrested for tax evasion.[24]

The Institutionalization of Corruption

More recently, a Diet member of the Social Democratic Party of Japan was charged in 2003 with skimming from the salaries of her secretaries. A former labor minister was sentenced on May 20, 2003, for taking 72.8 million yen in bribes.[25] In November 2007, it was revealed in testimony in the House of Councillors that senior members of the LDP and some high-ranking officials in the Defense Ministry had been "wined and dined" and treated to hundreds of rounds of golf by a top executive of the defense equipment trader Yamada Corp.[26] These cases have one thing in common: Neither the political system as a whole (in particular the electoral system) nor the internal mechanisms of political parties are equipped to address them as important issues of public concern and to take remedial action. The activities exemplified in each case were far from unusual. In fact, financial greasing of the political wheels has been standard practice for years as political leaders have accepted large sums of money to keep their faction operations going. Despite the commonplace character of such money transfers, the fact remains that much of it violates the law. Under the Political Fund Control Law and the Public Affairs Election Law, the flow of money in politics is supposed to be regulated. In fact, these laws have been routinely ignored. For example, the law limits contributions from a single source to 1.5 million yen. Yet Kanemaru had no compunction about accepting 500 million yen. Moreover, contributions over 1 million yen are supposed to be reported to the Home Affairs Ministry. Such reports are generally not made and the ministry lacks authority to investigate. There is no limit on the amount of money a politician can spend.[27] Finally, the Council on Political Ethics set up in the Diet to handle irregularities never held a session although it was created in 1985.

The laws passed to regulate political practices have been vague in content with weak enforcement provisions so political parties, especially the LDP, have had little reason to strengthen them. The problem of political malpractice, within the established political environment, has not been viewed as a legal one but rather one of impropriety or excess. Scandals have erupted and generated public controversy only when the character or magnitude of the activity appeared to exceed certain limits. There are several reasons for this institutionalization of corruption.

Party Philosophy

Part of the explanation for the pattern of financial scandal can be found in the LDP's style of governing. The LDP is not a party that defines itself in terms of ideology or policy positions but employs, instead, a "management" approach to government. It has been highly successful in retaining political power and has used it skillfully not only to advance the interests of the party but to promote the general welfare of the country and keep the electorate satisfied. Procedures by which the party can facilitate the resolution of differences over basic philosophies or individual policy matters are truncated because such issues lack clear public definition and do not normally receive formal expression. Moreover, the LDP has rarely been challenged to confront crises in the political system or deep divisions among the population. The LDP enjoyed an environment largely devoid of the kinds of controversies that could significantly affect voting behavior. This is not to say that Japan is a nation where everyone thinks alike. There are indeed important differences of opinion among the electorate but because of a political culture that discourages emphasizing differences and a unresponsive political system, such differences rarely become politically significant. Consequently, the LDP has been voted "into" power because of its constituency-based connections and its skills in managing the country's affairs. It has not been voted "out" of power by corruption because the issue has been insufficiently salient for most voters. That is, voters have not been dissatisfied with the performance of the LDP to the point that they would be willing to confront the uncertainties of rule by the opposition. The negative quality of public opinion is fairly shallow and is borne not of dissatisfaction with corruption as such, but with its magnitude and the lack of contrition by those caught practicing it.

Public Opinion

It is true that voters are tolerant of, if not entirely indifferent to, the peccadilloes of their politicians, but they are afforded little opportunity to express their discontent in a manner that would affect the political process. One important avenue by which public opinion manifests itself is the press. The Japanese press does not aggressively confront politically controversial issues or the behavior of government officials. The press rarely engages in investigative journalism and is generally reluctant to report in detail on matters potentially embarrassing to political figures. With what many regard as excessive zeal, the American press (and, to a lesser extent, that in Europe) diligently and almost tirelessly seeks flaws in the character, background, or performance of politicians. Such is not the practice in Japan. Japanese are not as vocal as are Europeans or Americans in expressing their views about government. In general, public debate and dialogue, at least as manifested in the press, is muted. Moreover, "taking the pulse" of public opinion, especially through polls, is much less a fixture of the political environment than it is in the West where the public's views on every conceivable subject are assiduously measured. Although they are not politically docile, the Japanese tend to be deferential to authority.

Ineffective Opposition

One of the main reasons the LDP has been allowed "to get away" with scandalous behavior on a fairly regular basis is that opposition political parties have not represented a real electoral alternative. The second largest party—the Socialists (Social Democratic Party of Japan [SDPJ])—has not been in a position to win a majority in the House of Representatives because they have not fielded enough candidates to give them control of the lower house should all of them win. Even a coalition among all opposition parties, something difficult to imagine in itself, would have been short of a majority. Only the departure of the Hata group from the LDP and the emergence of the Japan New Party, both centrist parties, made a coalition government possible in 1993.

The fundamental weakness of the opposition was evident in the 1990 and 1993 elections. Public sentiment, as measured by the 1989 vote, which installed a coalition of opposition parties in control of the upper house, appeared to put the LDP's control of the lower house in jeopardy. There was clear evidence of negative public opinion of the LDP over its Recruit involvement and sex scandals. But as it turned out, the following year voters found the opposition even less appealing than the LDP. So the LDP retained control of the House of Representatives by a substantial margin, winning 275 seats. In 1993, the LDP lost control of the lower house, but not by much, at a time when circumstances more favorable to the opposition would be hard to imagine. The LDP won 223 seats, with 36.6 percent of the popular vote.

The attractiveness of opposition parties is diminished by the fact that they have not escaped the taint of political scandal themselves. The DSP, SDPJ, and Kōmeitō have all been implicated in financial and other kinds of scandals in one way or another. Even the communists have had their problems. The co-founder of the Japan Communist Party (JCP) was accused of having betrayed one of his comrades to Joseph Stalin in 1939. The man was executed by the Soviet government.[28]

Money and Politics

The frequency of money scandals in Japan is due in large part to the way in which political parties, especially the LDP, are organized and operate. It is necessary for large amounts of money to be raised by parties and factions within parties in order to keep their people in office. For the LDP, failure to finance LDP politicians at the local level is less likely to bring victory to another party than to another faction of the LDP, because they compete with one another as much as or more than they do with the other parties. It has become increasingly difficult, however, for a single faction leader to raise enough money to satisfy the needs of all his faction's members. Thus several senior faction leaders may share responsibility for raising money.[29]

The LDP has neither a cohesive organization nor a mass membership. It is a coalition of factions of varying sizes, usually five, and voter identification with it is weak. Factionalization of the party was a product of the multiple-member district system by which members of the House of Representatives were chosen. In this system, candidates of the larger parties tended to compete against one another. Because they could have several candidates in each district, there is always the potential that they would divide the vote allowing a candidate from an opposition party to win. One way to minimize the problem was to limit the number of candidates, a common practice of the SDPJ.[30] The problem of candidates drawing votes from one another was mitigated by the fact that voters have stronger loyalties to individual candidates than to their parties.[31] Nonetheless, interfactional competition within the LDP was very important and may be the most significant in the entire party system.[32] For instance, the issue of choosing a successor to Shin Kanemaru and the future of the Takeshita faction attracted considerably more attention than did matters affecting other parties. The importance of factions has not disappeared with the new electoral system. If anything, there is even more competition among factions than there was under the old system.

Attaining a factional leadership position requires influential political and economic connections and the ability to raise money for the political needs of the faction members.[33] Membership in a faction is necessary not only for support in getting elected but as a channel for political advancement. For the LDP, interfactional bargaining is the process by which ministerial positions have been allocated. Top government and party posts are usually shared among major factions in proportion to their strength. Factions help fill the psychological need of party members for participation in a group.[34] But this identity does not equate with specific ideological or policy positions and members of different factions freely interact.[35] The interrelationships of faction members is an important source of opposition and competition within the political elite, which assumes even greater significance given the general weakness of interparty competition.[36]

Interfactional competition does not produce shifting patterns of membership allegiance. Changing factions results in loss of seniority, which is determined by the number of times an individual has been elected to the Diet as a member of a given faction.[37] Factional realignment does occur from time to time, especially after the founder of the faction has passed from the scene. On such occasions, there can be vigorous struggles for succession. The losers in such power struggles may decide that their fortunes would have greater promise if they combined with another faction. In the larger factions, a minority group might split off and join with a smaller faction to form a new and more influential faction. Such a split occurred when the Hata-Ozawa group in the Takeshita faction left to form its own faction consisting of thirty-five members of the House of Representatives and ten members of the House of Councillors.

There is little electoral competition within individual factions since they do not often support more than one candidate in the same district.[38] The weapons in the battle for political influence are raising funds, establishing connections in the economic world, placing people in the bureaucracy, and controlling the party leadership structure.

Other aspects of the faction system include its tendency to be highly responsive to outside pressures, which inhibits the capacity of the LDP and, by extension, the policy process to develop independence or to articulate the "national interest."[39] In the public's view, factions serve the personal ambitions of politicians and promote influence peddling. The power wielded by faction leaders has less to do with their political leadership skills or expertise in areas of public policy than with their connections and ability to raise money.[40]

The money needed by LDP factions comes primarily from business; the socialists are supported by labor unions. Kōmeitō received financial support through its connection to Sōka Gakkai. In the case of the LDP, donations are not intended to buy "special favors" but to keep in office the people who are sympathetic to the interests of business and who will promote a pro-business environment. There is a confluence of interest among the LDP, the bureaucracy, and the business community that is a powerful alliance, particularly in the absence of public opposition or challenges from other political constituencies.

Money raised by factions is normally not intended for personal use but to campaign and win the support of the electorate.[41] It takes a great deal of money to "service" constituents in Japan. Japanese are fond of gift-giving, and politics is not exempt. Diet members shower constituents with gifts on the occasion of births, deaths, weddings, and holidays, a relationship that voters have come to expect. "The notion of grass-roots politics is now almost unknown in Japan. It is the politicians who water the grass roots. With cash."[42] One avenue through which substantial sums of money are injected into people's pockets is public construction. The money is funneled through large construction companies that do little actual work themselves. They distribute the money to local construction firms but these firms do not do the actual work themselves either. They contract with a third level of firms that hire the workers and do the job. A siphoning of funds occurs at each level. Many of these firms have strong contacts with the LDP or government ministries.[43]

The closed construction bidding system even jeopardized relations with the United States. In the 1980s, the U.S. government requested that American firms be allowed to bid on constructions projects. Although the Japanese appeared to cooperate, in the event only Japanese firms were allowed full access to bid. Under the procurement system, only a few firms are permitted to submit bids on public works projects. "In this way, the procurement system limits potential conspirators on a project to a small number of designated bidders."[44] This illustrates the power of a triumvirate involving construction companies, public works bureaucrats, and politicians, especially from the LDP.[45]

It is unlikely that there will be a voter rebellion against a system in which the ultimate beneficiary is the local constituent. This situation is hardly unique to Japan. In the United States, voters have firm expectations that their own government benefits will continue and even increase while, at the same time, they demand lower taxes and criticize the government for fiscal irresponsibility. Japanese voters may, in the abstract, favor higher ethical standards for their politicians, but they seem to be unwilling to attain these standards at their own expense.[46]

It is in this connection that the Kanemaru affair differs significantly from other scandals involving the transfer of large sums of money to political operations. Apparently, a substantial part of the money raised by Kanemaru failed to find its way to the usual political channels. Much of it, apparently, was used to pay off mahjong debts and was left lying around the house in the form of cash and gold bars. Even for the jaded Japanese public accustomed to political shenanigans, this was too much.

Reform Proposals

A product of the Sagawa Kyūbin and other scandals was growing pressure from the public and from within the LDP itself in favor of reform. In 1992, a package of eighteen reform proposals was put forward designed to tighten controls over party finance and to impose meaningful penalties for violations. The opposition demanded that Kanemaru and Takeshita appear before the Diet to give sworn testimony concerning their activities. Due to eye surgery, Kanemaru was excused for a time, and his criminal indictment dramatically altered the situation. The LDP countered with the demand, later dropped, that several opposition politicians also appear before the Diet to explain their connection with scandals.

It was widely believed, however, that the problems of money and scandals would not be finally resolved until the electoral system itself was changed. This produced a variety of proposals to replace the multimember-district system with something else. The suggestions reflected the electoral potential of the different parties. The LDP embraced the single-member-district system, an alternative that was endorsed by 85 percent of the members of the party. The SDPJ and Kōmeitō favored a combination system with some seats selected from single-member districts and others chosen by proportional representation. The communists argued that the existing system should be made to work properly by enacting reapportionment to eliminate disparity between rural and urban constituencies.[47]

LDP confidence in the single-member-district system is predicated on the fact that the party is stronger in more districts than are the opposition parties. The opposition parties agree with this assessment and in fact project that the LDP would win as many as 90 percent of the seats under such a system. By contrast, the "first past the post" system might stimulate the development of an alternative party to the LDP, either through coalescence among the opposition groups or a split within the LDP along moderate/conservative lines, thus forming two entirely new parties.

The opposition parties, not unexpectedly, favor proportional representation, which would allow most of them to capture at least a few seats. Actually, this alternative is not unattractive to many members of the LDP since it could mean a permanent minority status for opposition parties and continuing LDP parliamentary dominance. Opponents of proportional representation find fault in such an arrangement and consider it inappropriate for Japan. In the view of most members of the LDP, proportional representation and multiparty systems tend to fragment power and weaken governing ability, making it the least likely alternative for ending political paralysis.

Advocates of proportional representation argue that it promotes equality of representation, which they regard as important even if it means a government that is diminished in its capacity to act decisively. Minority interests are better represented in the current system than they would be under single-member districts and its likely constituent, a two-party arrangement. Multiparty, proportional representation systems enhance the political influence of minority groups only in the absence of a dominant party, however. Advocates of proportional representation believe that such a system would give them the best chance of ending the LDP's reign. The expectations of most of them go no further than coalition government. In multiparty systems, small parties gain strength when they can broker their support in the formation of a coalition government.

In early 1992 an LDP panel proposed a system based on the model currently employed in Germany. It called for the number of seats in the lower house to be reduced from 512 to 471. Of these, 300 would be elected from single-member districts and 171 by proportional representation. Despite the latter provision, the opposition parties were not enthusiastic. The idea was attractive to the LDP for, among other things, a house with fewer members would mean a smaller number of people running for office. Assuming that the funds available for campaigning and other purposes did not decline, each politician could anticipate a larger share of the money.[48]

In the extraordinary session of the parliament that opened in early 1993, the LDP again proposed electoral reform. Four bills were introduced calling for changes in the election law and for replacement of the multimember-district system. The first bill proposed a single-member-district system. The second called for the establishment of a parliamentary panel to redraw electoral districts. The third was a revision of the Political Fund Control Law. It would have imposed a ban on the delivery and receipt of political funds among individual lawmakers; limited politicians to two fund-raising organizations (under existing law they could have any number); limited contributions from single organizations, such as companies or unions to fund-raising bodies to 240,000 yen per year; required reporting of corporate donations in amounts of 120,000 yen per year (currently 1 million yen); and required all donations of 10,000 yen (currently 1 million yen) be made public. The LDP's logic behind these proposals was to make political funds transfers more "transparent" and thus subject to the constraints of public opinion. The bill would have raised the maximum amount organizations could contribute to political parties to 200 million yen from 100 million yen. It would have raised the amount of single corporate donations that must be made public from 10,000 yen per year to 100,000 yen per year. The fourth bill would have provided public subsidies to parties running campaigns. These subsidies were to be drawn from a pool made up of money based on 250 yen per person. To receive money, parties would need five members in the Diet or 3 percent of the vote in the most recent election.[49]

The SDPJ and Kōmeitō introduced their own bill calling for a combination system with 200 single-member-district seats and 300 chosen by proportional representation. They also advocated a total ban on private financial transfers to politicians and parties.

With the fall of the LDP government, none of these proposals was enacted. The coalition government headed by Morihiro Hosokawa of the Japan New Party inherited the problem and committed itself to enacting reforms. The government approved a reform package on September 17, which included the following: a ban on donations to individual politicians; business and groups limited to making donations to political parties; disclosure required for donations exceeding 50,000 yen per year; public subsidy of political parties based on a pool of 335 yen per citizen; tax breaks for individual donations to political parties; strengthening anticorruption laws by making penalties 2.5 times greater; suspending candidacy rights if a relative is convicted of violating election laws; suspending for a period of time the rights to vote or run for those convicted of electoral law violation. The government proposed changing the electoral system to 250 single-member seats and 250 proportional-representation seats. Voters would cast two ballots: one for a candidate in a district and one for a party in the proportional-representation scheme.[50]

The legislation passed the lower house on November 18 by a vote of 270 to 226. On January 21 the bill was defeated in the upper house when seventeen members of the SDPJ broke ranks and voted against the measure. The driving force behind the reform effort had come as a result of party realignment. First a group of younger members of the Diet left the LDP and formed the Harbinger Party (Sakigake). Another force behind the reform effort was the Shinseitō, led by Ichiro Ozawa and Tsutomu Hata. Both of these groups split from the LDP in 1993. A compromise was finally reached, and legislation passed on January 29 creating a 500-member lower house: 300 single-member-district seats and 200 proportional-representation seats elected from eleven blocs.

Voters have two ballots: the first for a candidate and the second for a party. A candidate can run in both types of elections, but those winning in single-member contests have their names withdrawn from the proportional list. Dual contest winners for the proportional seats are chosen by the "close loser" method. The winner is the candidate who comes closest to the vote of the winner in the single-member-district contest.[51] The new system took effect on January 1, 1995.

How successful were these reforms? Reducing the frequency of scandal by controlling the flow of money into elections was effective to some degree. The outright buying of votes declined, but the election of 1996 actually cost more. This was because the new electoral system involved higher campaign costs. As yet the effort to bring about a party-centered electoral system has not been successful, and, if anything, there is even more emphasis on the *kōenkai* form of organization because in single-member districts, candidates have to rely less on the party. Nor has the electoral process developed a sharper policy focus. Most disappointing, perhaps, is failure to develop a viable opposition party structure.[52] And the scandals continue. In 1998, Ministry of Defense officials were convicted for collusion in an overpricing case. In the same year, the number two prosecutor in the Ministry of Justice resigned after being convicted of using taxpayer money to keep a mistress.[53]

Conclusion

It seems that financial irregularities in politics are less abuses of public trust than they are the consequence of the structure and style of Japanese politics. That these irregularities frequently get out of hand and lead to scandals is attributable, in large measure, to the weakness of the link between the government and the voter. The public cannot hold the government accountable through the electoral mechanism, nor can it provide the government with a mandate. Moreover, political irregularities as an issue have lacked sufficient saliency to provoke the electorate to make decisive changes. The 1989 upper house election may be interpreted as a "referendum" in which the voters displayed their displeasure with the LDP's performance. But the voters stopped short of turning the LDP out in the lower house election that followed. In the 1993 election, the opposition gave the voters little more than a whiggish, anti-LDP alternative, and the LDP won 227 seats. Under the old system of multimember districts, the LDP often received less than a majority of the popular vote. The "multiplier effect" of the multimember-district system and the fragmentation of the opposition has allowed the LDP to retain its dominance of the parliament. Insulated from voter sanction, the LDP not only ruled for four decades but was allowed the luxury of corruption.

Voter hostility toward LDP excesses had less to do with concern over corruption as such than with politician's blatant disregard for the "rules of the game." Traditional values, symbolized, for example, in the code of the warrior or *bushido*, impose standards for the maintenance of honor and demand retribution for violations of these standards. Voters do not expect ritual disemboweling of wayward politicians, although a few such gestures might be more effective in restoring public confidence in government than reform legislation. Politicians have displayed rather cavalier disregard for their responsibility for their own and their followers' actions. From Tanaka to Kanemaru, politicians have become less sincere in their expressions of repentance; after ritual apologies, it has been business as usual.

Political scandals plus mounting domestic and international problems focused public attention on the need for reform to an extent greater than at any time since the war. However, enacting legislation that nominally reforms the political process is one thing; rigorous enforcement is another. The long-standing practice of collusion between politicians and the bureaucracy together with the timidity of the judiciary suggest that "clean government" will not come about in a sudden rush of reform effort.

If the link between political scandal and political reform is weak, then what accounts for the fracturing of the LDP and calls for restructuring the electoral system? The answer to this question may be found in the growing political paralysis that afflicts Japan. The capacity of the multimember-district system and the party structure that it spawned to provide effective governance diminished. The proposal for a single-member-district system for the lower house had few serious advocates. The opposition parties feared, justifiably, that such a system would reduce their influence or put most of them out of business altogether. The combination arrangement finally reached has something for everyone. One thing is clear: if the faction system does not disappear, it will undergo significant change. But however the reforms work, they will not eliminate the need for money. Somehow voters have to be weaned from the services that they have come to expect from politicians. New styles of leadership and organization have to be invented. Under the new hybrid system, the LDP remains the dominant party supported by a minority of voters. Creating a system that will both respond to public sentiment and govern effectively requires a fundamental change in attitude on the part of the voters and the governing elite.

7

Political Participation

When the presidents and prime ministers of the world's leading democracies meet in one of their periodic summits, the Japanese prime minister is always among their number, although he typically stands unobtrusively at the end of the line in the group photograph. Japan is indeed a democracy; its citizens enjoy substantial personal freedoms and the civil liberties associated with an open society. But this state of affairs is not the consequence of a vigorous democratic politics. The people's will is only indirectly made evident in the governance of the country. As has been previously noted, Japan has all of the structural elements of a democracy. The way that this system operates, however, differs in many fundamental ways from that in democracies found elsewhere in the world. It is usual, for example, for the public to be directly involved in the competition for political power. One way in which this is achieved is where two or more political parties, each having a real chance of capturing power, compete in an electoral process. Another mechanism, found for example in the United States, involves special interests organized into pressure groups that compete with one another for favors from the government.

These forms of competition are not characteristic of the Japanese system. For one thing, the party system has not been competitive. The Liberal Democrats have in one form or another dominated the political process since World War II. Even when the Liberal Democratic Party (LDP) lost control of the government in 1993, it did not result from an effective challenge by other parties but, rather, from the collapse of the internal integrity of the LDP. From the end of the war until 1955, the combined strength of two conservative parties, the Liberal Party and the Democratic Party, constituted a parliamentary majority. These parties controlled the Cabinet, and thus the government and the policy agenda, except for one brief period when the Socialists managed to put together a coalition government. The Liberal and Democratic parties merged in 1955 to form the LDP, which dominated national politics until the 1993 election. At that time, several new parties came into existence and new party coalitions began to take shape. The ambiguity of parties as mechanisms defining ideological and policy options for the electorate is revealed by the formation of a coalition between the LDP and its traditional rival—the Japan Socialist Party (JSP)—after the post-1993 coalition fell apart.

If Japanese democracy does not follow conventional models, how then does it work? Is it necessary to redefine democracy to fit the Japanese case?[1] The absence of competition among parties does not mean that there is no competition for political power or that the public is powerless to influence government. First, voters tend to make an impact within parties, rather than through competition among parties. Second, the lengthy dominance of the LDP is not to be equated with a one-party dictatorship. The LDP has not been free to impose its will arbitrarily on a subdued population. It could, in fact, have been turned out of office if the public had become sufficiently outraged by its actions. The existence of just such a possibility has acted as a very important check on the government and its policies.

The voters were finally ready to end the domination of the LDP in the late 1980s, when political scandals, unpopular policies, and inability to enact reform undermined the effectiveness of government. Although the Liberal Democrats lost control of the upper house in 1989, they retained their majority in lower house elections the following year, albeit by a smaller margin. In 1993, following a number of defections, the LDP lost control of the lower house to a coalition of opposition parties led by the Japan New Party (JNP, or Nihon Shintō). The ability of the Liberal Democrats to hang on to power has been due not only to their own political skills but to the persistent inability of opposition parties to mount an effective challenge.

Some observers contend that Japan is moving toward a competitive two-party system. Until then the LDP continues to dominate. So far the party system has consisted of one and a half parties.[2] The largest opposition party—the Japan Socialist Party (JSP)—was, according to this view, but half a party. Other parties played only minor roles. The dominance of the LDP and the weakness of the opposition are the result of several factors. The first is the LDP's successful record in managing Japan's affairs. The LDP has had the good fortune to preside over the long-running expansion of the economy, the benefits of which have been broadly shared by the public. It is generally true that prosperity favors the ruling party. The opposition cannot claim credit for this prosperity and has generally been unable to exploit any issue of sufficient importance to attract additional numbers of voters

A second reason the party system is noncompetitive is the nature of the opposition parties. Parties in opposition to the LDP, and especially the JSP, have been handicapped in their efforts to capture power by their adherence to increasingly anachronistic ideologies. Not only are such ideologies of diminishing popular appeal, but the doctrinaire nature of such parties contributes to their lack of internal unity. The membership is inclined to fragment over philosophical disputes, thus diminishing the capacity of the opposition parties to pull together toward a common objective. In general, opposition parties have not developed broadly appealing policy agendas, nor are their organizational skills sufficient to mobilize enough voters to capture a majority in the Diet. Opposition parties have done well on occasion in local elections, however.

Third, the LDP's parliamentary strength has been magnified because of features of the electoral system itself. The percentage of LDP seats in the Diet has been greater than its share of the popular vote. The Japan Communist Party (JCP), in contrast, receives a larger percentage of the popular vote than it has seats in the Diet. These characteristics of the electoral system are discussed below.

Other explanations for the LDP's continuing success include the contention that the enormous expense of Japanese elections favors the LDP, which has more money at its disposal than other parties because of its links with business. The LDP also has the advantage of incumbency; being in power allows for the distribution of favors, something the opposition cannot do.[3]

The Electoral System

Voters elect a wide variety of public officials at the local, prefect, and national levels. Mayors and assembly members in villages, towns, and cities are chosen by popular vote. Governors and members of the assembly are elected for each prefecture. For the upper house of the national Diet—the House of Councillors—100 members are chosen by all voters in a national constituency and 152 are picked from the forty-seven prefectures and Okinawa. The more important election, however, is for the lower house of the Diet, the House of Representatives.

Before the reforms of 1993, the electoral system for the House of Representatives consisted of 129 medium-size, multimember districts. In each of these districts, voters chose from three to five representatives. There were also four two-member districts and one six-member district created as a result of the Public Offices Election Law of 1986. Even though as many as six representatives could have been selected from a given district, voters could cast only a single vote. This meant that candidates from the same party in a given district competed against one another.

This system weakened interparty competition and favored intraparty factionalism.[4] Parties are not competitive in this kind of arrangement since they can divide up the seats based on their relative strength. Even small parties could gain a seat if their constituency was geographically concentrated and sufficiently loyal.

The number of candidates a party fields was usually determined by the number likely to be elected. Running too many candidates potentially divided the vote to such an extent that a party with a smaller percentage of the total vote could win more seats than a party with a larger percentage of the total vote.

Parties fielding more than one candidate had to be careful that their supporters did not concentrate on one popular candidate at the expense of others.[5]

An important factor working to the advantage of the LDP was the over-representation of rural areas. The disparity in 1985 between seats ranged from 550,000 voters per Diet member in the most underrepresented district to 111,000 voters per Diet member in the most overrepresented. The under-represented districts, mostly urban, are those in which smaller parties such as the JCP and the Clean Government Party (Kōmeitō) have had their support. Strict apportionment on the basis of population could have reduced the size of the LDP's parliamentary strength in the old system.

Overrepresentation of rural areas was even greater in the House of Councillors where the most overrepresented districts had six times the representatives of the most underrepresented districts. When the electoral system was created in 1947, the seats in the House of Councillors were apportioned among prefectures on the basis of population. Despite the fact that cities have grown and the rural population has declined, the distribution of upper house seats was never reapportioned.

In a ruling handed down in April 1976, the Supreme Court declared the system of lower house apportionment unconstitutional. Since the overrepresentation of rural constituencies clearly favored the LDP, the government controlled by it was in no hurry to correct the situation. In keeping with the letter, if not the spirit, of the law, a few seats were added in the lower house, bringing the total number up to 511 in 1976. The number stood at 512 a decade later, when the number of seats was increased in eight districts and decreased in seven. These seats provided some additional representation for urban areas, but the overall balance among parties in the Diet was not significantly affected by the changes.

The low level of interparty competition at the district level is one reason for the weakness of party loyalty among voters. Most parties tend to put up candidates only when their chances of success are good. In elections from local to prefect levels, a high percentage of seats go uncontested.[6] Prefect governors, elected as progressives, typically move toward the center in order to broaden their political appeal. Others become independents, thus obscuring their party leanings.[7] Such a situation is not conducive to spirited partisanship.

The LDP introduced a primary election system in an effort to broaden the popular support base for party leaders and to control factionalism. But this move failed to achieve its objectives. Factions exploit the attachment of the voters to the local support organization during primary elections. In ballot-ing by mail, many voters turn their ballots over to their Diet member, who fills them out.[8] Thus the kōenkai (support group) of Diet members follow the member's instructions concerning which leadership candidate to support. "The traditional factional struggle did not abate at all; instead, it intensified and expanded its scope to the mass membership at the grass roots level."[9]

The kōenkai and local party leaders spend money to recruit new members into the support group on behalf of the member of the parliament. This cannibalism for factional support at the local level sometimes results in breakdown of stable intraparty relations, complicating the process of selecting the party president, who is generally the prime minister-designate.[10]

Getting Elected

The constitutional requirements for elections to the two houses of the Diet differ. Members of the upper house stand for election at regular six-year intervals. Lower house elections can be held anytime but after no more than four years. Occasionally, elections to both houses are held simultaneously. Campaigning for seats in the Diet, a process that is subject to very strict formal regulations,[11] is limited to a few weeks before the elections as is characteristic of parliamentary systems in general and in contrast to the American system. Door-to-door campaigning, signature drives, polling, providing food or drink, mass meetings, parades, unscheduled speeches, multiple campaign vehicles, candidate-produced literature are either illegal or strictly regulated, although the rules are not rigorously observed or enforced. Blaring sound trucks are, however, permitted, although they are not supposed to "arouse enthusiasm . . . for the purpose of the election campaign."[12] Public employees are precluded by law from engaging in electoral politics but they manage to get around the law.[13] Parties can spend freely on campaigns but they are prohibited from mentioning the names of candidates; only party policies can be discussed.[14] As a result, campaigns tend to be candidate-centered. The most common medium of communication between candidates and voters is the telephone.[15]

Voting procedures in Japan are, if not unique, at least unusual. Voters receive a postcard, which they submit at their polling place. They receive not ballots but a blank sheet of paper. Names of candidates are listed in the polling booth, and the voter writes the name of one of them on the piece of paper and, in the case of single-member-district elections, places it in the appropriate ballot box. The voter then receives a different colored piece of paper and proceeds to the voting booth for proportional representation voting where the parties running candidates are listed. The voter puts the name of the party of choice on the piece of paper and places it in the box for proportional representation votes. "To my knowledge, Japan is the only democracy that does not print ballots."[16] The political adage that money is the mother's milk of politics is especially pertinent in Japan. Getting elected is very expensive but no more so than in the United States. A portion of campaign costs is covered by the government, political parties provide additional financial resources, and factions are a source of money. But together these resources amount to less than a third of a politician's financial needs.[17]

In Japan there are rules limiting campaign expenditures, rules intended to keep the expense of running for office under control and prevent the abuses that attend dependence on outside financial support. Of course, there are ways of getting around the rules and, as a result, they have not succeeded in keeping the costs of elections down. Campaign spending limits are ignored, and financial disclosure reports are falsified. "What has been accomplished is the designation of most campaign expenses as illegal."[18] Legislative efforts to tighten up campaign financing have not restricted access to private sources of money. Despite the corruption that money in politics has brought about, voters have displayed a high level of indifference to the problem.[19]

The salary received by members of the Diet compares favorably with that of American members of Congress, but it is not adequate to meet all political and campaign expenses. There are several ways to raise additional money. One is to create a patron group, usually consisting of companies that make regular monthly contributions to the legislator's political coffers. This approach is favored by faction leaders, and their ability to create this kind of patronage is one of the tests of their leadership. Annual fund-raising events, such as parties or dinners, also generate substantial sums of money. A third way in which members of the parliament obtain money is the "bonus" paid out twice a year and at election time by faction leaders.[20]

Getting elected does not end the need for large sums of money. Expenses of members of the Diet are only partly covered by their salary and allowances. Substantial sums are spent on constituents to promote and retain their allegiance. The ability to raise these funds is a key qualification for becoming a faction leader, especially for Liberal Democrats.[21]

Substantial sums of money are spent by political parties, especially the LDP, to cultivate good will among their constituents. LDP members need money for cash gifts on the occasion of weddings or funerals. They also contribute to local festivals, meetings, and sporting events. These are all prohibited under the Public Officers Election Act, but the regulations are rarely enforced except during election campaign periods.[22]

The main funding conduit between the LDP and big business is the Federation of Economic Organizations (Keidanren). Keidanren decides how much each of its members should contribute, and the burden is divided up among individual companies. These funds, about $100 million a year, are sent to the National Association for Politics (Kokumin Seiji Kyōkai), an organization that is jointly administered by the LDP and Keidanren. The money is then channeled to the LDP. The largest contributors in order of amount given are banks, public works and construction, steel, insurance, and automakers.[23]

The LDP also borrows money from banks at highly favorable rates of interest. In the year before the 1990 election, the LDP borrowed $100 million.

Additional money comes from medium-size and small business and from special interest groups, or "tribes," that have an interest in specific areas of public policy such as education or construction. Although not widely discussed until the Recruit scandal, another way of raising money is the secret buying and selling of stock. This practice has been common among all parties except the JCP. The National Tax Agency estimated that, in 1988, Japanese business spent $32 billion on entertainment and gifts, much of the money finding its way into the hands of politicians.[24]

The ways in which citizens participate in campaigns common in American elections is missing in Japan, which is another reason why partisanship is weak among Japanese.[25] The extensive formal restrictions on campaigning that exist today stem from the 1920s when the conservatives were worried about the capacity of the Socialists to succeed in mass mobilization. Although the rules governing campaigns have not been effective in controlling corrupt practices, they have kept the voters from playing much of a role in campaigns.

Voters are limited in both their commitment to political parties and in their ability to discern what parties stand for by the fact that parties have not made clear their positions on the issues. This may have ended in the 2003 election, when the Democratic Party of Japan (DPJ) issued the country's first manifesto. This manifesto stated the party's position on the issues and included the signatures of all its candidates, showing their support. This put the LDP in an awkward position since it "had never been able to produce a coherent party platform."[26] Politics, elections, and political behavior in Japan are similar in many ways to those found in other democratic countries. The rise of conservative sentiment and the overall decline of political parties can be seen in Europe and North America. Yet Japanese voters seem willing to tolerate the peccadilloes of their leaders to a far greater extent than do Western publics. The Sagawa Kyūbin scandal is only the latest in a pattern of corrupt practices dating from the end of the war.[27] The Japanese also seem to have lower expectations regarding the efficacy of political action. Although they demand less of their government than do Americans, when the issue is considered serious enough, they can be mobilized. But there are also differences. One difference is the absence of policy expertise. There are few policy experts on politicians payrolls, nor are there many research institutions—"think tanks"—active in the political realm.[28]

The Role of the Press

The Japanese news media have a relatively small role to play in the political process and this is especially true at election time.[29] In all democracies, newspapers have lost much of their political significance to television. In Japan, newspapers have little, if any, influence in national elections. Candidates do not need them to "get their message across" nor do they seek editorial endorsement. Nor is television an important campaign mechanism either; candidates do not stage events to get on the nightly news. Unlike in the United States where millions of dollars are spent on television advertising alone, the Japanese employ a more direct and personal touch. They spend nothing on media advertising.[30] The key is having large sums of money to cultivate the voters between elections. Labor unions have been a source of money, and voters for parties on the left.

Japanese television is modeled after that in England. There is public television (NHK—Nihon Hosho Kaikan), which provides intellectually lofty programming, and commercial channels. The latter are much more widely watched but of considerably lower quality. "Commercial television is everything which NHK is not—sensational, lewd, repetitive, dishonest and stupefyingly banal. Naturally, people love to watch it."[31] Although the news media are not a particularly significant factor in the electoral process, they are politically influential in other ways. Public awareness of and sensitivity toward issues, such as the environment, are raised through media coverage.[32] The quality of news coverage is of the highest order, and the public is generally well informed. Nevertheless, Japanese newspapers are almost identical in content. Many papers, including the three largest—*Asahi shimbun, Yomiuri shimbun,* and *Mainichi shimbun*—are owned by the employees. Yet this does not translate into freewheeling editorial independence.[33] There is no distinctive orientation or point of view. Japanese journalists only rarely engage in "investigative reporting," preferring instead to develop close personal contacts with government officials and politicians. Exposés and in-depth reports of scandals are uncommon as they would compromise this relationship.

There are other outlets where a broad range of opinion can be found, as well as coverage of the less-conventional side of politics. There are weekly and monthly publications, many of which are owned and published by the larger daily newspapers, but which exercise substantial editorial independence nonetheless. Coverage of political scandals often appears first in these publications before being picked up by the mainstream press.

"Salacious, libelous, utterly unreliable, they are the most vital of all information for anyone who wants to know what the Japanese are really thinking."[34] These weekly magazines supplement the mainstream press and together give a reasonably accurate picture of what is happening in Japan. Formal restrictions are not imposed by the state on the press in Japan; the press imposes restrictions on itself. Reporters belong to "press clubs," which serve as conduits through which official press releases are issued. In actual practice, these press clubs restrict access to information and determine what journalists will and will not report. Close personal relationships are important not only between journalists and government officials but among journalists themselves. Japan has a long tradition of "press clubs." They were originally developed to facilitate government control of the press. Since the end of the war, these clubs have continued to exist, taking on a distinctly social quality. Journalists who are not members of a press club, especially foreigners, face many barriers to conducting their work.[35]

Within a given press club, individual journalists may operate in a very narrow orbit. Those assigned to a specific faction of a political party are called *habatsu kisha* (faction journalists). Moreover, they may very well be assigned to cover a specific politician within that faction. By so doing, they develop a very close personal relationship with that person. It is unlikely that they will jeopardize this relationship by reporting unfavorable information.

Journalists rely on officials to provide information, and journalists in turn provide officials with an important service in reporting this information. This system has been unflatteringly described as "announcement journalism." There is little independent investigation by journalists to confirm the accuracy of official announcements, nor is there much analysis or interpretation of the message that the government and officials want to get out. A reporter's reputation is not made by writing award-winning articles but by the contacts he or she has been able to develop. This does not mean that the media turn a blind eye to matters of public concern or the misbehavior of public officials. It does appear, however, that the Japanese have a fairly high tolerance level. "In general, the Japanese public places greater trust in the honesty of state officials than in the honesty of politicians or business leaders."[36]

Access to press status is extremely difficult. Every important government agency has its own press club membership which is carefully guarded. Reporters obtain information from agency press releases and through the close personal relationships that develop with officials through the press clubs. Gaining access to these clubs is difficult for Japanese and, until recently, impossible for foreigners. After years of pressure from foreign media, the Japan Newspaper Publishers and Editors Association decided in July 1993 that foreign journalists could become full members of the association, thus allowing them to join press clubs. Several foreign press groups quickly joined the Ministry of Foreign Affairs and Ministry of Finance press clubs, and applications were submitted to other ministries and government agencies. The pace of change, however, has been slow, as it is not particularly welcome within the Japanese press community and its constituents.

Another kind of censorship exercised by the press is limiting reporting on controversial or publicly sensitive subjects. Details on scandals involving important politicians have been noticeably absent from newspapers until the story has been revealed, usually by small weekly or monthly publications or the foreign press. After the taboo against being the first news source to report critical information has been overcome, then the various media are less constrained in covering it. The press did not discuss the issue of the crown prince's search for a bride even though it was widely known that he was so engaged, as was the name of the likely candidate. The story was not covered out of respect for the imperial system. There was considerable chagrin in press and government circles when the story broke in the United States.

Electoral Reform

After its election victory in 1993, the coalition government of Morihiro Hosokawa moved to fulfill its commitment to reform the electoral process. The bills passed the lower house in November but were defeated in the upper house on January 21 of the following year, forcing government leaders to negotiate with the LDP and amend the original proposals in order to win passage.

The new system enacted by parliament on January 29, 1994, established an electoral mechanism for the lower house, consisting of 300 single-member-district seats and 200 seats chosen by proportional representation. In the single-member districts, population disparity can be no greater than two to one. The proportional-representation seats are to be chosen from eleven newly created regional blocs. In order to qualify for a share of the seats, parties must receive at least 2 percent of the vote.

Reforms in political financing were also enacted in 1994. An immediate ban on corporate donations failed to win parliamentary approval, although such a ban was to go into effect in five years. The provisions of the Political Fund Control Act were strengthened to dilute the power of moneyed interests in Japanese politics. A new system of public funding was introduced that subsidizes political parties up to a maximum of 40 percent of the party's income for the previous year. Efforts to expand citizen involvement in election campaigns failed. The ban on door-to-door canvassing was retained.

Protest Politics

Despite the emphasis on orderly behavior, the observance of tradition, and the respect for authority, street politics is not uncommon in Japan. In fact, local protests to express grievances have a long history, going back as far as the seventeenth century.[37] Some of the most ritualized demonstration tactics found anywhere in the world occur in Japan. Demonstrators conduct their marches according to the same rules of organization as those followed by Japanese tourists. Each has distinctive badges, flags, leaders, and lockstep behavior.[38]

Much protest activity in Japan, like that in other parts of the world, is leftist in character. The most active protestors are students; older people do not have the time or energy to riot and demonstrate. Protests rose to a fever pitch over the renewal of the Mutual Security Treaty in 1960. The Vietnam war also provoked demonstrations. The construction of the Narita airport serving Tokyo was an occasion for pitched battles between demonstrators, who opposed it, and police. "Between 1971 and 1978 the students built forts and towers, tunnels and underground bunkers. A trench war cost the lives of four riot police and two protesters."[39] But such activities have diminished in frequency in recent years due to negative public reaction, the end of American involvement in Vietnam, continuing national prosperity, and the declining vitality of leftist ideologies.

The extreme form of protest is terrorism, and Japan boasts some of the world's most ruthless practitioners of this form of political action. The most notorious of such groups is the Red Army Faction.[40] Nine of its members hijacked a Japan Airlines plane to North Korea in March 1970. The group was also involved in the Narita airport riots, during which three police officers were killed by Red Army members using bamboo spears. But the group almost tore itself apart internally in 1972, when radicals killed fourteen members of the group, including five women. Several were tied to trees while naked and allowed to freeze to death.

In May 1973, five members of the Red Army Faction seized another Japan Airlines plane, this time in Libya. In February 1974 they blew up an oil storage tank in Singapore. But their most notorious exploit was the attack on Lod airport in Israel, during which twenty-six people were killed. Other issues occupying the attention of extremist groups are opposition to the emperor system (some homemade missiles have been fired at the royal palace) and general hostility toward capitalism.[41]

Another example of protest activity, which is essentially ritualistic character, is labor agitation.[42] Labor unions engage in their annual "spring offensives" to win new contracts for their members. But as was noted earlier, organized labor does not have a great deal of influence, so strikes, boycotts, and other labor action are not a serious threat to political and economic order.

A most extraordinary event occurred in March 1995, when an obscure syncretic Hindu-Buddhist sect called Aum Shinrikyō was implicated in the release of sarin nerve gas in the Tokyo subway system. Many passengers died, and hundreds of others were injured. This apocalyptic group, founded in the mid-1980s, had an international following, reportedly including 30,000 Russians, and anticipated the end of the world in 1997.[43] Police found not only large sums of money and gold in the possession of members of the sect but also the chemicals needed to manufacture sarin.

Not all protest activity is a reflection of radical ideologies. Occasionally, the general public begins an agitation if the government fails to take action on an issue of widespread concern. This can lead to demonstrations and protests.[44] Popular movements have a long tradition in Japan, going back as far as the mid-nineteenth century.[45] Since the end of the war, there has been the peace movement and opposition to nuclear weapons. An especially successful popular movement emerged beginning in the early 1960s in support of pollution control. Because business and industry were largely indifferent and the government inactive, a popular movement arose that eventually resulted in some very strong environmental legislation.

Citizens' Movements: The Environment

Japan's postwar economic development produced some of the worst environmental degradation of any industrial country outside the former Soviet bloc, leading one observer to note: "Japan has the worst pollution problems in the world."[46] This was probably an exaggeration and is certainly no longer true today. First, Japan has made considerable progress in alleviating the problems of pollution. Second, the degradation of the environment in industrialized areas of China has reached catastrophic proportions. Still, Japan has experienced major problems of its own, due in part to the small size of the country. Environmental stress has resulted from the concentration of industry and population in a small space, a condition that has been exacerbated by the rapid pace of economic growth. The infrastructure to deal with the increasing amount of waste generated by modern society has not kept pace with growth. Even such basic public services as removal of household sewage is primitive by modern standards. As recently as 1982, only about 20 percent of households in Japan were connected to municipal sewage systems.[47]

Economic reconstruction after the end of the war came at a heavy environmental price, a price that the public became less willing to pay as time went on. Although the classical beauty of the travel posters remained, it became increasingly harder to find. Degradation of the environment and the health of the people were systematically sacrificed in the interest of economic development.

> As development proceeded during the decades following the war, new highways and high-speed rail lines cut through the countryside; coastal beaches were converted into tightly concentrated industrial parks *(kombinato);* waterways became convenient sluices for washing away industrial waste products; parks and countryside were replaced by paper mills and petrochemical plants. Given the comparatively high availability and low

cost of oil, the government also decided in 1960 to shift Japan's energy supply from coal and hydroelectric power to this more available but heavily polluting form of energy. Through all of these shifts, business and government were primarily concerned with economic efficiency.[48]

From 1960 to 1968, Japan experienced a 270 percent increase in mining and manufacturing and a 450 percent increase in heavy-oil consumption. Private ownership of cars quadrupled during the same period.[49] (Japanese describe their intercity expressways as the world's longest parking lots.) These developments necessarily had a heavy impact on the environment.

Environmental deterioration reached a peak in the 1960s but the political and economic elites seemed indifferent to the problems. "The economic miracle became a noisy, smelly, overcrowded, unhealthy testament to human greed."[50] Industrial pollutants generated by dense concentrations of factories led to degradation of air quality. Tokyo residents began suffering the ill effects of smog in 1970 with the outbreak of numerous cases of respiratory complaints. The initial response was to build taller smokestacks in order to disperse the pollutants over a wider area and thereby reduce their concentration. Draining underground water supplies to meet growing human demand led to land subsidence and threatened surface structures. Effluent discharged into the sea damaged fishing grounds and ultimately caused serious health problems.

The most serious case in human terms and dramatic in political terms involved "Minamata" disease, or mercury poisoning. Between 1953 and 1960, forty-six people died and seventy-five others became seriously ill in Kumamoto prefecture as a result of mercury poisoning from industrial waste.[51] The source of the disease was traced to a vinyl chloride plant owned by the chemical company Chisso.

Despite the environmental disasters that seemed to be occurring with increasing frequency, public sensitivity was slow to develop. In part, the public was indifferent because the environment did not have a "constituency" among the existing coalitions of political interests. Consequently, neither the national government nor the leaders of industry felt compelled to take the initiative in correcting the situation. Rather they, and especially the Ministry of International Trade and Industry (MITI), stood in the way of efforts to address the issue. Government required everything be assessed in terms of its economic impact, while industry tried to cover up the situation. Mercury poisoning was identified as early as 1956 but was not recognized as a health problem by the government until 1968. In 1970 the Ministry of Health and Welfare set the acceptable level of cadmium (another health threat) in unpolished rice at one part per million after initially proposing a level of 0.4 parts per million.[52] As a result of government foot-dragging, the public reacted with suspicion and distrust of authority, an unusual phenomenon in Japan.

Although opposition parties took an interest in environmental issues, the LDP did not even address the subject until 1970. Trade unions were even slower to accept pollution as a "people" issue and thus appropriately a concern of theirs. Instead of leading these organizations to take the initiative in addressing pollution as a public policy matter, environmental degradation generated a popular grass-roots movement centered on those people most directly and seriously affected by pollution.[53] By the late 1960s, the environmental movement had become national in scope, and local governments switched from encouraging new plant construction in their cities to campaigning against such development.[54]

The local citizens' movement first sought compensation for victims of environmental damage caused by industry. It then brought pressure to bear on the government, forcing it, reluctantly, to take remedial action to correct the worst abuses to the natural environment and to public health.[55] After the process started to move, regulations governing air and water pollution were enacted. In 1970 alone, the parliament enacted fourteen laws dealing with pollution.[56] Administrative mechanisms to enforce them were established, and legal philosophies making the polluter responsible for damage were created.

A milestone in the campaign to clean up the environment was the passage of the Tokyo Metropolitan Environmental Pollution Control Ordinance in 1969. Given Tokyo's economic and industrial importance, the ordinance had far-reaching effects. It stated that people were entitled to a clean and safe environment as a matter of right. To ensure the observance of these rights, criminal penalties were sanctioned for polluters.[57] The ordinance gave citizens further standing to pursue their grievances through the courts. Local governments, which carry a large share of the enforcement burden, frequently demand performance standards from industry that are stricter than the national law requires.[58]

In at least one case, citizens successfully resisted the construction of an industrial project because of its potential pollution threat. There were prefect-level ordinances governing pollution on the books since the 1950s but they were not effective.[59] After the citizens' movement gained initial successes at the local level, the cause of environmental protection was taken up by the national government, in particular the courts, with a vigor approaching that originally displayed in opposition to any interference with economic growth. At the national level, a Basic Law for Environmental Pollution Control was passed in 1967. In its original form, it was weak and full of loopholes. Among other things, at the insistence of MITI, the law declared that protection of the environment must be "in harmony with the healthy development of the economy."[60] A law was passed in 1969 mandating compensation of victims. A 1970 law established procedures for settling environmental disputes, and the Basic Law was strengthened the same year.[61] This was followed in 1971 by the establishment of the Environment Agency, which carried the fight for environmental protection to the powerful economic ministries of the national government. The Environment Agency is located in the Prime Minister's Office and is headed by a director general with Cabinet rank. Despite this, the Environmental Agency was handicapped in its early efforts by the fact that its personnel were drawn from the ranks of MITI. It would be some time before the agency was able to recruit its own people and draw leadership from within its own ranks.[62]

The implementation of environmental regulations is a shared responsibility between the central and local governments. The central government defines environmental policy and sets standards. The prefect governments are responsible for monitoring. Enforcement is a cooperative effort involving central government bureaucratic agencies and prefect governments.[63]

A key reason for the citizens' movement success in forcing government response was the perception of the movement as disruptive of the normal political process. If this new form of political action had been allowed to go unchecked, traditional interests and institutionalized power would have been threatened. Thus the government responded to the issue of environmental degradation not entirely on its merits but to protect its control over policy and decision making.[64]

Japanese environmental protection efforts are very narrowly focused. Sensitivity over environmental issues developed in the context of health issues, especially the trauma associated with mercury and cadmium poisoning. Consequently, environmental law is most highly developed in areas of public health. Broader issues, such as aesthetics, endangered species, and multiple use of natural resources, receive comparatively less attention, and legislation in these areas is weak. The philosophy "the polluter must pay" pertains to human health and the living environment. "From the perspective of the compensation of victims of pollution, Japanese law is the most sophisticated in the world."[65] The Japanese borrowed two practices widely used in the United States. One is the environmental impact statement as an integral part of the economic planning and development process, and the other is the public hearing that allows for citizen participation.[66]

In the 1980s, the momentum of the environmental movement appeared to run out.[67] Litigation in this area disappeared, and the central government regained its control over the environmental policy agenda.[68] There is always the possibility of slippage in environmental protection, which could accelerate if the overall economic situation takes a serious turn for the worse.

"Civil society consists of sustained, organized social activity that occurs in groups that are formed outside the state, the market, and the family. Such activity on the part of groups and individuals cumulatively creates a domain of discourse, a public sphere."[69]

Pressure Groups

Unlike interest groups in the United States, Japanese groups do not rely primarily on external efforts to influence the policy process. Lobbying, campaign contributions, and public information programs are not unheard of in Japan, but there is also the practice of seeking direct involvement in government by getting someone from the group elected to office. Many politicians hold both public elective office and leadership positions in their organization.[70] The link between interest groups and government is further strengthened by the practice of retired bureaucrats obtaining jobs with interest groups, thus building bridges between these groups and government ministries.[71]

Professional Associations

Professional groups representing lawyers, engineers, physicians, and the like are not the important fixtures of the political scene that they are in the United States. Physicians have enjoyed a privileged status, being able not only to prescribe drugs but to sell them. They were able to limit the availability of birth control drugs until recently. But private health insurance companies do not exist in Japan. Drug companies have less influence than their American counterparts.[72] Professional associations do not have as much control over certification of their members as is the case in the West.

Business

There are several organizations representing the interests of the business community, the most important of which is the Federation of Economic Organizations (Keidanren, an acronym for Keizai Dantai Rengōkai). Organized in 1946 with the encouragement of the occupation authorities, it numbers among its members the industrial giants of Japan. Its two basic principles have been maintenance of a market economy and international cooperation.[73]

> Keidanren is a uniquely Japanese institution radiating the Japanese penchant for group rather than individual action, decision by consensus rather than majority vote and economic cooperation rather than competition, presenting a united front to the Government and Japanese society, and issuing guidance to the members.[74]

Other business groups include the Japan Federation of Employers' Associations (Nikkeiren). It is an organization of employers founded in 1948 in response to the vigorous, communist-backed labor offensive. Its main function is to coordinate negotiations with organized labor. The Japan Chamber of Commerce and Industry, the oldest group having been founded in 1878, is basically representative of smaller businesses and enjoys a considerable measure of power, even coming out on top in contests with Keidanren.[75] The Japan Association of Corporate Executives (Keizai Dōyūkai), founded in 1946, is an organization of progressive business interests, and is the least influential of all business groups.[76]

In addition to the effectiveness of business groups, economic interests also receive political representation as a result of the movement of top leaders between jobs in industry and government. Many retired bureaucrats go to work for industry and are expected to maintain intimate contact with their former colleagues in government. There is important linkage between the LDP and business and also between labor unions and the Socialist parties. This phenomenon accounts, to some extent, for the appeal of the Kōmeitō among voters who do not identify with either business or labor. These party issues are discussed in greater detail in Chapter 4.

Agriculture

On a per capita basis, the agricultural community is politically the most powerful in the country even though the number of full-time farmers has declined dramatically since the end of the war. In 1950, half the farmers devoted all their time and effort to agriculture. In 1989, less than 15 percent did so with the overwhelming majority holding salaried jobs of some sort. Today only about 5 percent of the population is classified as farmers. Despite the shrinking of the agrarian population, farmers have been consistent in their political loyalties. The LDP has been able to rely on a staunchly reliable voting bloc in farmers.[77] In return, the party resisted reforms that would dilute agriculture's influence by eliminating their overrepresentation in the Diet. Agricultural influence is not limited to the LDP, however, as farmer interests became more important for the Social Democratic Party of Japan (SDPJ).[78] The government has also protected agriculture's economic interests by maintaining a high price for rice and other products. A variety of trade barriers, covering such items as beef, citrus products, and apples have caused considerable friction with the United States.[79] Nevertheless Japanese farmers vigorously protest any action, no matter how limited, that they perceive jeopardizes their economic position.

Under continuous pressure from the United States, the Nakasone and Takeshita governments began reducing the public subsidy to Japanese rice farmers and also allowed expanded imports of beef and citrus products. The hostile reaction of the agricultural community brought about a partial retrenchment of the policy.[80] As trading nations moved toward a new agreement under the Uruguay round of General Agreement on Tariffs and Trade (GATT) talks in early 1993, the Japanese government and opposition parties remained adamant in their refusal to open the rice market, including the proposal to lift the ban and institute a system of tariffs. The fall of the LDP that same year and the changes introduced in the electoral system suggest a weakening of agriculture's influence.

The Agricultural Problems Association is operated by the leaders of various farm organizations and collects money for the LDP. Other groups include the Federation of Agricultural Cooperatives and the National Land Improvement Association. Nōkyō, the association of agricultural cooperatives, is the most successful farmers' group in establishing links with members of the parliament. Even though the number of farms and farmers has been declining for some time, agricultural interests have enjoyed inordinate political influence. One source of such influence, like that enjoyed by business, is the ability of politicians with farm interests to hold formal positions in both farm interest groups and the government.[81]

Labor

Historically, the working class in Japan has been politically weak. Beginning in the 1870s, efforts to unionize labor met with hostility and government repression. Union attempts to enhance the economic status of workers and political activities by labor in general were confronted by vigorous police repression after 1900 and the enactment of the Public Peace Police Law. Article 17 of the law allowed for suppression of union activities.[82] The fact that the supply of labor exceeded the demand further weakened its bargaining power.

The influence of labor has not changed much since the war, although its legal status is no longer in doubt. After a brief period during the occupation when the organization of labor was encouraged, unionization of labor has proceeded slowly. Overall it has lagged behind economic growth. Compared to other industrial countries, Japanese labor is extraordinarily weak as a political force. Unions have never been able to establish the degree of political independence found in the West, nor is their influence anywhere near comparable. In fact labor has not been an element of the support base underpinning the integrity of the regime.[83] Part of labor's problem is the fact that it has never been able to broker its support for political parties. Labor has been consistently affiliated with the JSP or the Democratic Socialist Party

(DSP).[84] The fact that these parties are permanently in the minority diminishes labor's political influence.

Today only about a fourth of workers are unionized. There are no strong "industry-wide" unions and federations consisting of several unions are weak. The General Council of Trade Unions of Japan (Nihon Rodo Kumiai Sohyokai or Sōhyō) was established in 1950 to separate the labor movement from the JCP. It maintained close affiliation with the JSP. In 1954 rightwing unions split off and formed Zenrō, later renamed the Japanese Confederation of Labor (Zen Nihon Rodo Sodomei or Dōmei), which was linked to the DSP. There were also two other union groups: the Federation of Independent Unions (Chūritsurōren') established in 1956, and the National Federation of Industrial Organizations (Shinsanbetsu) established in 1949. A new federation called the Japanese Private Sector Trade Union Confederation (Rengō) was created in November 1987, replacing all the above federations except Sōhyō which joined Rengo in 1990. Candidates running under the banner of Rengō have been elected to the Diet including eleven of twelve candidates who ran for House of Councillors seats in the 1989 election.[85]

In late 1989 Japanese labor unions underwent a major restructuring. A new federation called the New Japanese Trade Union Confederation (Shin Rengō) was formed, combining Rengō with a number of unions formerly affiliated with Sōhyō. Another new group the Japan Confederation of Trade Unions (Zenrōren), takes a more traditional view of the labor movement stressing class struggle. A third organization, the National Trade Union Council (Zenrōkyō), is mainly concerned with the plight of railway workers affected by the privatization of the Japan National Railways in 1987.[86]

In recent years, labor has begun moving away from its exclusive emphasis on increasing compensation toward worker-related issues, such as lower prices, especially the prohibitively high cost of land, and improving pensions. It has joined the call for an easing of import restrictions and for simplification of the tax structure. Labor also favors reforming the system by which goods are distributed and made available to consumers. Restrictions in this area, such as limiting access to markets by large department stores, have traditionally added substantially to consumer prices.[87]

This is changing as consumers are becoming more sophisticated. "Consumers . . . are growing far more independent and assertive in their relations with national government actors—so much so, in fact, that the gap between the local and national dimensions of consumer society may finally be closing."[88] Almost all labor organizations (94 percent) are "enterprise" unions, which means that all employees in a given firm, irrespective of their occupational category, are members of the union.[89] Although they are not controlled directly by management, these unions, at least as perceived by their members, have more in common with their own management than with other unions.[90] The leaders of such unions are themselves employees of the firm, although they are on leave and receive their salaries from the union. The compensation of workers in Japan compares favorably with that in other industrialized countries, but this is not due to vigorous union representation of worker interests in such areas as wages and working conditions. "Rather they function as an auxiliary to management in the personnel sector."[91] Nominally the governance of unions follows democratic principles. Nevertheless, workers are inclined to feel governed by unions rather than seeing them as representing their interests.[92] Unions are not, however, always compliant tools in the hands of management. If workers are arbitrarily discharged or regular workers are laid off, unions can fight effectively.[93] But all in all, unions have little impact on the routine operation of the company.[94]

About one-third of organized labor consists of public employees, who expend a great deal of energy on strikes over political issues, rather than wages, benefits, and working conditions. In contrast to industrial interests, public employees and their unions, such as teachers, have little personal contact with management, that is, the ministry most directly involved in their work. Educators do not have the close working relationship with the Ministry of Education that business has with MITI, for example. This means that those in the education field have little impact on routine policy administration.[95] Moreover, the fact that teachers have job security weakens their case for increased financial compensation. The teachers' union has been in the forefront of political activism. Before the war, the teachers' union was vigorously opposed by the government, which had the effect of driving union leadership into the arms of the radical left.[96] From the end of the war until about 1950, the Japan Teachers' Union (JTU) focused its efforts on improving teachers' salaries and teachers' rights. Subsequently it shifted its attention to Japan's military connection with the United States, which it opposed, as it did any Japanese rearmament.[97] Apart from its radical ideology, the JTU is also distinguished by its essentially negative orientation. It rarely proposes any substantive policy reforms, preferring instead to oppose government policy, or the Ministry of Education, or U.S. foreign policy, or capitalism.[98] The union has enjoyed some measure of success in getting its leaders elected to the Diet but has had little influence on policy.[99] In some areas, the JTU has been an effective counterweight to the power of administration, but it has also introduced politicization, instability, and intrigue.[100]

Because of the congestion and high cost of doing business, especially the price of real estate in the Tokyo metropolitan area, industries have begun to move their operations from urban to rural areas. This has weakened unions because there is less concentration of workers in cities who could be mobilized for political purposes. A combination of social, economic, and political changes has weakened organized labor to the point that no national body effectively represents labor.[101]

Students

Nearly 40 percent of college-age youth attend institutions of higher education. Tremendous status is associated with attending the "right" college. Admission is highly competitive, but the requirements for graduation are not very demanding. Hence being admitted is the important thing, and, having arrived, students do not find their studies intellectually taxing. This leaves them with considerable time for other things such as sports and politics.

Postwar student activism was more extensive than it had been during the 1920s and 1930s. Nonetheless, the vast majority of students are politically apathetic and do not participate actively in politics. Among those who are active, a few have been involved in right-wing nationalist causes. Most, however, have been ideologically influenced by communism. They have not been concerned about the welfare of the working class so much as they have been about the evils of U.S. military policy. Student demonstrations reached a peak in 1960 in connection with the renewal of the Mutual Defense Treaty and again in 1968–70 with regard to the Vietnam war. Demonstrations occur from time to time over such matters as visits of nuclear-powered vessels of the U.S. Navy.

The All-Japan Students Self Governing Association (Zengakuren) was organized on September 18, 1948, and was initially under the political domination of the JCP. In its early years, the group claimed as many as 300,000 members.[102] It advocates ending the Security Treaty with the United States and the removal of U.S. forces from Japan. In the past it favored return of Okinawa and opposed American "imperialism" in Vietnam. After the 1960 demonstrations, the group divided into a number of factions, some of which associated with the JCP, while others were even further to the left. When there was a confrontation among these groups in 1969, the police were brought in and universities were closed down for a time. This event disturbed the public and moderate students alike, thus weakening the cause of the left. In their own minds, students see themselves as sharing the interests of the working class. But workers do not believe that they have anything in common with students whom they regard as bourgeois.

In the past, politicization of students was enhanced by the special status accorded university and college campuses. Generally speaking, the police were disinclined to enter university grounds absent an emergency. This not only increased the capacity of students to assert themselves politically but also stimulated their sense of importance. All this changed as a result of political disorder on campuses during the 1960s. The government, particularly through the 1969 University Control Act, made it clear that it would impose stricter controls on universities than in the past. Afterward, the police were present on university campuses more often. As a result, student disturbances have diminished almost completely.[103]

Another possible reason for the decline in student political activism is suggested by evidence that students are becoming more conservative ideologically. This has not, however, translated into noticeable growth in the popularity of right-wing causes. The student movement has declined in strength, and demonstrations have become less frequent and less intense. Political apathy is not something peculiar to the Japanese student population but seems to be characteristic of youth in most industrialized countries.[104]

Part III

Society and Economy

8

The Social Order

Social Identity

Among the more important elements that make up the political culture of any country are collective ideologies and personal philosophies, the needs of the community and special requirements for individuals, the demands of the powerful and the not-so-powerful, all held together by a wide array of political institutions and government policies. In addition, the substance and tempo of politics are shaped by the social values and demographic characteristics of the people. In Japan, the latter category of influences is of relatively minor political significance. One of the most important social features of Japan is its homogeneity. Japan lacks the kind of racial and linguistic variety that can be found in many countries especially in Asia, factors that are defining influences in the political process. Likewise, religion, a decisive determinant of life for many people, especially those in the Middle East, is not a particularly important criterion defining personal or collective identity in Japan and plays only a restricted part in politics.[1] Most Japanese are of the same ethnic background, speak the same language, and subscribe to the same general set of beliefs. There are subtle social and cultural differences, but they account for little political contention. Rather than a mosaic of subnational populations that are socially and culturally distinguished one from another, Japan is a network of groups defined primarily in terms of interpersonal relations.[2]

A theme that runs throughout much of the literature on contemporary Japan is that groups are of central importance in the social system.[3] For some, this network of groups is perceived as tightly knit, resulting in a social monolith characterized by an almost seamless solidarity. This view is shared by those Western businesspeople who contend that one reason they are unable to penetrate the Japanese market is the strong sense of social solidarity and group loyalty. Another perspective, common among the Japanese themselves, is that Japanese society is so cohesive and fundamentally different that it has little if anything in common with other societies; it is, in a word, unique.[4] From another point of view, the group basis of Japanese society is a euphemism for a sophisticated and efficient method of social control.[5]

Social Status

If the social system is a vast network of groups, within the group itself individuals are ranked according to their status.[6] This ranking governs the way people relate to and interact with each other. There is also a rank-ordering process at work involving the groups themselves. This hierarchical ordering of society governs the way people see themselves and the way they interrelate in both intragroup and intergroup behavior.[7]

There is substantial homogeneity among members of different strata in occupation, educational achievement, and family background. For example, Japanese leaders in both business and government are highly typical: Most are university graduates in law, government, economics, physical science, or engineering.[8] Very few top executives have been educated in one of the social sciences or humanities, and almost 50 percent are graduates of a single institution of higher education: Tokyo University. Although study abroad is not a valued accomplishment, in fact it may be a liability,[9] most leaders have made several trips outside their own country. Almost all members of this elite group are highly literate and well informed.

This pattern continues across generations. Today's top leadership is composed of the sons of men who themselves had a relatively high occupational status. Very few of these are self-made individuals who have achieved fame and fortune without the requisite educational and family background. Approximately 61 percent of the current business leaders had fathers who were in upper occupational categories. But at the time these leaders were born, that is, around forty years ago, their fathers made up only about 11 percent of the population. Although 31 percent of them claim to have petit-bourgeois backgrounds, during their father's lifetime, the petty bourgeoisie constituted only 21 percent of the population. Less than 10 percent come from working-class backgrounds although this class included nearly 70 percent of the population. Moreover, this pattern has a long history. Most current business leaders claim that their grandfathers also occupied high-level occupations. In other words, 90 percent of top business leaders came from socioeconomic groups that accounted for only 30 percent of the population.[10]

It is sometimes argued that men of samurai background provided business leadership during the period of early industrialization. Their disproportionate numbers in leadership positions is due not to the fact that they were samurai but to their superior family connections, social status, and educational opportunities. Family influences have traditionally been very strong in determining choice of occupation and career advancement. This is especially true among business owners and top executives. Vertical mobility does not seem to have increased despite greater occupational opportunity resulting from industrialization.

Within the elite itself, the pattern of mobility is different. For those fortunate enough to enjoy elite status, the opportunities for personal advancement are considerable. The general population, in contrast, displays a high degree of occupational stability across generations. It is highly unlikely that a person could substantially advance his social status by extraordinary professional achievement, leading to rapid career advancement. Bright young "whiz kids" are not found among top leadership. For persons who are not members of the elite, opportunity for social advancement is limited. Over the years, the criteria defining social status have not significantly changed despite dramatic economic growth. The benefits of this growth have been shared throughout society, meaning more money for everyone. But this has not translated into economic and social mobility that would alter the pattern of social stratification.

The closed system of managerial leadership extends to Japanese foreign operations. Non-Japanese management personnel in countries outside Japan are largely excluded from the highest decision-making positions. Important decisions, and some not so important, are referred back to senior executives in Japan. Frustration and morale problems result as foreign nationals have been frozen out of top positions in companies in their own countries.[11]

The closed elite system based on family status and occupation is also evident in politics. Most politicians come from families with a tradition of political involvement. There is a pattern of family succession. Elected politicians are the sons (and a few daughters) of men who themselves were elected to office. Without the important personal connections that are associated particularly with family, it is very difficult for a newcomer to break into politics.

Compared to the United States, in Japan men with government, professional, and big business family backgrounds have a share of top business positions that is four times or greater. Although American business leaders do not, by any means, mirror the population, they are closer to representative than are their Japanese counterparts. Statistically, people of blue-collar or labor backgrounds have a slight chance of gaining top business positions in the United States. Business leaders (as well as those in government) with middle-class backgrounds are numerous in the United States. In Japan there is no chance for someone with a working-class background to make it to the top and very little chance for anyone from the middle class.

Even in rapidly expanding industries, there is no tendency toward greater vertical occupational mobility. Economic growth opens more types of job opportunities, but even here upward mobility is limited to a single track—education. "Higher education is the most important channel for occupational advancement in Japanese society."[12] But education tends to support the hierarchical system rather than function to circumvent it. Education itself has a rigid status hierarchy that closely parallels those found elsewhere in society. "The opportunity for higher education is largely predetermined by a given occupational status."[13]

Although the number of university graduates has been steadily increasing, this has had little effect on the recruitment of the administrative and managerial elites. The lack of opportunity for upward mobility has not produced significantly high levels of frustration, so far at any rate. Economic expansion has created jobs for the large numbers of graduates who seem reasonably satisfied with their social status.

The Individual and the Group

In the American system of values, individualism and privacy are given the highest priority. The Japanese place an equal emphasis on interpersonal connections and community life. The Japanese thus appear to Americans as a people unable to do much of anything on their own. To the casual observer, they appear to go about their business in groups of varying sizes at a pace reminiscent of the exaggerated hurriedness of a silent movie. As tourists, even in their own country, they scurry about, quickly getting on and off buses all the while dutifully following the pennant whose color identifies their particular unit. There is also usually an individual with a megaphone exhorting stragglers to keep up. They seem, to the outsider, only marginally interested in the sites, spending only enough time to take numerous pictures of each other. As with most casual observations, this one, while not inaccurate, does not tell the whole story.

Strong social forces promote close interpersonal links that are evident everywhere, from the schoolroom to the workplace. Students and their teachers remain together in a socially reinforcing environment far longer than would be true in the United States. Office workers sit in close proximity to one another, rather than in individual cubicles as is favored in the West. Even the boss himself is present in the communal work area rather than in a private office.

There is some question as to whether this approach improves efficiency. Although being close together promotes group solidarity, it also leads to the temptation to waste time in idle conversation. Japanese offices have only recently begun to take full advantage of modern computer technology and desks are still piled high with papers that require the attention and signature of everyone in the "loop."[14]

Much is made of Japanese-style "groupism," but to what extent is it really a departure from social practices found elsewhere in the world? Just how "unique" are they? Americans are probably inclined to exaggerate the distinctiveness of Japanese customs and social organization. Most Americans are probably uncomfortable with the notion that it is they who are different. In fact, a fairly pronounced sense of group solidarity is quite common throughout the world. It is the extent of the American emphasis on individuality that is unusual. What might be said about the Japanese is that the tendency toward groupism is carried to particularly high levels. All things considered, Japan is probably no more nor less "unique" than are other societies, except, perhaps, in the minds of the Japanese themselves.[15]

It is misleading to conclude that the social homogeneity of Japan means there is a complete absence of conflict. Conflicts occur in all societies as people compete for power, prestige, status, money, and anything else "worth having." In fact, the group basis of society is itself one source of interaction that can lead to conflict.[16]

> The group as a whole tends to be acutely conscious and assertive of its rights as a collectivity in dealing with outsiders, that is, with all individuals, groups, and agencies which are outside the in-group. Outsiders are normally to be met with indifference or, especially if they are in the same sphere of activity, with intense competition. A sense of radical separateness from outsiders and secrecy about the quasifamilial private life of the in-group are also common; candor and easy give-and-take do not often come naturally with nonmembers but formal propriety is generally respected.[17]

Japanese society is not free of those frictions and confrontations that lead to conflict. Rather, open conflict is avoided by careful observance of an elaborate and rigorous set of behavioral norms that channel potential disruptions into harmless rituals and symbolic activities.[18]

Many theories have been offered that purport to explain the group dynamics of Japanese society. One such theory suggests that groupism is a consequence of the social nature of paddy-type agriculture. Another is based on the importance of clans in Japanese history. Psychosocial theories stress the importance of power and honor in determining behavior.[19] Among the more popular contemporary theories are those involving family relationships and child-rearing practices.[20] Japanese children have close contact with their parents, especially with their mothers, which continues for a much longer time than is characteristic of American families, for example. Living arrangements encourage a strong dependency on others; it is virtually inescapable. Homes are small, making it difficult to escape to the privacy of one's own room. There is no central heating, so family members cluster around a space heater during cold weather. The psychological impact of such arrangements on children is considerable.

The phenomenon of interpersonal dependence, together with the fact that there are no major sociocultural divisions, means that as far as political demographics are concerned, uniformity and continuity characterize Japan. But this does not mean that there are no politically relevant divisions. It does mean that these divisions are comparatively subtle and not, generally speaking, particularly significant sources of political contention. Pressure groups, while they exist and in some instances—such as farmers—are quite effective, are not the important political fixture that they are in the West. Although this is attributable in part to social solidarity, it is also due to the attitude that pressuring the government for special favors is not considered ethical.[21] Not that special favors are not granted but that it is considered unseemly to ask for them.

Social Distinctions and Politics

Ethnic Groups

Japan's homogeneity is attributable mainly to the fact that, as an island nation, it has not been easily accessible. It has also never been the victim of a successful invasion, apart from World War II. The oceans have been effective barriers to the waves of migration that have swept over other areas of the globe. Even today, with greatly expanded population mobility resulting from ease of travel and extensive commercial interaction, there are comparatively few foreigners living in Japan. Most non-Japanese live apart from the rest of society and find it extremely difficult, should they choose to do so, to become an integral part of society and culture. "Convinced, accurately enough, of the uniqueness of their culture, the Japanese are also likely to think that it is so subtle and complex that no one who is not born Japanese and reared in Japanese society can ever truly become part of it."[22] This attitude frequently leads to a general indifference toward racial sensitivities and subsequent charges of Japanese racism. For example, the justice minister once observed that prostitutes, like American blacks, destroy neighborhoods.[23]

Koreans, who were brought in as laborers, make up the largest foreign community, numbering about 650,000. Many were forced to go to Japan and work in the factories and mines as World War II drained Japanese manpower.[24] Koreans were even pressed into service in the Japanese military. Even though many Koreans are second- or third-generation residents of Japan, most have not become Japanese citizens despite a growing trend among younger Koreans to seek naturalization. In the same group, intermarriage with Japanese is also becoming more frequent.[25] These Koreans are only partly assimilated, even though they speak Japanese (often as their first language)[26] and they are not physiologically distinct from the majority population. Until recently, they have been formally denied jobs in bureaucracy and in public schools; only forty Koreans had been hired as teachers by 1990.[27] As aliens they were denied the right to vote and they have generally been treated with contempt.[28] They were, until 1992, when the Japanese government agreed to abolish the practice, required to be fingerprinted as aliens and carry identity cards bearing their picture.[29] Koreans will continue to be treated as aliens until they acquire citizenship, which involves passing a background check and adopting a Japanese name.[30] Unemployment among Koreans in Japan is high, exceeding the rate among blacks in the United States.[31]

There have been occasions in the past when Koreans have been the victims of gross brutality at the hands of the Japanese. For example, in 1923 an earthquake struck Japan. In the ensuing confusion, rumors, promoted by official police broadcasts, began to circulate that Koreans were setting fires, looting shops, poisoning wells, and planning to attack Japanese. Many Koreans were massacred at the hands of the Japanese, who were quick to conclude that the rumors were true.[32] In the 1930s, many Koreans were active in the Japan Communist Party (JCP) and thus were suppressed in the sweep against leftists under the Peace Preservation Law.[33] After the war ended, the Korean connection to communism earned them the suspicion and suppression of the U.S. occupation authorities.[34] Today the Korean community has little political influence, a situation that is not likely to change in the foreseeable future.

Among the organizations representing Koreans is Seiwakai, which consists of Koreans who have become naturalized citizens. Because naturalized Koreans do not want to call attention to their ancestry, this group does not have a large membership. Another group, Chongnyon, includes those favoring North Korea and has supported repatriation rather than assimilation. Its membership dwindled as the attractiveness of North Korean society has paled when compared to that of the South. Mindan, the group supportive of South Korea, has tended to favor assimilation and improvement of the social and economic condition of Koreans in Japan. The latter two groups reflect the antagonism between the two Koreas, a situation exploited by the Japanese government to neutralize the political effectiveness of the Korean community in Japan.[35]

The Japanese attitude toward non-Japanese is not lost on potential immigrants, such as the world's growing refugee population. Even Vietnamese, who are culturally and ethnically closer to the Japanese than to, say, Americans, do not always look to Japan as a haven. After a great deal of international pressure, the Japanese government agreed to grant permanent residence to 10,000 Vietnamese "boat people." Many Vietnamese took advantage of the opportunity, but others preferred to take their chances on gaining admission to the United States.[36] There are about 100,000 illegal immigrants in Japan. Despite cultural barriers, the lure of employment is strong; there are opportunities for work, especially in low-status jobs that the Japanese themselves avoid because they are considered dirty, dangerous, or demeaning.[37] There has been an influx of Chinese, despite barriers to their entry. In 1989 some Chinese tried to enter the country by passing themselves off as Vietnamese. The Japanese contended that these people were not genuine refugees seeking relief from persecution, but only economic opportunists, and sent them back to China.[38]

As the numbers of refugees, especially from Southeast Asia and China, increase, the pressure on Japan to admit at least some of them has grown in proportion. This issue is complicated by the fact that the international status of refugees is frequently ambiguous as many of them do not qualify as "political" refugees, that is, those fleeing persecution for their political or religious beliefs. The numbers of people seeking asylum include many who are simply willing to take a chance, even at the risk of their lives, for the opportunity for a more materially rewarding life. No country has been willing to open its doors completely to such immigrants, fearing a floodtide of foreign job seekers. The United States does much the same thing with respect to Haitians, Salvadorans, and others lacking skills or financial resources.

The Japanese face a major dilemma. On the one hand, there is the reality of the thousands of foreigners in their presence, most not genuine refugees. These people are willing to take the lowest-status employment, jobs that the Japanese themselves are inclined to avoid, thus there is real demand for their labor. On the other hand, the concern for social harmony has led the government to pursue a vigorous policy of expatriation of illegal immigrants. To deal with the labor shortage problem, the government advises employers to modernize, thus eliminating the need for unskilled workers.

The Dowa, or "village people" formerly known as Burakumin or Eta, are a caste of untouchables who trace their ancestry to ancient times. They are underprivileged and oppressed, traditionally holding only the most objectionable and "polluting" jobs, such as leather working, where they earn half or two-thirds of the average national income per household. Their main political organization is the Burakumin Emancipation League. In the mid-1970s the league became very assertive, demanding better services from the government for their community. Increased government spending, especially on education programs, rewarded their militancy, which included occasional violent behavior.[39]

Burakumin have endured extreme forms of discrimination and oppression especially in marriage and employment. The parents of a potential marriage partner will abort the marriage if the other potential spouse has a Burakumin family background. Employment may also be denied if the person has Burakumin background.[40]

Another oppressed group is the aboriginal Utari, or Ainu, whose ancestors were among the earliest inhabitants of the Japanese islands. Fewer than 20,000 Ainu survive today as a culturally identifiable group in Hokkaido. But the Ainu do not receive special attention because the Japanese government does not recognize them as a distinct, minority people.[41]

Women

Apart from foreigners and minority ethnic groups, women are the clearest victims of social discrimination and this includes both their public and private lives.[42] The women's liberation movement is less in evidence in Japan than in some other modern industrialized countries. In fact the feminist movement is weaker now than it was in the past and "has deteriorated into a politically irrelevant source of amusement and object of ridicule."[43] Viewed from a broader historical perspective, however, the status of women is one of the most dramatic areas of social change in modern Japan. Moreover, although the public manifestations of feminism may be less evident than in Western countries, Japanese women already enjoy something Western women very much desire—that is a strong social bond among themselves, a "sisterhood."[44]

The prewar status of women was little more than that of chattel, a situation consistent with other parts of Asia, especially China. Although divorce was easy for men it was almost impossible for women. They were largely denied education beyond the primary level, as learning was not considered necessary for women. In the minds of the elite who ran the country, "women were thought to be less intelligent than men, more emotional and so less rational, less reliable, vindictive, potentially dangerous if not rigorously disciplined, and worst of all, silly."[45] Postwar reforms attempted with considerable success to change this. Women were given full legal equality in the 1947 constitution, including the right to seek divorce, which many did. Beginning in the 1960s, the divorce rate began to increase and reached an all-time high in 2002 of 2.3 for every 1,000 people.[46] This was due to several factors. First, social attitudes toward divorce have changed; it does not carry the stigma of failure to the degree that it once did. Second, women now have greater opportunity to be financially self-supporting and can risk separation. Third, a breakdown has taken place in women's attitudes of the mutually exclusive distinction between wage earner and homemaker. Many women now demand more from life than being a good wife and mother.[47]

But divorce remains a risky business for women. Some are unable to support themselves and their children on their own because of inadequate income and the continuing discriminatory nature of the employment marketplace. Thus Japanese women will put up with more than their Western counterparts to make a marriage work or, at the very least, last. There is also the vestigial stigma associated with divorce, which is still viewed by many as a social disgrace.

Although conditions are better today than they were before the war, women are a considerable distance from enjoying full reproductive rights. Contraceptive practices exist in a shadowy area of the law, in which, until recently, birth control pills could only be prescribed for therapeutic purposes, not for preventing pregnancy as a matter of family planning. On September 2, 1999, the government approved contraceptives for general use. But this came about only after the government had approved Viagra after only six months' deliberation. Media attention and outrage by women's groups finally brought action on the pill.[48] Physicians had opposed allowing their use for birth control in order to protect their lucrative abortion practices. Physicians are also able to sell the drugs they prescribe, a practice that would be considered conflict of interest in many countries. The government was fearful that easy access to birth control would further diminish Japan's already low birth rate.[49] Having been legalized, the pill is still not easy to obtain. Women must undergo exams much more frequently than is required of women in the United States, the cost of which can be substantial. This reinforces women's suspicions regarding the safety of the drug, resulting in few users. Women's reproductive freedom is driven less by self-interest and social acceptability than by official priorities. As far as women have been concerned, the state has required them to either provide babies or labor.[50] "The Japanese people have been badly served by their government, as well as by interest groups and the media, all of which have pursued their own agendas with little regard for individual needs, reproductive health or rights, or accurate and even-handed information."[51]

The expectation, widespread before the war, that women should be "good wives and wise mothers" did not allow for significant opportunities for educational advancement. After the third grade, girls and boys were educated in separate facilities with the latter being prepared for a life of work and responsibility. Girls' futures were seen as limited to the home, and little formal education was needed for that. University education was not available to women. As a consequence of the reforms introduced during and after the occupation, however, women moved quickly into the educational system. In 1955, 47.4 percent of females in the appropriate age group were enrolled in high school, whereas the figure stood at 82.7 percent in 1970. In 1955 only 14.9 percent of the women students went on to higher education, but this increased to 23.5 percent in 1970.[52] By 2002, female enrollment in four-year universities had reached 38 percent. The same year, the female enrollment in two-year private colleges was 89 percent. However, the total enrollment in these colleges has declined.[53]

Women have made great strides in moving up the social ladder at least in education, yet there is still a considerable distance to go before they achieve anything approaching equality. Many women choose to enroll in junior colleges, rather than compete for places in the more prestigious four-year colleges.[54] Many parents are not willing to send their daughters to four-year colleges because they think it would interfere with their marriage plans. Those women who attend college are most likely to major in literature, nursing, or home economics.

The number of female graduates is relatively small, but this is not due to their being denied admission to higher education. Because colleges and universities in Japan are open to women, the limited number of graduates results from the fact that a college degree is of considerably less importance to women than it is to men. Given the nature of the Japanese employment system, education is the most important determinant of job status. But less than 30 percent of Japanese companies will even consider hiring a woman for a managerial or technical position. In the remaining 70 percent of companies, most jobs open to women are as assembly-line workers, secretaries, and clerks.[55] There are also very few women in professions, such as medicine and law.[56]

As far as female employees are concerned, many companies value penmanship, attractiveness, and manners more highly than achievement or skill. Many women work as "office ladies" which consists mainly of serving as a hostess and bringing tea to male workers. In addition to physical attractiveness, the attributes required for this work are grace and charm.[57] The larger companies compete for the best applicants for these jobs. But good looks are not enough. Office ladies must pass a written exam and an oral interview, at which it is not uncommon for them to be accompanied by their mothers.[58] Most of them have high school or junior college education. But advanced university education, especially in technical fields, is not relevant.

Women with limited education or lacking the attributes of office ladies make up a large part of the labor force in light industries, such as textiles and electronics. Still others can find work as waitresses, sales clerks, or elevator attendants.[59] In almost all of these jobs, women employees are considered "temporary." Their temporary or part-time status also means that women do not receive fringe benefits, training opportunities, family and housing allowances, and other income supplements accorded to permanent workers.[60]

One area where women are experiencing expanding job opportunities is with foreign firms. Both Japanese women seeking employment and foreign firms doing business in Japan that need employees face the restrictions imposed by Japan's rigid social system. Japanese men are accustomed to doing business the Japanese way and are reluctant to adapt to the different procedures used by foreign firms. Japanese women are largely frozen out of Japanese business, so they are not rigidly socialized into Japanese business practices. Hence they are less biased and more inclined to learn new ways of doing things, which in turn affords them greater opportunity for getting a better job.

Another major area of employment opportunity for women is in education. Although women make up 50 percent of elementary school teachers, the percentage declines at the higher levels of the educational system.[61] There are few women teaching in universities and colleges and almost none to be found among researchers and scientists. Of course, this pattern is also generally characteristic of Western societies.

Not only are women denied access to top jobs, but they face discrimination in other ways. Although women make up 39 percent of the workforce, their compensation is only 53 percent that of male workers. They are also excluded from many of the training programs necessary for career advancement. They have little job security because most are classified as "temporary." The great majority of women working in factories are younger, single, or in their early years of marriage. They are expected to quit their jobs and stay home when they begin to have children. Even if a woman resisted the social pressures to remain home with her children, to be a working mother entails other obstacles, the most important of which is the lack of child-care facilities. There is a trend for females in their mid-thirties to return to the workforce after family responsibilities have diminished.[62] The rapid turnover of employees keeps wages low, an important factor in Japan's ability to keep prices down and to sell its products on the world market.

The social and economic status of women is changing, but it is doing so at the same slow pace that is characteristic of the rest of society. The Japanese seem little disposed to use the instruments of public policy to accelerate this process. Nor is there an inclination to use the courts to improve equality, despite the fact that the constitution contains major civil rights provisions. Although some litigation has been initiated, women are disinclined to sue their employers for redress of civil rights grievances for two reasons. First, women who are likely to be "troublemakers" will probably not be hired. Second, suing one's employer goes against the grain of company loyalty.[63]

Instead, Japanese women and society in general seem content to accept a pace of social change that corresponds to the transformation of the underlying value structure of the society. Women will experience better employment opportunities when there is a consensus that such would be good for the country. It is not likely to come about through the enactment of laws by the national government.

Politically, women do not constitute an independent political bloc. They do not, for example, vote solidly for candidates who favor "women's issues." Few women are not active in politics, and not many run for elective office, although the number is growing. Moreover, in the elections of the late 1980s and the early 1990s, the gender issue was a factor of some significance. There were more women candidates, and female voters seemed more influenced by the scandals of the time than did male voters. One important development in the late 1980s was the emergence of a new leader of the Japan Socialist Party (JSP)—Takako Doi, a woman who later became speaker of the House of Representatives. These and other developments have only marginally stimulated interest and greater political activity among women.[64]

Political Groups

Political groups whose members share a common commitment to ideological or philosophical systems are few. Organized religion, in the formal Western sense of churches, is not only unimportant in determining political identities but it has little significance in defining social relationships.[65] Although the Japanese have spiritual values, they do not prefer institutionalized religion.[66] Nothing like the Catholic Church, with its considerable political influence in many parts of the world, exists in Japan. A minority of the population belongs to various Christian denominations. Shinto, an ancient religion that entails worship of ancestral deities and reverence for the natural world together with the spirits associated with it, continues to play an important role for some Japanese, although many of its spiritual values are widely shared.[67] The association of Shinto with right-wing ideologies and the authoritarian politics of the 1930s and 1940s diminish its contemporary political significance.

There are several reasons for the weakness of institutionalized religion in Japan's civil society, according to Helen Hardacre. One is the fact that public opinion is negatively politicized toward religion. Another is the rise of and confrontation with Aum Shinrikyō, which produced a strong reaction and tightening of government regulation of religion.[68]

An exception to the limited role of religion in politics is found among some Buddhists. Many Japanese who do not find a home in the established groups of society are attracted to the Value Creation Society (Sōka Gakkai), which was organized in 1930 as a layman's affiliate of the Nichiren Shoshu sect of Buddhism. It became popular after the war and experienced extraordinary growth in membership, appealing especially to housewives and laborers. Its membership includes few professionals, farmers, or persons with high levels of education.[69] The Clean Government Party (Kōmeitō) was founded in 1964 and carries the Sōka Gakkai philosophy into the political arena.

In March 1995, the religious cult Aum Shinrikyō killed twelve people by releasing sarin nerve gas in the Tokyo subway system. Four of the five Aum members who had committed this act were convicted and given the death penalty. The fifth was sentenced to life in prison.[70] This group, basing its theology loosely on Hinduism and Buddhism, was classified as a "criminal religion" in that it committed many acts of violence, often against its own members.[71] Followers of the cult, many of whom were highly educated scientists, apparently were seeking a higher form of spiritual enlightenment than could be found in more conventional belief systems.[72]

There are some right-wing groups, mostly ultrapatriots and holdovers from the war period. These people have been active from time to time and have committed assassinations. They were involved, as was the left wing, in the disturbances that resulted in the cancellation of the visit of U.S. President Dwight Eisenhower in 1960. The right wing is weak for a variety of reasons. For one thing, postwar nationalism has tended to be essentially nonpolitical, stressing instead local customs, family patterns, traditional art forms, and mundane aspects of everyday life.[73] The right also lacks funds and receives little support from the general population. Moreover, the military, which is under firm civilian control and enjoys little popularity, is not looked on as an expression of patriotism. Philosophically, the right wing is out of touch with contemporary reality and is badly divided along ideological and personal lines.[74] Conservative interests, which are often frustrated and alienated in socialist regimes, are not attracted to right-wing causes. The Liberal Democratic Party (LDP) has effectively represented conservative interests, including an expanding constituency that favors a militarily stronger Japan.[75] In general the police have been able to keep track of extremist groups of all persuasions, thus weakening their ability to operate clandestinely.

The cause espoused by the political right was illustrated by a quixotic incident involving Yukio Mishima, a leading literary figure of ultranationalistic persuasions. In November 1970, he tried to persuade members of the Self Defense Force to take over the government by a coup d'état and repeal Article 9 of the constitution. His efforts produced more laughter and derision than enthusiasm. He probably anticipated failure, so in a melodramatic gesture, he staged a suicide in the traditional samurai manner by disemboweling himself, an event that generated considerable interest in the West, perhaps even more than in Japan.

9

The Economy

Japan's postwar economic recovery, and its penetration of international markets during the 1970s and 1980s, was viewed by many as miraculous. This was Japan's second display of rapid industrial expansion and growing technological sophistication; the first was the period of economic modernization during the second half of the nineteenth century. In both instances, Japan's pursuit of economic growth at first attracted little attention from the rest of the world. Japan was thought to pose no significant threat to the economic interests of others.[1] Even Japan's military activities in China during the 1890s and its defeat of Russia in 1905 did little to alter the prevailing view that Japan was only a regional power. But with the victories over Nationalist Chinese, British, French, and American forces in the 1930s and 1940s came the realization that the Japanese challenge to global strategic interests had to be taken seriously. Later, having defeated the Japanese, the world's major powers sought the return of the familiar and comfortable pattern of international relations governed by the promotion of their own self-interests. American patronage of Japan after World War II provided a welcome cloak of obscurity and time to rearrange national priorities. "Washington's tutelary shadow was a convenient screen behind which they could reach the center of the stage without upsetting anyone."[2] But this convenient arrangement could not last forever. Economic exploits in the 1970s and 1980s brought the Japanese once again the full and occasionally hostile attention of the international community.[3]

When Japan embarked on its national development program in the late nineteenth century, it was well positioned to achieve economic growth. As early as a century before the Meiji Restoration in 1868, the expansion of agricultural productivity generated capital, which was then being used for the maintenance of a social order that by the middle of the century had become largely functionless. After the Restoration, the role of the professional warrior class, or samurai, disappeared, along with the feudal system of which it was a part. With the coming of the unified state, revenue used to support the samurai could be redirected into economically productive investment. Moreover, the samurai themselves constituted a pool of manpower, much of it educated and literate, now available for economic and political modernization. "And it may be, then, that the rapid transformation of Japanese society in the Meiji era was in large measure achieved because of the tools, training, education, leadership and experience brought to it by members of the former feudal class."[4]

Despite their basically feudal character, Japan's political and economic institutions were not altogether primitive in the broad organizational sense. The modernization of the 1880s and 1890s was based on significant institutional precedents and substantial human and financial resources.[5] By the mid-nineteenth century, market activities, industrial employment, and commercial ventures had attained a fairly high level of sophistication, providing the foundation for later expansion.

The economic development process was encouraged by political leadership, which recognized not only the need for economic growth but also that such growth was dependent on the maintenance and strengthening of national unity. Stimulated by government policy, commercial and financial organizations developed in the form of several large business houses. Western economic methods were accepted, including the technology of modern industry and the management practices needed to run them. Pursuit of economic modernization and national integration contributed to the development of a vigorous nationalism in which there was a broad popular sharing of national goals.

Japan's developmental experience is distinctive in that very early in the process education was assigned a high priority. Learning was not the preserve of the social elite but was seen as a means to the end of national growth. To achieve this end, education became an integral part of the value system of the Japanese both individually and collectively. As a result, economic demands were met with adequate manpower possessing skills appropriate to sustain economic development.

Japan managed the transition from an agricultural to an industrial economy without experiencing the massive social dislocation that frequently attends this process. Rural poverty and urban unemployment were problems of much smaller magnitude in Japan than in other countries during the early stages of industrialization. The combination of private entrepreneurship and government support led to rapid growth in the manufacturing sector. This meant a corresponding decline in the economic predominance of agriculture during the second half of the nineteenth century. On the eve of World War II, agriculture's share of the gross domestic product (GDP) stood at just 19 percent. Still, the population in the agricultural sector, including forestry and fishing, continued to make up 45 percent of the total number of persons employed. There was a renewed emphasis on agriculture, following the period of industrial decline brought on by World War II. The number of persons employed in farming increased to 53 percent of the population in 1947 but declined again soon thereafter.

The Post–World War II Economy

Japan's economic development after the end of World War II was truly re-markable, especially when viewed in light of the condition of the country at the conclusion of hostilities in 1945.

> The war economy, which had been starved, pounded and beaten virtually to its knees by mid-summer of 1945, came to a standstill upon surrender. There was no longer purpose to ninety percent of end-product output. Oriented wholly for war, facing a completely uncertain future, with no incentive or authority for reconversion to peace-time purposes, silent war plants, desolate of workers, remained only so much economic debris, part to be salvaged for reparations, part to be slowly turned to meet reconstruction needs, and part to rot unused and unprotected from the elements.[6]

After overcoming enormous difficulties during the late 1940s and early 1950s, the Japanese economy began to expand. The gross national product (GNP), which was $1.3 billion in 1946, had increased to $290 billion by 1972 and has continued to increase since. Today, only the economy of the United States exceeds that of Japan in size. But Japan no longer achieves the double-digit growth rates that it once did, and, in fact, the economy experienced contraction in the 1990s.

Not only was the importance of rebuilding war-ravaged economic structures recognized, but emphasis was placed on the introduction of innovative pro-cesses. "The truth of Japan's dizzying climb out of poverty is that, unencum-bered by ideological baggage and having little regard for her own economic history, Japan wrote her own success story. She filled the blank landscape with new institutions and new relationships of her own devising."[7] Spend-ing large sums of money on the frontiers of science was not thought to be in Japan's best interest. The criterion guiding research and development efforts has been the prospect for commercial success, an approach to technological innovation that was influenced by the fact that little capital was available. The Japanese relied on the research and development efforts of other countries and then bought the finished product or process, often at bargain-basement prices, when it had reached a state of significant market potential.

Japan's economic success has been attributed to many factors, ranging from national character to restrictive international trade practices. Each of these different points of view has some merit, but much of the credit for the economic "miracle" goes to a highly skilled labor force committed to hard work and quality products. The very latest technologies have been introduced, giving Japanese industry significant competitive advantages. Japan has not been burdened with a heavy military expenditure, which was 1 percent of GDP during the cold war years compared with 6 percent in the United States. A cohesive national economic development strategy has contributed to growth and has helped to produce a favorable international trade balance.[8] The success of this strategy has been due in large part to the efforts of the government. "Japan's decision-makers have run their country for well over a century now with three objectives: independence, survival, and control—the independence of their country from foreign domination, their own survival as a ruling elite, and their continued control of key economic and political levers."[9]

Economic Characteristics

In broad outline, the Japanese economy has several distinctive features. First, the economy consists of two tiers, which differ significantly from each other.[10] One level is highly sophisticated and is heavily involved in export activity. The second level is oriented toward the domestic market and to the supply of all manner of manufactured components for larger firms such as those in the automobile and electronics industries. This second tier of small and medium-size firms is technologically much less sophisticated than the first although it employs more than 80 percent of the workforce.[11] It is at this level that elements of backwardness and poverty are found in the system.[12] The economy, particularly the second tier, is highly structured and rigid, serving the interests of producers and distributors, not those of consumers. Overall, the economy has not been a hospitable environment for foreign economic interests or foreign competitors.

One of the distinguishing characteristics of the economy is a national strategy that emphasizes capital expansion at the expense of both public and private consumption. The financial resources generated by economic growth have been reinvested to produce further growth. Neither the social infrastructure nor the working public have been prime beneficiaries. Investment in education, welfare, and retirement has not matched the overall rate of growth. Consumers and taxpayers have been burdened with high levels of protection, especially of agricultural products.[13] The high personal savings rate, together with forced savings through high prices, continues today. Richard Katz notes: "Firms took their newfound profits and reinvested them in new factories and equipment. Not the frugality of the Japanese households, but the increased profits of Japanese corporations created Japan's extraordinary national savings."[14]

The emphasis on capital formation has come at the expense of personal consumption; the share of national income received by labor has declined.[15] "The average Japanese was working hard to subsidize exports."[16]

Japan's national development strategy is based on more than good intentions and wishful thinking. It is embraced by an industrial development policy that "involves the government's use of its authority and resources to administer policies that address the needs of specific sectors and industries (and, if necessary, those of specific companies) with the aim of raising the productivity of factor inputs."[17] The goals of this policy include increasing economic efficiency, reducing excess competition, and protecting basic materials production for the domestic economy.[18] Although basic materials have been protected, they have not been made more efficient and they are not competitive at the international level.[19] Japan's economic success led many in the United States to argue that the lack of such an industrial policy placed the American economy at a competitive disadvantage. "Thus, from the perspective of Japanese economic advantage, the individualistic business culture of the United States was the perfect, if unwitting, complement to Japan's corporatist order and nationalistic industrial policy."[20] Until the economic crises of the 1990s, Japanese enterprises were primarily financed with borrowed money, a practice that differed from that found in most other industrialized countries. Whereas Western companies have somewhere around 60 percent equity investment, leaving 40 percent borrowed money, the Japanese had only 20 percent equity and 80 percent debt.[21] This led to a lack of transparency in the flow of information between companies and investors; the relationship between investors (banks) and companies in Japan was private and opaque.[22] This began to change in the 1990s, with more emphasis being placed on stocks and bonds.

This does not mean that banks directly control businesses; rather, it is a reflection of the linkage and interdependence among various economic institutions. Companies also tend to hold substantial shares of each other's stock; independent shareholders are thus not in a strong position to influence the decisions of management. Companies can resist pressure from holders of equity to deliver profits, thus allowing for an emphasis on long-term goals.[23] The payment of dividends to shareholders is not irrelevant; the payment of dividends is critical to the company's ability to raise equity capital. But "when the shareholder's claim to a return on his investment is met by the Japanese company, the shareholder has little or no further voice in corporate affairs."[24]

The reliance on banks for financing has begun to change somewhat. One reason is the banking crisis of the 1990s, which substantially weakened the capacity of banks to make loans. Another reason is the accumulation of "internal wealth" by some of the more prosperous companies, which can serve as their own banks.[25] Even when corporations issue bonds or equity, the purchasers are usually banks.[26]

The relationship between government and business in Japan is functionally much closer than in any other industrialized economy.[27] Although the government does not take a direct role in the management of companies, it does take an active part in shaping and stimulating economic performance. Government-backed credit is used to support capital development, and government is deeply involved in planning.[28]

The government protects industry from foreign competition, especially fledgling industries.[29] Except for a few industries, such as shipbuilding and aluminum, Japan has not confronted major problems of noncompetitiveness.[30] In a few areas, especially aluminum, the government has encouraged reduction in production capacity.[31] Following the 1973 decision by the Organization of Petroleum Exporting Countries (OPEC) to increase the price of petroleum, the Japanese aluminum industry could not compete with countries that possessed their own cheaper sources of energy. As a result, by 1987 aluminum-refining capacity had fallen 97 percent.[32] Downsizing encounters little public opposition because it is perceived as a necessary trade-off in favor of long-term economic growth.

In seeking to explain the rise of Japan to the position of a major economic power, much has been made of the unity among labor, business, and government.[33] "The emergence of government-guided capitalism was one of the two major elements of the new economic order that transformed Japan after the war. The other was a novel style in relations between workers and management. Its essence was an uncommon harmony between them within the structure of the company."[34] The perception of Japan as an economic monolith is expressed in the term "Japan, Inc." One author sees worker involvement in and loyalty to the company as akin to the caste system in India.[35] Although there are very strong elements of group solidarity, the Japanese economy is far from uniform. Lifetime employment and company loyalty, which have begun to disappear, were found only in larger corporations. The employees of small firms have less job security and are less inclined to identify themselves with their place of work.[36]

The importance of top-to-bottom socioeconomic solidarity may be overstated. Of perhaps greater importance to Japan's success is the relative absence of divisive and adversarial relationships. Intraindustrial price competition is minimized thanks to government policy that views this American-favored practice as disorderly.[37] Class-consciousness and conflict over class-related issues are missing. If the tiny portions of the population that are either very rich or very poor are excluded, the distance between the top and the bottom of the earnings pyramid is not great.[38] Japan exceeds almost all OECD countries in equalization of income distribution and is far ahead of the United States. CEO compensation is much less than that in the United States, and management would not give itself millions in bonuses while laying off workers or cutting salaries. Japanese companies prefer to reduce dividends to stockholders than to lay off workers.[39] During periods of economic decline, such as the 1990s, the unwillingness to lay off workers has led to underemployment and excess labor in some industries.

Another reason for the stability of the system is the extent of vertical integration among businesses. The big companies that make cars or electronic equipment rely on hundreds of suppliers that are tightly integrated into a production system. These suppliers are not owned by the larger end-user company, however, but are part of a network of companies all sharing in a productive enterprise. This system works well because there are so few opportunities for stoppages to occur within it. While Japan was experiencing rapid economic growth, Western economies often faced labor problems. American producers had to stockpile parts from suppliers, even those it actually owned, because of potential labor problems.

Finally there is the characteristic that has attracted the most foreign attention: the emphasis on trade. The high priority given to exports in the Japanese economy is a function of economic reality. Most industrial raw materials must be purchased abroad, and to pay for them Japan relies on the sale of its own manufactured goods to other countries. It is not the case, however, that the Japanese economy is totally dependent on trade for its survival. Despite the attention given to exports, the backbone of the economy is the domestic market.[40]

Yet it remains true that prosperity nationwide is tied to the growth in exports.[41] The trade picture is further clouded by the fact that Japan imports heavily from foreign companies that are Japanese owned. Two-thirds of the entire growth in manufactured imports from early 1980s to mid-1990s was from Japanese overseas subsidiaries.[42]

Major Strengths

According to Edward J. Lincoln, Japanese products have often enjoyed price advantages over their foreign competitors for several reasons.[43] First is the Japanese approach to quality control, ironically based on methods developed in the United States. Second, the Japanese took advantage of an inventory control system called "just-in-time production" to reduce costs, a process developed by the Toyota Motor Company in the 1930s. In this process, a manufacturer maintains only enough parts on the production line to keep it running for a short time, as little as one hour. Only about three-fifths of the day's production is kept in stock; the rest is "in the pipeline," so to speak. Third, there is "close cooperation in the movement of new technologies and products from concept to production."[44] Fourth is the cooperative relationship between subcontractors and the corporation. Fifth is an emphasis on continuous change in product design and the processes of manufacturing. Improvements are continuous, rather the result of one major breakthrough.[45] Sixth is a corporate philosophy that places less emphasis on short-term profits than on long-term market share. Finally, there is the substantial worker commitment to the welfare of the company. There are fewer occupational ranks from top to bottom and greater cooperation across functional departments.[46]

Japan enjoys a significant competitive advantage in many product areas because of manufacturing flexibility afforded by the existence of a large number of smaller producers. As a consequence, Japanese producers have been able to effect important product changes more easily than their counterparts in other countries, where greater reliance on mass-production techniques inhibits continuous design modification.[47] This flexibility means that Japanese manufacturers can concentrate on product quality and consumer demand, rather than being limited to a competitive relationship with other manufacturers defined primarily by prices.

Another distinctive feature of Japanese industrial organization is the fact that companies avoid diversification. Unlike American firms, where mergers and acquisitions are common, resulting in conglomerates of companies whose activities are completely unrelated to one another, Japanese companies, even the bigger ones, prefer to limit themselves to a single, clearly defined industry.[48] After 1987, Japan surpassed the United States in industrial expansion and modernization. In 1989, the Japanese spent about $750 billion on capital development, compared with $500 billion for the United States.[49] Some of this investment went into the modernization of traditional industries, such as steel production, enabling the Japanese to compete with producers with lower labor costs, such as South Korea. Other areas of industrial development are particularly relevant to export industries, giving the Japanese important competitive advantages over other countries. Japan established a lead in the development and use of industrial robots, with the result that there were more such cost-cutting tools in use in Japan than in the rest of the world combined. Japan also took the lead over its foreign competitors in areas of computer-controlled manufacturing processes. Automation not only reduces labor costs, but increases product quality and reliability. Such technical achievements are possible, in part, because of the availability of skilled manpower, in particular engineers and technicians. Particular emphasis has been placed on electrical engineering, which has made possible Japan's achievements in the field of consumer electronics.[50]

In response to the Japanese challenge, American manufacturers undertook massive restructuring efforts. Companies shed large numbers of employees in an effort to bring costs down. More sophisticated manufacturing processes were introduced, which not only helped reduce costs further but increased quality. By the 1990s, the beleaguered American automobile industry had rebounded to a point where it could compete with the Japanese, not only on a cost basis but on product quality as well. But by the turn of the millennium, U.S. automakers were again in financial difficulty, due in part to an emphasis on large sport utility vehicles, which became less popular when gasoline prices rose.

Japan has enjoyed an advantage in international trade by virtue of the fact that the world's largest trading companies have been Japanese. This gave them a substantial market penetration capability. The tight linkages among Japanese companies, working through these trading companies, allowed them greater worldwide market access than was typically enjoyed by Western companies.[51]

That some of the world's largest banks have been Japanese has been another economic advantage.[52] After the merger of the Tokyo and Mitsubishi banks in 1995, the Japanese could claim to have the world's largest bank. But the bursting of the bubble economy left Japanese banks with a heavy load of bad debts. Government efforts to prop up the banking industry led to further mergers and restructuring of banking methods. The Japanese also gained control of many foreign banks. In California, for example, the Japanese gained a controlling interest in the state's larger banks. Because of high savings rates and low inflation, banks in Japan have access to a money supply that is cheaper than that available to their foreign competitors.[53] Clyde Prestowitz observes that the Japanese do not fully appreciate the advantages this low cost-of-capital gives them. It "allows managers to concentrate on improving their operations rather than preparing their golden parachutes."[54]

The improved competitiveness of American and European industry changed the market for Japanese producers. They would no longer be able to focus their efforts on increasing their share of global markets. The market-share strategy had succeeded in the past but had come at the expense of profits. To increase profits in the face of Asia's financial difficulties required draconian efforts to reduce costs.[55] Modern economic progress requires substantial investment in the search for new scientific and technological discoveries. The United States has historically spent more on research and development (R&D) than has Japan, but much of that has gone into military-related activity. Half of the American R&D budget comes from the federal government, and half to two-thirds of that goes to military-related research.[56] There is considerable expenditure on space-related research, a source of important innovations. American space technology became increasingly military in its applications during the Reagan years and the emphasis on the Strategic Defense Initiative

(SDI).[57] After the September 11, 2001, attack massive amounts of money were committed to "homeland security" in addition to an expanded military budget.

After the Soviet Union disintegrated in 1989, the U.S. financial commitment to SDI was reduced. In 1994, the new Republican majority in Congress sought to increase spending on the program, which was being continued in its R&D aspects. Because it requires a substantial investment of financial and manpower resources, the Japanese were invited to assume a share of this work. At first, the Japanese were interested not in the military applications of the SDI but, rather, in possible spin-offs of marketable products. After the September 11 attacks, the concept of strategic defense was revived in the form of national and regional missile defense systems intended to defend against rogue states. Tokyo joined the effort after North Korea developed nuclear capability and an effective delivery system.

Research that is "nonmilitary" might produce results with distinctly military applications, however. The Japanese developed a special paint to enhance television reception in high-rise buildings. The nonreflective effect of this paint against electronic waves can also be used as a "cloaking device" on airplanes, hiding them from radar.[58] This technology had great significance for the American "stealth bomber" program.

The Japanese approach to R&D is distinctive in that most expenditure comes from private enterprise and only a small share from the government. This does not mean the government is indifferent to the pattern of R&D expenditures since much of it is in response to government policy.[59]

Major Weaknesses

The heady years of seemingly limitless economic success ended in the 1990s, when major problems developed. Everyone who visits Japan is stunned at the high cost of living.[60] There is a gap between nominal income and purchasing power; Japanese goods are often cheaper in the United States than they are in Japan. The currency realignment that sent the dollar–yen exchange rate from $1:300 yen to one dollar for a little more than 100 yen in 2008 made Japanese goods more expensive abroad but Japan continued to have massive balance-of-payments surpluses.

Another problem is the distortion in financial assets associated with real estate, which is highly overvalued and led to the so-called bubble economy and its ultimate collapse. Adding to the real estate problem is an ineffective and inefficient land use policy, particularly in the form of tax policy. "This is because extremely low property tax rates encourage land holding, high sales tax rates discourage sale of land, and low inheritance taxes on land encourage inheritance in the form of land rather than other types of assets."[61] A major economic problem is the concentration of economic resources in the Tokyo region and their sparse distribution in other parts of the country.[62] In addition to bad loans, the banks had other problems. In 1995, Daiwa Bank in New York was forced to suspend operations because of violations of U.S. banking laws.

Developing weaknesses in the economy have led to calls for liberalization and reform. However, there is as yet no agreement on a new model political economy because of an inability to resolve basic issues regarding what this model should be. Derek Hall suggests that while there is agreement on the need for reform and that this reform should be Japanese in character, there is no agreement on the precise dimensions of such reform.[63]

The Japanese Worker

Rapid economic development after the end of the war was helped by the existence of a reservoir of industrial manpower in the form of underemployed agricultural workers. Here again, the Japanese experience is different from that found elsewhere in the world. Many third world countries also have surplus agricultural labor, but this manpower pool is largely illiterate and lacks the skills necessary for industrial employment. Moreover, Japanese workers have a high incentive to learn new skills and are able to do so thanks to the existence of educational opportunities provided by business and industry.

Among the important factors determining social status in Japan, in addition to education, are age and gender. Of the three, only education is something over which the individual has some measure of control. Nevertheless all of them are significant manpower variables. The rigidities of age differentials that characterize Japanese society would startle Americans used to laws against age discrimination and a powerful political lobby representing senior citizens. Compulsory retirement at fifty or fifty-five is common, and the retirement benefits are relatively modest.[64] This does not mean that workers are just callously thrown on to the human "scrap heap." Retirement does not necessarily mean unemployment, and many workers, especially in the white-collar categories, find other work, although probably at lower pay. Most workers who have retired from larger firms find work in small and medium-size firms, where three-fourths of the workers forty-five and older are employed.[65] There are fewer retirees in Japan than in other industrialized countries, but this will change as a result of the aging of the population.[66] It is also true that pressure from the aging workforce has led to liberalization of retirement policies, and many employees are now retained beyond age sixty.[67]

The circumstances of the workforce had changed in other ways. For one thing, companies are not hiring as many new employees as they once did. Payrolls are reduced by expanding the practice of hiring temporary or part-time workers, who do not receive the same level of benefits as regular full-time employees. "The percentage of 'non-regular' workers that accounted for 18.8 percent of the labor force in 1990 reached 30 percent by early 2005."[68]

The role of women in the workforce has changed greatly since before the war, but it is still an essentially male-oriented system. In this respect, Japan differs from the United States or Western Europe only in degree. Career women are still often perceived as a disruption of company personnel systems. Women normally work while they are single, and two-thirds of married women have jobs, but they typically quit work to have children. A common fixture of Japanese companies is the "office lady," who, in addition to other duties, serves tea to other workers. Although there have been proposals to enact laws granting equal employment opportunity, most managers and many women prefer the existing setup. The unmarried office ladies see their situation as affording the chance to earn spending money and have fun, opportunities that are less likely to be available during marriage, especially while raising a family.[69] They also are free from the pressure-cooker environment facing men, who need to continuously prove themselves and advance in the company.

Work performance and advancement within the system are largely a function of interpersonal relations. Group identity is defined by such criteria as friendship, colleagues, skill categories, and age. Assuming the necessary qualifications and seniority, a worker can expect promotion only if he has cultivated the proper relationship with his superiors. The importance of "pleasing the boss" weakens solidarity among workers collectively in relation to management.[70] The importance of maintaining the goodwill of supervisors is greater for workers in smaller enterprises than for those in the big corporations.[71]

Worker Compensation

The wage structure in Japan stresses length of service, age, and education, plus a variety of allowances, rather than explicit job classification.[72] Basic wages, which vary depending upon the type of work involved, are supplemented by additional allowances for education, housing, family responsibilities, travel to work, increases in the cost of living, and punctuality. Retirement, sick leave, and insurance programs also exist; universal medical insurance was introduced in 1961. Although the level of social welfare spending has increased, benefits received by Japanese workers are not as generous as those enjoyed by workers in the West.[73] One of the most important elements of the wage system is the payment of semiannual bonuses, whose size depends on the profitability of the firm. During the years of rapid growth, the bonuses often amount to several months' basic wages.[74]

Workers also receive extra pay for productivity, plant efficiency, and overtime, which workers typically put in. Other benefits include subsidized meals in company canteens, cheap dorms for single workers, public baths, haircuts, health coverage, athletic facilities, vacation resorts, housing subsidies, and retirement benefits. One advantage of a pay system that emphasizes benefits and add-ons is that it encourages performance. Workers can borrow money from a group co-op, but if they are unable to repay, the company intervenes to straighten out their personal finances. There is considerable involvement of the company in the personal lives of the workers. This is generally not resented since it is viewed by most as constructive.[75] Not only does the employer take an active interest in his workers' personal lives, but so does his wife. She might become involved in discussing the marriage plans of employees or try to help them with personal problems. Most often, the boss's wife directs her activities and interests toward employees' wives.[76]

The Japanese save a very high percentage of their incomes compared to the population in other industrialized countries. Workers must save for their old age because retirement benefits are not sufficient to meet all their needs. Moreover, people save because government policy has not encouraged consumer spending, a factor that contributes to the emphasis on exports.[77] In the 1960s, savings from households plus the surplus of tax revenues over expenditures fueled corporate investment.[78] There are also other incentives to save. As much as 30 percent of total income may come in the form of bonuses, which are perceived as "extra" and thus likely to be stashed in the bank. Although savings have not traditionally been taxed, in 1986 new legislation was passed, which, among other things, began implementation of a policy of taxing interest on bank accounts and encouraging consumption. Japanese savers invest only 10 percent in stocks and mutual funds; most goes into bank deposits, which earn less than 2 percent as of July 2008. This is due not to conservative practices and risk aversion but to the fact that under Japan's system most stocks must be bought in lots of 1,000, which would require a substantial outlay.[79]

Labor has shifted its attention from an emphasis on higher wages to increased leisure time. Many industrial workers make more than their American or German counterparts, but they also work more hours and have fewer opportunities to "enjoy life." This is now changing, with greater emphasis on holidays and benefits.[80] Workers are also becoming sensitive to the higher cost of living in Japan, not a little of which is caused by government subsidies of exports and agriculture. Overall, consumer prices are considerably higher in Japan as they are in the United States.[81]

As the economy continues to grow and the population ages, there is a growing shortage of unskilled and semiskilled labor. Many smaller firms descend into bankruptcy because of their inability to recruit workers. The shortage is being met in part by immigrants, a situation that itself has generated political controversy.[82] The Japanese do not warm to immigration on the grounds that it would be socially and culturally disruptive.[83] Many enter the country anyway, attracted by the possibility of employment. The Justice Ministry estimated that there were 70,000 illegal immigrants working in the country in 1989 and more than twice that many by the turn of the century. Illegal immigrants continue to enter the country at a rate in excess of 10,000 per year. These people take jobs considered unpleasant by the Japanese. Immigrant workers receive half or three-fourths the compensation that a Japanese would receive.[84]

The commitment to a work ethic is so strong among the Japanese that they seem to have little time or much interest in anything else.[85] Beginning in the early 1970s, the five-day, forty-hour work week was introduced, yet today many Japanese continue to work five and a half or six days a week. Even though the forty-hour week did not mean a loss of income for wage earners, it was not universally welcomed, due in part to tradition and particularly to the lack of leisure-time outlets. Many people believed that they would lose their commitment to productive activity if they had another day off. "The extra day of imposed idleness makes the brain too soft," observed one worker. But perhaps the biggest barrier to encouraging the Japanese to work less and play more is the lack of opportunity to take advantage of more time off and the high cost of recreation. The newspaper *Asahi shimbun* observed: "The scope and content of the options available in Japanese leisure are far too limited. The ordinary home is too small to hold weekend parties, and there are no public facilities where citizens can enjoy weekend sports." There are also mundane problems like the lack of babysitters. This commonplace activity by means of which thousands of American teenagers earned their first income is a practice not well received in the Japanese culture.[86]

Not only are Japanese workers industrious, but they constitute probably the most orderly labor force in the world, due to a combination of management philosophy and cultural influences. The Japanese are less inclined to identify themselves by profession or skill but, rather, by the place of employment. Americans would say, "I am an engineer." A Japanese person would say, "I work for Toyota." This tendency has weakened as Japanese workers have become more mobile. Still, Japanese workers' productivity is linked to their immersion in the company.[87] Some view this immersion as a pernicious process designed to intimidate the worker and rob him of his individuality.[88]

In Japan, the incidence of labor disruption is among the lowest of all industrialized countries. The amount of time lost due to strikes measured in thousands of man-days in 1987 was 256 in Japan, 501 in France, 4,606 in Italy, 3,546 in England, and 4,469 in the United States. Moreover, the figure for Japan has continued to decline.[89] This is not to say that there is total tranquility on the labor front. There have been some long and bitter strikes, notably among seamen and railway workers. For the most part, and especially among manufacturing industries, strikes have been mainly confined to the "spring offensive" and have been short and ritualistic in character. These strikes are called when negotiations are in progress and are intended more as a demonstration of labor solidarity than an effort to pressure or threaten management.

The salary system covering both workers and managers does not create the wide disparities in levels of compensation that prevails in the United States.[90] Top executives in Japan rarely receive more than $200,000 a year including benefits. Compensation packages amounting to several million dollars are common among the elite of American business.[91] The pattern of equitable income distribution was threatened during the period of the "bubble economy" of the 1980s, when some people were able to realize substantial sums of money through real estate speculation. Because of the exploding value of real estate, those fortunate enough to own property were able to borrow against the value of their holdings and then invest in the stock market, where sizable fortunes could be made.[92] This produced some resentment among those less fortunate. Most people cannot afford to purchase even a small apartment in a major city. If they do so, it is assumed that their children will pay off the mortgage. This speculative binge collapsed, however, trapping many of the newly rich.

The tranquility of the workplace is the result of not only management practices but also collective psychology. Repeated surveys indicate that workers and managers alike prefer a work environment based on harmonious relationships, rather than one that is "impersonal" and based on objectives and especially skill-related criteria.[93] This "organic" approach to capitalist enterprise stresses the humanistic side of economic activity.[94] It treats the worker as a human being, rather than as an input element of the production process akin to raw materials and machinery.[95]

What is even more significant than the absence of strikes is that production has not been handicapped by disputes over work rules, work conditions, or resistance to technical innovation by labor. The emphasis on automation, which made Japan the world leader in that field, drew little organized resistance from workers.

Lifetime Employment

One of the most widely publicized aspects of the Japanese economy is the system of lifetime employment. In return for this security, the employee makes a commitment to the firm. His success is defined in terms of the company's success, hence he has a strong psychological attachment to it.[96] Traditionally, it has not been common for workers to shop around for better jobs nor have they used offers from one firm as leverage to increase their salary with another.[97] But this practice has eroded significantly. Workers are more inclined to seek better employment opportunities, and employers are less reluctant to lay off unneeded employees. Temporary workers and contract employment are also more common. White-collar employees can be reassigned to the assembly line, and since assembly-line workers are often regarded as temporary, the result gives the appearance at least of avoiding layoffs. Even at its peak, the lifetime employment system did not cover everyone, being limited mainly to larger corporations and the public sector. Small manufacturing and merchandising firms cannot afford the luxury of permanent jobs for their workers, and at this level there is more movement of workers from one employer to another.[98] The lifetime employment system has been subject to strain during times of economic difficulty. After the 1973 oil shock, many firms, including some of the larger ones, were forced to cut staff. In order to minimize layoffs, employees were required to take off uncompensated time. This amounted to loss of income of 10 percent or more for some workers. In other firms workers were required to take "voluntary" early retirement.[99] As a result of these developments, in general "Japan's social protection system is unraveling."[100]

To avoid layoffs in the manufacturing sector, many companies created subsidiaries in the service sector, ranging from hairdressers to restaurants. "These subsidiaries were established less to make money than to absorb excess employees."[101] During the economic downturn of the 1990s, smaller services operations were no longer viable. Such operations have to be subsidized or close down.

Despite the widespread belief that there is, or soon will be, a labor shortage in Japan brought on mainly by the aging of the population, the fact is there is considerable underemployment. Moreover, the economic decline in the early twenty-first century resulted in significant unemployment. But the emphasis placed on education puts workers in a better position to learn a new job. Japanese workers are inclined to spend more time on self-education than do their foreign counterparts. Education is probably the single most important key to success not only in gaining employment but in career advancement.

Although labor–management relations serve the larger social interest of the country, there are some exceptions. Lifetime employment and a wide range of other benefits do not extend to employees of smaller firms. Since mortality among these firms is high, job security is poor, which tends to drive wages down. Unions have had little impact on job protection. Even in large companies, many workers on the fringes do not benefit from the system. Many workers are considered "temporary," even though they might actually work for the firm for long periods. Others retire and are then rehired at lower salaries. In manufacturing, many women are hired on a temporary basis, for low wages, and then released if they marry. Nevertheless, women, particularly older ones, are coming to occupy a more prominent and permanent place in the labor supply.[102] There is, of course, little assertion of individual "rights" of the employee, but that philosophy is not an important element of the social value structure.

Economic growth has benefited Japanese workers, and they expect further rewards. Despite the outward appearance of tranquility, there is much to suggest that the Japanese worker is not altogether happy with his lot. Recent surveys indicate that job satisfaction is low, although manifestations of this, such as absenteeism, are missing. Younger workers' commitment to the traditional values of loyalty, competitiveness, and hard work is weaker than that of their predecessors.[103] The notion is becoming more prevalent that hard work does not necessarily result in an improved lifestyle. Japanese workers produce things not for themselves, but for foreigners.[104]

Japanese Management

It has become nearly an article of faith that Japanese methods can work wonders in running industrial and commercial enterprises. Yet the firms that are regarded as models of this approach are invariably exceptional. Not all Japanese companies are so well off or so well run. Moreover, many Western companies are as well managed as the best Japanese firms.[105]

Japanese business has little use for the inspired amateur with a general education. Instead, the pattern is one of systematic training in the disciplines relevant to work being done. A majority of those in higher authority in business and industry have an education in science and technology. Most of the seats on the boards of directors of leading companies are occupied by professional engineers and individuals educated in some branches of applied science.

Managers are not only well trained in the technique of their occupation but are also emotionally involved in the fortunes of their firms to an extent seldom seen in the West. They are often so completely devoted to the business they serve as to leave little scope for private social activities other than those in which they are associated with fellow managers. A precise definition of responsibilities is superfluous since every member is first and foremost a member of a team that identifies itself with the firm's interest.

Management defines corporate interest in much broader terms than is generally true in the West, where profit is the main preoccupation. There is a greater concern for ensuring long-term viability and market share, not just short-term profits.[106] The health of the firm is seen in the general context of

the national welfare, rather than the other way around. "The [Japanese company] is not simply an economic institution, but is a deeply social institution, working out its destiny in a competitive economic environment."[107] The government is not there to be exploited, nor is it perceived as a threat, depending on circumstances, but as a partner. Overall management philosophy stresses public good over private gain. Individual self-aggrandizement is certainly not part of this philosophy, as reflected in the fact that top Japanese executives make considerably less than do their American counterparts.[108] Indeed, in the Japanese view, the high level of compensation received by American executives is one of the shortcomings of American business.

The Role of Exports

National prosperity has been linked to the maintenance of a perpetual balance-of-payments surplus. This has been achieved by Japan by selling more abroad than it buys—a highly satisfactory arrangement for the United States, which regularly buys more than it sells abroad. "The importance of the current account surplus is so imbedded in the thinking of Japan's decision makers that to secure it they have been willing to sacrifice much of the prosperity that could otherwise have been theirs. They have seen to it that the surplus was not consumed domestically; instead, they have invested it overseas, where it finances the deficits of trading partners."[109] Japan accepts payment not in gold or yen but in dollars, "a currency that has lost two-thirds of its purchasing power over the past three decades."[110] These dollars are then recycled back to the United States to fund additional imports.

The Japanese economy in general and the employment system in particular are not immune to the changes that are affecting other countries. The tremendous pressures exerted on Japan by its trading partners produced adjustments in the domestic economy. For certain sectors of the economy, these adjustments were traumatic. Major dislocations at the international level, such as the Asian currency crisis in the late 1990s, have made economic transformation all the more painful. Some observers see the process as being more than just painful. One of the less optimistic forecasts suggests that

> Japan will be a society composed of a large number of workers who are
> equalized in a corporate hierarchy regardless of age and educational back-
> ground. They will be controlled by a lesser number of real business elites
> who have survived hard competition in climbing up to their position. . . .
> To the average Japanese white collar worker, the company will no longer
> be a community based on paternalism and familism, but an arena of fierce

competition with fellow workers, not only in terms of actual performance but also in potentialities and overall quality as a human being. This is an inevitable consequence for Japanese management if they are to prosper in the new global economic order.[111]

Another observer saw Japan facing "wrenching economic and social decisions in the next few years—decisions that will determine its economic direction for years to come."[112] These dismal forecasts are based on the proposition that Japan's economic security relies on its enormous trade surpluses, which are bound to end as a result of international pressure. Trade restrictions imposed by Japan's trade partners and the substantial decline in the value of the dollar will force the Japanese to consume more of their own products or face serious economic problems. By the turn of the century, the gloomy prognoses seemed to have come to pass, as Japan endured a prolonged economic slump. Despite the weak dollar, the pattern of huge trade surpluses in Japan's favor continued due to the buying power of the U.S. economy.

What is it that keeps Japan from being an "open" trade partner? The Japanese often argue that the United States has more formal tariff barriers than they do. Formal tariff barriers are out of fashion, so the main obstacle to imports into Japan is procedural.[113] Included are practices that have existed so long that they would be difficult to change. One such procedural constraint is the government's power over businesses, ranging from control over finances and taxes to the issuance of licenses. Given this power, the government offers "administrative guidance" to businesses regarding the nature and quantities of imports.[114] This guidance is the product of domestic political and economic concerns, not market forces such as consumer demand.

Lengthy and cumbersome customs procedures are another aspect of the system that increase costs and delays to importers.[115] The Japanese often insist on their own standards, testing, and certification procedures, duplicating, in many cases, those employed in other countries. In the interest of promoting a national development policy, the government purchases from domestic producers even though the costs may be higher than those of foreign sources. Under the law, depressed industries are given preferential and protective treatment. At the other extreme, promising but often risky high-tech industries are cultivated and protected by the government.[116] Foreign applications for patents are sometimes delayed for as long as ten years, allowing Japanese producers time to develop the process or idea to the point of commercial viability. Finally, the distribution system in Japan is notoriously complicated, making it difficult for importers to gain access.[117] A law, only recently modified (the Large-Scale Retail Store Law), requires neighborhood approval, meaning small shop owners, before any store larger than 600 square yards can open.[118]

As a result, few large supermarkets, whose capacity to buy in volume allows for considerable saving to the consumer, are found in Japan.

In April 1998 the Diet approved a proposal to replace the Large-Scale Retail Store Law with the Large Store Location Law. The intention was to make it easier to open large stores. But groups representing small retailers criticized the proposal and, due to fears that the LDP would suffer at the polls, the final version bowed to these interests.[119]

The government restricts competition and protects small stores through a labyrinth of licensing requirements. As recently as the 1990s, more than three-fourths of retail outlets in Japan employed four or fewer workers, compared with slightly under 45 percent in the United States. Opening a supermarket requires forty-five different licenses, and 200 pages of applications under nineteen different laws. "This includes separate applications to different agencies for licenses to sell meat, fish, milk, bread, tofu, pickles, ice cream, cakes, tea, frozen foods, box lunches and so forth."[120]

Japanese consumers continue to subsidize their American counterparts as well as the Japanese manufacturers, who depend on high domestic prices to stay in business. Construction costs, cement and steel prices, and insurance rates are high but the profits are reinvested in business. Efforts to change this situation through trade negotiations and regulatory reform meet with limited success. "Fears of economic dislocation and unemployment seem to outweigh concerns about efficiency losses due to the high price of goods."[121]

Japan's approach to managing the economy differs significantly from European or American practices. The Japanese favor regulatory mechanisms and restraint of competition. The Europeans have used state ownership of industry and have undertaken major efforts to redistribute income. Americans have preferred legal efforts to promote competition and prevent restraint of trade together with rate setting, although the latter is less used today.[122]

The formal rules governing economic activity prohibit collusion, price-fixing, and similar activities. Nonetheless, cartels exist in many areas of the economy that engage in precisely these activities. Cement and construction are notable examples of price rigging through trade associations. The activities of these associations are technically in violation of the law but they are tolerated and even encouraged by the government. The associations impose penalties on companies that refuse to go along with the rigging of contracts. The government ignores such activities.[123]

An area of frequent and intense dispute between Japan and its trading partners concerns agricultural products. There are two major constraints limiting the Japanese government's ability to be a more accommodating trade partner in this area. The first is the considerable political influence wielded by the agricultural community. In the wake of economic recovery after the war, the rural population declined in both numbers and economic influence. Today only a small portion of the population is engaged in farming, and many are part-timers who receive only a portion of their income from farming. Agriculture's share of GNP is only 3 percent. Yet farmers' consistent support for the LDP earned them the party's gratitude and protection from foreign competition. For example, the government buys rice and sells it to traders at fixed prices that are ten times higher than those of American-grown rice and seven times higher than those of rice grown in Thailand.[124] In the late 1980s agricultural imports increased, but the hostility this produced among farmers and the political difficulties confronting the LDP led to retrenchment. Even in the political shakeup of 1993, political parties did not attempt to broaden their popular appeal by offering themselves as champions of the consumer. The Hosokawa government did permit rice imports but only because there was a serious shortfall in domestic production.[125]

The second barrier to liberalized agricultural trade is the support for agricultural industry by the public and its apathy regarding the high cost of food. Restrictive agricultural trade policies endure because of the general political consensus on the need for a stable and guaranteed food supply, even if this means paying higher prices than those on the world market. Protectionism continues because consumers have not objected to paying more, nor have taxpayers rebelled over budget deficits and tax subsidies for agriculture.[126] Consumers are not inclined to blame farmers for high prices. Consumer advocacy groups do favor lower prices, but not at the farmers' expense. The public tends to favor government subsidies for producers to lower costs to consumers and to protect the farmer's livelihood.[127]

The privileged status of agriculture is changing. The United States has demanded for years that Japan open its domestic market to more American agricultural products. Although this is happening at a pace maddeningly slow for Americans, it is being done. After years of stalling, the Japanese finally opened their market to American apples. Moreover, the political influence of agriculture may be declining. The new electoral system ending the multiple-member district arrangement that benefited the LDP and agriculture gives greater voice to urban voters. But perhaps more important than changes in electoral dynamics is a growing awareness among urban wage earners that they are paying heavily to subsidize farmers. By reducing the amount of money they pay for food, urban families could spend more on other products thus enhancing their lifestyle.

Meeting the Challenge

The Japanese were able to achieve extraordinary economic growth during the 1950s and 1960s. They unnerved Americans and Europeans and seemed poised to become the world's number one economy. But by 1973, Japan had turned suddenly into an "underachiever."[128] Japan's economic success during the period of high growth was the result of a combination of industrial policy and poor economic performance in Western countries. Striving to meet the Japanese challenge, countries in the West, especially the United States, restructured their economies and increased efficiency. By the end of the century, the Japanese business model, which had come to be envied worldwide, was seen as a liability. Japanese firms lacked creativity and competitiveness and were thus at a disadvantage in an increasingly globalized economy. "Interestingly, however, this debate was more a feature of western analysis of Japanese management and less in evidence within Japan itself."[129]

The Japanese were faced with a problem of their own making. Industrial policy calling for support of selected industries lured more companies into that industry than could be supported. But, having backed that industry, the government could not permit failure. Allowing the weak to fail in order to strengthen the industry "was considered a violation of an implicit social contract, a source of disorder and confusion."[130]

The Japanese strategy for meeting the challenges posed by the changing international economic environment is multifaceted. Changes include the shift from energy-intensive industries, which are being moved to other countries with lower labor costs, to knowledge-intensive activities. The Japanese are moving away from the practice of allowing others to pioneer high technology by engaging in this type of R&D themselves. Greater efforts are being made to integrate Japan into the world economy while, at the same time, retaining Japan's leading role in it.[131]

The Japanese have maintained their share of world markets by emphasizing quality rather than price. This strategy is becoming harder to sustain because of the increasing value of the yen. Still, foreign consumers have developed loyalty to Japanese products and are willing to pay more for their cars or electronic goods comfortable in the knowledge that they are getting their money's worth, even at higher prices. Many Japanese manufacturers have been very successful in developing strong consumer loyalties to their products. In 2008, Toyota had become the world's largest manufacturer of motor vehicles and was an innovator in the marketing of fuel-efficient hybrids. The American flagship automobile company, General Motors, teetered on the edge of bankruptcy.

The emphasis on automation has allowed Japanese manufacturers to remain competitive on price even in the face of the rising value of the yen. Automation, of course, puts pressure on the employment system to create alternative job opportunities or, if there is unemployment, encourage early retirement. At one of Hitachi's plants, the time required to assemble a videocassette recorder was reduced from three minutes to 1.7 minutes by the introduction of robots. By so doing, the number of workers was reduced from thirty-three to four.[132] The Japanese are able to achieve these results without creating unemployment and labor unrest in part because the population growth rate is only 0.6 percent. More significantly, the median age is increasing. Together this means there are fewer people in the labor pool looking for jobs than is the case in other countries.

Another approach to maintaining competitive advantages is to move industry out of Japan into either low-labor-cost countries or into consumer countries. This process, which exports industrial capacity from Japan, has been dubbed "hollowization" It keeps Japanese companies in strong internationally competitive positions, but it reduces the amount of wealth and jobs created within Japan. "Most of those imported TV's, for example, are made by Japanese companies in Southeast Asia. Clearly such 'captive imports' (called 'reverse imports' by MITI) are not positioned or priced to challenge the cartelized price and industry structure at home. Japan has an unfortunate pattern. When imports are unavoidable, the approach is: buy the foreign producer, not the foreign product."[133]

Imports, however, have not resulted in significant structural changes in Japan's noncompetitive industries. Despite talk of hollowization, domestic production has been replaced by imports in only a few areas, specifically aluminum smelting, apparel, and, to a lesser extent, lumber and furniture.[134]

The Japanese are also trying to anticipate the demands and needs of the future by developing key innovative industries. To date these have included semiconductors, robotics, computers, office automation, telecommunications, pharmaceuticals, and biotechnology. The strategy has been clearly successful only in the first two areas and marginally so in the others. The Japanese got into mainframe computers just when the industry was shifting to smaller personal models.[135] Despite American gains in the semiconductor industry, Japan is likely to continue to pose a competitive challenge to the United States in many aspects of computer technology.[136] In the other areas, Japan is generally behind its competition and its protectionist stance creates antagonism.

Finally, a new approach began to manifest itself during the late 1980s. For years the Japanese passively accepted foreign criticism of its economic practices. But as Americans became upset over purchases of companies, ball teams, and real estate by Japanese investors, their attitude changed. Increasingly, the Japanese view the United States as behaving irrationally. Choice properties are put up for sale, and when the Japanese buy them, often paying premium prices, they are faulted for it.[137] Since Americans do not display a similar concern over European investment, the Japanese have concluded that the problem may have a cultural foundation. Accordingly, they have begun to expand their cultural diplomacy by, among other things, financing Japanese studies in American schools.[138] The Japanese have also begun to speak out more, being less defensive of their own practices and more critical of those of other countries.

The Post-Bubble Economy

The bubble economy was brought about largely because of speculation in the stock and real estate markets. These collapsed, leading to a prolonged period of economic stagnation. The economy was saddled with a mounting national debt, a systemwide financial crisis, and currency instability. The shrinking value of assets made it difficult for borrowers to obtain loans, and many existing loans backed by these assets became nonperforming, thus limiting the ability of financial institutions to lend. Problems were exacerbated by the government's erratic fiscal policy.[139]

The bad debt problem was due in no small measure to corruption. Favored investors, including politicians, bureaucrats, and organized crime, "received guarantees of high positive rates of return on their equity portfolios."[140] Small business received loans to speculate in stocks and real estate. "These scandals implied that the bubble and its aftermath involved more than just a simple speculative mistake that could hit any economy. The causes included extensive unethical and corrupt behavior within the existing system—behavior that was difficult to detect until outright corporate failure revealed an inner rot."[141]

In 2007, the U.S. housing market was hit by a financial crisis brought on by the proliferation and securitization of "subprime mortgages." When home buyers confronted payment requirements that they were unable to meet, mortgage default rates began to rise and property values to fall. Mortgage companies sank and the ripple effects then spread to banks and on through the increasingly globalized financial system. Japan had a somewhat similar problem in the 1990s, when housing loan companies, called *jusen*, made loans based on inflated land values. After the bubble burst, the loans could not be repaid. The government used public money to liquidate the failed jusen. "It was widely seen as a means of covering up the greed or ineptitude of government bureaucrats, elected officials, mobsters, LDP-connected farming cooperatives and banking corporations."[142]

One area where collusion and profiteering take place is in the construction industry. Construction costs in Japan are very high due to collusion among bidders. In order to spread the wealth, they agree in advance on which company will win the contract, freezing out foreign bidders, whose bids may be as much as 45 percent lower than those of Japanese companies. According to Katz, "construction lies at the heart of Japan's daisy-chain of inefficiency."[143]

The close relationship between the construction industry and the LDP led to considerable overconstruction, especially in office buildings.[144] After the collapse of the bubble economy, rents for these buildings dropped sharply, making it difficult for owners to pay back the bank loans that had been taken out to fund their construction.[145]

The banking crisis proved particularly intractable due in part to its magnitude but also to the lack of political will to fix it. Insurance companies were also hard hit because they invested heavily in banks.[146] From 1998 to 2002, the government spent 10.433 trillion yen on failed financial institutions, leaving 8.7 trillion yen remaining in bad loans.[147] Banks also made bad loans for foreign purchases. In 1993, a group of Japanese banks led by Mitsubishi Bank sold the Hyatt Regency Wakoloa resort hotel in Hawaii to a Hilton Hotels subsidiary for 25 percent of the construction costs.[148]

The Ministry of Finance (MOF) took a conservative approach to the bad debt problem. Rather than risk a shakeout that would eliminate weaker financial institutions, the MOF kept them afloat to avoid the ripple effects of bankruptcies and unemployment. One MOF approach to restoring profitability was to encourage banks to pursue overseas investment.[149] But as banks moved to eliminate their nonperforming loans, they continued to make bad loans, thus leaving the basic problem more or less intact.[150] The result weakened not only the reputation of the MOF but that of Japanese banks, whose international ratings declined.[151]

Throughout the 1990s, Japan seemed unable to climb out of the economic doldrums. One problem was the Asian financial crisis, which affected not only the weaker economies, such as Indonesia, but also the Asian tigers, such as South Korea. Despite changes in the electoral system and the advent of non-LDP governments, economic reform proceeded at glacial speed.[152] The economic system that had allowed Japan to catch up with and even surpass the West had become obsolete by the turn of the century.[153]

By 2006, economic conditions were improving, thanks to export growth and progress in restructuring the corporate and banking sectors. Public debt, however, continued to grow, reaching the highest level among advanced industrialized countries, as measured by percentage of GDP. Japanese education, despite its problems, continues to produce a population with the skills necessary for a modern economy. Another positive sign is the continued high expenditure on R&D.

The aging of the population is a continuing worry. Without substantial immigration, the size of the workforce will shrink, and the Japanese are not enthusiastic about immigration. Workers can realize some benefits by postponing retirement. The labor pool can be expanded by increasing the number of women in the workforce. In addition, underemployment and worker inefficiency are problems that should also be addressed.

There were mixed economic signals at near the end of the first decade of the twenty-first century. The shake-out from the burst bubble continued, with land prices still falling.[154] A positive sign was the decline in the rate of unemployment to 5.1 percent, the lowest in two years. However the value of the yen increased in relation to the U.S. dollar, making Japanese exports more expensive. Overall, the economy continued to navigate the slow road to recovery.[155]

Part IV

Public Services

10

Education and Health Care

Among the most important needs of society are intellectual renewal and physical well-being. These issues are dealt with in turn in this chapter.

As part of society's continuous regeneration, new members are inculcated with the customs, traditions, rules, and values peculiar to their cultural milieu. The importance of technology today places additional demands on the process of intellectual renewal: expanding ability to generate and interpret information. Such ability requires not only the skill of literacy but technical and substantive knowledge as well. The responsibility for both socialization and imparting skills rests primarily on the education system. Japan's rise to international prominence is attributable, in part, to its education system. This system has produced students who perform at or near the top on basic skills tests, resulting in not a little envy elsewhere in the world.

Japan's health-care system is another a source of envy, as the Japanese have one of the highest life expectancies in the world. The health-care system is also among the least expensive, certainly in comparison to the United States, and the most accessible. However, costs will necessarily go up as the median age of the population increases.

Education and the Social System

Societies differ in their social and cultural characteristics. People locate themselves within their social landscapes in many ways: class, caste, tribe, religion, and race are the more common criteria. Although it is by no means completely homogeneous, these kinds of social distinctions have less significance in Japan than in many other countries.

Class consciousness and class status play a limited role in social and political life. About 90 percent of the population consider themselves middle class. Even those who view their occupational status as "working class" think they are socially in the "middle" of the social hierarchy.[1] Race is important only to the extent that the small minority of the population that is not Japanese is discriminated against. Institutionalized religion is of limited significance in shaping social processes.

An important factor in defining social status in Japan is education. The amount and type of educational achievement and the formal examinations that are a measure of it help determine location in the social hierarchy.

Theoretically, if education serves to define social status, and since it is something that can be acquired rather than inherited, then it should be an avenue for movement from lower social status to higher social status. In the real world of Japan, however, such opportunity is limited. The problem is that access to educational opportunity is generally not available to those who would most benefit from it to improve their social status. An individual's educational opportunities are constrained by social position. An important predictor of educational attainment is family. Thus, it is unlikely that a member of a family with low educational status attainment can change his or her social position by gaining the "right kind" of education. But it is likely that a person from a family with high-status educational background will acquire the same kind of education as have other members of the family.

The importance of education in the social order began to develop during the period of modernization in the nineteenth century. The most up-to-date approaches to education were introduced during the Meiji period when a new system, which departed radically from traditional education, was introduced. Based on contemporary French models, the new system was contained in the Fundamental Code of Education, introduced in 1872. A three-tiered educational arrangement was created, consisting of primary, middle, and university levels. By 1886, three or four years of primary schooling were becoming compulsory. Four years were made a national requirement in 1900, and primary education was free. The standard was increased to six years in 1908. The long-standing commitment to education has produced a literacy rate that approaches 100 percent.

As Japanese society became more affluent after 1868, demands for educational opportunities increased. More people sought to improve their educational qualifications in order to acquire better jobs. A powerful social expectation developed linking education to superior employment opportunities. Implementing this link required a process to measure educational performance objectively. What emerged was a system of standardized examinations. Performance on these tests determined not only the student's educational future but the range of employment opportunities as well. The education system up to and including the university level had a distinctly vocational quality about it. The process was highly selective and afforded only the narrowest opportunity for social and economic mobility. Education did not necessarily mean greater opportunity to move upward in social status, but the lack of education nearly guaranteed downward mobility.

In the late nineteenth and early twentieth centuries, educational philosophy was an integral part of a tightly knit sociopolitical system revolving around the emperor. Since a high premium was placed on loyalty in this system, education was called on to provide rigorous socialization.

In an effort to promote orthodox beliefs, the Ideological Control Bureau was created in 1934, followed by the Nationalism Instruction Bureau in 1937. To promote a proper public orientation toward the state, the Research Institute for National Spirit and Culture and an Education Reform Council were created. These efforts were augmented during World War II by even more vigorous attempts to promote ideological orthodoxy. Emphasis on intellectual conformity fell heavily on education.

Education underwent fundamental transformation after the war ended. As part of their commitment to change Japanese society away from its imperial roots and toward democracy, the U.S. occupation authorities applied themselves to an overhaul of the process and substance of Japanese education. The philosophy behind this undertaking contained three basic principles: equal opportunity, broad knowledge aimed at personal enlightenment, and respect for academic freedom and autonomy. The indoctrination aspect of education was one of the main areas receiving the attention of occupation authorities. Their objective was to make the education system more supportive of democratic values and practice. To this end, centralized control of education was ended, and authority transferred to elected school boards at the prefect and major city levels. American educational ideas and philosophies were introduced, curriculum was revised, and textbooks rewritten. The pattern was reversed beginning in 1954, when the Diet passed legislation curtailing the political activity of teachers and their unions.

The Education System Today

The contemporary system consists of four levels: the primary (grades 1–6), which is compulsory, the lower secondary (grades 7-9), which is also compulsory, the upper secondary (grades 10–12), and higher (college and university). The curriculum, at least through high school, is very demanding. The Japanese school year is longer than its American counterpart. Until recently, Japanese students attended school five and a half days a week, from September 1 to July 20.

Students are socialized into a process of intense group involvement early in the educational experience. Students sit in the same seat, in the same classroom, with the same classmates and teacher for long periods of time. The bonds of group solidarity are further strengthened by student participation in school routines, such as cleaning classrooms and serving lunch. Students scrub floors and wash windows, promoting the spirit of teamwork and psychological identification with the institution. Students take turns serving meals to their classmates, a practice intended to promote mutual self-respect. This means that students are assessed not only in their academic work but in all aspects of their behavior. "Today, the web of control in Japanese schools is so systematic that it is extremely difficult for students to escape."[2]

Although the rate of school attendance is high and the dropout rate is low, the situation has begun to change in recent years. Students are less engaged in school, and many are leaving early. This is probably a reflection of the erosion of traditional values and culture. The education system is structured hierarchically, not necessarily in terms of quality but in terms of prestige, which is measured by the employment prospects awaiting graduates.[3] The academic hierarchy and the employment hierarchy closely parallel each other.[4] At the apex of the pyramid are the great national universities, especially Tokyo University. There are also elite high schools whose students have a good chance of going on to one of the top universities. Interestingly, competition to gain admission at the top-level schools, where applicants roughly equal spaces available, is not as intense as at the middle level, where there may be as many as eight applicants or more for each opening.[5] At the next level are the better private universities and the elementary, middle, and high schools affiliated with them. Unlike the better public institutions, however, these are expensive, catering only to the financially well off. Nearly two-thirds of all universities are located in the Tokyo metropolitan area, as are most important government agencies and business headquarters. Next are the public and private institutions, whose reputation is lower than that of the elite schools. At the bottom are public elementary and high schools attended by students of limited economic means or those unable to gain admission elsewhere. Unlike the other institutions, this latter category of schools does not require entrance examinations. Their graduates do not typically go on to higher education, entering instead one of the many vocational education and training institutions followed by employment in commerce or industry.[6]

The Ministry of Education determines the content of curriculum and chooses which textbooks can be considered for adoption. The issue of textbooks has been especially controversial. The Ministry of Education controls the content of textbooks through a three-step process. Writers first submit their manuscripts to the Ministry of Education, which, if it sees merit in them, sends proofs to around 800 scholars, teachers, and professors, who render an appraisal and an opinion. The manuscript is then reviewed by about forty Ministry of Education officials, after which it is sent to a committee of twenty private citizens appointed by the ministry. In the case of history textbooks, these citizens have often held very conservative views.[7] The entire range of social studies material is subject to an ideological screening, but so are textbooks in math, physical science, music, and art. Local school boards make selections from the approved list for use in the various courses. Many critics see this process as pernicious. "It is important to observe that these unjustified interventions in the educational process constitute one of the most serious problems plaguing postwar Japanese education."[8]

This process was challenged in court on the grounds that it violates constitutional freedoms. In a decision handed down March 19, 1986, the Tokyo High Court ended a twenty-year legal battle over the issue of government control of the content of textbooks. The court found that such control does not violate constitutional guarantees of academic freedom and freedom of expression. This decision also had international ramifications. It contributed to Chinese and Korean concerns that the Japanese government was seeking to rewrite history and soften language describing Japanese atrocities during World War II.

A number of changes were made in the education system beginning in 2002. The curriculum was reduced by about a third, and the school week shortened to five days. More emphasis was placed on developing learning in the broad sense, rather than the usual exam-driven process. Universities were given greater flexibility in determining administrative and educational goals. Not all of these reforms were welcomed by the educational community, especially the five-day week. The overall result has been a general decline in academic standards and achievement.

With the shortened school week, less material can be covered and the pace of instruction has slowed. The reforms were intended, in part, to address the problems of school violence and nonattendance. But they do not appear to have had that affect. Top students continue to do well, but the performance of middle- and lower-level students has declined.[9]

Literacy

The achievement of near-universal literacy and high levels of educational performance, at least as measured by standardized exams, are not attributable to lavish financial support. Japan does not rank among the leaders in expenditure on education when compared to other developed countries. The most important influence in shaping overall educational attainment is a general social value and expectation that everyone will be able to read. Another factor is intellectual discipline and commitment on the part of students. In general, Japanese students take their schooling seriously. There is also the pressure of the examination system, which tends to focus the mind and concentrate efforts. Even if Japanese students have neither great intellectual curiosity nor a commitment to learning for its own sake, they will try hard in order to avoid the embarrassment of a poor showing.[10]

Curriculum

The high rate of literacy and educational attainment in general are due in no small measure to the fact that nearly all students have the same native language. In all education systems, teaching language is the first task of the schools. Although Japan does not have to carry the added educational burden of multilingualism, teaching language is complicated by the fact that Japanese is written in more than one script. The Ministry of Education has adopted a standard vocabulary of 1,850 Chinese characters, called *kanji*, about half of which are learned in elementary school and the rest later. These characters involve as many as twenty strokes and require memorization, unlike a phonetic alphabet, in which words can be "sounded out." (Although it is linguistically different from Chinese, Japanese traditionally was written using Chinese characters.) There are two other scripts, *hiragana* and *katakana*, that are used for grammatical reasons and for writing foreign words. Each of these has forty-eight symbols. Typically, Japanese children are able to read in these scripts before they enter the first grade.[11] The Latin alphabet is also used to write proper names and in the many English and other European-language books that are available in Japan. Arabic numbers are used, as is a Japanese system of numbers.

The curriculum emphasizes math and science, and Japanese students have compared favorably in those subjects with their counterparts around the world. Although students are expected to memorize a vast amount of material, not all learning is by rote. There is also hands-on education stressing experience, observation, and experimentation.[12] There is a popular adage that a student who has more than four hours of sleep a night will definitely not get into one of the top colleges.

The education system is geared to the passing of examinations. "No single event, with the possible exception of marriage, determines the course of a young man's life as much as entrance examinations, and nothing, including marriage, requires as many years of planning and hard work."[13] Examinations occur in the course of regular schooling and, most importantly, are decisive in gaining admission to the more prestigious high schools and universities. Students begin preparing for these examinations as early as the primary grades or even before. Those students who have the aptitude, and of course many do not, hope ultimately to pass the entrance examination to one of the top universities. Each university has its own examination, so failing one means that a student may try for another. The examination may also be retaken, which many do hoping to gain admission to the institution of their choice.

Until high school, students are treated more or less equally. It is common for students of all ability levels to be in the same class, following the same pace of instruction. Teachers and parents do not accept the notion that there are fundamental differences in ability among students. Differences in performance are seen as the result not of aptitude but of a lack of effort by students, teachers, and parents. Treating everyone equally in this way reflects the Japanese trait that seeks to avoid calling attention to oneself. Identifying "slow learners" in order to place them in a learning environment suited to their capabilities would be resisted by students and parents. This approach means also that no one fails or must repeat a grade because of poor performance.[14] Fast-track approaches or special programs for the "gifted" also are missing for the same reasons. The overall performance is quite high; only a few are passed through the system without having learned much along the way.[15]

From high school on, the stress is on merit in a process designed to identify the most gifted and highly motivated.[16] The egalitarian approach to education gives way to a rigorous sorting process, in which students are grouped together on the basis of ability, motivation, and job orientation. After ninth grade, students take examinations that funnel them into senior high schools and vocational schools of varying quality. Students may have to travel some distance from home in order to attend the school of their choice. Grades and teacher recommendations count, but the most important factor is the entrance examination. Not all students, of course, are "driven" by the desire to achieve high educational status; only about 10 percent have such aspirations.[17] For the rest, school is a less trying experience.

Standardized examinations do not stress creative or interpretive ability but, rather, test analysis and recall of specific information. There is also considerable emphasis on math and natural science problem solving. Many of the better high schools rush through the prescribed curriculum in two years and devote the entire senior year to review of material likely to be on the examinations. Examinations from previous years are studied to provide guidance on how best to prepare. There are even entrance exams for vocational schools, such as those for cosmetology, which have or would like to have good reputations.[18]

Why Do Students Work So Hard?

Concern for the future of their children often leads parents, especially mothers, to considerable effort and expense to ensure admission to the best schools.[19] This begins as early as kindergarten or even before. Mothers have even been known to attend school to take notes for their children who have fallen ill.[20] It is widely assumed that gaining admission to the better kindergartens is all-important because it can insure success later. Demand for admission to the better kindergartens is so great that examinations and other criteria may not be enough to decide who gets in. In some cases, a lottery is needed.[21] In one instance, unable to devise an exam for two-year-olds, preschool authorities decided to determine the children's abilities by testing the mothers instead.[22]

Homework is sometimes so difficult that students cannot do it alone. Mother's are called on for help. As a result mothers are inextricably involved in their child's education.[23] Success or failure reflects on the parents and teachers as well as the child. In the event of poor performance, parents and teachers may receive as much as, or more criticism, and embarrassment, than the student.

Preparation for the exams has spawned a lucrative industry in cram schools called *yobikō* and *juku*. The government recognizes many yobikō, and the larger ones may have as many as 35,000 students in their branches. The juku are smaller, privately run operations, usually with a neighborhood clientele.[24] There are three types of such schools. The first, the most elite, has as its sole purpose to train children to pass the examinations. There are even special schools to train three- and four-year-olds for kindergarten examinations.[25] Parents pay as much as several thousand dollars to send children to these schools. The second type, juku, is intended to help students master the regular curriculum. A third type devotes its attention to vocational pursuits, including music, art, and sports.[26] There is also a brisk business in practice exams, correspondence courses, and drill books that supplement the public school system.

There is a stark contrast between the academic environment of colleges and the cram schools whose function is to gain admission into college. Although college itself is pretty casual, the cram schools entail six-day weeks of lectures, memorization of vast amounts of material, and the abandonment of social life. Some of the juku have their own entrance exams, while others prepare students to take the entrance exams of the better juku.

Twice a year, in February and March, the competition for admission to high schools and colleges takes place. This time is known as "exam hell." In preparation for these exams, some students spend almost their entire adolescent years with little time for anything but study. Families focus their attention on deciding to which schools application should be made; students themselves often have little voice in the matter.[27] Critics note the negative side of this. "Under the pressure of their parents' expectations, and forced into endless studies intended to ensure later success in our society's entrance examination madness, our children are being robbed of their childhood."[28]

Japanese students display a high degree of persistence in completing school tasks, at least in comparison to American students. This is due mainly to family expectations. The Japanese stress application and effort in education, while American parents are more likely to emphasize ability or motivation and are thus inclined to be passive in relationship to their children's education.[29]

The pressures of education have created concern that the quality of adolescent life has declined.[30] School club activities no longer draw the numbers of students that they once did. Young people spend increasing proportions of their time in academic pursuits and less in exercise and leisure. While Japanese children are becoming taller and heavier thanks to richer diets, they have less endurance and strength. There are also problems of bullying (*ijime*) and absenteeism resulting from refusal to go to school (*tōkō kyohi*).[31]

Higher Education

The contrast between K–12 education and higher education in Japan is striking. Although there is much to admire in the former, the latter is a national embarrassment. McVeigh's observation is typical. "Japan's universities and colleges, taken together, are a national educational failure."[32] Despite concern for the quality of higher education and frequent calls for reform, little has actually been done. This concern is nothing new, however. In the late 1960s, the highly charged political atmosphere of the time encompassed education and led to riots and campus disruptions. Disorder became so severe that many institutions, including prestigious Tokyo University, were closed for more than a year. Among the student grievances was dissatisfaction over higher education.

In international rankings, Japanese students collectively score at or near the top on standardized math and science exams. Japan's population in general is almost totally literate in a language of daunting complexity. These accomplishments are a credit to the enterprise of the Japanese as a people and to the effectiveness of their educational system, at least through high school. Given the importance of learning in Japan's economic success, it is perhaps paradoxical that very little credit for the nation's postwar attainments is attributable to the system of higher education.

Until the reforms that followed World War II, higher education was limited, very selective in its admissions, and elite in its product. Private academies and Buddhist monasteries in some ways resembled higher education in the modern sense. But the first real university was not established until 1877 in Tokyo. At first, Tokyo was the only imperial university (designated as such in 1886), with the exclusive charge of enquiring into "abstruse principles of learning in accordance with the needs of the state." The preeminence of Tokyo University Law Faculty graduates among the bureaucratic elite, a phenomenon that continues today, was established when such graduates were exempted from the civil service exam under the Imperial University Order of 1886. Other imperial universities were soon established in Kyoto and elsewhere, and in 1903 "professional schools," another type of university, were authorized with their mission limited to providing advanced instruction in the arts and sciences. The University Order of 1918 granted university status to private and prefectural or municipal institutions.

Few men and hardly any women had the opportunity to pursue advanced learning at these institutions. Only the intellectually gifted were chosen and, after completing their university studies, graduates assumed important positions in society. This practice was not unlike that followed in Europe, after which it was in fact patterned. The European and Japanese systems were designed to produce educated manpower to meet political and economic needs, not to create broad opportunities for social development.

Reforms introduced during the occupation affected higher education in several ways. In an effort to make access to higher education available to a broader range of students, additional universities were created, mainly by reorganizing and upgrading existing colleges. Enrollment at the university level increased slowly, however, until it began to accelerate in the 1960s, stimulated by rapid economic growth.

Changing the specialty emphasis that characterized university education before the war and adding general education requirements together with the expansion of enrollment from 1960 onward resulted in two problems: overall decline in the quality of higher education and a differentiation among institutions based on prestige. The more established institutions had greater prestige, especially the old imperial universities, and they attracted the better-qualified students. University status correlated with employment status; the more prestigious the university, the better the jobs its students could expect upon graduation.

Students

For some families, gaining admission for their children to an institution of higher education is of the greatest importance. The focus of all this effort and the ultimate test of the students' academic preparation and intellectual ability, to say nothing of his or her subsequent position in life, come at the time of university admission exams. Two exams are given: one general exam is used mainly by public universities and by some private institutions. The second exam is one devised by each university. The standardized test in effect determines who is qualified to take the specific university tests. In keeping with the latest reforms, an effort was being made to reduce the number of exams students face and the burden that they carry. To increase their chances of admission to a school of their choice, students take the exams for several universities or departments within the same university.[33] It is not uncommon for students to take several such tests.[34] This can be very expensive, as the private universities charge 30,000 yen (approximately $280 at the current rate of exchange) to take each exam. Universities whose prestige is in the lower ranks hold their exams first. Some students aspire no higher than such schools, while others take these exams in order to guarantee themselves admission of some kind. They then take the exams of higher-prestige universities at a later date. Once admitted, students have a short time (approximately ten days) to pay the full year's tuition and fees, which are not refundable. Most private universities now permit delaying this charge until the results of national university exams are known. Nonetheless, admission fees can be $2,500 or more, and tuition is twice that for arts students and three times for engineering students.

Many students take the entrance exams for the second or third time. Those students, called *rōnin,* who fail to gain admission anywhere or to the university of their choice may spend a year or more cramming in preparation to repeat the tests until they succeed or give up. One consequence of the emphasis placed on educational success is a suicide rate among Japanese youth that is 30 percent higher than in the United States, although by no means are all suicides in this age group attributable to educational stress.[35]

The disparity between the number of applicants and the number of spaces available in universities has all but disappeared. The number of people in the university-entering age group (eighteen) has declined. There are simply fewer students seeking admission because of demographic trends, and the younger student is not being replaced by persons in older age categories. The "non-traditional" student is a phenomenon that has not yet begun to appear in any significant numbers. Another factor contributing to the decline in the student population pool is the high cost of education, which is making it increasingly difficult for families to carry the burden, especially if they have more than one child to educate. In addition, there was a substantial drop in the number of applicants in the 1990s associated with the weakening of the economy.

By the time they have been admitted to a university, Japanese students have spent a good part of their lives in rigorous preparation for that event. Compared to the time and effort spent qualifying for advanced study, after having entered an institution of higher learning, students discover that the demands made of them have diminished substantially. "There is undoubtedly a persistent feeling that university life may provide a moratorium on overtax-ing one's intellect."[36] The course work is not demanding, and having been admitted, a student is virtually guaranteed a diploma. "Social constraints put the school administration and faculty in a position where they feel obliged to permit graduation of students who worked so hard to get into college."[37] The years of higher education for students are more like a vacation than a time of serious study. It is a welcome pause before entering the pressured environment of employment and married life.

Universities and colleges vary in their academic standards, as do departments and programs within them. Students attend class irregularly, some hardly at all. Lecture notes are copied and sold, a process facilitated by the fact that some professors make few changes in their courses from year to year.[38] Course exams are not demanding, if they are given at all, and students who do not pass can retake them. In some courses, there are few if any requirements apart from class attendance. Of those who enter the various institutions of higher education, 95 percent ultimately receive degrees.[39] In the United States, getting into college is easy but graduating is another matter. Less than 50 percent of those who enter American colleges and universities ever receive a degree. Graduation from college in Japan, in and of itself, is not looked on as a particularly significant accomplishment. It is not an achievement in which the student takes much pride, nor does it confer much status. The status is achieved from having gained admission—particularly to an institution with a good reputation.[40]

The low quality of higher education is not without exception. After the first two years of "general education," students, especially at the major national universities, need to establish good academic records in order to compete for choice career assignments. There is also the prospect of even more exams for admission into government service, a reality that creates a seriousness of purpose for many students.[41] Technical schools—in engineering, for example—are more demanding of students than liberal arts schools.

Having been substantially liberated from the demands of study, many students find themselves in the unfamiliar situation of having a great deal of spare time on their hands. In the 1950s and 1960s, a popular outlet for student energies was politics, particularly of the radical left-wing variety. Many activities, including mass public demonstrations, were directed at a wide range of issues, a favorite being U.S. foreign policy, which was regarded as imperialist. Today politics has less attraction for students, most of whom have turned their attentions elsewhere. The radical student movement has all but disappeared in Japan, reflecting a worldwide phenomenon. Japanese students have only begun to discover the pleasures of drinking and other social pursuits and are limited in engaging in them by the fact that universities do not have on-campus student housing, which makes it difficult for students to spend much time together. Socializing is also limited by the fact that many students at universities in the larger urban areas may spend as much as four hours per day commuting between their homes and campus.

The Issue of Academic Status

The old imperial universities, such as Tokyo and Kyoto, are at the top of the status hierarchy, followed by a select group of private institutions that also have good reputations. The academic demands of private universities are generally lower than are those of the public institutions, and they tend to be overcrowded and understaffed.

Students who gain admission to one of the top universities can be confident of good jobs after graduation. Especially coveted is employment with big corporations or powerful government agencies. While ability and performance are increasingly important criteria for advancement, educational pedigree remains a decisive criterion. "It is still the case that the university one has succeeded in entering is likely to determine one's chances of getting the security of an elite position in a government department or large firm."[42] For university graduates, especially from institutions of lesser standing where there is greater competition, job hunting can be a trying process involving long trips, more exams, and lengthy interviews.

Most universities have placement services that generally are effective in obtaining employment for their graduates. Moreover, there are connections between certain universities and specific companies. Employers look for more than intelligence and aptitude in their applicants; they are also interested in compatible personnel. "A good employee is one who is a blank page on which the company can write what it wants."[43]

Faculty

Faculty salaries at institutions of higher education are comparable to those of managers in medium-size companies. However, because of the high cost of living in Japan, the living standards of most professors are somewhat more modest than those of Western academics. There is little salary difference between professors with the same number of years of service, nor is there much difference among academic fields.

The governing structure of universities is not always transparent. In the case of private universities especially, it is not always easy to identify persons who exercise real authority or the procedures by which they are selected. In a formal sense, the decision-making process parallels that of business and government. The consensus-based approach works for the latter two because each has an end-product and the cooperation of everyone is enlisted in achieving that end. The same can be said of education at the K–12 levels, where results, as measured by student performance on exams, are readily identifiable. Universities have no such product standard. Each unit within the university protects its prerogatives with feudal zeal, which means that even routine decisions can take considerable time. Cooperation among departments can be extraordinarily difficult, requiring a considerable investment of time and effort.

The relatively low level of academic achievement in higher education is not limited to students. Members of the faculty are not very productive by Western standards, although there are exceptions. Limited productivity is due in large part to the fact that research scholarship is not a principal function of Japanese universities. Research and development work more often takes place in private corporate laboratories and research institutes, rather than within the system of higher education.[44] Few Japanese academics have won international recognition for their work. Researchers in Japan have not emphasized research of the "theoretical" variety.[45] This kind of work the Japanese have generally left to others. Rather than seek important discoveries "on the frontiers of science," Japanese research efforts tend to be concentrated on the "applied" side, which, is where human and financial resources are committed.[46] University based research is constrained by a number of factors: rigid governing hierarchies, inadequate financing especially for facilities, poor programs at the postdoctoral level, weak ties to industry and limited involvement by foreign researchers.[47]

Professors, who are tenured immediately upon being hired, really need not do much of anything apart from teach their classes unless they desire promotion, which requires demonstration of scholarship through publication. For many professors, there is ample time for other pursuits, including textbook publishing, involvement in juku, consulting, and administrative work. It is not uncommon for professors to teach at more than one university; a few teach at three.[48] This is especially true for professors in large metropolitan areas.

Financing Higher Education

Public institutions receive their financing mainly from the government, whereas private universities rely primarily on student fees. Unlike universities in the United States, those in Japan receive little support from private contributors. There are organizations connected to individual universities to which supporters, especially alumni, may contribute, and these sums can be deducted from the donor's tax obligation. Endowments established by and in the name of corporations are not common.[49] Private schools must rely on bank loans for the construction of physical facilities and on tuition and other fees to pay them off and to maintain the institution. Public institutions, in contrast, receive less than 20 percent of their operating budget from student fees. Keeping students in college and attracting more of them is thus an economic necessity at private schools.[50] The costs for technical schools, such as medicine and engineering, are considerably higher. As universities compete for students from a shrinking population pool, the result is unlikely to have a positive effect on the quality of the educational experience.

Problems of Higher Education

In 2006, the government of Shinzo Abe revised the Fundamental Law of Education. Revisions included language emphasizing respect for tradition and calling on education to foster patriotism. Patriotism was defined in the bill as "cultivating an attitude which respects tradition and culture, loves the nation and homeland that have fostered them, while respecting other countries and contributing to international peace and development."[51] A requirement that students and teachers stand and sing the national anthem (*kimigayao*) at enrollment and graduation ceremonies led to lawsuits by teachers. Other patriotic rituals, such as displaying the flag *(hinomaru)*, likewise generated controversy. The emperor had previously stated, on October 28, 2004, that he preferred these exercises to be voluntary.[52]

The Tokyo board of education mandated the singing of the national anthem and the display of the flag. Several teachers refused, and their contracts were cancelled. These teachers and numerous others punished for the same reason later filed lawsuits.

Despite the increasing attention given to deficiencies in the system of higher education, some problems remain and tend to worsen as time goes on. The education system is rigorous and demanding through high school and the entrance exam system allows for the establishment and maintenance of high standards. It also raises the level of performance expectation, meaning that students are going to work harder. But this hard work ends after graduation from high school. Higher education is a brief way-station on the way to employment. It serves as "the last grading and classifying function of the state-sanctioned socializing machinery."[53] This system has worked pretty well for those Japanese companies that do not want highly specialized graduates but, instead, prefer recruits with excellent general skills who can then be trained in company-sponsored programs. But business is also beginning to complain that new recruits lack maturity and social skills, aspects of learning and growing up that the education system does not effectively provide. Higher education, in particular, has given little, if any, attention to such matters.

The issue of educational quality at the university level is a matter of serious concern for Japan, given the fact that the knowledge/information race not only is accelerating but has more participants. Japan has invested heavily in applied aspects of education, particularly engineering. But the sophisticated academic resources needed to sustain past successes and to build upon them are underdeveloped. This extends even to libraries. "It often seemed to me as if libraries were run purely for the convenience of their administrative staff rather than for academic purposes."[54] In an effort to increase emphasis on theoretical or basic science, the Japanese have begun to enter into cooperative ventures with foreign research organizations, especially in the United States. The Japanese were involved in the American "supercollider" nuclear physics project, for example, before it was cancelled by the U.S. Congress.

The conformity-oriented and highly selective university admission process has contributed to a growing problem of rebellious behavior and disorder in the schools. Violence involving students, and juvenile delinquency in general, although still small in scale by Western standards, appears to be on the increase.[55] Considerable interest and concern over this phenomenon has been generated in the press, which has emphasized the growing dimensions of the problem.[56] It is not clear whether this behavior reflects a weakening of the traditional emphasis on personal discipline or if it is the consequence of something new, an expression of frustration and alienation brought on by the social and psychological demands of modern urban society. In any event, the education system in Japan, as elsewhere, is a primary mediator of social stress.

Education and Japan's Future

Part of the difficulties encountered by education today has to do with the changes, particularly those affecting the family, that attend modern industrialized and urbanized society. Moreover, Japan today, as in the past, draws on and is influenced by ideas and practices found elsewhere, especially in the United States. Educational philosophies and social customs that stress individuality over conformity find greater receptivity among contemporary Japanese youth than was the case with former generations.[57]

In some respects, Japanese and American systems of education are converging. The former are moving away from the lockstep approach that relies heavily on exam-driven pedagogy. School uniforms are less popular, and more "individual growth" ideas are being favored. In the United States, by contrast, there is a perceptible movement toward exam-driven education. The No Child Left Behind philosophy of the Bush administration places heavy emphasis on performance on standardized tests. Among the results of such an approach is a "teach to the test" pedagogy.

American higher education has become a target of a variety of criticisms. Among these are grade inflation, declining performance standards, overpaid and underworked faculty, excessive administrative overhead, overemphasis on nonacademics such as sports, and the lack of vocational utility of university degrees. These are the same criticisms being made of Japanese universities. Thus the two systems have much to learn from each other. Japanese universities seem to be striving to become what American universities used to be. American universities appear to be becoming what Japanese universities are now.

The shortcomings in the education system are overshadowed by its contribution to Japan's economic success. And there are other benefits to the Japanese approach to education. As Ronald Dore observed, "Japan's approach to education has the added advantage of postponing the youthful self-indulgence that has undermined other societies by keeping adolescents glued to their studies for most of their waking hours."[58] Education in Japan, like that in all countries, must be continually responsive to society's changing tastes and needs. However, whether Japanese education possesses the kind of adaptability and initiative necessary to confront the evolving demands made of it is uncertain.

Health Care

For the most part, as concerns their health, the Japanese subscribe to the principles of modern science, in particular the model of biomedicine. Many people also avail themselves of folk remedies and traditional healers, a practice also not uncommon in the West. A person who is sick might seek relief from a visit to a Buddhist or Shinto shrine or, if unable to do so, might send a family member instead. Hot spring baths and over-the-counter medications are popular, as are various herbal remedies. Acupuncture is also employed. While the Japanese accept the germ theory of disease, some traditional ideas surrounding hygiene endure. There is the inside-outside notion with the outside being dirty. This view underlies the shoe removal and house-cleaning rituals commonly practiced in Japan. The word used for the common cold is *kaze,* which literally means "wind." Outside wind is said to cause colds, and the cold itself is considered a wind inside the person.[59]

National Health Program

Like every other modern society, except for the United States, Japan has a state-supported program to underwrite health care. The earliest public health insurance system in Japan dates from 1927. The U.S. occupation disrupted the progression toward a socialized medical delivery system by dismantling the wartime system in favor of a free market approach, but Japan soon returned to the socialized model.[60]

Today there is no single national health insurance system. Instead, there are many individual insurers. These insurers are required to offer a basic package of coverage and may include additional benefits, such as funeral expenses and maternity leave. About 63 percent of the population is covered by the Social Insurance System (SIS), which consists of about 1,800 providers called health insurance societies. These entities cover people who work in companies or offices. Employers pay 50 to 80 percent of the cost, and the rest is covered by employee premiums. The remaining 37 percent of the population, consisting of the unemployed, retirees, and the self-employed, are covered by the National Health Insurance (NHI) system, which is funded by the government and the insured. The NHI, with about 3,400 regional plans, was set up in 1958 and is administered through local governments.

Health-care coverage is basically the same for everyone, but it is made available through a complicated insurance scheme involving more than 5,000 different programs on the basis of either employment or residence. Employees and their dependents, the latter including the elderly with low incomes who are themselves dependents of their children, are enrolled in Employee Health Insurance (EHI), either in company-specific plans or in a national program for smaller firms managed directly by the government. Self-employed people or those who do not work, which includes most retired pensioners, have insurance provided by their municipal governments under a scheme called Citizens' Health Insurance (CHI). The government provides a subsidy to CHI from general revenues to compensate for individuals with low incomes. There are also transfers from EHI plans to CHI to cover the heavy costs of health care for the elderly. Economic stagnation beginning in the 1990s has been a problem for the insurance system. Declining revenue from employee contributions has resulted in an increase in workers' contribution rates. The problem is especially acute in CHI, as laid-off workers and those with low incomes have enrolled.[61]

Japan has used the "socialized" medical system since 1961. The Japanese variety of national health-care coverage means that all citizens have some form of medical insurance that is guided by the government. There are many similarities between the Japanese system and the United Kingdom's national health insurance scheme. In fact, Japan used the U.K. approach as a model in developing its own program. In this medical system, employees and their employers each pay 50 percent of the employee medical insurance fee. That is about 18 percent of employees' monthly salaries. When employees visit a doctor's office or receive medical treatment, their medical insurance currently pays 80 percent of the total cost and the employees pay 20 percent. However, amendments to the Health Insurance Act implemented after April 2003 required employees to pay 30 percent of the total medical cost.

In addition to the SIS and NHI systems, there is a third type of insurance for long-term care. This program was started in April 2000 to address the growing need for health care among the aging population. The program is paid 50 percent by the government and 50 percent by the insured, who must be at least forty years old. Qualification for long-term insurance requires approval by a regional review board. Users must be sixty-five or have a certifiable condition requiring more than ordinary care.

Costs

The cost of health care in Japan is considerably less than that in the United States and comparable to that in European countries. Japan spends 7.6 percent of its GDP on health care, compared with 13.1 percent by the United States. Fees for medical services are set by the government and are universal. These fees are standardized nationwide and are set by the Medical Fee Table. The cost of drugs is set by the NHI price list. Costs covered in part or in full by health insurance include in- and out-patient care, home care, and dental care; prescription drugs; long-term care expenses; home nursing expenses for the elderly; prosthetics; and cash benefits for childbirth. Costs that are not paid include additional fees for hospital care (such as for a private room); routine physical examinations; some dental treatments; over-the-counter drugs; daily expenses (such as for food) incurred in health facilities for the elderly; and some prosthetics, including eyeglasses. The Japanese health-care system has energetically utilized cost controls for both primary and secondary care.

The insurance system is a combination of private insurers, government subsidy, and co-payments. Co-payments are capped at approximately $600 per month, which makes the effective co-payment rate about 15 percent. Health-care providers are mainly private, and hospitals must operate on a nonprofit basis. There are 1.9 physicians per 1,000 population, compared with 2.7 in the United States.

The fee schedule is universal. Differences in physicians' qualifications do not translate into different fees. "Services provided by a newly licensed resident are paid the same amount as those by a well known specialist."[62] The fee schedule does not recognize any differences among facilities or regions. A given procedure costs the identical amount whether performed in a big Tokyo hospital or in a small rural physician's office. Physicians not only prescribe drugs but dispense them through their own pharmacies, an arrangement that has led to overmedication. Kickbacks from the pharmaceutical industry to physicians to encourage them to prescribe their products contribute to the problem.

In the United States, the more sophisticated the procedure, the higher the fee. This applies in particular to surgery. In Japan, surgical fees are often below the cost for providers. Increasing the number of surgical procedures would not increase revenue but would actually result in a net loss. Therefore, ordering low-cost services, such as laboratory tests, is more profitable.[63]

The aging population and the economic stagnation beginning in the 1990s have sent the overall medical system into deficit. The cost burden on general government revenues has increased because fewer people are paying into the insurance pools.

Increasing health-care costs led the government to introduce a 3 percent sales tax in 1989. It was increased to 5 percent in 1997. The tax was very unpopular, but was necessary, as the government was incurring substantial deficits. Nonetheless, "Japan has managed to keep the amount the state contributes to medical care well below that of comparable industrial countries, at the same time as keeping the amount spent per head below that in most European countries and less than half that of the USA."[64] One result is a limit on access to health care; another is a black market in delivery of sophisticated medical services that are not otherwise available or are too expensive. People with sufficient financial resources can afford to pay for them.

National health-care expenditures rose from about 1 trillion yen in 1965 to nearly 20 trillion yen in 1989, or from slightly more than 5 percent to more than 6 percent of Japan's national income. In addition to cost-control problems, the system was troubled with excessive paperwork, long waits to see physicians, assembly-line care for out-patients (because few facilities made appointments), overmedication, and abuse of the system because of low out-of-pocket costs to patients. Another problem is an uneven distribution of health personnel, with cities favored over rural areas.

The Japanese government passed amendments to the Health Insurance Act in 2002 that increase the burden on the public. For example, the government increased patient cost-sharing for insured persons from the current 20 percent to 30 percent as of April 2003. At the same time, the government required an elderly patient to pay 10 percent of the total medical cost, instead of the then-current fixed rate of 1,000 yen a month (about $8 per month).

Aging Population

One of the most important factors shaping the dynamics of society is the median age of the population. In societies where the median age is, say, fifteen, the needs for education, jobs, and housing are the highest priorities. The large and growing workforce allows for rapid economic expansion and a growing tax base. In societies where the median age is forty, the highest priorities are health care and retirement benefits. The workforce grows slowly or even contracts. Contributions to tax revenues and retirement programs fall on a diminishing population. Japan is in this latter category.

In 1920 there were 36.2 live births per 1,000 population. In 2000 there were 9.5. Thus Japan faces not only an aging population but a shrinking one. Other countries are also experiencing a decline in the birth rate of what might be called the "native" population. But, overall, the populations are not declining or aging because of the influx of immigrants. Moreover, these immigrants tend to have higher birth rates than the "native" population. In the United States, for example, it is estimated that the Hispanic population will triple by 2050. Japan, however, does not welcome immigrants. Given this combination of factors, Japan faces a challenging demographic future.

The birth rate started declining about 1950, when the postwar baby boom ended. The fertility rate in 1997 was 1.39 compared with a maintenance rate of 2.08. At the current rate, the population (excluding immigration) started declining in 1997. The total population should drop to 67 million by 2100. The over sixty-five population will increase from 15.7 percent of the population in 1997 to 32.3 percent in 2050. The Medical Service Law was amended in 1985 to respond to the challenges posed by an aging population. The effort included a better distribution of medical services and set the number of hospital beds per district.

One cause of the low fertility rate is later marriage. In addition, a small percentage of births are to unwed mothers. The government has been trying to come up with incentives to encourage women to have more children, so far with little effect.

Free health care for the elderly was ended in 1983, replaced by the Health Care for the Elderly Law, which "created insurance funds for the retired (but not yet over the age of seventy) and the elderly (over the age of seventy)."[65] Medical care costs for those over age seventy are five times greater than for those under seventy. This cost comprises one-third of national health-care expenditures and is project to reach half by 2025.

The nursing care insurance system, which began in 2000, is based on the German nursing care system and has been modified as needed. This nursing care insurance system has four main characteristics . First, it requires all Japanese citizens who are forty and older to participate by paying a nursing care insurance fee. Second, this insurance account is independently used and is not shared by the other medical insurance systems. Third, the government develops outlines and policies for this nursing care insurance, yet commercial companies can provide actual care services. Fourth, relatively few health care workers serve each patient in the Japanese medical system. In 2000, for every 1 million people, there were 821.4 registered nurses and assistant nurses (roughly half of these are registered nurses), 19.3 nurse-midwives, 29.0 public health nurses, 201.5 physicians, 71.6 dentists, and 171.3 pharmacists. Compared with Western European countries, there are less than half the number of nurses per 1 million people.[66]

Medical Services

Basic health care is comparable to that in other industrialized countries and better than in some. Routine health maintenance is good, as indicated by the long lifespans. The average lifespan in 2000 was 77.64 years for Japanese men and 84.62 years for women, and it is expected to continue increasing as a result of health care and lifestyle. The Japanese, generally speaking, have a healthier diet than people in the West, certainly in the United States. But with the advent of fast food, there is a growing problem of obesity among younger people. Moreover, the infant morality rate is low, only 3.7 per 1,000 live births. Sophisticated diagnostic procedures are widely available. Japan has the highest number of computer tomography (CT) and magnetic resonance imaging (MRI) scanners per capita of any country. The capacity to provide advanced (and expensive) medical services, such as organ transplants, is less than in the United States. Where Japan lags the rest of the world is in the area of preventive health care. Japan is a country of heavy smokers, and the government has done little to mitigate the practice through public education campaigns. HIV-AIDS awareness is low, and the number of cases has dramatically increased.

Physicians fall into two occupational categories: those who work in their own offices, and those who work in hospitals. Actually, the majority of physicians are salaried employees of hospitals. Hospitals are not open to private-practice physicians, who, thus, cannot attend their patients there but, rather, must do so in their own clinics. This system differs from that familiar to Americans but actually is the most common practice in Europe and around the world. Hospitals can be further divided into those that are privately owned, public hospitals run by the government mostly at the local level, and university hospitals. Another distinctive feature of the Japanese system is that private-practice physicians and those working in hospitals receive the same fee.[67]

The physician-patient relationship is quite different from what Americans are used to. Patients do not typically make an appointment to see a physician. Instead, they go to the doctor when they feel the need and are accepted on a first-come, first-served basis. This often results in long waiting times, which is the inevitable result of the virtually free access to hospitals and physicians. Given this opportunity, it is to be expected that many people will choose prestigious medical centers rather than a local physician. The long waiting times are mostly found at the medical centers. In part because of complaints about these waiting times, the Ministry of Health, Labor, and Welfare (MHLW) has been trying to reduce demand for care at large hospitals in favor of private-practice physicians. To this end, the ministry has proposed reducing the consultation fees paid to medical centers and making patients pay more if they choose to visit such centers without a referral. This approach does not really work, however, because while it is unattractive to the centers, which receive less money, it is attractive to patients, because it makes the prestigious centers more accessible to those who can afford them.

Consults are short, lasting only a few minutes. Physicians are not in a position to become personally acquainted with their patients, although over time they become familiar with their patients' health condition. The emphasis on privacy in medical practice is much less in evidence than in the United States, where patients meet the physician in a private room. In Japan, curtains might separate patients as medical staff move among them. "Outpatient departments resemble a factory assembly line in some hospitals—for example, with patients in stirrups lined up in partitioned rows as the gynecologist goes through the internal examinations."[68] The surrogate-patient approach is sometimes employed if the ill person is unable to see the physician in person: the surrogate describes the symptoms and receives a prescription or recommendation for further intervention.

It is increasingly the case in the United States that physicians are limiting their practices to a specialty, primarily because they can make more money. In Japan, doctors are trained as specialists, but most of them practice as primary-care physicians. Specialists are found in the largest hospitals. Most office-based physicians work alone in that they try to deal with all the problems of every patient with whom they consult. There is also less specialization in other fields. Nurses, medical social workers, and medical records librarians do not specialize through some kind of academic accreditation process.[69] Japanese medical practice differs in other ways compared to that found in the United States. For example, physicians have substantial clinical autonomy in deciding what course of action to take. They do not need preapproval from the insurance company for any procedure or medication, but they are subject to after-the-fact reviews that can result in denial of payment.[70]

On the negative side, physicians have tended to withhold information from patients and even mislead them about their condition. "In particular, patients complain about drugs dispensed without explanation of intended effects, let alone side-effects. Also patients are usually not allowed to look at their own medical records unless a court order is secured."[71] This poor record of information disclosure is largely attributable to the short time available for consultation, which is encouraged by the fee schedule and the traditional, standoffish attitude of older doctors. Another cause is simply the fact that much information is not recorded. The Medical Service Law was revised in 1997 to address the problem, requiring physicians and medical staff to provide adequate information to patients so that they would be in a better position to make informed decisions. The fee structure was also made more transparent.

Not much can be accomplished in the "three-hour wait, three-minute consultation." As a result, the emphasis is on ordering tests and prescribing drugs. Japanese are subjected to more tests and take more drugs than their Western counterparts. Often these offer little benefit except to the pharmaceutical and medical equipment companies. The result is a kind of "tragedy of the commons" problem as the Japanese are overexploiting the health-care system.[72] The number of medical errors is probably lower in Japan than in the United States, because the rate of complicated procedures that are more likely to produce errors is lower in Japan. Only about one-third as many surgeries are performed in Japan per capita relative to the United States. However, errors may go unreported because in Japan records are not well kept and monitoring systems are less developed. In the United States, record-keeping is exhaustive in part because of the potential for litigation. There has been a recent increase in the number of errors reported, probably attributable to a greater willingness of staff and patients to speak out.

Eighty percent of Japan's hospitals and 94 percent of its physician-run clinics are privately owned. Patients are free to select care providers, and competition ensures an adequate number of facilities, except in rural areas. Investor-owned, for-profit hospitals have been prohibited. But in July 2003, in response to calls from advocates for market-based health care, the creation of new investor-owned hospitals in specific localities (called "special zones" for deregulation) was permitted. This was intended to meet a need in rural areas. However, these hospitals would not be allowed to charge fees over and above those allowed by the fee schedule. All services would be paid by the consumer, with no reimbursement at all from public health insurance programs. It is unlikely that there is much of a market for such a costly approach to medical care services. Wealthy people are already able to seek treatment abroad. This narrow opening for market-based medicine is unlikely to widen. It is opposed by the MHLW and the Japan Medical Association. Moreover, public opinion polls indicate the public is opposed to a system in which the quantity and quality of care is a function of ability to pay.[73]

On balance, the Japanese health-care system is superior to the one in the United States. It is more equitable and costs less. A major reason for the high cost of health care in the United States is administration. As much as 40 percent of the cost to Americans of health care is paperwork. Japanese do not have the same degree of access to highly sophisticated (and expensive) procedures like organ transplants that Americans do, assuming that they have insurance or can afford it. Despite increasing costs and an aging population, the Japanese health-care system is not likely to change much in the near future. Campbell and Ikegami conclude: "Our guess is that the system will not look very different ten years from now—which is not necessarily a bad thing, since by international standards of access, cost, and fairness, health policy in Japan has been quite successful."[74]

11

Public Safety

Ranking high among basic needs, alongside food and shelter, is personal security. All societies fulfill these requirements, some more effectively than others. Unfortunately, the guardians of safety themselves occasionally pose the greatest threat to the persons and property of citizens. Drawing on European experience, the Japanese established a centralized police system in the 1870s. The police became an important tool of the government, and the temptation to use police power for political purposes soon led to its abuse.[1]

In an effort to mitigate the abuse of police power, the U.S. occupation tried to decentralize the police. The control of police forces throughout the country by the Home Ministry had been a primary means of suppressing dissent and promoting the orthodoxy of the emperor-centered state. After the war ended, the Home Ministry was abolished, and each community was given control over its own police services.

Decentralization of the police was not universally welcomed, however. Japanese conservatives opposed the move on the grounds that decentralization would render the police ineffective and unable to meet the threat posed by communist agitation. The occupation authorities themselves began to have doubts about the new organizational structure. "Such a system contained weaknesses, a fact which GHQ [General Headquarters] no doubt thought would contribute towards the democratization of the nation's police system. It did, but as Communist disturbances attained ever more serious proportions, the inefficiency of the new police system made itself increasingly felt."[2] Local governments, which were given responsibility over police, found themselves facing heavy financial burdens. In response to the costs and the perceived threat of communist subversion, central controls over law enforcement were shortly reinstated. In the Reform Police Law passed by the Diet in 1954, the police were reorganized along prefectural lines with the general management of the system under a national Public Safety Commission.

Crime Rates

The Japanese approach to the maintenance of public order places more emphasis on the Confucian notion of using social pressure to ensure proper behavior than on the coercive power of police. "No industrial nation has weaker formal law enforcement."[3] Postwar Japan has been a safe and remarkably crime-free society. By American standards, the crime rate is low, but it has been increasing, especially in petty theft, such as shoplifting, robbery, and crimes committed by groups of people or gangs.

Juvenile crime is especially worrisome to authorities. "Since the 1970s, for example, juveniles have comprised at least 40 percent, and sometime more than 50 percent, of those arrested for penal code violations."[4] In 2004, crimes committed by persons under age fourteen increased 3.3 percent over the previous year. Of these, 80 percent were charged with arson. Child abuse cases were up 45.9 percent, many involving acts committed by juveniles against one another.[5]

The jail population is also increasing. As of the end of 2005, there were 79,055 people (including pretrial detainees) incarcerated in the country's seventy-two correctional facilities.[6] At the end of 2003, the prison population was 116.6 percent of capacity. The increase is due to an overall growth in crime and a tendency of courts to give longer prison sentences.[7]

Part of the problem is the large number of hard-to-clear petty crimes. The clearance rate is somewhat misleading, since the actual number of crimes in Japan is lower than in the United States, for example.[8] Most recent figures show the crime rate in Japan to be 19.177 per 1,000 population and 80.064 per 1,000 population in the U.S. There were .005 murders per 1,000 population in Japan and .043 in the U.S. There were 55,766 assaults and 296,486 burglaries in Japan and 2,238,480 assaults and 2,191,875 burglaries in the U.S.[9]

Statistics suggest that the effectiveness of Japanese police has been declining. The crime rate has increased steadily over the past decade, and in 2002 the crimes dealt with by police increased 3.1 percent.[10] Felonies committed by organized crime have also increased.[11] At the same time the prosecution of crimes reached an all-time low in 2001 of 19.8 percent of criminal cases. The arrest rate has declined steadily since 1994. The number of major crimes, such as murder and armed robbery, almost doubled over the past decade.[12]

The Criminal Justice System

It is simplistic and misleading to directly equate crime rates with the effectiveness of law enforcement. In the United States, the crime rate has declined, a development often attributed to tough sentencing guidelines and increased numbers of police officers. One clear result has been a boom in prison construction. Although having more officers on the beat and criminals in jail aid in the deterrence of crime, other factors may be more important. An older population is one such factor. Another is a political culture in which voluntary respect for the law is a shared value.

It is possible to force obedience through intimidation. Authoritarian regimes may have low crimes rates because of massive application of coercion. But this is likely to endure for only a short time, and even then such societies do not operate effectively. Consider, for example, totalitarian systems such as the former Soviet Union, which had little violent crime and streets that were safe to walk at night. But such safety comes at great cost. Behavior is forced in a police state, and people go about their business with little enthusiasm. Despite its great-power status, the Soviet Union achieved little apart from military strength and some notable accomplishments in space technology. With the demise of police state controls, criminal activity has become widespread.

Japan has both an aging population and a disposition among its citizens to obey the law. This obedience is a product of social expectations to conform, rather than the fear of punitive retribution imposed by agencies of the state. "Japan's homogeneous society, deeply loyal to a historic tradition that provides a sense of moral order, is knitted into a framework of group relations that provides its people with both a sense of place and a sense of self and that creates a strong commitment to social norms. The result is a people whose respect for law and order is reflected in one of the lowest crime rates in the world."[13] Furthermore, breaking the law (or rules of any kind) is not an individual matter for which one person is held accountable; it brings shame and embarrassment to one's family, friends, and associates.[14] This, of course, produces an environment that pressures people to avoid activity that violates formal legal rules and discourages unconventional and deviant behavior of all types.

In fact, the formal coercive powers of the Japanese state are limited. For example, Japanese courts do not exercise contempt powers, so bureaucratic agencies cannot ask the judiciary to ensure that their orders are enforced. The criminal justice system relies on "confession, repentance, and absolution" rather than punishment in the form of fines or imprisonment.[15] This is not to say that there are no jails, but incarceration is limited mostly to habitual offenders. Japanese prisons house approximately 80,000 inmates, in a total population of approximately 127.8 million, compared with more than 2.2 million in American jails with a total national population of approximately 301 million.[16]

To be tried by a jury of one's peers is a legal custom predicated on an abiding distrust of the state. It is an article of faith in the United States that a fair trial requires a jury. But sometimes, even with one, a fair trial is hard to come by because of juror bias. Jury trials are not a fixture of Japan's legal system although they once were. When they did exist, defendants rarely chose trial by jury, probably in the expectation that penalties imposed by citizens would be more severe than those decided by judges. Most cases today are heard by a single judge. For more serious crimes, murder and rape, for example, a three-judge panel is employed. Because of concerns over the fairness of the justice system, a jury process is being introduced. The criminal justice system is conceived within a broad social context. The fundamental object of the criminal justice system is not, strictly speaking, to deter, rehabilitate, or punish. Rather, it is seen more as a process of "reeducation" in which the lawbreaker is reminded that illegal activity is not socially acceptable. Everyone is assumed to know what correct behavior is, and there is a low threshold of tolerance for misbehavior. Criminal activity is rather like sin, for which society requires atonement. An individual who breaks the rules is not excused because of psychological stresses or inadequacies in the economic or social environments, but these might determine what must be done by way of expiation.

There is a parallel here with education, in which society assumes equal ability among students, and differences in performance are a matter of effort. Likewise, a criminal knows better; he has a recognized place in society and must learn to live up to expectations.[17] It is expected that the citizenry will behave correctly; there is no notion that illegal behavior is somehow tolerable if one can get away with it.[18] Deviation brings about sanctions that are more social than legal. The lawbreaker is not brought before a neutral bar of justice but, rather, is made to face the disapproval of society.[19]

The workload of Japanese prosecutors, at least by American standards, is light. American prosecutors carry a felony case load nearly three times that of their Japanese counterparts and twice that of even the busiest Japanese office.[20] Those individuals who are brought to trial face almost certain conviction. This does not mean that judges are biased or irresponsible. One reason is that that prosecutors screen out before trial almost all cases with even a remote risk of ending in acquittal.[21] Another reason for the high conviction rate is that the legal deck is stacked in favor of the state, for, in contrast to the United States, Japan has few procedural safeguards protect the rights of the accused. Police, who rarely make court appearances, work closely with the prosecutor, who takes an active role in directing police in their investigation. Evidence is given to the prosecutor in writing, as is the testimony of witnesses. Prosecutors conduct their own investigations, and they alone have the authority to bring charges against a defendant, with the result that there is "more charging power in the prosecutor in Japan than in almost any other democratic country."[22] Japanese defendants do not have the right to confront their accusers. Judges have considerable latitude in deciding what they will and will not accept as evidence. However, judges exercise little such discretion because of the thorough and exhaustive case presented by the prosecutor.[23] An accused has little opportunity to challenge or discredit the case against him. Nevertheless, it cannot be assumed on the basis of this that Japanese jails are full of innocent victims who have been "framed" by overzealous authorities. In the unlikely event that an accused is acquitted, he is entitled to compensation from the state for his trouble.

The Japanese criminal justice system employs neither the guilty plea nor the practice of plea bargains, at least in the ways that they are used in the United States. Defendants can choose a streamlined summary procedure and receive a light sentence or the full-blown trial process, which might result in a more severe sentence.[24] Although the right to bail exists, it is not often used. But this does not mean that every offense results in full legal proceedings. In practice, prosecutors have a considerable range of discretion as to how far to proceed against an accused.[25] An offender may be let off altogether depending on such factors as personality, age, and the background of the accused plus the nature and circumstances of the crime and, significantly, what has happened since.[26] Prosecutors have the option not to prosecute, even though assured of a conviction, if they decide that it would be in the interest of society and the accused not to do so.[27] In such cases, a major determining factor would be the prospects for rehabilitating the offender.[28] If an offender displays genuine contrition and makes restitution to the victim, he is not likely to face prosecution. First offenders are not likely to go to trial unless they fail to show remorse. Although almost all trials result in conviction, there are very few acquittals, a jail sentence is not likely and if one is imposed it would probably be for less than three years.[29] Nonetheless, more than half such sentences are suspended; probation is seldom used. This contrasts with the United States, where a defendant who receives a jail sentence usually spends at least some time in jail. As a result, the Japanese incarceration rate is only about 20 percent that of the United States.[30]

Capital punishment by hanging is an option available in the Japanese criminal justice system, putting Japan on the list of 20 out of 193 members of the United Nations that condone the practice. Although it has not been the practice of the Ministry of Justice to announce in advance the dates of executions or divulge the names of those condemned to this penalty, only the number of those hanged is announced. However, in 2007, the names and dates of execution of four convicts were announced. Between 1946 and 1993, 608 prisoners were executed. Since 2003, 10 executions have taken place, with 104 prisoners remaining on death row as of August 8, 2007. In late 2006, a seventy-five-year-old man who could neither walk or stand without assistance was hanged, provoking Amnesty International to express concern and mobilizing opposition among Japanese.[31] Japanese courts are as likely to impose the death penalty for certain crimes as are those in the United States, although fewer capital crimes are committed in Japan.[32] One characteristic of the entire criminal justice process is the minimal role played by defense attorneys. If an offender makes a confession—a common phenomenon—the prosecutor has the option of a summary procedure that avoids formalities. A fine can be imposed, which, under the law, cannot exceed approximately $1,500, but is usually less than $350. This system places a very high premium on the integrity of the criminal justice authorities. The emphasis upon confessions has led to a rise in cases of police and prosecutors pressuring and sometimes mistreating suspects. Suspects can be jailed for up to twenty-three days, during which they can be subjected to considerable pressure to confess.[33] A suspect who maintains his innocence might face prosecution, which would not have occurred had there been a confession. Those proclaiming their innocence might also draw longer sentences.[34]

Because it has been the practice until recently to impose jail sentences relatively rarely, the Japanese prison population is comparatively small. Prison has not occupied a central place in the Japanese approach to law enforcement. The social disgrace and humiliation of being convicted of a crime and having one's name appear in the newspaper is usually seen as sufficient punishment.[35] The main emphasis is on psychological rehabilitation. If the accused displays genuine contrition, apologizes for his acts, and promises to live a proper life, incarceration is unlikely. Exceptions are habitual criminals and persons involved in drug-related crimes, for whom jail time is considered appropriate. While in jail, inmates are subjected to an intense work regime, which is considered the most effective road to reentry to society as a productive citizen.[36] The criminal justice system is also not used as a means of political or social oppression. Advocates of unorthodox views or minority groups who might swell prison populations in other countries are missing from Japanese jails.

In recent years, it has come to light that prisoner abuse is not uncommon in Japanese jails. After two prisoners died at a Nagoya prison, seven guards were indicted for abuse. Perhaps an equally severe problem is poor health care. A report revealed in May 2003 that 238 prisoners had died under suspicious circumstances, probably including inadequate medical attention.[37] Opponents of gun control maintain that the easy availability of firearms in the United States does not increase violent crime but actually deters it: more guns, less crime. Although this may be a rather implausible argument, one thing is beyond dispute. People cannot shoot one another if they have no access to guns. In Japan, the private possession of firearms is practically nonexistent.[38] Only persons involved in law enforcement may possess handguns, and most police officers have never drawn their weapons in the line of duty, much less had occasion to fire them.[39] Even the possession of antique handguns requires a license, and then the gun must have been manufactured before 1867. Hunting is nonexistent in all but the more remote areas of the country, so few firearms are kept for that purpose. All guns must be registered, including those used for sport, and their owners must be demonstrably proficient in their use. Obtaining a permit, even for a shotgun for trap shooting, requires hours of classroom and practical exercises. Permits to own firearms are denied to anyone with a criminal record.[40] Not many Japanese are attracted to the "survivalist" or soldier-of-fortune lifestyle, nor are many interested in the technology of firearms, pursuits that lead many Americans to collect guns. The Japanese are concerned about the smuggling of handguns into the country. Although the number of guns is not large, the increase in gun availability has contributed to violent crime.[41]

Another significant area of contrast between the Japanese and American approaches to criminal justice is the recruitment of prison personnel. Serving as a corrections officer in an American jail or prison is not considered attractive employment. Those who seek such work are, as a rule, not highly skilled or trained. By contrast, Japanese correction officers must compete in a highly selective recruitment process. Moreover, the centralization of the Japanese system allows for the maintenance of high standards, whereas in the United States the decentralized nature of the system leads to a wide disparity in standards.

The impressive effectiveness of the criminal justice system does not always extend to the control of organized crime. Japan has as many as twenty times more gangsters as does the United States.[42] Curiously, organized crime figures and the police have a familiar, although tense, relationship. Because of their financial power and political connections, members of organized crime groups rarely get caught in the periodic sweeps made by police; they know about such sweeps in advance. But to avoid causing the police to "lose face," the criminals will leave behind some contraband so that the police efforts were not a total failure. The gangsters are also helpful in keeping foreign drug traffic out of Japan and in managing the commercial sex industry. Potential problems are kept at a tolerable level, not out of moral concerns but simply as a matter of business.[43]

The swaggering organized crime figures, called *yakuza*, draw on a long tradition going back as far as the seventeenth century, when bands of samurai bandits terrorized the people.[44] The yakuza are known for, among other things, the initiatory practices of tattooing and cutting off the tips of one or both of the little fingers. These organized crime gangs are involved in all manner of criminal activities as well as legitimate business. They are also heavily involved in politics, having relatively open relationships with politicians, for whom they raise money and serve as bodyguards.[45] The Japanese public is remarkably tolerant of organized criminal activities.

Although there is comparatively little violent crime, there has been an increase in economic crimes, such as the fraudulent use of credit cards. Drug use, especially among juveniles, is increasing among the general population, as is the crime associated with it. Of considerable concern is the increase in crime among youth. Persons under eighteen account for almost 43 percent of criminal activity although it often involves such "low end" crimes and extorting lunch money from fellow students. Another worrisome development is the popularity among teenagers of motorcycle gangs. These gangs and their followers are inclined to engage in unruly and sometimes violent behavior.[46]

There are youth gangs and occasional revolutionary groups that engage in lawbreaking. Terrorists have also been present from time to time, such as the Japanese Red Army. Another problem for the police are public demonstrations, which are highly stylized and require considerable police sophistication in crowd control. Demonstrators have helmets and protection against tear gas, and they march in choreographed order. Due to the nature of the job, riot control police are usually rotated to other work after three years.

It has already been noted that there is much less civil litigation in Japan than in the West. Part of this is due to the fact that the system is inaccessible to most people, who, even if they wanted to do so, would find going to court an unsatisfactory alternative. Japan has only about 10,000 lawyers, compared with 600,000 in the United States. Very few of those who try are able to become lawyers in Japan because of the extremely difficult bar examination. It is next to impossible for foreigners to accomplish this feat, and as a result, few practice in Japan. The number of lawyers, and judges, is limited, and persons accused of crimes cannot expect vigorous intervention on their behalf by a lawyer. The social expectation in Japan is that everyone will cooperate with the police, including especially those accused of criminal offenses. In the United States, a person charged with a crime is immediately in an adversarial relationship with the legal authorities. The accused is likely to start stressing his or her rights, especially to counsel, and not give information freely to police. The authorities are viewed as the adversary, perhaps even the enemy, and it is perfectly acceptable to do everything legal to frustrate their efforts. It is the responsibility of the authorities to make a case; the accused need do nothing or indeed everything to prevent it. A common occurrence, seen especially on television news programs, is an attorney stoutly protesting the innocence of his client, contending that the charges, the trial, or the resulting conviction are a miscarriage of justice. In the system employed in Japan, the authorities must also prove their case, but there seems to be greater confidence in their integrity and ability. A Japanese attorney is truly "counsel" to his client, rather than his champion and spokesman, as in the United States. Because he spends little time with his client, the Japanese attorney does not develop a "defensive strategy" and coach his client on what to say and how to say it. In fact, the attorney is likely to assume that his client is guilty and seeks the most satisfactory resolution of the situation, not victory as such. Attorneys do not have free access to their clients, but must get permission from the police or the prosecutor to see them.[47]

In the United States, the public views the jury system as a check on the potential abuse of power by police and prosecutors. Because the defense does everything in its power to undermine the prosecution's case, there is the temptation to cheat in order to win a conviction. Moreover, prosecutors, chiefs of police, and sheriffs are usually elected, making them responsive to public opinion. The public may not always be free of bias in a criminal case, especially if it is a celebrated one. It is not uncommon for the office of prosecutor to be used as a platform for attaining higher political office, tempting the occupants of such offices to sacrifice justice to personal ambition. Such political distractions are largely missing in Japan, removing at least some of the threats to the integrity of the criminal justice system.

The Police

One of the reasons for the low crime rate is the effectiveness of the police. "The social presence of the police is pervasive, unofficial, and low-key."[48] Americans do not have a particularly warm feeling for law enforcement officers and do not readily interact with them, at least in their official capacity. In Japan the attitude is more positive although recent ineffectiveness of some public servants has shaken this attitude somewhat. Nonetheless, by American standards it is still high. A December 1998 poll conducted by the newspaper *Asahi shimbun* revealed a substantial level of public trust in the police. More than 70 percent of respondents said they were trustful or somewhat trustful.[49] In Japanese society there is much greater physical proximity and interaction and less concern for privacy than in the United States. Japanese citizens are much more likely to call on police officers for a variety of problems and to cooperate with them than are Americans. This social environment contributes significantly to police effectiveness and the low crime rate.[50]

Despite its generally positive reputation, all is not well in the world of Japanese law enforcement. One problem is embezzlement from police slush funds. Another is the corruption that is endemic in police control over the *pachinko* industry. As mentioned above, police have long had the reputation of being tolerant of organized crime.[51] Police are distributed throughout populated areas through the use of small police stations called *kōban*. Police keep track of visitors and the comings and goings of the population. They visit each household twice a year to collect data on who lives there and the kinds of valuables that they keep. Such visits are also an opportunity to pass on crime prevention information. Citizens do not object to this invasion of their privacy; in fact they welcome it. Police provide counseling and advice on personal and family matters.[52] There are also foot patrols, and the use of bicycles and scooters is commonplace. It appears that, in cities at least, the main task of Japanese police officers is giving directions.[53] The cordial relationship between the public and the police has begun to deteriorate in recent years due, no doubt, to the stresses of modern life.[54]

The recentralization of the police after the occupation has been accompanied neither by an abuse of police power nor by its exploitation for political purposes. Overall supervision of the police system is the responsibility of the National Safety Commission. The commission, under the jurisdiction of the prime minister, is composed of a chairperson and five members appointed by the prime minister with the consent of the Diet. Police are attached to the forty-seven prefect governments and coordinated through the National Police Agency (NPA). The NPA, headed by a director general, has overall supervisory control over police activities. Police at the prefect level are under Prefectural Public Safety Commissions, which usually consist of three members. Because each political jurisdiction does not have its own independent police force, there are no problems of overlap or conflict between different police jurisdictions.

The typical Japanese police officer is between twenty and thirty-five years old, better educated than average, well trained, and male.[55] Few women are engaged in police work, although their numbers are growing. Not long ago, few women were on routine patrol duty. Women's police roles were generally limited to issuing parking tickets, counseling juveniles, directing traffic, and doing plainclothes work against shoplifters and pickpockets. Now more women are found doing routine police work.[56] Police officers in rural areas enjoy high social prestige, but their counterparts in the cities have somewhat less prestige. Nevertheless, the job continues to attract more applicants than there are openings. One reason for the appeal of law enforcement careers is the favorable work environment. "The police in Japan are probably the most fortunate police force in the world, having a light work load and a highly enabling formal legal system."[57] Pay for Japanese police officers is comparable to that of American counterparts, although they work longer hours. They are also not allowed to take on extra jobs, such as serving as security guards, in their off hours. Serving as a police officer is one of the few occupations leading to occupational mobility. The sons of many police officers are able to attend the better schools and universities and thus receive higher-status employment.[58]

Despite the problems mentioned above, Japanese police maintain a high degree of professionalism and enjoy a favorable popular reputation. While on duty, officers may not smoke or eat outside the station. They are expected to be polite, professional, and dutiful in their relationship to the public. In general they are better behaved than their American counterparts. Throughout Japan the number dismissed for misconduct is only about half that of New York City alone.

There is an elite quality about the self-image of Japanese police. The personal bonds of loyalty and camaraderie among members of the force are particularly important among younger officers working in the cities. Officers have a strong sense of loyalty to their commanders, who, in turn, manifest great concern for the welfare of their men. In fact, police organization and behavior recall much of Japan's imperial past, especially the samurai tradition with its warrior's code of conduct.[59]

Although police scandals are not as common as they are in the United States, their reputation is tarnished from time to time by some startling ineffectiveness and charges of corruption.[60] In an incident in September 1984, two police officers were charged with robbing banks to pay off loan sharks. During the same year, three men on death row had their sentences overturned after the courts ruled that their convictions had been obtained by force.[61] Since then, four more death-row inmates were acquitted after having their cases retried.[62] Johnson notes that in order to maintain their harmonious relationship with police, prosecutors regularly indulge police misconduct including mistreating suspects under interrogation.[63] In 1995, the sarin gas attack in the Tokyo subway system put pressure on the police services as never before. The authorities moved quickly in searching the many properties of the Aum Shinrikyō sect. Nonetheless, public confidence in the ability of government to protect citizens suffered a setback.[64]

Vice and Victimless Crimes

Activities that do not involve personal injury or property damage, but are nonetheless regarded as "crimes," reflect the cultural values of society. In some Muslim countries, consuming alcoholic beverages is a punishable offense because it violates religious tenets. In the Netherlands, businesses that provide sadomasochistic diversions are subject to the law to the point that special arrangements are required to enable customers to escape in the event of fire.

The use of state police powers to maintain standards of morality or to prevent and punish immorality is little in evidence in Japan. The Japanese tolerance of vice and victimless crime is not the result of moral bankruptcy. Quite the contrary, "because there is strong consensus about moral issues, morality is regulated through informal controls. These controls are vested

in the community rather than in the law, the courts, or the police."[65] Police
are generally little involved in the suppression or control of these activities.
This is not to say that vice is open and widespread; gambling is formally
controlled, as is pornography, while prostitution has been illegal since 1956.
The attitude of the police, which reflects that of the general public, is that
if there is no public problem, then leave the matter alone. Drunkenness, for
example, is not looked on as criminal behavior even when it takes place in
public. In such cases, police normally limit their involvement to helping the
tippler home.[66] The issue of pornography and vice is a complicated matter,
with the Japanese displaying an almost bizarre inconsistency. Censorship has
enjoyed a long tradition in Japan, devoted mainly to upholding official political
orthodoxy and preventing obscenity. After the war, "freedom of speech" was
guaranteed by the new constitution. Article 21 states: "Freedom of assembly
and association as well as speech, press and all other forms of expression
are guaranteed. No censorship shall be maintained, nor shall the secrecy of
any means of communication be violated." Although the language of Article
21 seems straightforward enough, other portions of the constitution in fact
qualify it. Since 1947, official censorship of anything other than obscenity
has ceased. It would appear that Article 21 would preclude even that. However, Article 175 of the penal code prohibits the sale, distribution, or public
display of obscene material. The Supreme Court upheld the constitutionality
of this provision in 1957. The legal context regarding obscenity is vague and
ambiguous. In the *Lady Chatterley's Lover* case, the Supreme Court upheld
the government's authority to censor literature on the basis of obscenity, cit-
ing the public welfare provisions of Articles 12 and 13 of the constitution.
The "public welfare" provisions of these articles open a large loophole by
means of which not only obscenity but all constitutional rights can potentially
be restrained. Article 12 states: "The freedom and rights guaranteed to the
people by this constitution shall be maintained by the constant endeavor of
the people, who shall refrain from any abuse of these freedoms and rights and
shall always be responsible for utilizing them for the public welfare." Article
13 states: "All of the people shall be respected as individuals. Their right to
life, liberty, and the pursuit of happiness shall, to the extent that it does not
interfere with the public welfare, be the supreme consideration in legislation
and in other governmental affairs."

Since "public welfare" begs for definition, the court invented the doctrine
that, in obscenity cases at least, public welfare is defined in terms of "prevailing social norms, which are the norms of sound men of good sense." Going
a step further, the court assigned to itself the responsibility of maintaining
such norms through the "clinical role" of the courts in promoting a moral
sense among the public should it become insensitive to obscene writings.

Despite such an interventionist philosophy, the courts have not been active in protecting the public welfare, mainly because there have been few threats to "prevailing social norms." Judicial indifference to obscene writings is not a problem because most media maintain self-censorship codes. These self-imposed restraints on the public availability of material, which could be regarded as morally objectionable, conform to what is presumably the judicial test of obscenity. This is a presumption since the issue is rarely tested in court, so the exact legal parameters of obscenity are not known. The prevalence of self-restraint by publishers does not mean, however, that obscene material is nonexistent, only that there is a clear, self-imposed disposition to avoid testing the limits of the law.

When the pop music star Madonna published her collection of photos detailing her sexual fantasies, the book soon found its way to Japan. It caused something of a stir and was not allowed to enter the country until certain offending parts had been carefully excised. This episode illustrates the curious inconsistency in Japan's approach to sexually explicit material and to the issue of freedom of speech and press in general. Photo magazines are carefully edited, but comic books can be graphic in detail. What is objectionable in a "sex" book is permissible in a book of "art." Pornographic movies are available, but with details obscured. Prostitution has been illegal since 1956, but colorful advertisements, a practice that itself is nominally illegal, adorn telephone booths, announcing the services of call girls. Information on a wide range of sex services can be found at train stations or in magazines available at newsstands. Sex shops with gaudy exteriors, called "soap lands," provide commercial sex to Japanese men. Foreigners are typically denied entry.

The commercial sex industry thrives in Japan, but it nonetheless carefully avoids overstepping the bounds of propriety. Enforcement procedures involve few instances of fines or jail sentences. Publishers of material deemed inappropriate are likely to be warned by a visit from the authorities or perhaps in the form of a letter. The message is that this sort of thing cannot be allowed to continue and failure to comply properly can lead to unfortunate consequences. The matter usually ends there; the actual application of police powers is normally unnecessary to gain compliance. Publishers of magazines and other material may lose the services of their printers, who, in turn, fear loss of other business because of their association with something objectionable. Ultimately, these informal sanctions are effective because of the docile character of the consuming public, which accepts what it gets. If there is a "demand," there most likely will be a "supply." Since consumers are not aggressive in their demands, suppliers are unwilling to accept the risks and costs of so soft a market. An exception to this is organized crime, which, of course, operates outside normal social and legal contexts.

Apart from direct official efforts to censor obscenity, the government has also used privacy and libel laws to limit freedom of expression. Under Article 230 of the criminal code, statements that cause injury are libelous whether or not they are true. This formulation does not extend to matters of a public nature or to the realm of politics, however, where press reports need only meet the test of whether they are true. In practice, the press rarely takes advantage of its potential power to report in detail on individual politicians or other highly visible public personalities. Prosecutions for libel can be employed to discourage anything that might be taken as disrespectful to the imperial family.

Political Corruption

A curious exception to the public intolerance of crime is the widespread practice of financial malpractice among political parties and politicians. One of the most celebrated examples of this concerned former prime minister Kakuei Tanaka. On October 12, 1983, Tanaka was found guilty of accepting more than $2 million in bribes to arrange the purchase of Lockheed aircraft by Japan's largest domestic airline, All Nippon Airways. He was sentenced by a three-judge Tokyo district court to four years in prison and a fine equal to the amount of the bribes, or $2.1 million at the current exchange rate. Tanaka appealed to the Tokyo High Court and the case eventually went to the Supreme Court. The appeals process took ten years; the original indictment was on August 16, 1976.[67]

Despite this, Tanaka continued to hold his seat in the Diet and remained the most powerful party politician in the country for more than a decade. This eventually came to an end, however, as his health began to deteriorate.

The Recruit scandal of the late 1980s involved less illegal activity than what was widely regarded as political corruption. Nevertheless, many top politicians, especially in the Liberal Democratic Party, resigned from office or were forced to assume a lower public profile. Overall, the Japanese voter has been remarkably indifferent to personal and financial corruption among politicians.

In recent years, politicians and the public media have made frequent reference to a "crime wave" sweeping Japan and most of it is attributable to foreigners and youth. David T. Johnson argues in a recent study that the claims of increases in crime are either exaggerated or the result of changes in police reporting techniques. Moreover, given the small number of actual crimes, even a slight increase can be magnified in percentage terms. Recent scandals have encouraged police to polish their image by more rigorous crime reporting. It is true, however, that the public is feeling less secure about crime and personal safety. This in turn has resulted in a "get tough" approach to crime, including longer jail sentences and more frequent use of capital punishment.[68]

Japan's record in the area of public safety is enviable. The low crime rate is due to a combination of efficient law enforcement and a society in which there is a low threshold of tolerance for crime.[69] It is also true that the usual factors associated with crime, such as poverty and racial conflict, are not major social problems in Japan and are thus of relatively little significance. To its critics, Japan's social achievements have come at the cost of dehumanizing its citizens. The "system" is all-powerful, infallible, and faceless.

Part V

Japan and the World

12
Foreign Relations

Japan's foreign relations, those of a formal sort having existed for a relatively short time, have been shaped by two dominant factors: isolation and dependence. As an island nation, Japan has been kept from the kind of direct and continuous contact that is commonplace for countries sharing common land borders with their neighbors.[1] The isolation produced by physical separation from other societies has not been offset by an inclination by the Japanese to venture forth from their home islands on expeditions of discovery and conquest, until recently at any rate. This isolation has been a major influence on Japan's national development and self-awareness. Despite its physical detachment and limited direct interaction with other civilizations, however, Japan has not been impervious to influences from outside. Many intellectual and cultural practices imported from other countries have combined with indigenous patterns to form the Japanese way of life. The knowledge that much of its civilization is of foreign origin has encouraged a sense of insecurity bordering on inadequacy that demands psychological reinforcement and compensation.

Contributing to a collective sense of vulnerability is a lack of material assets. Physical isolation and absence of desirable commodities, resources, or market potential helped spare Japan from foreign invasion and exploitation. But the same deficiencies that helped keep Japan safe from predators also served to retard its material advancement. To accomplish economic modernization, Japan found it necessary to rely on external sources of supply for raw materials and the technologies to make use of them. Hence, though isolated from the rest of the world, Japan was dependent on it.

Over the past two centuries, the combination of isolation and dependence has been important in defining the psychological environment within which the Japanese conducted their foreign relations. One product of this environment is a very strong sense of national identity, of belonging to Japan and to the Japanese race. This nationalism is expressed in the idea that "the Japanese people, sharing a divine origin of the Sun Goddess *Amaterasu,* were united in the framework of the *kokutai* which could be described as a sort of family state with the emperor as the father of the Japanese nation."[2] This exceptionalist ideology has manifested itself in a fairly distinctive way. Although there has been a pervasive sense of inferiority bred of insecurity relative to the outside world, this is offset by a strong motivation to assert the country's status in the international community. The feeling of playing in a game defined in terms of someone else's rules produced uncertainty as to the role Japan should take in shaping world events. But national ambition and fear of being isolated internationally led Japan to assert what it considers its proper world role.[3] This ambition includes the desire, still not clearly defined, to have a say in determining the rules, although the Japanese remain vague about how to accomplish that end.

World War II demonstrated the failure of military efforts to achieve an important place in international relations. If defeat in war were not to result in permanent obscurity, then international relationships had to be redesigned and rebuilt from the ground up. From the status of a major world power with extensive overseas possessions and even greater ambitions, Japan found itself treated as an international pariah struggling for mere survival. After the occupation had ended and they had secured their economic footing, the Japanese discovered that they were no longer competitive in international power politics, having become far outclassed by the "superpowers." Moreover, they remained economically vulnerable because of their dependence on outside markets and sources of raw materials. The promotion of its status in the world, a driving force behind Japan's domestic and foreign policies since the nineteenth century, depended on the development and inspired implementation of new techniques of foreign relations.

Foreign Political Relations

The first task facing the postwar government was to undo the wreckage left by the war. Only then could it begin the process of rebuilding working relations with other members of the international community. After successfully confronting the economic crises, Japan initiated a cautious campaign to rebuild its overseas connections. From the very outset, these overtures had a decidedly trade-oriented character. Treaty relations with Taiwan were established in 1952. Although there were no formal reparations, the Japanese did make sizable investments that served as recompense. In subsequent years, trade between the two grew rapidly. Reparations were paid to some countries, such as Burma in 1954, while agreements were reached with other countries under which they would receive quantities of capital goods: the Philippines in 1956, Indonesia in 1958, Laos and Cambodia in 1959, Thailand in 1962, and South Korea in 1965.[4] These agreements helped smooth the way to the opening and development of markets in Southeast Asia. Since then, Japan's relationship with other Asian countries has been similar to that of the United

States vis-à-vis Latin America. Each is viewed by their weaker neighbors with a combination of fear and distrust mixed with envy and admiration.[5]

Restoring normal relations with its former enemies proved difficult because the acts of brutality committed by the Japanese army against the people of conquered Asian countries left a bitter legacy that would not be easy to overcome.[6] Even though more than sixty-three years have passed since the end of the war, distrust of the Japanese endures, often not too far below the surface. "Almost none of Japan's relationships in East Asia can be described as warm."[7] They are suspected, not without reason, of trying to impose their will by peaceful means, having failed to do so through military action. As one writer noted in 1989: "Japan's neighbors thus looked more and more like offshore extensions of the constantly aggrandizing Japanese economy. The Greater East Asia Co-Prosperity Sphere of World War II vintage had come out of mothballs."[8] Suspicions are openly displayed when Japan, by word or deed, bruises the feelings of its former adversaries.[9] In its relationship with some countries, such as that with North Korea, Japan must deal not only with the legacy of World War II but with the complexity of contemporary international security issues.[10]

Another issue that has come up only recently, adding to Japan's postwar embarrassment, concerns "comfort women," women in areas occupied by the Japanese army who were recruited to provide sexual services to Japanese troops. The Japanese government claims that these arrangements were voluntary and contractual, for the most part. The women and their advocates claim that they were forced and demand compensation and apology. Typically, the Japanese government has been stingy with both. In Confucian societies, public disclosure of such relationships is considered embarrassing to all concerned.[11]

One issue that is virtually guaranteed to pique foreign sensitivities and suspicions is the official treatment of the World War II period, especially in history books. In an effort to cushion the impact of the war on national pride, some important language is sometimes altered. Japanese military actions in northern China in the 1930s are described in these books, with approval of the Ministry of Education, as "advances" rather than "aggression," as the authors of earlier texts had written. The Chinese, Koreans, and others take strong exception to this, regarding it as a brazen effort by the Japanese to obscure the nature of their wartime behavior, leading eventually, perhaps, to denial that they had committed atrocities.[12]

Many in Japan who are concerned about the country's prestige consider public statements of apology ingenuous, merely empty words intended to mollify critics. Privately they deny Japan that committed any atrocities and contend that Japan's colonial rule was fundamentally positive.[13]

The issue of Japan's wartime activities became a topic of heated international discussion after Emperor Hirohito's death. Many world leaders, including the President George H.W. Bush, attended the funeral in February 1989. American veterans' groups and others around the world protested the attention given to Hirohito, because in their view he was in many ways culpable for Japanese atrocities during the war.

The success of the Japanese in developing overseas markets and their tendency to keep themselves apart from local people led to demonstrations of resentment against them.[14] Protests and riots marred the visit of Prime Minister Kakuei Tanaka to Southeast Asia in January 1974. Ostensibly the rioting was directed against Japanese "economic imperialism," but the grievances were really the result of feelings injured by the sometimes abrasive Japanese manner and style of behavior. The demonstrators could not name specific cases of Japanese exploitation, but they "could cite chapter and verse on where they thought they had been snubbed, or excluded or insulted or treated unfairly by the Japanese."[15]

Hostility is based on more than national pride and Japanese insensitivity, however. The Japanese have employed trade practices that tend to be favorable to themselves. In its trade relations with Malaysia, for example, to whose market Japan has free access, "Japan has resorted to the deplorable use of protectionist devices to ensure the continuation of its less competitive industries and agricultural production."[16] Only Malaysian raw materials are allowed into Japan duty-free; light manufactured goods, such as shoes, face restrictions. The Japanese practice of protecting even the most noncompetitive economic activities means loss of export opportunity for foreign producers and substantially higher costs to Japanese consumers.[17]

Attitudes toward trade relations became more complicated as Japan's importance in international relations increased. The record of economic success resulted in what one writer called the Japan as Number One Syndrome. "There is an increasing tendency for even the ordinary people of Japan to overestimate Japan's worth and throw their weight around."[18] Japanese scholars and newspapers noted smugness among their compatriots, a feeling that perhaps Japan is indeed superior to the rest of the world. In 1953, 20 percent of Japanese surveyed believed that they were superior to Western peoples while 28 percent believed that they were inferior. In 1968, 48 percent thought that Japanese were superior, while only 11 percent thought they were inferior.[19] In response to American complaints that doing business in Japan is nearly impossible for foreign firms, the Japanese reply that foreign firms should try harder. In this way the Japanese, in their own minds at least, shift the blame for trade problems onto the shoulders of others and absolve themselves.

Japan–China Relations

Because of its size, the extent of its population, and the potential for economic development, China has occupied an important place in Japan's foreign policy considerations. From the end of the war to the 1970s, however, relations between the two countries were minimal. Because of circumstances dictated by the results of the war, Japan was obliged to follow the policy path set down by the United States. Washington, which officially regarded the communist takeover of China as illegitimate, maintained that the "legal" government was the Nationalist regime on Taiwan. Until 1962, China maintained close relations with the Soviet Union and had a friend in India, which regularly supported Beijing's position in the United Nations. That year, Moscow and Beijing formally split over issues ranging from ideology to foreign policy. The same year, China sacrificed the friendship of India by going to war to adjust their common border. In addition to these issues, China was caught up in the turmoil of the Cultural Revolution from 1966 to 1977; it had few friends and seemed uninterested in acquiring any. Two things changed all this. One was the restructuring of U.S. foreign policy after the end of the Vietnam war and the subsequent withdrawal of U.S. forces from the Southeast Asian mainland. The second was the death of Mao Zedong and the failure of his political heirs to continue his legacy. The new leadership sought different approaches to national development.

As part of the process of disengaging from Vietnam, the United States began normalizing relations with China. Under these altered circumstances, Japan opened diplomatic relations with China and broke its ties with Taiwan in 1972. Japan's trade with China soon blossomed, increasing from $1.2 billion in 1972 to $3.8 billion in 1975. This was 3.3 percent of Japan's trade but over 25 percent of that of China. Despite the political break, Japan's economic ties with Taiwan continued to expand. Indeed, the pattern of growing economic linkages was characteristic of Japan's relations with all the countries of Asia from the 1970s onward.

After a period of initial excitement about the development potential of the "Asian Giant," the growth of economic and commercial activity slowed, due to China's continuing political instability, its lack of roads, bridges, and other infrastructure limited capacity to absorb outside investment. These problems have since been largely overcome.

China's almost limitless need for investment capital and technology attracted many countries, including Japan. In 1978, two agreements were signed: the Sino-Japanese Treaty of Peace and Friendship and the Sino-Japanese Long-Term Trade Agreement. These agreements facilitated the development of commercial links between the two countries. During the 1970s, Japan eagerly entered into economic deals with China providing financing, technical aid, and joint venture partners. But China's difficulties in sustaining the pace of economic development often led to cancelled contracts and losses to Japanese investors.[20] Faced with a variety of problems ranging from an inability to achieve economic targets to political troubles in Tibet, the Chinese government was forced in the late 1980s to retrench its reform agenda, which necessarily caused the Japanese to scale back their plans for Sino-Japanese cooperation. After the Tiananmen incident of June 1989, the Japanese reduced their economic activities in China. Although prospects for continuing political instability in China raised doubts about the wisdom of quick reentry into the Chinese market, scarcely a year had passed before the Japanese moved to restore their "special historical relationship" with China.[21]

In addition to economic and political constraints on Sino-Japanese relations, there is the enduring Chinese suspicion of Japanese intentions. Japan's military buildup and its contemplation of a greater international role for itself fueled distrust. The Chinese view Japan's military activity as greater than that needed for defense, suspecting that Japan might be contemplating "projecting" its military power to other parts of Asia. There is also concern in China over the possibility that Japan will develop a nuclear weapons capability, a concern fueled by the uncertainty of North Korea's nuclear intentions.[22] There is also Japan's claim to some small islands in the East China Sea, believed to contain oil reserves, which rekindles Chinese fears of an aggressive Japan.[23] For their part, the Japanese are concerned about China's long-range intentions given its military modernization efforts and its actions relative to disputed islands in the South China Sea, the Spratlys, for example.

These problems notwithstanding, the two countries share a number of foreign policy interests. At the security level, there is mutual concern over tensions in Korea and the strategic implications of a post-Soviet Russia. Trade relations are enhanced by virtue of the compatibility of their economies. The Chinese have raw materials for export and need industrial equipment and technology. Japan's economy depends on the importation of raw materials and the means of industrialization are readily available for export.[24] From the 1990s onward, China's economy expanded at an extraordinary rate while that of Japan remained mired in stagnation.

Japan–Russia Relations

Japan's relations with the Soviet Union soured when Moscow abandoned the 1941 neutrality treaty with Tokyo and entered the war on the side of the United States and its allies. Japan viewed the Soviet entry into war just shortly before Japanese military operations were ended by the use of the atomic bomb as opportunistic. The Soviet army further added to Japanese ire by prolonging their advance into September after the emperor's surrender statement of August 15. Soviet brutality against Japanese nationals in captured territory and the detention of nearly 600,000 prisoners of war, in some cases for years, contributed to enduring Japanese hostility toward the Soviet Union.

Some Japanese territorial possessions and a great deal of war matériel were in Soviet hands when hostilities ended.[25] The Soviet forces turned over a quantity of captured guns and ammunition to the Chinese Communists, then fighting a civil war against the Nationalist government of Chiang Kai-shek. Although not itself a major victim of Japanese aggression, the Soviet Union responded with hostility and suspicion toward Japan that was more firmly entrenched and endured longer than did that of any other country. This atmosphere of distrust only began to change slightly with the demise of the Soviet Union itself.

The coldness of the relationship between the two countries continued in the post-Soviet period despite a considerable potential for economic cooperation. The Russian Far East is rich in natural resources, but the financial and technical capability to develop them has been lacking. The Japanese frequently express interest in the possibilities of investment in the region, but little has actually been accomplished for several reasons, especially the unresolved Northern Territories issue.

In 1954, the Soviet Union announced that it was prepared to normalize relations with Japan. After extensive and difficult negotiations, all outstanding issues between the two countries left over from World War II were settled, with the exception of the territorial question. In a joint declaration issued on October 19, 1956, the state of war was ended and normal diplomatic relations were established.[26]

Japan lost many territories as a result of World War II. Taiwan, which it had controlled for several decades, reverted to China. The Koreans achieved their independence from Japanese colonial rule. The United States occupied Okinawa, which it returned in 1972, and a host of lesser islands in the Pacific. The Soviet Union took over those islands in the Kurile chain under Japanese control and repatriated the 16,000 Japanese citizens living there. The Soviet forces and later the Russians have never left. The Japanese claim that four of the islands—Etorofu, Kunashiri, Shikotan, and Habomai—are legitimately theirs and continue to seek their return.[27] Japanese interest in the islands is sharpened by the fact that they are located in a rich fishing area, but their main significance is their strategic location and their relevance to Japanese national pride.[28]

The Soviet Union gained control of the islands under the provisions of Allied wartime agreements, principally the Yalta agreement of February 11,

1945. These territories fall into three categories: South Sakhalin; the Northern Kuriles; and the Southern Kuriles, Shikotan, and the Habomai group. In a treaty with the tsarist government in 1855, Japan agreed to a border in the Kurile chain between Etorofu and Urup islands. Moreover, under the agreement, Russia and Japan would share jurisdiction over Sakhalin. In an 1875 treaty, Japan gave up its Sakhalin claim in return for control of all the Kurile islands. The southern islands, Etorofu and Kunashiri, Japan claims, were not referred to in the treaties as the Kuriles and they, together with Shikotan and the Habomais, were *never* under Soviet rule. Japan regained control over South Sakhalin as a consequence of the Russo-Japanese War of 1904–5.[29]

In the 1951 Peace Treaty ending World War II, the Japanese renounced "all right, title and claim" to the Kuriles and South Sakhalin, but the treaty made no mention of beneficiaries of this act. The signatories of the treaty—which did not include the Soviet Union—therefore did not regard these territories as belonging to the Soviet Union but, rather, as being in a state of international limbo; presumably the problem was to be resolved later.[30] The Soviet Union took the position that there was no possibility of coming to terms with Japan after the latter renewed its Mutual Security Treaty with the United States in 1960. In 1973, Japan offered the Soviet Union $3 billion in development credit if it would discuss the islands issue. The Soviet leaders refused because, among other reasons, they had a concern that settling the islands dispute with Japan might encourage China to pursue its own territorial claims.[31] Until 1988, the Soviet Union refused to accept the idea that the islands issue was something dividing the two countries. It contended that the issue had already been settled.[32] The Soviet leaders softened their position in December 1988, when the foreign ministers of the two countries discussed the question, but they made no progress.[33] A Soviet "peace offensive" in Asia, the pressing need for Japanese financial and technical help for Soviet economic reforms, and a proposed visit by President Mikhail Gorbachev to Japan in spring 1991 created an atmosphere in which some movement on the Northern Territories issue seemed inevitable. Accordingly, in September 1990, the Soviet foreign minister Eduard Shevardnadze stated that his government was willing to negotiate the Northern Territories issue.[34]

After the collapse of the Soviet Union, movement toward resolution of the islands dispute all but ended. A planned visit by President Boris Yeltsin was cancelled, causing great displeasure among the Japanese, who believed that they were being treated rudely. When Yeltsin finally got around to making his trip, there was no progress on the island matter.

This unresolved legacy of World War II was an important pivot around which Japan's relations with the Soviet Union revolved.[35] From Japan's point of view, Soviet insistence on retaining control of the islands was an exercise in imperialism. The Soviet claim to the islands is unjust and its hostile attitude toward Japan increased the possibility of armed conflict. Japan's persistent demand for a satisfactory resolution of the issue and its defense preparations, including especially the Mutual Security alliance with the United States, exacerbated the Soviet sense of vulnerability. From the Soviet point of view, Japanese actions undermined Soviet security. One consequence of this situation was a negative view of the Soviet Union among Japanese. One survey, for example, showed that 34 percent of the Japanese respondents perceived the Soviet Union as a country that could be trusted, while 55 percent of Americans and 73 percent of West Germans viewed the Soviet Union favorably.[36]

The crisis in the Soviet economy, which only worsened under Gorbachev's leadership, led some countries, particularly Germany, to offer economic assistance. Strategic relationships and the economic plight that persists in much of the former Soviet Union, has created broader bargaining opportunities for central and eastern Europe. Exploiting this opportunity, Poland, Hungary, and the Czech Republic joined NATO. Russia has expanded its links with South Korea, a development intended, in part, to encourage greater flexibility by Japan. However, Prime Minister Toshiki Kaifu announced in mid-1990 that his government was unable to extend economic assistance without resolution of the territorial dispute.[37]

The Northern Territories dispute was not the only issue dividing Japan and the Soviet Union. Soviet official embrace of Marxism-Leninism was not conducive to warm relations with the Japanese, who generally view all such ideologies, especially the revolutionary sort, with suspicion. American anxiety about the Soviet threat was also a factor limiting the scope of Soviet–Japanese relations. In 1987, the Toshiba Machine Company sold eight computer-guided, highly sophisticated milling machines to the Soviet Union, giving it the ability to mass produce a more silent submarine propeller.[38] This action resulted in official American retaliation against the company. The incident also served to point up the ambiguous nature of Japanese foreign and security policy.[39]

The plentiful supply of petroleum since the energy shortage in the 1970s diminished Japan's desire to develop Siberian energy sources; the sense of urgency to improve relations between the two countries evaporated. The Japanese government remained suspicious of the peace offensive initiated by Gorbachev and continued by his successor, a strategy that generally worked well elsewhere in Asia. The Japanese suspect that what the Russians really want is Western and Japanese technology and a more benign strategic environment.[40] Consequently, efforts to promote trade and secure Japanese investment capital in the former Soviet Union have produced modest results.[41] In the 1990s, Japan's own economic problems and lawlessness in Russia dampened enthusiasm for investment. The pattern changed, however, after the price of petroleum reached $100 a barrel in 2007. Moreover, greater economic and political stability under Russia's President Vladimir Putin created a more favorable environment for Russo–Japanese cooperation. Japan's involvement in the cold war manifested itself in other ways. For example, its admission to the United Nations was delayed because of Soviet opposition. In a tit-for-tat game of diplomacy, nations favored by the Soviet Union were blocked by the United States and its allies while the Soviet leaders returned the favor with regard to countries sponsored by the West. Then in 1956 Japan and several other countries were admitted in a package deal. From the time of its admission until the late 1980s, Japan kept a low profile in the world body despite its extensive economic concerns. It is not unfair to say that apart from trade issues, the Japanese, until recently, took little active interest in matters of international politics.

But this has changed. Unwilling to forego all opportunity for leadership roles in the United Nations and other world organizations, the Japanese have begun to assert themselves. This has taken the form of seeking important positions in various international agencies. They contend that their significant financial contribution to world activities should be recognized by granting them a larger voice. This includes, in particular, a permanent seat on the UN Security Council. This has not been forthcoming, however, and Japan continues to contribute more to the financial requirements of the world body than the Japanese think is consistent with their influence. To this end, Japan has sought to affect the administrative and financial mechanisms within the United Nations.[42] With the elevation of terrorism to the position of the number one international security issue and the U.S.-initiated war in Iraq, Japan has moved to play a more direct, although secondary role.

Japan and Eastern Europe

The suddenness with which the communist regimes in Eastern Europe collapsed caught the world by surprise. After the initial euphoria brought on by the return of long-lost freedoms had worn off, the depth and extent of social, political, and economic problems became evident. Replacing communist governments with something else proved far from easy. One of the more obvious problems was the need for fundamental reconstruction of the security relationships that had been built up since World War II. For Japan this presented no serious difficulties because it had not played a role in European security matters. Another concern, one in which the Japanese do have a keen interest, was the dilapidated state of the economies of the former Soviet bloc.

In January 1990, Prime Minister Kaifu, while on a European tour, announced a major aid package to Poland and Hungary. Each country would receive $500 million in loans spread out over three years. The Japanese government would also underwrite $350 million worth of investments in Poland and $400 million in Hungary by Japanese companies. It was also announced that Suzuki Motors Company planned to undertake a joint venture with Hungary to manufacture cars. This deal, part of the aid package, involved a substantial Japanese government subsidy. The Japanese government was also giving the green light to Japanese bankers and businessmen interested in investing in Eastern Europe.[43] Since then, Japan has continued a relationship with countries of Central Europe as a matter of normal business.

Japan and the Third World

Since World War II, Japan has had little to do with most of the countries that make up the third world, especially those outside Asia. But even with its Asian neighbors, Japan's relations have not been warm. Former adversaries in Southeast Asia view Japan with distrust. The situation improved when Japan undertook a campaign to re-establish itself internationally by, among other things, extending development assistance. Japan has invested heavily in the "newly industrialized countries" of Asia, such as South Korea. Japan has invested in the rapidly growing Indian economy. Lack of economic opportunity limits Japan's involvement in Bangladesh. Political instability in Nepal precludes outside investment and dampens other possible interests. The war in Afghanistan and the political disintegration of Pakistan have ended Japanese interests in those countries, apart from security issues.

From the 1970s onward Japanese salesmen were found in increasing numbers in parts of the world where their previous presence had been limited or nonexistent. Trade with and investment in Latin America and the Middle East grew dramatically. The importance of petroleum in the modern industrial economy meant a substantial Japanese stake in the future development of the Middle East. Despite its limited ability to influence the course of political events in the areas, Japan has continued to use its economic strength to promote its interests in this volatile region.

Relations with Africa, a continent with which Japan had little historical contact, were established in the 1970s. In its dealings with Africa as elsewhere, however, Japan has been guided by the twin objectives of obtaining raw materials and securing long-term market access. In the case of Africa this has meant that Japan has not put forward a policy reflecting sensitivity or appreciation for the character of African political realities. Japan sought to protect its commercial dealings with South Africa and Rhodesia as the white-dominated governments of these countries were coming in for increasing criticism from the world community and calls in the United Nations for economic sanctions. Japan responded with delays and foot dragging.[44] As one author notes, Japanese policy has been devoid of "a proper understanding of political and economical aspirations in Africa in general and in particular, of racism in Rhodesia and South Africa."[45] Japanese foreign policy has not shown appreciation for or even interest in the political, economic, and social problems of this part of the world.

Other Developments

As a formal ally, Japan had little room for independent maneuver in areas where U.S. policy impinged on Japanese interests, principally in Asia. From the Korean War to the end of the Vietnam War, the Japanese had to work within a strategic context dominated by the United States.

Japan's subordination of its foreign policy interests to American strategic doctrine and its junior-partner status began to change with the end of the Vietnam War and liberalization in China. The Nixon Doctrine signaled the U.S. intention to reduce substantially the American presence in Asia. Another important American action was the return of Okinawa, taken as a consequence of World War II, to Japanese control. Relations between the United States and China moved toward normalization, and China undertook to play a more conventional role in international relations. All of these developments created opportunities for the Japanese and made it easier for them to pursue their own interests.

Beginning in 1985, Japan took a more active interest in the activities and operation of the United Nations. In addition to advocating reform and restructuring of the world body, the Japanese vigorously sought to increase the number of Japanese nationals working for the UN, especially at upper levels. They also encouraged the United Nations to take a greater role in international peace-keeping operations and in June 1988 Prime Minister No-boru Takeshita declared his country ready to cooperate. However, Japanese participation in such operations did not enjoy popular support and passing the necessary legislation proved extremely difficult. In 1988, Japan proposed an international panel to address the problem of the civil war in Cambodia and assumed an active role in this process itself a year later.[46] Reflecting the increase in its international economic status, Japan indicated that it would assume a greater role in developing the policy of the International Monetary Fund.[47] In a substantial departure from previous practice, the Japanese have begun to take an interest in such matters as civil rights, refugees, and the status of women.[48]

The crisis in the Persian Gulf after Iraq's invasion of Kuwait prompted a reassessment of Japan's policies regarding use of its military forces. The debate over whether more than money should be used to advance its international interests was among the most emotional and heated since the war, with the military being uncharacteristically vocal in advocating a change in Japan's traditional defense-oriented strategy.[49] Short of providing actual combat units, the Japanese government was willing to back UN sanctions against Iraq. But there was considerable opposition even to this from the Democratic Socialist Party and the Japan Communist Party. Prime Minister Kaifu finally got legislation through the House of Councillors, with the help of the Clean Government Party (Kōmeitō) only after promising to reduce the defense budget.

Relations with the United States

Former U.S. ambassador to Japan Mike Mansfield, to the chagrin of many, especially in Canada and Britain, described the U.S. relationship with Japan as the most important in the world, bar none.[50] Although he may have overstated the case, it is not a gross exaggeration. Considering the shared strategic and economic interests, the bilateral connection between the two countries has rivaled that between the United States and Europe. It is not likely that this is true psychologically, however. In addition, the relationship between the United States and Japan has been contentious more often than that between the United States and Europe. "The extensive differences in structure and practice between the two economies guaranteed that conflict would arise. . . . Such friction also affected relations between the United States and its European trading partners. But the cross-investment linking the U.S. and the Western European economies eased tensions by giving each power a voice in the other's system."[51] For the first few years after World War II, U.S. policy was to make Japan an international nonentity. Japan was to have no military role and a limited economic one. This changed with the advent of the cold war, and Japan became an important partner in the American containment strategy. "The significance of the alliance to both governments and the growing interdependence of the two economies produced a far more compelling sense of common interest at the heights of power than would have been the case without the Cold War."[52] Japan welcomed American protection, seeing in the Korean and Vietnam wars evidence of its own vulnerability. But apart from being helpful in a logistical sense, Japan took no active part in these conflicts. In fact, both wars helped stimulate the Japanese economy. Wars are prodigious consumers of equipment and supplies, which the Japanese were only too willing to provide. The substantial income derived from these conflicts, which were highly unpopular in the United States, fueled the growth of industry in Japan. To a significant degree, the early postwar economic advancement of Japan was financed by the American taxpayer.

Japan continued to play the junior partner role until the Vietnam War brought about a fundamental restructuring of U.S. policy. After Vietnam, the Nixon Doctrine stated that the United States would leave land wars on the Asian continent to Asian nations, which had to expect to carry the primary burden of their own security; Americans would play only a supporting role. In this context, the United States encouraged greater participation in security matters by its Asian allies, especially Japan.

Major changes in American strategic thinking in the 1970s occurred at a time when Japan was becoming a major factor in the world's economic system. The balance of trade was shifting in Japan's favor; Americans drove more cars made in Japan; and many American industries, such as television and cameras, were virtually eliminated by Japanese competition. The relationship had entered a new phase marked by increasing stresses and strains. Serious adjustments were in store for the U.S.–Japan relationship.

In 1971, the Nixon administration delivered two "shocks" to Japan. In July, President Richard M. Nixon revealed his plans to open relations with China by visiting Beijing. This announcement came as a surprise to the Japanese, who had not been informed, much less in advance. However, American leaders assured them there would be no agreements with China that would prejudice U.S.–Japan relations. The second shock came in August, when the gold standard was discontinued. The American dollar was allowed to "float" and find its own value relative to other currencies on the basis of actual market forces. It was expected that the value of the dollar would decline, making it cheaper and the yen more expensive, thus enhancing the competitiveness of American exports. To make matters worse, from the Japanese point of view, a 10 percent surcharge was imposed on imports to the United States.

During the 1980s, the atmosphere of U.S.–Japan relations took on a friendlier quality. President Ronald Reagan and Prime Minister Yasuhiro Nakasone enjoyed good personal relations, calling each other by their given names.[53] Despite the surface cordiality, serious differences remained, ranging from American imports of cars and steel to the touchy question of Japan's desire to continue killing whales when most of the world had agreed to stop. Despite efforts to control it, the trade deficit continued to grow through the 1980s. During the Reagan years, the deficit rose from $12 billion in 1981 to $58.6 billion in 1986. Americans tended to blame the trade imbalance largely on Japanese import restrictions, while the Japanese faulted American budget deficits and a strong dollar.

The American trade deficit soared in the 1990s, fueled by a strong U.S. economy and economic weaknesses in Asia. Financial collapse in Indonesia triggered similar crises in Thailand and South Korea. The problems of these economies were exacerbated by the stagnation of the Japanese economy after the end of the speculative bubble period. Meanwhile, the U.S. economy survived the bursting of the dot-com bubble. The stock market reached heights unanticipated by the most optimistic investor. Given the strength of the American economy and the weakness of those in Asia, the imbalance in trade increased. To make matters worse, the Japanese yen appreciated indicating a deflationary trend and making it even more difficult for the Japanese to stimulate economic growth. After a period of slow economic recovery in the early twenty-first century, the Japanese economy appears to have stalled again.

Security Issues

In the area of defense policy, the United States and Japan generally shared a common view of the Soviet challenge, but there were frequent disagreements over specifics. Both countries appreciated the significance of Soviet military capability, but there were widely differing views over what the Soviet Union was in a position to do with this armed might. The United States generally saw Soviet activities in Asia as part of a global challenge. Japan was more inclined to view the matter from a narrower regional perspective, particularly as concerns the Kurile islands and the vulnerability of Japan's commercial sea-lanes. As the Soviet challenge receded after the dissolution of Soviet hegemony in Central Europe, the case for major military efforts to maintain the security of Asia began to disappear. In early 1990, U.S and Japanese officials agreed that the U.S. troop presence in East Asia and the Pacific could be reduced by at least 10 percent.[54]

Overall, Japan has not been in a good position to play a military role on the scale preferred by the United States. Even though the 1 percent of the gross national product (GNP) barrier limiting military expenditures was abolished,[55] the public revenues simply do not exist for massive rearmament. The Japanese government, confronted by the twin problems of unbalanced budgets and public hostility toward tax increases, has not had revenues at its disposal to finance substantially greater military spending. To complicate matters, the United States, consistent with the Reagan supply-side economic philosophy, pressured Japan in late 1986 to cut taxes in order to stimulate economic growth. Greater Japanese (and German) economic expansion were perceived as the engine required to promote growth in the international economy. At the same time, North Korean missile activity and nuclear weapons development encouraged the Japanese to be more attentive to their security requirements.

The Japanese public has demonstrated its willingness to pay for a military establishment, but not at the level that American taxpayers are willing to tolerate. The United States, during the cold war years, devoted in the neighborhood of 6 percent of its GNP to the military, with considerable public support. Japan held its expenditures to around 1 percent, and there is little public enthusiasm for increases. Americans are willing to shoulder a major responsibility for security in all parts of the world; the Japanese have to date shown little interest in assuming a greater share of that burden except as it affects them directly.

Many Japanese are convinced that expanding their military capability would be counterproductive, and significant changes in security policy would likely provoke a reaction from Japan's neighbors. Japan can draw important lessons from the Soviet experience. Soviet policy, driven by insecurity, was Janus-faced. The Soviet Union was an imperial power with a vast and heterogeneous empire.[56] For several hundred years, the leaders of the Russian/Soviet empire took advantage of every opportunity to acquire additional territory. The latest chapter of this process was the thrust into Afghanistan. Showing its other face, the Soviet Union felt very insecure, seeing itself threatened from all directions, a factor that also contributed to the Afghan involvement. These two aspects of Soviet policy played on each other. The Soviet Union was insecure because it was an empire; all empires are insecure. More territory was added to enhance security, that is, the border was continually pushed outward. Central Asia was added in the late nineteenth and early twentieth centuries to protect the southern flank. European satellites were acquired after World War II to protect against invasion from the West. With such an extended frontier, security concerns became ever greater, although ironically they emanated more from within than from without.[57] The Soviet Union was destroyed not by external attack but from internal decay, a common fate of empires.

Nuclear deterrence strategy evolved from the brinksmanship philosophy of "massive retaliation" when Soviet aggression was to be met with an all-out nuclear counterstrike to a more flexible doctrine called "graduated response." As the twentieth century drew to a close, nuclear deterrence strategy was no longer driven by the cold war. Today nuclear strategy addresses such issues as nuclear proliferation and the problem of "rogue states." The current nuclear powers are disposed to maintain their nuclear monopoly and show little interest in nuclear disarmament. The issue of deterrence is now relevant primarily to those countries without nuclear weapons that calculate their security might be enhanced if they had them, such as India and Pakistan, both of which tested nuclear weapons in 1998. Some countries, including Iraq and Libya, determined the pursuit of nuclear technology to be too costly in both financial and political terms and abandoned the effort. North Korea has an active nuclear technology and weapons program and has been known to be in the export business. But in 2007, Pyongyang agreed to shut down its weapons-related reactor. Iran has been developing nuclear technology, with assistance from Russia, which it claims is for peaceful purposes only.

Despite changes in the international security situation, the U.S.–Japan relationship endures. The Mutual Security Treaty has been reaffirmed, and the two countries pledge to continue their cooperation. The United States maintains its forces in Japan although the American presence is not universally welcomed. In Okinawa in particular there is hostility toward the American presence.

Japan will continue to play an important and probably expanding role in the international security system. Following enactment of legislation allowing Self Defense Force (SDF) personnel to participate in the occupation of Iraq, the first contingent arrived in early 2004 but were subsequently withdrawn. An expanded Japanese military seems to be less unpopular among Japanese than it was in the twentieth century.

Development Assistance

On occasion, U.S. global concerns, once driven by anxieties about the Soviet Union, led to requests for Japanese involvement in areas of little, if any, concern to Japan. This included American encouragement for Japanese foreign aid to countries outside the scope of Japan's foreign policy interests.[58] That there has been Japanese cooperation is more a reflection of Tokyo's desire to mollify the United States than any effort to pursue an expanded foreign policy agenda.

In response to the demands for greater support for the world economic system and an expanded strategic role, increases in official development assistance (ODA) and defense spending were part of the budget forecasts up to 1992. Japan's foreign aid philosophy is now entering a new phase. Until the late 1970s, aid was tied to the promotion of exports and economic interdependence, especially with countries in Asia. Now there is greater emphasis on humanitarian assistance and aid to promote strategic interests.[59] Japan led the world in ODA until 2001 when the United States became the world's top donor. In 2007, Japan gave $7.691 billion in ODA while the U.S. gave $21.763 billion. This amounted to .17 percent of Gross National Income for Japan and .16 percent for the United States.[60] The U.S.-sponsored involvement in Iraq and Afghanistan has expanded the burdens on other members of the international community for development programs.

As part of its economic recovery program after World War II, Japan's foreign aid program was at first tied to export promotion. There has been an enduring impression that ODA is more in the form of loans, which must be repaid, than grants, which are not. The latter are preferred by recipients, of course.[61] There have also been persistent charges that Japan links development assistance to enhancement of its international economic position.[62] The Japanese respond that their efforts are not appreciated; they give to more countries than any other single donor. When Japan refused to actively participate in the first Gulf War but, instead, provided $15 billion to help cover the costs, its efforts were dismissed as "checkbook diplomacy."

Technical Competition

A whole range of industrial and technological issues have divided the United States and Japan. The more Japan moves ahead, the more the United States sees itself as threatened and casts about for defensive measures. With the reversal of its economic fortunes in the 1990s, Japan retreated into protectionism. One dramatic case in point is the aircraft industry—both civilian and military. The Japanese want to expand their involvement in supplying international aviation. American firms, such as Boeing, are interested in pursuing joint ventures with the Japanese but in a rather peculiar way. The Japanese are suspected of an inclination to exploit knowledge of aviation technology obtained from the United States in order to expand their own exports and thereby undercut their American partners. Accordingly, Japanese engineers and others working on joint ventures in American aircraft industries are kept away from certain sensitive information. Military aircraft, such as the F-15 built under license by Mitsubishi, may be less prone to malfunctions than models built in the United States. Nevertheless, the technology of the plane's fire control system is not made available to the Japanese.[63]

In 1987, Japanese politicians and business leaders debated the issue of developing a new fighter plane for Japanese use. This was called the FSX project. The United States wanted the Japanese to build a refinement of the American F-16. This way the United States would retain its leadership in basic aircraft design while obtaining access to Japanese technological refinements.[64] The Japanese viewed the U.S. position as an attempt to restrict Japanese technological progress. The Americans argued that Japanese production of major weapon systems significantly increased their costs.[65] The feeling grew in Japan that it should pursue "technonationalism" and develop its own plane with the intention of becoming a major competitor in the world aerospace industry. Among Japanese it is felt that Japan can build a superior model to American types.[66] This is precisely what worries many people in the United States.

Agreement between the two countries was finally reached in November 1988.[67] The Japanese agreed to a refinement of the F-16 but won so many concessions from the Americans that the deal was a major victory for them.[68] A year later the project had run into trouble. The cost of producing the plane had nearly doubled, making it considerably more expensive than the American-produced F-16. Delays in delivery raised the possibility that the plane might become obsolete before it ever became available.[69]

It is clear from this episode that Japan is not only increasingly able but also willing to challenge American domination of the bilateral relationship. In fact, the Japanese are gaining an increasing share of the development of technologies that will make up tomorrow's weapons. Reflecting American recognition of Japanese technical advancements, joint development of technologies to make submarines less detectable, missile guidance systems and improved rocket engines were announced in March 1990.[70] When the United States pointed with pride at the success of its "smart" weapons during the first Gulf War, the Japanese noted that many of the sophisticated components that made these weapons work were made in Japan.

In other areas, from advanced computer chips to high-resolution television, the Japanese work from a strong technological and industrial position. By exploiting their advantages, the Japanese confront the United States with a continuing challenge. "Unless Americans overcome their lingering complacency, pay more attention to getting into the marketplace the fruits of technology that they pay for, and/or team up more closely with the Japanese, they may find themselves on the sidelines of future global competition."[71] Due in large measure to the declining value of the dollar, which made U.S. exports more attractive to foreign buyers, the United States began to recapture its competitiveness by the mid-1990s. By 2007, the dollar had fallen against all major currencies. While a cheaper dollar helps exports, it also increases the costs of everything imported into the U.S.

The Japanese are aware of the sensitivity of Western peoples to the Japanese economic invasion. Japanese purchases of American real estate provoked considerable public anxiety.[72] In appreciation of this, the Japanese began reducing their highly visible economic presence and cultivated better public relations through, among other things, philanthropic efforts. Japanese interests that contribute substantial sums to American educational institutions, for example, are allowed to write off these donations against their taxes.[73] Some American state governments have requested loans from Japan to build roads, ports, and similar facilities.[74] With the end of the good times, though, the Japanese were forced to sell many assets, often at a fraction of their purchase price.

The Nuclear Issue

Another area of contention between the United States and Japan related to both trade and defense is the development of nuclear technology. American policy framed in the context of aiding the recovery and growth of Japan through development assistance generally, and the Atoms for Peace Program in particular, promoted nuclear technology to help meet the need for electricity. American collaboration with Japan in developing the nuclear power industry was formalized at the government level in 1958 by an Agreement for Cooperation.[75]

Japanese nuclear facilities were built on American light water reactor technology, with the fuel provided by the United States. A key condition of American enrichment services to provide the fuel for these reactors is safeguards for peaceful use through the International Atomic Energy Agency. Spent fuel from Japanese reactors has been sent abroad for disposal or reprocessing. The United States has required prior approval for such shipments. A controversy emerged in the 1970s, when Japan expressed the desire to develop nuclear fuel self-sufficiency by doing its own reprocessing. Because a by-product of reprocessing is plutonium, which can be used in nuclear weapons, the Japanese proposal conflicted with American nonproliferation concerns and legal requirements.

Despite its opposition to nuclear weapons, Japan was slow to join the nonproliferation regime. It signed the Nuclear Nonproliferation Treaty but did not do so until February 3, 1970, only one month before the treaty was to go into effect. It took another six years for the Diet to ratify it. In addition to reprocessing facilities, the Japanese wanted to develop breeder reactors, which produce more nuclear fuel than they consume. The administrations of Gerald Ford and Jimmy Carter opposed such development, but Ronald Reagan's administration was more accommodating. Under an agreement signed in November 1987, the United States removed a requirement that spent fuel from Japanese reactors sent to Europe for reprocessing had to be approved on a case-by-case basis. Despite congressional opposition on the grounds that the agreement allows for a potentially dangerous traffic in weapons-grade plutonium, the administration pressed ahead.[76]

The Japanese government wants to expand the total amount of electricity coming from nuclear sources. The achievement of this goal has proved difficult, however, for a variety of reasons. The nuclear industry in general, especially in the United States, has declined. Nuclear power has become highly controversial because of safety considerations, Japan has experienced several "accidents," and there is a declining rate of growth in demand for electricity. Proposed nuclear facilities in the United States have been cancelled, including some already under construction. The industry that produces equipment for nuclear plants declined sharply. Japanese reliance on nuclear power has resulted in the need to develop the industrial capacity to provide the plants, equipment, and replacement parts to keep the reactors working. Japan has succeeded to such an extent that Japanese nuclear technology surpasses that in the United States. It takes less than half as long to build a nuclear plant in Japan, they produce substantially less radioactivity to which workers in the reactor environment are exposed, there are fewer unplanned shutdowns, and the operating processes are generally more sophisticated.[77]

The Japanese nuclear power industry suffered a major setback in February 1991, when a series of problems resulted in emergency flooding of the reactor core at a nuclear power plant. Some radiation escaped into the atmosphere.[78] Despite vigorous government efforts to expand nuclear power as a substitute for foreign oil, public opposition, which has always been substantial, is growing. Public anxiety over the safety of nuclear power was heightened in October 1999, when another accident occurred. Workers in a plant processing nuclear fuel placed 35.2 pounds of uranium— instead of 5.2 pounds—in nitric acid in order to produce uranium dioxide. A nuclear fission process released significant quantities of radiation into the surrounding atmosphere. The inept handling of the accident was even more disturbing than the accident itself. In 2007, another nuclear accident occurred when a reactor was damaged by an earthquake. Nonetheless, pressure to expand nuclear power will continue as demands for petroleum expand, producing sharp increases in price.

Foreign Economic Relations

In 1973, the Organization of Petroleum Exporting Countries (OPEC) raised the price of oil, resulting in a 450 percent jump in its cost to Japan.[79] Because Japan imports nearly all of its energy supplies, this development was a major economic shock, producing double-digit inflation; the price index went from 100 in 1970 to 180 in 1976. A second, but much less severe, oil shock occurred in 1978–79. Because they import not only oil but also most industrial raw materials, the Japanese grew nervous over the potential that other commodity producers would seek to emulate OPEC and develop their own cartels, a costly prospect for Japan. Projections of economic growth dropped from the usual range of around 10 percent to 5 percent or less. Officials in the Ministry of International Trade and Industry (MITI) were forecasting the "complete collapse" of the economy if the problems were not dealt with effectively.[80] Inflation continued for some time at a rate of 25 percent, and there was increased unemployment. The lifetime employment system was strained as companies found themselves with too many employees. Japan was experiencing trade disadvantages, and it was feared that exports would stagnate.

Japan consumes substantially less oil per capita than does the United States. Still, Japan tries to achieve further economies by reducing consumption, especially by increasing efficiencies in industrial machines, electric motors, and other consumers of energy. Other regulations included a speed limit of 50 miles per hour and a maximum of 68 degrees Fahrenheit for domestic heating. These last two rules have little significance since roads are so narrow and crowded most of the time that it is rarely feasible to drive over 50. Typically houses are so poorly heated that it is improbable a consistent temperature of 68 degrees can be attained.[81]

The experience of the oil shocks, inflation, and political scandals bruised the Japanese sense of optimism. Malaise and social decay were perceived and extensively commented on by both Japanese and foreign observers. Bombings by political radicals in downtown Tokyo, increasingly frequent and lengthy strikes, and inept political leadership did not augur well for the future.[82] Overall, the inadequate response to the oil crisis contributed to the malaise of the 1990s.[83]

Although the Japanese responded to demands from foreign economic interests for access to the domestic market by lowering many formal trade barriers, often-elaborate administrative regulations remained that served just as effectively to limit imports. "The amazing thing . . . is that there were no *formal* barriers in the cartelized industries. That would have been politically untenable in light of U.S.–Japan trade friction."[84] In reply to complaints that their policies restrict trade, the Japanese often put the blame on foreigners. They lack language skills, do not understand the local system, are too impatient, or fail to satisfy specific Japanese tastes. Such observations about foreign firms and business people are true as far as they go. Nevertheless, the Japanese probably exaggerate the importance of such factors in restricting the level of imports.

To some extent, American trade problems are self-inflicted. In the 1950s and 1960s, the United States, in the interest of containing the Soviet Union, pursued a policy of promoting solidarity among its allies. One aspect of this solidarity was to restrict trade with the Soviet bloc. As an inducement to cooperate with this policy, the United States allowed its trade partners access to the American market while permitting these partners to retain barriers to American goods.[85] They were so weak and the United States so strong that this was not seen as a serious problem. But American allies grew accustomed to such privileges and were reluctant to give them up. Changing the rules of the international trade game proved difficult for the United States faced with enormous trade deficits.

American manufacturers expect to sell most of their goods to domestic consumers. The Japanese rely heavily on foreigners to buy a substantial portion of the products of their industries. The emphasis on trade is the result of several factors. One is the poor performance of Japanese labor in increasing its share of economic growth. Historically, if workers earned more, they could have bought more. "At the heart of Japan's post-1973 anorexia is its low personal consumption."[86] Today, the Japanese worker is among the highest paid in the world, yet consumption is weak because of the high cost of goods and services. There is also the problem of the extremely high cost of real estate, especially in the Tokyo area, and limited space. Thus Japanese dwellings are typically small, leading some observers to suggest that the Japanese have a "rabbit hutch" mentality. Japanese consumers appear satisfied with a modest standard of living, compared to those in other countries with similar levels of income. This is an oversimplification and an increasingly inaccurate one, as the Japanese are becoming more concerned about quality-of-life issues including material rewards.[87]

In contrast to Western countries, where imports satisfy a substantial part of consumer demand, the Japanese purchase little made abroad. From 1975 to 1986, the percentage of domestic consumption satisfied by imports rose in most Western countries, while in Japan, which already has a very low ratio of imports to domestic consumption, it actually declined.[88] It is true that the Japanese consumer has a high degree of product loyalty, especially to products made in Japan. This may be in part devotion to national symbols, but the Japanese are also quality conscious. Many foreign goods, while cheaper, may also be of lower quality. Japanese consumer habits are beginning to change as a result of the appreciation of the yen, which has made foreign goods increasingly competitive, at least in price, in the Japanese domestic market. Moreover, easing trade barriers will make imports more broadly available and thus more attractive to consumers.

Another reason for the emphasis on trade has been the failure of the government to pursue actively policies intended to stimulate domestic demand. Public financial support of housing construction, for example, is quite small. Total housing investment as a percentage of GNP has declined steadily since 1979.[89]

International Trade Pressures

Under mounting pressure from abroad, the Japanese took steps to open up their markets. In December 1985, for the first time in its history, the Tokyo Security Exchange (Nikkei) granted seats to foreign firms. Three were from the United States, two from Britain, and one from Hong Kong. Foreign banks were also allowed to open securities subsidiaries in Tokyo, something that Japanese banks cannot do. This concession was in response to Western pressures and threats of retaliation. Britain threatened to close the London securities markets to countries that excluded British firms. The West Germans had prohibited Japanese banks from underwriting German bonds until German banks were allowed to operate in the Tokyo securities market. Nevertheless, this partial opening did not satisfy Western bankers, as those denied seats on the Tokyo Stock Exchange saw little prospect of gaining them in the near future.[90]

One persistent sore point is the domestic petroleum market, to which foreign oil companies have enjoyed little access. Under the Petroleum Industry Law enacted in 1962, the government exercises control over the industry through licensing. The industry is inefficient, and profits are low. In gasoline distribution, relative to demand there are more outlets in Japan than in the United States.[91] In the winter of 1984–85, this practice drew extensive publicity embarrassing to the government when a small Japanese trading company challenged the legality of the system.[92] Although the arrangement was formally lifted the following year, MITI, which controlled the issuance of import licenses, provided new ones only to those least likely to use them. This included the biggest domestic refiners, whose business depends on keeping the market closed. Foreign concerns and small Japanese traders wanted the government to dismantle the arrangement in which Japanese refiners customarily sold gasoline at very high prices in order to cover loses on the sale of politically sensitive products such as heavy fuel oil (for industry) and kerosene (for home heating).[93]

Toward the end of 1985, Japan succumbed to international pressures to realign its currency. Undervalued for years against the dollar, the yen appreciated 20 percent in the last quarter of the year. By mid-1988, the dollar had lost half its value against the yen. It was widely hoped that the rise in the value of the yen would relieve the balance-of-payment deficits that Japan's European and American trading partners had been amassing for years. It was also believed that a higher-valued yen would force the country to rely more on its domestic markets to consume the products of industry and less on exports. But after several months of continued decline in the value of the dollar, the trade imbalances persisted, sometimes at levels even wider than before. In 1988, the overall trade deficit of the United States began to shrink, largely on the strength of expanding American exports, not declining imports. Despite the continued depreciation of the dollar to levels well below 100 yen, the trade deficit with Japan continued. When Japan and other Asian countries experienced economic difficulties in the 1990s, they imported less and the United States imported more, leading to even greater trade imbalances.

Japanese exporters confounded foreign expectations that the trade deficit would quickly ease. The volume of Japanese exports continued to remain high because of consumer demand and willingness by manufacturers to absorb some of the increased costs through lower profits. The expectation that Japan's exports would rise in price proportionate to the currency differential, thus making Japanese products less attractive, was not immediately fulfilled. Although prices did in fact rise, the increases have been limited, in part, because the Japanese have moved many manufacturing processes offshore. Due to lower production costs, especially labor, many Japanese products are now made in Korea, China, and Southeast Asia. Moreover, American producers did not take full advantage of rising import costs to lower their own prices to make their products more attractive and thus gain greater market share. They preferred, instead, to continue with high profit margins.[94] The Japanese continued to sell cars, American producers continued their high profits, the consumer paid more, and the trade deficit remained a problem. The Japanese did not deviate from their past strategy of protecting market share, even if this meant diminished profits.[95]

The Japanese have made a number of concessions that ostensibly opened up their domestic markets. Tariffs on American computer parts were eliminated, and the duty on many other electronic products was reduced 20 percent. A major development was the acceptance by the Japanese of foreign test results for pharmaceutical products. This meant that importers would not have to duplicate the time-consuming and costly process of repeating laboratory tests already done abroad before the products could be sold on the local market. Restrictions that limited the ability of outside firms to bid on major construction projects and to gain access to the Japanese telecommunication market were eased by agreements negotiated to liberalize these markets.[96] Some agricultural import markets have also been liberalized, but the Japanese remained adamant in excluding rice imports until they were forced to open their market due to bad weather.[97] Only after poor domestic crops in 1993 did the government open the door to foreign rice. But Japanese consumers still have limited access to foreign rice.

An increasing chorus of American and European criticism of restrictive practices in electronics and microchips led the Reagan administration to impose tariffs on selected Japanese goods, amounting in some cases to 100 percent. This was in retaliation for what the U.S. government contended was Japanese dumping of microchips on world markets at prices below production costs.[98] Foreign firms were not able to compete, thus the Japanese were able to gain a greater share of the market. It is widely believed in the West that the Japanese agree, reluctantly, to change their import-export policies but move with glacial slowness in implementing them. "Trade disputes between Japan and the United States have typically ended with Japanese promises followed by no action whatsoever," observed one businessman.[99] The Japanese do not see it this way. They see themselves making one concession after another, only to be met by still more demands.[100]

The trade problem took another turn in 1988, when the U.S. Congress enacted the Omnibus Trade Bill, which revised the 1974 Trade Act. Among other things, the bill strengthened provisions for sanctions against unfair trade practices. This "Super 301" list was implemented by the administration of George H.W. Bush in 1989 and included Japan along with India and Brazil. Japan and Brazil were dropped from the list in 1990. President Bill Clinton threatened to invoke 301 when trade negotiations appeared deadlocked, but last-minute agreement prevented a confrontation.

American leaders think that Japan erects barriers to imports, whereas the Japanese see the American trade deficit as a result of too much spending, too little saving, and inadequate education in the United States. An effort to address these issues took the form of the Structural Impediments Initiative, in which the two countries suggested to each other how changes might improve trade. An agreement was reached in April 1990 under which, among other things, the Americans promised to improve education and the Japanese promised to make it easier for American companies to open branches in Japan.

The refrain heard from Western business people and politicians that all they want from the Japanese is a "level playing field" suggests that if the Japanese would just play fair all would be well in the world of international trade.[101] It is true that the Japanese bureaucracy sees its responsibility as gaining and retaining competitive advantages for its own producers, not in making it easier for foreign commerce to make a profit in Japan. This is only part of the story, however. All countries, including the United States, try to protect their industries.[102] The Japanese jumped to such an enormous economic lead that their competitors are inclined to emphasize, perhaps too much, unfair play.[103] In fact, moreover, Japanese imports have increased about 40 percent annually over the past three years, and this is in manufactured goods, not low value goods or raw materials. At the same time, exports have remained at basically the same level.[104]

The Japanese see themselves being made into scapegoats for problems and failures that are not entirely of their own making.[105] Besides, they have their own problems. Much of their heavy industry, steel and shipbuilding, for example, have been placed in a weak competitive position vis-à-vis low-cost producers like South Korea, China, and Taiwan. In some cases, weak performers are kept afloat by spreading production cuts across an entire industry. But this is not a permanent solution to the problem. Many Japanese companies are opening overseas factories in order to gain a better political relationship with the host country, in addition to economic advantages, such as cheap labor. The result is less employment at home. Although wages have increased, the rate has begun to slow down.

The United States continues to run a substantial balance-of-payments deficit with Japan. The recessionary problems of the 1990s blocked the upward movement of the yen against the dollar. Japan and other countries running surpluses with the United States, such as China and oil-exporting countries, continue to subsidize American deficits. "The United States has permitted Japan to flood its economy with exports provided that Japan is willing to accept dollars as payment and reinvest those dollars back in the United States."[106]

As Japan's economic power has grown, so has the desire to play a greater institutional role at the international level. This means, for example, expanded Japanese contributions to the International Monetary Fund and the World Bank. Japan is second to the United States in contributions to the United Nations. Its new financial status also means greater influence in determining international policy for Japan. Despite its expanding international involvement, Japan's foreign policy remains unfocused. "What still seems to be missing in Japanese foreign policy is some definition of what that policy stands for."[107]

In many ways, the relationship between Japan and other countries has developed at a pace exceeding their capacity to adapt. People have difficulty adjusting their self-image to changing realities. Americans, for example, have difficulty shaking off the complacency associated with being the world's most powerful nation. Many in the West see Japan not as a vigorous competitor but as a threat.[108] The relationship between Japan and its international partners becomes increasingly complicated as the number and variety of interests involved grows. To official government-to-government relations must be added industrial and commercial contacts and even official representations from American state governments.[109]

One of the most striking things about Japan's postwar foreign policy has been its low visibility. Although Japan is becoming more active on the stage of international relations, its role remains primarily economic. It has little interest in the many controversies that occupy the attention of many governments. This low-key approach is sustained by public opinion, although there is a growing nationalist spirit calling for a more assertive foreign policy. The international environment is also beginning to change. The Japanese have been denied the luxury of treating the rest of the world as one big marketplace. Japan's response, however, has been slow. The changes that have occurred have been incremental. Japan's responses to the two Gulf Wars, to international terrorism, and to international peacekeeping operations have been minimalist and came about only then after intense international pressure and internal political debate.

13

Defense

A series of redefining challenges to domestic and international politics have rolled over Asia during the course of the last several centuries. Most countries in the region were ill-equipped to deal with these challenges when they first began to appear, and some remain so even today. Europe's discovery of a comparatively easy and swift access route to Asia by sea was followed by exploitation and colonization, which had not only long-term political but also cultural consequences. The Dutch in Indonesia, the French in Indochina, the Spanish in the Philippines, and the British on the Indian subcontinent and elsewhere created new political structures and introduced, among other things, alien languages, religions, and philosophies. China, although spared direct colonization—there was too much competition among European countries and China was too big and unified for that—nevertheless experienced the corrosive effects of Westernization on its own institutions. The Europeans exploited China economically and tried with some success to impose European culture on it. One consequence was the demise of the centuries-old, Confucian-based, emperor-centered system sooner than would have been the case had China been left to develop in accordance with its own internal dynamics.

Eventually the Europeans began to lose their imperial grip, confronted as they were by the rise of national self-determination and, especially after World War I, by their own weakness. The erosion of European domination of Asia, a process that was accelerated by the two world wars, was largely completed by the end of the 1940s. The decline of European influence was matched by a corresponding rise in the power of Japan, which began to play an increasingly important role in Asian affairs by the end of the nineteenth century. This new role was a major departure for Japan, which, throughout most of its history, had been a provincial backwater, content to pursue a policy of isolation, especially toward the West. Even with its immediate neighbors, Japan had traditionally maintained only limited and intermittent formal relations. For their part, other countries were not much interested in Japan. In fact only on two occasions, in the thirteenth century, did the outside world attempt physically to force its way into Japan. In these efforts, the Mongols were frustrated, not by effective Japanese resistance, but by logistics and bad weather. Interrupted in its march toward great power status by defeat in World

War II, Japan has since developed great economic strength and has become, in that category at least, a rival of the United States as world leader.

Following the Meiji restoration in 1868, an ambitious program of political and economic modernization was undertaken, an effort that was so success-ful that within a few decades Japan had become an important participant in inter-Asian relations. Japan met the challenges posed by Western domination in the area and in so doing introduced a second major challenge to Asia. At the time of Japan's ascendancy, other East Asian countries showed no similar talent for national development. For a variety of reasons, they fell victim to modern technology in the hands of countries able and willing to use it. In the case of China, bound by its own traditions, coming to terms with the modern world was inhibited by Western exploitation and interference. Soon China, as well as other countries in Asia, would find it severely outclassed by Japan in employing the tools of national power in international relations.

From Hot War to Cold War

After the cataclysm of the Great War of 1914–18, world leaders experimented with a variety of different approaches in an effort to avoid another such di-saster. Most failed, including among the more novel of them the League of Nations and arms limitation agreements. One effort by the victorious Allies, and favored especially by the French, sought to impose punitive measures on Germany to the extent that it would not again be in a position to threaten world peace.

After World War II, innovative efforts to develop institutions and processes for the promotion and maintenance of peace met with greater acceptance on the part of the international community than had similar efforts following World War I. Among these, the establishment of the United Nations was probably the most significant. Other efforts, reminiscent of the post–World War I period, included an attempt to restrict Japan's war-making potential. By placing Article 9 in the new Japanese constitution, the U.S. occupation intended to prevent Japan from posing a threat to peace by denying it the right to develop a military. This approach to preventing war is more than anything else a measure of the American faith in the efficacy of laws to solve problems. But the effort has not been completely successful, not because of a desire by the Japanese to revive their militaristic past but because of the changing realities of world politics. The constitution had barely been put into effect when the idea emerged, warmly endorsed by the United States, that some kind of armed capability beyond that of ordinary police was called for to meet a perceived threat to Japan's internal security.[1]

The American architects of Japan's nonmilitary status soon began to have second thoughts about their efforts. Japan's march toward domination of Asia appeared to have ended with its defeat in World War II. The defeat of Japan and the other Axis powers resulted, among other things, in the rapid expansion of communism. Promoted by the Soviet Union, communism in a very short time came to enjoy considerable success in Asia and eventually extended its writ to Mongolia, North Korea, Indochina, and, most important, China. The advent of communism was the third major development in modern Asian international relations. In the late 1940s and early 1950s, the communists appeared to be well positioned for further successes in South and Southeast Asia as well as elsewhere in the world.

As discussed in Chapter 2, the dramatic changes in international strategic relationships that immediately followed World War II brought about a fundamental revision of U.S. foreign policy. The view developed in the foreign policy establishment that a permanently demilitarized Japan would be a serious handicap to the maintenance of security and stability in Asia. The bold expansion of communism resulted in yet another transformation and challenge affecting Asian international relations: the cold war. In an effort to contain the spread of communism, the United States assumed the leadership of an international coalition intent on deterring Soviet-backed aggression. This effort included not only a military component, but also concern for the internal political stability and economic development of potential communist targets. Countries threatened by communism were not only vulnerable to the Soviet Red Army but to subversion and takeover from within.

A way around the restrictions of Article 9 was found in the simple expedient of calling it (the military) something else. Created in 1950 as the Police Reserve, and renamed the Self Defense Force (SDF) in 1954, the original contingent consisted of 75,000 men. Even though this was not a large force, raising it was not easy. The troops had to be paid more than other government personnel because "this was the only means at our disposal for attracting the kinds of recruits we wanted."[2]

Now the cold war is over, the Soviet Union is no more, and the world is experiencing another period of redefinition, one where the new patterns of Asian international relations are not yet clear. One thing is apparent, however, and that is Japan will continue to play an important role in Asian affairs. It is also likely that the U.S. role will change and perhaps diminish in Asia now that international security issues, as defined by the cold war, no longer exist. The military power that the Soviet Union employed to promote its interests in Asia has been inherited mostly by Russia, which now lacks a clear mission. As the former component parts of the Soviet empire determine their new identities and relationships with one another, the military resources (apart from nuclear weapons) once controlled by the Kremlin to project Soviet power have become of greater interest to the newly independent states in their relations with each other than to the outside world. The role of the United States in world affairs also, for new and different reasons, varies considerably from what it was during the twentieth century.

Most Japanese have been willing to tolerate the existence of their country's military forces, but only so long as they are maintained at relatively little cost and keep a low public profile. Nevertheless, when it was first established after the war, the military was widely perceived as something illegal and unconstitutional.[3] Political parties have been divided on the question of the appropriateness of Japan possessing a military and have not agreed on its role in foreign relations. The Japan Socialist Party (JSP) throughout most of its history regarded the SDF as unconstitutional. Conservative politicians, especially in the Liberal Democratic Party (LDP), have not only supported the existence of Japanese armed forces but have gone so far as to favor altering or removing Article 9 from the constitution.

In the first few years after the war, the need for military force was conceived in the context of internal security. In the late 1940s and early 1950s, communism was spreading in Asia and left-wing sentiment was growing in Japan. The force levels required to meet this challenge were thought to be small, mainly infantry equipped with light weapons, something that could be acceptable to the Japanese without seriously compromising their no rearmament status. Responsibility for the external security of Japan, however, fell largely on the United States. A formal arrangement to divide security responsibilities along these lines was proposed as early as 1947. This shared approach to preserving Japan's security was attractive to both countries. The United States did not want American personnel dealing with internal Japanese security matters. For their part, the Japanese realized that they could not defeat a determined Soviet attack. Territorial security on this scale could come about only if Japan were part of a larger security arrangement. Moreover, the international climate was such that Japan's rearmament would be looked on with great suspicion by its neighbors and would also have serious domestic political repercussions. The cost of rebuilding the military made that an unattractive alternative, especially in view of the weak economic condition of the country.

Opposition in the United States to any security role for Japan was silenced by the communist takeover of China in 1949 and by the Korean War, which followed soon after. American worries about communist expansion developed rapidly and John Foster Dulles, who would become secretary of state in the administration of Dwight Eisenhower, encouraged the Japanese to assume more responsibility for their security by building up an army of 350,000 troops plus naval and air forces. Dulles wanted Japan to play a role in regional defense, leaving the United States free to pursue global responsibilities. The

Japanese remained uninterested in such a high level of rearmament and in any strategy calling for their increased involvement in security matters until well into the 1970s.[4]

The importance of Japan in Asian security issues increased as a result of the Korean War. The danger of the entire East Asian landmass coming under the domination of communism seemed more than just a remote possibility. Japan's role as a forward staging area was vital to American defense plans. One consequence of the Korean War was the resurrection of Japanese industry. In early 1952, while Japan was still under the control of the occupation authorities, hundreds of factories, previously designated for dismantling and shipment abroad as reparations, were reopened under Japanese control. UN forces in Korea used much of the output of these factories.[5]

The Japanese Defense Establishment

To formalize the U.S.–Japan defense relationship, the Mutual Security Treaty was signed in 1951. The language of the treaty stipulated that it be renewed at ten-year intervals, in 1960 and 1970, after which it would continue in effect unless abrogated by either party after giving one year's notice. The alliance was not popular in Japan, and political leaders were forced to sell it to the public by emphasizing its economic benefits, rarely mentioning its security aspects.[6] This bilateral agreement was an element of the American strategy of containment that called for the creation of a series of multilateral and bilateral security alliances surrounding the Soviet bloc. Eventually, this alliance system came to include the North Atlantic Treaty Organization (NATO), the Central Treaty Organization (CENTO), and the Southeast Asian Treaty Organization (SEATO), together with several bilateral alliances like the Mutual Security Treaty with Japan.

Under the defense treaty, Japan agreed to the stationing of U.S. troops on its soil. The presence of a foreign military force has been highly controversial. The U.S. presence in Japan is governed by the Status of Forces Agreement (SOFA). Although the SOFA creates an "inequity favoring the United States,"[7] the Japanese government has considered the alliance vital to the country's security. It is seen in Tokyo as enhancing the credibility of the American deterrence, thus making American defense assistance more reliable. As the Japanese government sees it, if Japan is to avoid a major military buildup, there is little choice but to rely on the armed strength of the United States. Neither country got everything it wanted in the treaty, however. The Japanese failed in their efforts to gain a formal American security guarantee and a pledge for cooperation and consultation.[8] The Americans failed to persuade the Japanese to undertake a military buildup. The United States did agree that U.S. troops stationed in Japan would not be used elsewhere without Japanese consent.[9]

Internal security problems largely disappeared with economic growth, and anxiety about communist subversion abated after years of stable conservative government. The possibility of internal disorder was present from time to time, as was demonstrated by the riots in 1960. Such problems have diminished in frequency and scope and, in any event, are not likely to require military force to suppress. Thus the justification for Japanese military capability rests mainly on external security considerations.

Since 1979, the Defense Agency has defined the role of the Self Defense Force in terms of six functions:

1. to maintain an adequate surveillance posture at all times;
2. to act and take the steps required to respond to domestic insurgency with external support, organized personnel infiltration, arms smuggling, or the covert use of force in Japan's nearby sea and airspace;
3. to rebuff cases of limited and small-scale aggression, in principle, without external assistance. If this is difficult, the SDF should continue resistance and overcome aggression with U.S. cooperation;
4. to effectively function in the fields of command communications, transportation, rescue, supply and maintenance;
5. to carry out extensive education and training of SDF at all times;
6. to carry out disaster relief operations in any area of the country when required.[10]

The significance of Japanese military preparations in the context of global or regional security matters has been highly ambiguous. The Japanese military had not fired a shot in anger since World War II until March 23, 1999, when three Maritime Defense Force destroyers fired six times at two North Korean vessels that had entered Japanese territorial waters and refused orders to halt. The two boats escaped undamaged. That exchange did little to test the effectiveness of the SDF. In the absence of such tests, a conventional measure of military capability is the amount of money spent. Despite dramatic changes in international politics and strategic relationships and the expansion of Japanese international interests, there has been little public enthusiasm for expanding military capability. As a matter of policy, the Japanese imposed on themselves in 1976 a limit on military spending of 1 percent of the gross national product (GNP). This allowed for actual increases in expenditures while preserving an important psychological constraint.

The United States repeatedly pressured the Japanese to increase their military spending, something widely resented in Japan.[11] This issue was pressed vigorously during the years of the military buildup under the administration of Ronald Reagan. After that, military outlays increased 5 percent annually in real terms. Since the demise of the Soviet Union, increases in military spending have been minimal.

In April 1996, President Bill Clinton and Prime Minister Ryutaro Hashimoto reaffirmed the status of the security alliance between the two countries. They also initiated a review of security policy in light of changes in the security environment brought on by the Gulf War, North Korea's nuclear program, and China's evolving strategic agenda. The United States, recognizing the sensitivity of the American presence on Okinawa, agreed to reduce slightly the number of American personnel there, but the basic problem remained. American military personnel commit crimes in Okinawa that generate considerable public hostility. Most Okinawans agree with Jaime Gher: "The harsh reality is that United States SOFAs and current United States military practice protects United States troops at the expense of the local people."[12] Although Okinawans and many other Japanese have a negative view of the American presence, Americans are not altogether pleased either. The United States wants to elevate Japan's "junior partner" role in the alliance in order to defuse concern in the United States over Japanese "freeloading on defense."[13]

The U.S.–Japan alliance was a product of the cold war and now that the cold war is over, the rationale for the alliance needs redefinition. Continuation of the alliance serves several purposes of benefit to both countries. The United States continues to use Japan as a forward staging area, placing military forces in close proximity to potential problem areas in Asia. The alliance also gives the United States access to Japan's defense-related technologies. Without the agreement, Japan would be less likely to share these technologies. For Japan, the alliance spares it the necessity of expanding its own military capabilities, and everyone benefits from the absence of incentive for an Asian arms race.[14] Japanese modesty about their military strength and frequent American criticisms that they are not doing their fair share in the area of international security give the impression that Japan is militarily weak. This is far from an accurate assessment because, in fact, Japan ranked behind only the United States and the Soviet Union in military spending.[15] True, a nuclear capability, long-range transport aircraft, a high seas fleet, and most "assault" weapons are missing from the weapons inventory, in keeping with Japan's defensive orientation. The industrial and technological capability for producing a whole range of modern weapon systems does exist, however.

Organization of the Military

The administration of the military establishment is the responsibility of the Japan Defense Agency (JDA). The Self Defense Force, which is divided into three branches—army, navy, and air force—was initially under the director-general of the JDA. This subministerial level was designed to downgrade the status of the military consistent with the postwar political climate. The military is now under the supervision of a cabinet-level minister. Like many government ministers, the one heading the JDA does not remain in office for long, often less than a year—hardly long enough to become familiar with the job much less make a policy impact.[16]

The mission of the SDF has been limited, until recently at least, to local defense. To meet this local defense obligation, Japan began building up its forces as early as 1954, the year the SDF was formally created. This expansion has continued ever since. The Japanese military consists of approximately a quarter of a million personnel, 90 percent of the equipment for whom is produced by Japanese industry.[17] The ground forces have a wide variety of modern tanks, armored personnel carriers, artillery, and helicopters. The air force has near-state-of-the-art aircraft, mostly fighter-interceptors, plus an array of ground-to-air missiles. The navy has over 200 ships of various types, including submarines, destroyers, and frigates, two of which employ the ultra-modern Aegis Air defense system.[18] In late 2007, the Maritime Self-Defense Force (MSDF) announced that it had successfully tested this system as part of the Theater Missile Defense program developed in cooperation with the United States. The navy also has a large array of aircraft, intended mainly for antisubmarine and reconnaissance duty.[19]

In addition to the SDF, the United States maintained more than 50,000 military personnel in Japan and Okinawa until the wars in Iraq and Afghanistan necessitated the "redeployment" of U.S. forces. The United States operates a wide variety of weapons systems on or out of Japanese territory. The forces of the two countries engage in frequent joint exercises, and an agreement was signed in 1978 for joint military planning. Apart from expenditures on their own military establishments, the Japanese contribute to the expense of maintaining the American presence. Japan spends far more to offset American basing costs than any other country hosting U.S. troops.

The SDF is a volunteer force, although the government has not totally closed off the possibility of conscription in the event of a serious emergency. Military service does not command very high public prestige, thus recruiting is not always easy and does not attract the best talent. Selling the SDF to the public as a disaster relief agency has the disadvantage of diminishing its combat readiness.[20]

For obvious reasons, the Japanese have a "nuclear allergy." This attitude is expressed in the Three Non-Nuclear Principles: no manufacture, no introduction, and no positioning of nuclear weapons on Japanese soil. It is an open secret, however, that U.S. military forces possess such weapons and that they are frequently located on Japanese territory. In 1981 former U.S. ambassador Edwin Reischauer casually remarked that American ships routinely visit Japanese ports carrying nuclear weapons. Although there was a public furor over this episode, the Japanese and American governments typically deal with the matter by ignoring it.[21]

While its nonnuclear intentions are no doubt genuine, Japan is only a short technical step away from acquiring nuclear weapons. There is the technology and industrial capacity, and weapons-grade nuclear material is obtainable. Nearly 25 percent of Japan's electricity comes from nuclear plants, which, with reprocessing, could produce large quantities of plutonium suitable for bombs. It is unlikely, however, that the Japanese will be attracted to the nuclear option, especially given popular opposition.[22] Japan signed the Nuclear Nonproliferation Treaty (NPT) in 1976.

Projecting Japanese Military Power

The Japanese began to broaden their involvement in strategic affairs in 1981, when Prime Minister Zenko Suzuki committed Japan to defending sea-lanes up to 1,000 nautical miles from Tokyo.[23] The pledge, which was renewed by Prime Minister Yasuhiro Nakasone, requires expansion of Japan's naval forces, including, presumably, more than antisubmarine efforts, and represents a major change in strategic thinking. It presumes not only the desire to acquire the capacity to take meaningful action but the willingness to become involved in areas outside the immediate vicinity of Japan. The Japanese have in fact been in no hurry to implement this policy, especially since the demise of the Soviet Union. The United States has pressured Japan to obtain the hardware needed to fulfill the 1,000-mile patrol commitment. Much of this hardware, of course, would come from American manufacturers such as Boeing, which makes the AWACS aerial surveillance aircraft. Japan said it could use four such planes, while members of the U.S. Congress argued that the job would require as many as fourteen.[24] Augmenting their own reluctance to enlarge their military posture, the Japanese are encouraged to take a go-slow approach because their military is viewed with deep suspicion by other Asian countries.[25] But these same Asian states also see Japanese military strength working to their advantage. The Chinese, for example, see a stronger Japan as a complication for Soviet and post-Soviet strategy and thus a positive contribution to Chinese security.[26]

The development of an expanded naval capability does not appear to be the product of an evolving Japanese strategic doctrine, but rather is an incremental response to specific issues.[27] One such issue is the idea of bottling up the Soviet/Russian fleet by closing the straits through which its ships operating out of Vladivostok must go to reach the Pacific Ocean. Another issue is Japan's vital sea access to Persian Gulf oil, which is 6,000 miles away and perceived as vulnerable. There seems little point in patrolling one-sixth of this sea route, however, unless that is where the greatest threat is perceived to be. It is far from clear that such a threat exists, for two reasons. No country in Asia, including Russia, has any conceivable reason to quarrel with Japan to the point that shipping is jeopardized. Second, no country in the region, apart from Russia and the United States, has the naval capability to disrupt shipping.

Rather than serving to enhance Japan's capacity to act unilaterally on security matters, the expanded naval strategy reflects an increasing willingness to assume a greater role in joint defense efforts with the United States. However, this policy has less to do with security matters than with political concerns. For one thing, the policy is not fully consistent with public opinion. But it is not likely to generate serious opposition because the public sees military spending in general as a cost of maintaining good relations with the United States.[28] Indeed, it is accepted that the defense budget is more a reflection of American desires than Japanese.[29] Nevertheless, Japanese compliance in building up its military and expanding military cooperation with the United States does not necessarily mean that the Japanese fully agree with the American strategic point of view.

In late 1984, a joint American–Japanese advisory group suggested that the Japanese contribute to multinational peacekeeping efforts. Prime Minister Nakasone rejected the idea at the time, but an expanded UN role for Japan including a military one would come about in time. Japan has made financial support for peacekeeping operations available for some time. The idea of Japanese personnel participating in peacekeeping operations was raised again by Prime Minister Toshiki Kaifu in 1989. Japanese naval escorts accompanied vessels carrying plutonium back from reprocessing in Europe to protect them from terrorist attack.[30]

Japanese forces participated in the occupation of Iraq for a while, although they eventually withdrew. They have continued to provide logistical support for U.S. efforts in the Persian Gulf. As part of their "nonmilitary" stance, Japan formally prohibits the exportation of military hardware. Although it is generally true that they are not a major military supplier, the Japanese do sell a variety of items (i.e., dual-purpose) that have direct or indirect military application. Trucks, for example, require little more than a coat of paint to become military vehicles. Some in the West are skeptical that Japan can resist the potentially lucrative arms business. "A close look reveals that Japan is exporting arms, albeit on a very small scale, and that Japan's industrial structure and the character of new weapons are bound to lead to an increase in these exports and eventually to the abandonment of the 1967 ban on arms exports."[31]

There is more to the development of weapons technology than strategic threats or economic benefits. There is growing pressure from within the Japanese defense establishment to develop military technology in order to enhance career opportunities. Defense officials have traditionally had second-class status within the political and bureaucratic structures. Development of defense industries would give them a greater measure of respectability and expand postretirement job opportunities in the private sector, something enjoyed by other government officials.[32] The vacuum created by the end of the cold war may produce a more favorable environment for the institutional interests of the Japanese military.

The North Korea Problem

In the twenty-first century, Japan's main security concern has been North Korea and its nuclear program. This program began in 1964 and relied on a Soviet-supplied research facility at Yongbyon that employed uranium mined in North Korea. North Korea joined the International Atomic Energy Agency (IAEA) in 1974 and signed a safeguards agreement in 1977 covering its two nuclear research facilities. Under pressure from the Soviet Union, on December 12, 1985, Pyongyang joined the NPT, which required complete inspection of nuclear facilities by the IAEA. It took seven years to fulfill the requirements of a safeguards agreement, something that usually takes around eighteen months. The Soviet Union had promised to provide four light-water reactors if North Korea joined the NPT, but these reactors were never delivered. However, Pyongyang only agreed to IAEA inspections in 1992. It announced its intention to withdraw from the NPT and the safeguards agreement on March 12, 1993, and from its commitment to the IAEA the following June.

In August 1988, North Korea launched a missile that traveled through Japanese air space. The Japanese considered this event a serious security issue and took extreme measures in retaliation. Tokyo put its military forces on alert, suspended food aid, ended participation in the effort to normalize relations with North Korea, refused to proceed with normalization talks, and threatened to condemn North Korea in the UN Security Council.

Another issue plaguing relations between North Korea and Japan concerns Japanese citizens who had been kidnapped by North Korea to teach language and train spies. The North Korean leader, Kim Jong Il, admitted to this and apologized. In a further irritant, North Korea tested a medium-range missile, the *Taepodong-I*, in August 1998. At first, the United States claimed that this test was part of a weapons development program. Later American experts agreed with the North Korean claim that the test was an unsuccessful satellite launch.[33] On October 9, 2006, North Korea tested a nuclear device, a test that was thought to be only partially successful. It is expected to eventually have an intercontinental delivery capability, enabling it to reach the United States with nuclear weapons. Anticipating this, the administration of George W. Bush moved forward with the "national missile defense system" by deploying radar systems and antimissile batteries in Alaska. North Korean actions, especially missile developments, brought about international condemnation. In the UN Security Council, the United States sponsored a resolution that would impose an arms embargo, a ban on all trade relating to weapons of mass destruction, a freeze on funds related to missile and nuclear programs, freezing bank accounts that allegedly contained counterfeited U.S. dollars, and a ban on trade in luxury goods. The proposal also called for international inspection of all cargo to and from North Korea. The resolution passed, but difficulties arose immediately over enforcement, especially the inspection of ships sailing to North Korean ports.

Japan and International Peacekeeping Operations

Until 1991, Japan avoided seriously confronting the many complicated issues involved in the development of a mature foreign policy. At the beginning of the year, a U.S.-led coalition attacked Iraqi forces that had invaded Kuwait and drove them back across the border into Iraq. Japan, as a major world economic power and one obtaining a substantial portion of its petroleum needs from the Middle East, was pressured to take active part in this undertaking. International expectations of Japanese involvement and uncertainty as to what form their participation in international affairs should take produced intensive debate in Japan. When the allied forces entered Kuwait, Japanese personnel were not among them. Japan did contribute $13 billion to the Gulf War effort, which was paid in full by year's end, unlike Saudi Arabia and Kuwait, which were in arrears in their payments.[34] Despite the amount of money Japan had committed, the other participants did not appreciate Japan's contribution. Americans were dissatisfied and accused Japan of "checkbook diplomacy," and the Kuwaitis, when thanking their liberators, did not mention Japan.

There is a persistent demand from the United States and other countries for direct Japanese participation in international peacekeeping operations. These operations include the many efforts by the United Nations to interpose itself between warring factions in the hope that nonviolent solutions to political problems can be found. Despite the idealistic nature of these operations, involvement in them remains a matter of considerable political controversy in Japan. Proposals introduced by the LDP government to permit Japanese military personnel to take part in UN peacekeeping operations failed to pass in the parliament when first proposed. The JSP and other opposition parties were against an expanded Japanese international role that might in any way involve the military. The opposition controlled the upper house and was able to prevent the enactment of the legislation authorizing peacekeeping participation. Eventually a bill was passed, but the government was forced to make significant concessions to the opposition in order to win passage of the measure in the upper house. The resulting law virtually prohibited the use of armed force except in self-defense by Japanese personnel. This restraint placed limitations on Japan's ability to participate in peacekeeping operations, as the experience in Cambodia eventually proved (see Chapter 12).

On June 15, 1992, the Diet passed the International Peace Cooperation Law after much interparty haggling and an ox-walk (see Chapter 3) by the opposition. The end result was so restrictive that the Self Defense Forces can be used in peacekeeping operations in only narrowly limited circumstances. The legislation stipulates that specific authorization in the form of a parliamentary act is required *in each case* before peacekeeping forces (PKF) can be dispatched. PKF operations that have been initially approved must be re-authorized every two years. The enabling law itself was to be reviewed after three years. The personnel for such activities, called the International Peace Cooperation Corps, include troops from the SDF and nonmilitary personnel who observe elections, help refugees, and provide other services.

Before the government can ask the parliament for authorization to send peacekeeping personnel, five conditions governing the situation had to be met. (1) There must be an agreement among the combatants to stop fighting. (2) The disputing parties must agree to accept UN peacekeeping forces. (3) All parties to the conflict must adopt positions of neutrality. (4) PFK may use arms only in personal self-defense, not to protect personal property or territory. (5) Forces will be withdrawn if the agreement to stop fighting is breached.

Responding to the second Persian Gulf War and the demands for Japanese participation in the coalition occupying Iraq, the Diet passed legislation allowing SDF participation on July 4, 2003. In December the Cabinet approved a plan for approximately 1,000 troops to be sent to the southern part of Iraq to engage in humanitarian work and rebuilding infrastructure. It was decided to send personnel to this part of the country because it was safer.[35] But their arrival was not universally welcomed, as some Iraqis protested that the Japanese were providing jobs for local people. The demise of the Soviet Union radically rearranged international priorities. The new situation was particularly problematic because the main defining element of international affairs—the cold war—had ceased to exist. Deciding its new role in the "new world order" is complicated for Japan by two things. First, public opinion is badly divided over the nature of Japan's international role and the methods to be employed to fulfill it. There is still a strong pacifist tendency running through public opinion, producing uneasiness over the use of armed force. The issue is further complicated by Article 9 of the constitution. Still popular with the public, Article 9 limits Japan's role at least in military terms. Second, the government is fundamentally incapable of assuming leadership and setting a course. This political paralysis can be attributed to the nature of the political process and especially to the factional rivalries within the ruling LDP. When the LDP lost its majority and was forced to seek coalition partners, the prospect of a government able to act decisively diminished even further. Public opinion and party fragmentation together weaken the ability of the government to act. As a result, the decision-making process at the national level is usually incoherent, leaving most power to be exercised by the bureaucracy.

Constraints on Expanding the Military

Public Opinion

Except for a few die-hard right-wingers, the Japanese public has accepted the verdict of World War II. There has been little talk that the war was lost because of "a stab in the back" by cowardly politicians, because of the perfidy of their allies, or because of the incompetence of their generals. Japan lost the war because the enemy was stronger. Thus there is little popular support for efforts to correct the mistakes of history, at least not by using the failed methods of the 1930s and 1940s.[36]

Although the Japanese public shows little enthusiasm for remilitarization, attitudes toward the SDF are ambiguous. Public opinion polls reveal strong, if not necessarily consistent, views on matters of national security. More than 80 percent of those surveyed regularly support the SDF, at least in concept. But the armed forces are viewed with suspicion.[37] The inconsistency between public support for the SDF and negative attitudes toward the military may be explained in part by the fact that many people see the SDF as an emergency or disaster relief agency.[38] (The reputation of the SDF as a disaster relief agency was tarnished in 1985, when some survivors had to wait fourteen hours for rescuers following a plane crash, and in the 1994 Kobe earthquake, when rescue efforts were slow.)[39] There is little public support for a combat role for the SDF, but there does appear to be a growing acceptance of the need for Japan to be able to provide for its own defense.[40] Support for the acquisition of nuclear weapons is, however, practically nonexistent. As far as the U.S. military presence is concerned, the Japanese public is generally supportive but has little confidence in the reliability of the United States in the event of war.[41]

Article 9

A second major constraint on the growth of the military establishment is Article 9 of the constitution. A strictly literal reading of this provision would seem to preclude any military, no matter what it is called. The issue of the constitutionality of the SDF has severely tested the Supreme Court's concept of the nature and scope of judicial review.[42] The first constitutional challenge to the SDF came in 1952, when the leader of the left-wing JSP asked for a declaratory judgment that the National Police Reserve (the predecessor of the SDF) was unconstitutional. The court held that constitutionality could not be determined in the abstract. A dispute in law between two parties in which the issue was present would have to be raised.

Another test came in 1959, when a suit was brought over the enlargement of a U.S. military base. At issue were the Mutual Security Treaty, which allowed for the American presence, and whether the constitution precluded Japan's participation in it. Opponents of the treaty took their case to the streets, and there were numerous disturbances. At the district court level the decision went against the treaty on the grounds that it constituted a violation of Article 9. When the case was appealed to the Supreme Court, the court held that the constitution did not forbid self-defense as such or the posting of foreign troops in Japan.

In 1962, two people were charged with cutting a communications cable belonging to the SDF. Their defense was that if the SDF was unconstitutional they could not be acting illegally. The court dodged the issue by finding that the cable did not relate to self-defense so the constitutionality of the SDF was not relevant.

On September 7, 1973, the Sapporo District Court held the SDF to be in violation of Article 9. The particular case dated back to 1969 and also involved the Mutual Security Treaty, which opponents said violated the constitution. At issue was the construction of a Nike Hercules surface-to-air missile base on land under the jurisdiction of the Ministry of Agriculture and Forestry. The government had asked the ministry to rescind its designation of this area as a forest preserve in order to allow the missile base development. The ministry had agreed, and local residents brought suit challenging the constitutionality of the SDF. The government argued that all nations have the inherent right of self-defense and the SDF was not "war potential." The district court held that Article 9 renounced all armaments, including those for self-defense. The SDF violated the second paragraph of Article 9 in terms of scale, equipment, and capacity. Hence the construction of the missile base was unconstitutional.[43] The lower court opinion was not upheld by the Supreme Court. It took refuge in the doctrine of "acts by government," which is predicated on the idea that the courts cannot offer judicial judgments on national acts of a political nature.

There have been other cases, all having one thing in common. In each case, the Supreme Court has shown a strong disinclination to rule on the constitutionality of the SDF, a matter that it views as mainly political and therefore outside its jurisdiction. As long as military policy is seen as defensive, Article 9 will not be a hindrance. But once Japan adopts a more ambitious military program—one that cannot be described convincingly as defense—then serious constitutional issues, ones that the court may not be able to avoid, are likely to arise. This constraint has led to proposals to alter Article 9 to allow for expanded military activities.

Some observers contend that by using the "acts of government" doctrine, the Supreme Court has abdicated its authority to judge broad matters of constitutionality, because most issues that are likely to come before it are going to be political. The Japanese have apparently decided that such matters should appropriately be decided in a broader political arena, rather than by a handful of judges using legalistic reasoning. Conservative politicians have always believed that Article 9 unduly constrains Japan's security interests, but the public has shown little interest in changing it. After the events of September 11, 2001, and the development of a North Korean nuclear capability, attitudes changed. All four candidates for the presidency of the LDP in 2003 claimed that Article 9 needs to be amended. Moreover, the interpretation of Article 9 allowing for "defense" has been broadened to include consideration of a doctrine of preemption if it is determined that an attack on Japan is imminent.[44]

Budget Constraints

If the Japanese public seems uninterested in a broader military program, the LDP government has been supportive. Yasuhiro Nakasone became prime minister in 1982 and soon acquired the reputation of a hawk on security matters. He advocated the abandonment of the 1 percent ceiling on military expenditures. In December 1984, government leaders agreed to a 6.9 percent increase in defense outlays over the level in the 1984 budget. Still, the amount remained below the magic level of 1 percent of GNP. As part of his campaign to take a more "realistic" view of defense matters, Nakasone proposed in late 1985 that the 1 percent limit be formally dropped, rather than just let the issue "fade away," the approach favored by most Japanese politicians. Opposition factions within the LDP, together with other parties, cooperated to force the prime minister to back down. There was probably more maneuvering for influence within and between parties here than real differences of opinion on a major policy issue. Nevertheless, the fact remains that the Japanese were not eager to cross the psychological threshold limiting defense spending.[45]

In 1986, the fiscal-year budget called for expenditures that pushed the figure for military expenditures to over 1 percent of GNP, and the limit was formally abolished by Cabinet decree in January 1987. The 1989 budget called for further increases in defense amounting to 5.9 percent. This was the third year in a row that the 1 percent barrier had been breached, if indeed only slightly.[46] Even with substantial increases in spending for defense, the military budget was only 1.006 percent of GNP in fiscal 1989.[47]

Economic problems from the 1990s onward made expansion of the military budget problematic. To lift the country out of the economic doldrums, the government allocated substantial sums to construction projects and other infrastructure. This left less for the military, which was seen as having less of a "pump-priming" effect.

Japanese Strategy in the New Millennium

International security relationships defined by the cold war in general and American security doctrine in particular provided a comfortable ordering of world affairs for Japan. But despite their low-key approach, the Japanese have not been indifferent to the potential of hostile challenges. Regional rivalries and conflicts have been sources of concern, particularly the ever-present danger of a renewal of hostilities in Korea. The proposed withdrawal of U.S. troops put forward by the administration of Jimmy Carter would have, in the view of the Japanese, seriously compromised the stability of East Asia. The continuing confrontations between Vietnam and the member countries of the Association of Southeast Asian Nations (ASEAN), on the one hand, and Vietnam and China, on the other, were viewed as threatening to Japanese interests.[48] The North Korean nuclear program is worrisome because it could force Japan to develop its own nuclear deterrent.

The Japanese have not had an ideological animosity toward communism like that which drove U.S. foreign policy during the cold war. Although the seriousness of their differences was a major factor, there were few substantial issues dividing them from the Soviet Union. The lack of resolution of these issues was (and still is) mainly a consequence of Soviet and Russian intransigence. The Japanese consistently favored better relations with the Soviet Union, mainly to exploit the considerable potential for commercial development in Asia. But this relationship remained limited because of Soviet hostility toward Japan, especially the continuing occupation of four islands in the Kurile Island chain that the Japanese consider their "Northern Territories."

Nevertheless, physical security occupied a secondary place among Japanese priorities. Instead, emphasis was placed on economic security. "Japan's approach to the issue of security has been that of an expanding international trade company, not that of a nation-state."[49] Japan's economic interests have not been threatened in any direct military way by any power, including the Soviet Union. The Japanese have instead worried about the possibility that their alliance with the United States would draw them into a war between the United States and the Soviet Union.[50] There was concern about the general challenge posed by the Soviet military presence in Asia, a presence that was viewed as an overall complication rather than a specific security threat.[51] This view is not likely to undergo much change as Soviet interests are assumed by the Russian Federation.

Japan's traditional concern about China, particularly with respect to the future of Korea, diminished during the 1980s with the growing compatibility of foreign policy views among China, Japan, and the United States. The Japanese have been given little cause for worry that China might seek to reassert its ancient imperial claims, at least until recently. Friendliness among the United States, China, and Japan, however, added to the paranoid suspicions of the Russian government, which contributes to regional tensions.

Viewing the world through an expanded window of opportunity encouraged the Japanese to unburden themselves of the legacies of the past, an exercise not always well received by other countries. Prime ministers from Nakasone to Shinzo Abe attempted to overcome the problems of postwar guilt. They have encouraged, especially Abe, the revival of Japanese national pride. As part of their "settling Japan's postwar accounts," any prime minister courts controversy if he visits, or discusses, the Yasukuni Shrine, which honors Japan's war dead. The shrine commemorates the 2.5 million Japanese who died in battles dating from the period of the Meiji restoration in the nineteenth century. Not only are soldiers included in the list but so are others, including the young girls who blew themselves up with grenades rather than surrender to U.S. forces during the battle for Okinawa in World War II.[52] These visits provoke strong public reaction and protests from abroad, especially from China.[53] The emperor's visit to China and Prime Minister Morihiro Hosokawa's apology for Japan's World War II actions helped dampen international suspicions of Japan.

In a speech given in Vladivostok in 1986, Soviet leader Mikhail Gorbachev announced a major change in Soviet foreign policy. The traditional suspicious and confrontational posture was to be abandoned in favor of a more conciliatory approach to relations with other countries, especially those in Asia. Gorbachev's gesture was followed by high-level mutual visits by Soviet, Japanese, and Chinese leaders. The Soviet Union floated trial balloons concerning the islands issue, including suggestions that they be leased to the

Japanese or that the two countries share ownership. Although the Japanese want nothing less than sovereignty, these moves were taken as an indication that the Soviet leaders may have been willing to seek a solution.[54] The process was derailed, however, with the collapse of the Soviet Union. Gorbachev's successor, Boris Yeltsin, faced with even further fragmentation of his truncated state, was unable to act on the islands issue. Under Vladimir Putin, there has been no progress on the issue.

The end of the Soviet Union did not mean the end of the Soviet arsenal, most of which came into the possession of the Russian Federation. If Soviet military strength was all out of proportion to legitimate security concerns, the same weapons in the hands of the Russians pose continuing uncertainties. Before being eliminated by the Intermediate-Range Nuclear Forces treaty of 1987, the Soviet Union had as many as 135 SS-20 multiple-warhead missiles in Siberia, many of which were presumably targeted at Japan.[55] The Soviet Pacific fleet was the largest in the Soviet Navy, consisting of as many as 800 ships. Despite its size, however, this fleet consisted mainly of coastal defense elements and submarines. There were only two aircraft carriers, the largest of which was less than half the size of the massive American attack carriers of the Nimitz class.[56] The Russian Navy is now deteriorating from lack of maintenance, and the Russian government has been willing to sell off some of it to raise much-needed funds. The expanded Soviet involvement in Indochina after the withdrawal of the United States was also a source of some concern to the Japanese.[57]

The Japanese have never been confident that the United States could be relied on to defend them. Administrations from Richard Nixon to Bill Clinton took pains to define publicly the narrow limits within which U.S. troops would be used. And when they have been used, as in Somalia in 1992 and in Haiti in 1994, both efforts ultimately ending in failure there has been public clamor to bring them home. The Iraq War and the preemptive doctrine of the Bush administration have created an environment in which Japan's military role, as well as those of other countries, is transformed.[58] Thus the Japanese have come to see the appropriateness of greater self-reliance.

The Japanese are confronted with pressures to increase their military involvement emanating from three directions. First there was the diminished American commitment to Asia after the Vietnam debacle and the demands of the war on terror. Quantitatively the American presence remains considerable and even expanded during the Reagan administration. The American preoccupation with the Middle East creates doubt about the U.S. commitment to Asia and the reduced American presence leaves something of a power vacuum, which the Japanese, among others, do not want to see filled by Russia or China. The Japanese are thus drawn to expand their own involvement.

The events of September 11, 2001, the Iraq War and the North Korean nuclear weapons program are the most recent, and potent, pressures for Japanese military expansion. Japan participated in the occupation of Iraq, is deploying an antiballistic missile shield, and talks seriously about amending Article 9 of the constitution. Japan is on the threshold of important changes in its strategic posture. The Japanese have become much more active on the strategic scene in part to meet American demands that they do more, but also to enhance their own international importance. In addition to penetrating the 1 percent of GNP barrier to military spending, they signed an agreement in 1983 permitting defense technology transfers with the United States, something prohibited up to that time. More significantly, the Japanese government expanded the notion of "self-defense" to include protection of American naval vessels by Japanese forces even in the absence of a direct attack on Japan. They have also dropped their passive posture vis-à-vis arms limitation negotiations. Before the Intermediate-Range Nuclear Forces agreement between the Soviet Union and the United States was signed, Japan pressed for guarantees that Soviet SS-20 missiles would not be moved from Europe to East Asia.[59]

The existence of a large Soviet/Russian military presence in East Asia exerts pressure for expanded Japanese military spending.[60] It is not that the Japanese believed that their own security was seriously threatened by Soviet military strength. Rather, such military strength gave the Soviet Union at least a symbolic advantage over Japan in international relations generally. However, the demise of the Warsaw Pact and the political disintegration of the Soviet Union reduced, if it not eliminated, this justification for a broader Japanese military commitment.

The combination of these pressures has resulted in a slow but steady expansion of the Japanese military. Given Japan's rapid economic growth rate, even with an expenditure of only around 1 percent of GNP, the increase in actual military spending is considerable. At this rate, Japan has become the fourth-largest military power in the world, as measured by force levels, rather than expenditures.

In the twenty-first century, the international security environment has taken on dimensions fundamentally different from those that existed as recently as the 1990s. Typically, Japan has been slow to respond to these changes. The first priority was to develop a response to the September 11, 2001, attack on the United States. The Bush administration moved quickly, threatening to leave Tokyo behind and putting it in a position of appearing to be an unreliable ally. Japan joined the war on terror, although somewhat reluctantly and on a limited basis. "Japan's policymakers decided early on that the events of September 11 were of such magnitude that Japan was obligated to make a human contribution to combating terrorism."[61]

The decision to take a more active role in international security matters was stimulated by the nuclear weapons program of North Korea. Even before September 11, the United States and Japan had realigned their security relations in 1997 with Japan assuming a broader role in assisting U.S. operations in a vaguely defined area surrounding Japan. In 1999, the SDF was empowered to provide logistical support for U.S. forces "during an emergency." In 2003, the parliament considered bills allowing for the mobilization of the SDF in the event of a "military attack situation." These developments were clearly in reference to North Korea.

In the first Gulf War, Japan did not actively participate but contributed a substantial sum of money to fund the operation. For this, it was accused of "checkbook diplomacy." Japan was reluctant to get involved in the Iraq War but feared that failure to support the U.S. effort might jeopardize U.S. willingness to back Japan in the North Korea issue. The Diet thus passed the Iraq Reconstruction Support Law in July 2003, allowing for humanitarian and logistical support. In December 2003, SDF troops were dispatched to Iraq, although they were assigned to a "noncombat" role.[62]

The government of Shinzo Abe advocated a stronger defense posture and moved toward amending Article 9 of the constitution to allow it. Japan joined with the United States in developing a theater missile defense shield. Japan joined in the Six-Party Talks (United States, China, Japan, Russia, South Korea, and North Korea) that addressed the problems posed by North Korea's nuclear weapons development program. The talks succeeded in late 2007, as North Korea agreed to dismantle its nuclear program. But uncertainty returned in January 2008, when Pyongyang failed to meet one of the deadlines previously agreed to. Agreement was eventually reached. North Korea began dismantling its nuclear program and in a largely symbolic gesture, blew up the cooling tower at its nuclear facility.

Part VI

Conclusions

14
Problems and Prospects

Until the crises of the 1990s tarnished its image, Japan was frequently portrayed in the popular media of the West and by many of the large number of scholars who study it as a dynamo of economic and social, if not necessarily political, efficiency. This view is still embraced by "revisionists" who contend that Japan's economic difficulties are only temporary and that it will emerge from them even stronger than before. Americans marvel at the quality of Japanese goods and buy them in prodigious quantities. But there has also been concern that Japan's economic efficiency has taken jobs away from Americans and generates such a favorable balance of trade that Japan can buy up America. When the Japanese purchase a famous landmark, such as Rockefeller Center, many, especially politicians, react negatively. The U.S. Congress frequently fulminates over Japan's "unfair" trade practices. Japan's assault on American national pride is ironic given the fact that U.S. investors have been buying up entire economies, particularly in Latin America, for decades.

Many explanations are offered to account for modern Japan's rise to prominence, ranging from a distinctive national character to a national industrial policy. The Japanese are also perceived as having the advantage of social homogeneity, which reduces the conflicts that dissipate social energies. They are also seen to possess a single-minded and tenacious commitment to the pursuit of economic development. For the most part, these explanations are accurate as far as they go. But the Japanese also owe a great deal to opportunities made available in the world during the period since the end of World War II. By carefully assessing these opportunities, together with a futuristic orientation and a large measure of luck, the Japanese have been enviably successful.

But Japan, like all modern societies, entered a postindustrial phase of development that is considerably more complicated than what was encountered in the past. Postindustrial politics are, in many respects, a reversal of the patterns commonly associated with "modernization." There is less of a tendency toward integration at the national level and greater orientation toward local or community-based issues. People are personally concerned about problems and less inclined to turn to the government for resolution. In postindustrial societies, established forms of political organization, especially legislatures and political parties, show diminishing capacity to handle the tasks before them. Reformation and modernization of these institutions are slow. To fill the void, citizens' movements energize the political process to take action on issues delayed by the entrenched power of political and economic self-interest. But at the same time, citizen involvement tends to fragment political power, leading to further paralysis of the governing process. "Single-issue politics," which is predicated on citizen involvement, makes it nearly impossible to define, much less attain, the national interest.

The Institutional Dimension

The postwar political system of Japan is often analyzed in the context of two general issues: the first concerns the degree of success experienced by the Japanese in rehabilitating themselves, beginning with the reforms introduced during the U.S. occupation; the second addresses the character and health of democracy in Japan today in much the same way politics in the United States or Britain would be viewed. Both approaches reflect an ethnocentric bias that judges the prewar political system of Japan as morally inferior and defective, a condition that can be remedied only by becoming like us. The intent of the occupation was to reconstruct Japan in precisely that way. If the Japanese were more like us, then not only would they be materially and ethically better off, but they would no longer pose a threat to international peace and security. Despite the self-serving superficiality of this point of view, the fact remains that much of the institutional structure introduced by the occupation remains in existence. But it does not always work the way it is supposed to, and the Japanese are not entirely happy with it.

The second issue—the state of democracy—is at once more productive of interesting discussion and philosophically ambiguous. One problem is that democracy, like freedom, is one of those terms that has become nearly unusable because it is freighted with emotional baggage. For purposes of this assessment, democracy is not an absolute concept but a relative one involving two essential variables. The first is the extent of meaningful popular participation in political decision making. This participation is meaningful to the extent that there are real choices. Participation is not just a ritual exercise, but makes a difference in the outcome of political events. Or, to put it another way, democracy is a process that acts to counter or impose limits on the exercise of arbitrary political power. The second is the existence of formal and transparent rules governing the exercise of political power. Critics of Japanese government see the system as deficient.[1] The occupation reforms have not been fully absorbed; they exist in form, the Japanese go through the motions, but they do not really believe in what they are doing. A spiritual commitment is lacking. According to this point of view, for example, the parliament does not function as a truly representative body in which popular will is transformed into public policy. The parliament is nothing more than a rubber-stamp agency to legitimize decisions made by a self-perpetuating economic and political elite. But this is not really a fair, much less complete, test. The more important question is the extent to which the acts of decision making and the decisions themselves are at variance with public desires. The bureaucracy and the powerful economic interests cannot work their will with complete indifference to what is publicly acceptable. Japanese government is arguably kept within tighter limits of public tolerance than is that of the United States, where the fragmentation of government encourages the pro-liferation of special-interest constituencies. The Japanese system favors the *general* interest over *special* interests. True, government provides considerable support for industry, but this support does not disproportionately favor the rich. Among other consequences of this system is a leveling of rewards and a constraint of opportunities. Americans are inclined to view such a process as undemocratic. But should democracy stress the general welfare or promote individual initiative?

A different view holds that democracy does not work in Japan because the system is so effective and pervasive that people not only have little influence on it but are themselves substantially controlled by it.[2] This is not oppression in the dictatorial sense but, although subtle, oppression nonetheless. People are not necessarily conscious that they are being manipulated and even de-prived of their freedom. Conformity is not based on overt coercive threats of punishment imposed by the state such as jail, threats that could be viewed as external to the individual. In Japan, conformity results from the individual's need to participate in and draw support from the system. Thus, for their critics, the Japanese are not really happy; they just think they are.

Part of the vulnerability of democracy in Japan is perceived to be its tenuous link to traditional political culture. Democracy is not an indigenous develop-ment, but was borrowed from outside and was to some extent imposed. The absence of strong cultural ties to other democracies, especially those in the West, deprives the system of external reinforcement. Japan's ties with the West are based on common interests rather than shared values. If the international environment changes significantly, these common interests could disappear and the Japanese would have little difficulty realigning. "Japan's current dedication to democracy, an open society and material affluence is not some-thing that grew inexorably from purely Japanese roots; it is the product of a particular set of international circumstances and under other circumstances might well be superseded by other imperatives."[3]

It may very well be true that democratic values are not well established in Japan due to their nonindigenous origin. But the same can be said about much of Japanese culture. The Japanese have been extremely successful in synthesizing cultural elements that originated in other countries with their own value system and sense of national purpose. They have always been responsive to the international environment, which suggests a higher degree of adaptability than may be the case in those societies characterized as "tradition bound."

The Political Process

To be fair, no political system is effective and democratic solely as a consequence of its broad constitutional framework. Constitutions are easy to write; making them work is another matter. The Japanese political process has a number of potentially serious flaws. Among the more readily identifiable is the weakness of the political opposition, especially as it pertains to political parties. These parties can claim little credit for the success of postwar Japan. While itself by no means perfect, the Liberal Democratic Party (LDP) has at least been in tune with political realities. The opposition parties have been consistently out of touch with one basic law of democratic politics: Political parties exist to gain control of the machinery of government, that is, to exercise power. Parties that are content to merely serve as vehicles for the personal advancement of their leaders or to perform educational functions by propagating a doctrine are at best sideshows. Only the LDP seems to understand that control of political power will always remain fugitive unless an election is won. The Japan Socialist Party (JSP) finally grasped the matter, but too late for it to become truly competitive. It is still not clear whether the new electoral system will produce party realignment and a more competitive party system.

One serious flaw in the political system and one that has drawn considerable attention is pervasive corruption and public indifference to it. Corruption exists in all political systems, to widely varying degrees. It is impossible to eradicate it altogether in any political system. But if the practice distorts the political and policy processes, it poses a substantial threat to, if nothing else, the ethical integrity of the system. Corruption contributes to cynicism and public indifference. The Japanese voter appeared poised to confront this issue in the 1989–90 elections but ultimately failed to do so, and the 1993 election fell short of a popular mandate to change the political environment. Public cynicism seems to be growing, as indicated by the low voter turnout in recent elections. Meanwhile, scandals involving public officials continue seemingly without letup.

There are two main reasons for the LDP's continuing domination. First, the opposition parties—the success of the Democratic Party of Japan to the contrary notwithstanding—have not inspired public confidence. The public is not sufficiently put off by LDP misbehavior to throw it out, nor is the prospect of an opposition victory seen as sufficiently attractive to vote it in. Second, and more fundamentally, the voters themselves share the benefits of political corruption. Basically, politicians are no more corrupt than their constituents, who still expect favors from their representatives. In the final analysis, the benefits of political corruption are fairly widely distributed.

Another concern, voiced mainly by Americans, is the passivity of the judiciary. Especially in the area of civil rights, a vigorous court system is seen not only as the main protector of these rights but as the agency most capable of enlarging and enriching them. Its critics see the court system in Japan as serving the interests of the state, not the people. But there is another side to an activist judiciary. Very few countries, other than the United States, have a judiciary that plays a determining role in deciding matters of basic public policy. There are several good reasons for this. For one thing, some issues are extremely contentious—abortion, for example. The only way a workable solution, to say nothing of a satisfactory one, can be attained is through an extended process of political compromise. Courts are generally unsuited to make such judgments. Another problem is the tendency of legislatures to finesse or postpone action on issues that may be politically sensitive or unpopular, in effect deferring such matters to the courts. Thus the effectiveness of the legislature as a link to the public and basic decider of public policy is diminished.

There is growing evidence that changes are taking place in the basic values that guide the political process. For example, one scholar sees Japan moving from a traditional political culture to a modern one.[4] The traditional culture has the following characteristics. Society is divided into groups that tend to be exclusive of one another. These groups, based on families or work enclaves, have a certain tribal characteristic in that they do not substantially interact with each other. The system is authoritarian in the sense that a simple authority structure exists which enjoys an unchallenged domination of society. People are highly competent in specific subjects and the performance of technical tasks is of considerable importance. This specialization leads to compensation patterns largely of a materialistic nature.

The modern system that typically replaces the traditional one has in many respects the opposite characteristics. It is open, in that there is more movement among social groupings. Egalitarian values replace the rigid hierarchical structure of traditional society. Competence is measured more in general characteristics or "citizen" values and less by technical specialties. The value structure is less material-oriented, stressing instead universal or humanistic values.

There is evidence that this transformation is indeed taking place in Japan, but it is not doing so at a very rapid rate. The results of elections since the 1990s have confirmed that Japanese voters remain conservative and, if anything, are becoming more so, something that seems to be characteristic of voters in other democratic societies. The conservative drift is manifested in parties on the left that have been trying to shed their radical philosophies and project more moderate images. The JSP abandoned its roots, denounced doctrinaire socialism, and made a serious effort to place itself somewhere toward the middle of the mainstream of public opinion, and, as a reward for its efforts, has largely disappeared. New parties are reform-oriented, but are barely distinguishable on philosophical or policy grounds. Moreover, they tend to come and go at a bewildering rate.

The Changing Social Context

There are some signs that a political culture is emerging that is not as firmly rooted in conservative values. Although the group orientation remains strong as does emphasis on the collective good of the whole, another dimension is also becoming evident. That is the "what's in it for me" attitude. The commitment to work for its own sake is weakening. Many younger Japanese do not get personal fulfillment out of work to the extent their parents did. There is increasing concern for leisure-time activities. A Labor Department survey revealed that 30 percent of salaried workers spend less than three waking hours on weekdays at home with their families. The impact of such a practice on conceptions of self-worth for both men and women, the integrity of the family, and child development psychology is considerable. It is reasonable to expect that this practice will change as the criteria for personal development evolve. As Japanese acquire more disposable income, they are inclined to want to enjoy it. The memories of hard times recede into the past and postwar generations are less driven to achieve economic security. The appearance of religious cults such as Aum Shinrikyō suggests the existence of a spiritual vacuum that is no longer filled by the ethics of hard work.

As far as long-term developments are concerned, among the more significant factors is the changing age profile of the population. The median age is increasing. While this means added burdens on some public service sectors, mainly health care, the development has distinct implications for a postindustrial society. One obvious consequence is a shrinking labor force. Another is expansion of certain kinds of consumer demands characteristic of an older population, including travel, adult education, recreation, and retirement amenities.[5] An aging population also means the character of the workforce must change. Workers will stay on the job longer, and retirement will be postponed. "Temporary workers" can expect to become less temporary.

More women will enter the workforce, in higher-paying and status jobs, and will remain there longer.

Increased prosperity and the advancing median age of the population have created a shortage of certain kinds of labor. In part, the shortage of workers will be offset by increasing worker efficiency and postponing retirement. But there is a whole category of jobs that no Japanese wants because of pay, status, or working conditions. Other countries address this problem through immigration. In the United States, for example, the "illegal alien" problem is the result of a labor shortage in areas like agriculture. Apart from the issues of space (the Tokyo metropolitan area is overcrowded), housing (it is expensive), public services (they are inadequate), there is the matter of social prejudice. The Japanese simply have a very low threshold of tolerance for others in their presence who are not Japanese, and this extends to other Asians. "Not only are the Japanese incapable of assimilating those of obviously different physical strains but their racism is so strong that they cannot readily assimilate even those who display no physiological differences."[6]

One distinctive feature of Japan, a sense of community, is beginning to decline. The diminishing role of agriculture has eroded the integrity of village-based communities. Geographical and economic mobility mean dispersal of family members and a weakening of links among them. Industrialization has resulted in the transformation of towns into metropolitan areas and the appearance of new towns; neither development is characterized by a strong sense of community.

The process of urbanization has also changed the character of cities. Small family enterprises will diminish in number, replaced by supermarkets and the like, thus removing a focal point of neighborhood activities. As the pressure from abroad to open markets continues, one area of development will be American-style merchandising. This will further erode mom-and-pop approaches. "The urban neighborhoods retain little of their former neighborhood community character, and in any case such neighborhoods, once considered typical of Japanese urban life, are no longer."[7] Apartment blocks housing working- and middle-class people with few community bonds have replaced such neighborhoods.

The rapid pace of economic change has inevitably left its mark on the social system. The rural, agricultural, community lifestyle that was characteristic of the country as recently as a century ago has been replaced by one in which job and employment group provide individual identification. The dynamics of social change have especially affected the status of women. Sexual equality does not exist in Japan, or anywhere else in the world for that matter. But in few other places has the status of women changed as dramatically as it has in Japan. This can be seen in a number of ways. Today nearly a third of the workforce is female, with all that implies in terms of roles and attitudes. From having no opportunity for higher education before the war, women now pursue advanced degrees in large numbers. There are more women active in politics.[8] They vote in higher percentages than men, and now they run for office and (occasionally) serve on the Cabinet.

The divorce rate, though one-fifth that of the United States, is rising. Part of this may be due to increasing sensitivity and awareness among women of their rights. A willingness to endure family involvement in mate selection is declining. Women are less inclined to put up with unhappy marriages. In this sense the divorce rate may be a healthy sign, indicating improvement in the status of women. But there is also the matter of children and broken homes. The incidence of single-parent families, almost all of which are headed by women, has risen by more than 13 percent in the last decade. Still, only 7 percent of families are single-parent in Japan and 87 percent of single mothers work compared to 20 percent and 60 percent respectively in the U.S. Female expectations of life's rewards seem to be changing. There is growing discontent among women with their traditional roles as mother and housekeeper. The willingness to equate their personal happiness with a process that involves sacrificing themselves for their husband's career appears on the way out.

Male attitudes and values seem to be changing at a slower pace than those of women, however. But that is also not unique to Japan. Japanese men are reluctant to surrender what they consider their privileges in sexual relationships, and they are only slowly coming to terms with the evolving nature of the family. In the workplace substantial barriers remain for women seeking more than menial or semiskilled employment. The "office lady" is a phenomenon that is not likely to disappear any time soon.

The traditional commitments to family and workplace as principal determinants of lifestyle are undergoing important transformation. Workers today, because of greater life expectancy and early retirement, are spending less than half their lives in a milieu defined by employment. Women are committing a smaller percentage of their lives to child rearing and more to alternatives, such as work.[9]

Although the extent of social pathologies is significantly narrower than in the West, especially in the United States, Japan is beginning to experience increases in a variety of problems. The suicide rate is rising especially among men in their forties and fifties, normally a period of stability and professional achievement. Stress and depression are more common features of the life experience of professional men. Among young people, the stress of exam competition induces many of them to take their own lives. Drugs, discipline, and "bullying" problems in the school system have increased. However, as noted in Chapter 7, the *crisis* aspects of these problems may be exaggerated. The high place that education occupies in the social value system means not only a literate population but one well positioned to take advantage of the information and communication revolutions that are currently occurring worldwide. But along with this comes erosion of traditional values. Today's youth often display anomie rather than commitment to hard work and group loyalty.[10] Given their substantial wealth, the Japanese are now in a position to work less and enjoy themselves more and to place greater stress on pluralism and individual identity.

Economic Development

The government of Japan is trying to use economic development not only to serve the ends of economic betterment of the Japanese people together with enhancement of Japan in the world community, but also to address social problems. As was mentioned above, there is a labor shortage, which is not only an economic but a social problem. Many job openings attract few applicants because they require low skills or no skills at all and, thus, are unattractive to Japanese workers. If importing workers to meet the need is unacceptable, then the alternative is to export the jobs. Hence, industrial and foreign policy converge in the realm of overseas investment and development assistance. Those manufacturing processes that entail low labor-skill levels are being automated or exported to other countries. This strategy is likely to succeed because of the declining workforce and the weakness of organized labor, which has never been effective in protecting jobs. The result is not unemployment but continued emphasis on the development of economic activities that are not only profitable but also socially acceptable.

With the movement of some industries out of Japan to countries with low labor costs or to consumer countries in the West, and with the introduction of new industries in Japan based on innovative technologies, a number of political changes are likely. The numbers of jobs in the blue-collar (that is, industrial) category will decline, but there will be increased employment in the service sector. The changing labor market will contribute to the decline in the influence of certain political constituencies, such as those drawing their strength from industrial unions, a process that is already well under way. Other institutions, such as the bureaucracy, will also be affected. The influence of such agencies as the Ministry of Economy, Trade, and Industry will decline since Japanese business, which is becoming increasingly internationalized, will be less dependent on government help and protection. The repercussions of economic internationalization should also extend to political parties, which will develop appropriate philosophies and policy agendas. The expansion of Japan's global interests means that Japanese business will be less dependent on the support of government to guarantee prosperity.[11]

The much-vaunted lifetime employment system has always been less extensive than commonly supposed in the West, but even among the large corporations "temporary" personnel and early retirement limit the significance of the practice. Moreover, the economic stagnation that began in the 1990s led to layoffs and substantial unemployment. The changing complexion of the economic system in Japan could mean that companies may be less inclined to make the same kind of commitments to employees as in the past. Moreover, the potential of a lifetime job with one company holds less appeal for younger people than it did for their parents. However, the shrinking labor force will likely result in greater job security for everyone as competition for personnel becomes more intense.

The decline in the value of the U.S. dollar beginning in the mid-1980s, falling to around 85 yen to the dollar by the mid-1990s, and about 103 by mid-2008, has long-term implications for the Japanese economy. The higher-valued yen means Japanese goods sold in the United States cost more for Americans, who are then less likely to buy them. Japanese companies willing to accept lower profit margins can absorb some of the higher costs. Production costs can also be reduced by greater efficiencies. But this cannot go on forever. Among the first to feel the squeeze have been the smaller companies that serve as subcontractors for larger producers. Eventually the Japanese must stimulate their domestic consumption or the economic engine will stall, given its heavy export dependence.

Japan was able to weather the energy crises of the 1970s by increasing efficiencies, finding new cost-saving methods, and accepting lower profits. In addition, the increased value of the yen against the dollar worked to Japan's advantage in oil imports. The international price of oil is denominated in U.S. dollars, so even when the price of petroleum goes up, it takes fewer yen to buy a dollar's worth of oil.

Nonetheless, the dramatic run-up in the price of petroleum to more than $140 a barrel in mid-2008 affects Japan in a number of ways. First, energy necessarily costs more. Second, the United States, the world's number one consumer, and least efficient user of petroleum, is especially hard-hit by sharp price increases. Third, the increase in the price of petroleum is due in some measure to rising demand, especially from the rapidly expanding economies of India and China. These two countries pose a challenge to Japan's competitive position. Fourth, the increase is also attributable in part to instability in the Middle East, a matter of concern to Japan, given its dependency on the region's petroleum exports. On the positive side, there is considerable opportunity for expansion in the Japanese domestic market. Consumers are faced with artificially high prices in everything from foodstuffs to real estate. Public services have a wide range of possible expansion from sewers to senior citizen centers. Improving the service sector of the economy would benefit

Japanese and Americans alike because many American businesses are well established in these areas of endeavor. Changes in retail merchandising would benefit the Japanese consumer, who now pays high prices and would also create opportunities for outside investment. But this will not be easy. Small stores, and the voters who own them, will try to protect themselves against competition from supermarket and chain stores.[12]

The rising value of the yen is beginning to have an impact on the big corporations. Profit margins for the big companies are shrinking, which means, among other things, that they are sometimes unable to pay the substantial year-end bonuses that workers have come to expect.

International Relations

Two factors dominate Japanese foreign relations. First, there is the continuing friction with allies and trade partners. This is due in large measure to the drive for economic supremacy by the Japanese and the concomitant lethargy displayed by the West in anticipating and meeting the challenge. But the problem is also due to a lack of understanding of Japan as a nation and as a political system. It is widely assumed that Japan is like any Western nation, with the same expectations and understanding of the rules of the game.

The Japanese sometimes try to have it both ways—arguing, on the one hand, that they are just like other capitalist countries and, on the other, that they are different, perhaps even unique. "The nation as a whole believes itself to be utterly unique; there is no other place in any way like Japan."[13] To many Japanese, outsiders cannot possibly understand them, and international frictions stem from this lack of understanding. The second factor is an expanding level of Japanese participation in international affairs in areas outside economics and a growing assertiveness in defining the way these affairs are conducted. Japanese are more active in international organizations, more generous in dispensing foreign aid, and a significant military factor. They are also less inclined to passively accept "Japan bashing" from abroad. They are less inclined to accept blame for trade problems or to tolerate exclusive Western control over the international monetary and financial systems.

Japan has expanded its international security activities but, in so doing, has created additional ambiguities. Part of the problem dividing Japan from its Western allies derives from the fact that the latter's attitude toward Japan is inconsistent. On the one hand, the West often regards Japan as another country like itself. While Japan is expected to behave like a European nation, it is not exactly treated like one. Japan is welcomed to the extent that it looks and acts like a Western country. If it behaves in ways different from those customary in the West, the Japanese are suspected of something devious.

American and European pressure on Japan to open its markets, reduce exports, and play a greater role in financing third world development may encourage the Japanese to look elsewhere for friends. For a long time, they have desired to expand their economic connections with China, and, to a lesser extent, with Russia. These efforts have not been as productive as the Japanese would have liked because of Chinese political instability and structural weaknesses in the economy. The Russian attitude toward the Northern Territories issue and security matters in general have limited opportunities in that quarter. But the politics of both countries have changed. The collapse of the Soviet Union and the modernization and liberalization campaign in Russia was welcomed by Japan, and it was among the first to restore economic ties with China after the Tiananmen Square massacre in 1989.

Despite the fall of the Soviet state, no breakthrough in Russian relations with Japan has occurred. For a number of reasons, the Japanese remain cool to their northern neighbor. Memories of Soviet detention of Japanese citizens and the enduring Northern Territories issue slows the process of improving relations wirh Russia.[14]

The Japanese have become less inclined to passively accept criticism from abroad; they are more disposed to launch verbal and other kinds of counterattacks. As Yuji Aida, an emeritus professor from Kyoto University, observed: "The knee-jerk impulse of Japanese intellectuals to apologize for wartime sins both real and imagined reflects not a lofty, moral consciousness but an obsequious desire to ingratiate themselves with the victor."[15] The Japanese have begun to criticize the United States for many shortcomings, including the tendency to emphasize short-term profits, overcompensation of executives, the federal deficit, and inadequate savings.[16]

Japanese foreign policy is guided, as it has been since the last century, by the desire to improve Japan's standing in international relations. The Japanese see everything in hierarchical terms: "they are obsequious to superiors but haughty toward inferiors, and exceedingly preoccupied with self."[17] The world is a given to Japan, a framework within which to operate. Thus the foreign policy task is to adapt to this framework, not to change it.[18]

Japan's relations with South Korea and Southeast Asia involve strong economic bonds. The Japanese have been actively involved for years in investment, market development, technology transfer, and the purchase of raw materials. The result has been increasing integration of the East Asian economic system, a development that could, in time, rival that of the European Union. But this regional economy has been clearly dominated by one country—Japan. "Japan's neighbors thus looked more and more like offshore extensions of the continually aggrandizing Japanese economy. The Great East Asia Co-Prosperity Sphere of World War II vintage had come out of mothballs."[19]

Quality of Life Issues

The national consensus that focused energies on industrial development at the expense of everything else is dissolving. Pollution, urban congestion, and modest public services are giving rise to demands for an enhanced quality of life. From Bucharest to Prague to Manila to San Salvador and a host of other places, people are demanding a better life. This trend is not likely to bypass Japan. Japanese consumers are going to absorb a growing percentage of their own goods in pursuit of the good life.[20]

Among the areas where this is becoming evident is housing. Faced with astronomical prices and limited space, public restiveness will require sacrifices by some for the benefit of others. Farmers, who now work parcels of land to produce noncompetitive crops, will have to see their land turned into housing to relieve congestion. Another area is public services, ranging from sewage disposal to recreation. Developing the infrastructure of the country is likely to replace economic growth as the nation's highest priority.

Appendix A
The Constitution of Japan, November 3, 1946

Preface

We, the Japanese people, acting through our duly elected representatives in the National Diet, determined that we shall secure for ourselves and our posterity the fruits of peaceful cooperation with all nations and the blessings of liberty throughout this land, and resolved that never again shall we be visited with the horrors of war through the action of government, do proclaim that sovereign power resides with the people and do firmly establish this Constitution. Government is a sacred trust of the people, the authority for which is derived from the people, the powers of which are exercised by the representatives of the people, and the benefits of which are enjoyed by the people. This is a universal principle of mankind upon which this Constitution is founded. We reject and revoke all constitutions, laws, ordinances, and rescripts in conflict herewith.

We, the Japanese people, desire peace for all time and are deeply conscious of the high ideals controlling human relationship and we have determined to preserve our security and existence, trusting in the justice and faith of the peace-loving peoples of the world. We desire to occupy an honored place in an international society striving for the preservation of peace, and the banishment of tyranny and slavery, oppression and intolerance for all time from the earth. We recognize that all peoples of the world have the right to live in peace, free from fear and want.

We believe that no nation is responsible to itself alone, but that laws of political morality are universal; and that obedience to such laws is incumbent upon all nations who would sustain their own sovereignty and justify their sovereign relationship with other nations.

We, the Japanese people, pledge our national honor to accomplish these high ideals and purposes with all our resources.

Chapter I: The Emperor

Article 1:
    The Emperor shall be the symbol of the State and the unity of the people, deriving his position from the will of the people with whom resides sovereign power.

Article 2:

The Imperial Throne shall be dynastic and succeeded to in accordance with the Imperial House Law passed by the Diet.

Article 3:

The advice and approval of the Emperor in matters of state, and the Cabinet shall be responsible therefor.

Article 4:

(1) The Emperor shall perform only such acts in matters of state as are provided for in this Constitution and he shall not have powers related to government.

(2) The Emperor may delegate the performance of his acts in matters of state as may be provided for by law.

Article 5:

When, in accordance with the Imperial House Law, a Regency is established, the Regent shall perform his acts in matters of state in the Emperor's name. In this case, paragraph one of the preceding Article will be applicable.

Article 6:

The Emperor shall appoint the Prime Minister as designated by the Diet. The Emperor shall appoint the Chief Judge of the Supreme Court as designated by the Cabinet.

Article 7:

The Emperor shall, with the advice and approval of the Cabinet, perform the following acts in matters of state on behalf of the people:

(1) Promulgation of amendments of the constitution, laws, cabinet orders, and treaties.

(2) Convocation of the Diet.

(3) Dissolution of the House of Representatives.

(4) Proclamation of general election of members of the Diet.

(5) Attestation of the appointment and dismissal of Ministers of State and other officials as provided for by law, and of full powers and credentials of Ambassadors and Ministers.

(6) Attestation of general and special amnesty, commutation of punishment, reprieve, and restoration of rights.

(7) Awarding of honors.

(8) Attestation of instruments of ratification and other diplomatic documents as provided for by law.

(9) Receiving foreign ambassadors and ministers.

(10) Performance of ceremonial functions.

Article 8:

No property can be given to, or received by, the Imperial House, nor can any gifts be made therefrom, without the authorization of the Diet.

Chapter II: Renunciation of War

Article 9:

(1) Aspiring sincerely to an international peace based on justice and order, the Japanese people forever renounce war as a sovereign right of the nation and the threat or use of force as means of settling international disputes.

(2) In order to accomplish the aim of the preceding paragraph, land, sea, and air forces, as well as other war potential, will never be maintained. The right of belligerency of the state will not be recognized.

Chapter III: Rights and Duties of the People

Article 10:

The conditions necessary for being a Japanese national shall be determined by law.

Article 11:

The people shall not be prevented from enjoying any of the fundamental human rights. These fundamental human rights guaranteed to the people by this Constitution shall be conferred upon the people of this and future generations as eternal and inviolate rights.

Article 12:

The freedoms and rights guaranteed to the people by this Constitution shall be maintained by the constant endeavor of the people, who shall refrain from any abuse of these freedoms and rights and shall always be responsible for utilizing them for the public welfare.

Article 13:

All of the people shall be respected as individuals. Their right to life, liberty, and the pursuit of happiness shall, to the extent that it does not interfere with the public welfare, be the supreme consideration in legislation and in other governmental affairs.

Article 14:

(1) All of the people are equal under the law and there shall be no discrimination in political, economic or social relations because of race, creed, sex, social status, or family origin.

(2) Peers and peerage shall not be recognized.

(3) No privilege shall accompany any award of honor, decoration or any distinction, nor shall any such award be valid beyond the lifetime of the individual who now holds or hereafter may receive it.

Article 15:

(1) The people have the inalienable right to choose their public officials and to dismiss them.

(2) All public officials are servants of the whole community and not of any group thereof.

(3) Universal adult suffrage is guaranteed with regard to the election of public officials.

(4) In all elections, secrecy of the ballot shall not be violated. A voter shall not be answerable, publicly or privately, for the choice he has made.

Article 16:

Every person shall have the right of peaceful petition for the redress of damage, for the removal of public officials, for the enactment, repeal or amendment of laws, ordinances or regulations and for other matters; nor shall any person be in any way discriminated against for sponsoring such a petition.

Article 17:

Every person may sue for redress as provided by law from the State or a public entity, in case he has suffered damage through illegal act of any public official.

Article 18:

No person shall be held in bondage of any kind. Involuntary servitude, except as punishment for crime, is prohibited.

Article 19:

Freedom of thought and conscience shall not be violated.

Article 20:

(1) Freedom of religion is guaranteed to all. No religious organization shall receive any privileges from the State, nor exercise any political authority.

(2) No person shall be compelled to take part in any religious acts, celebration, rite or practice.

(3) The State and its organs shall refrain from religious education or any other religious activity.

Article 21:

(1) Freedom of assembly and association as well as speech, press and all other forms of expression are guaranteed.

(2) No censorship shall be maintained, nor shall the secrecy of any means of communication be violated.

Article 22:

(1) Every person shall have freedom to choose and change his residence and to choose his occupation to the extent that it does not interfere with the public welfare.

(2) Freedom of all persons to move to a foreign country and to divest themselves of their nationality shall be inviolate.

Article 23:

Academic freedom is guaranteed.

Article 24:

(1) Marriage shall be based only on the mutual consent of both sexes and it shall be maintained through mutual cooperation with the equal rights of husband and wife as a basis.

(2) With regard to choice of spouse, property rights, inheritance, choice of domicile, divorce and other matters pertaining to marriage and the family, laws shall be enacted from the standpoint of individual dignity and the essential equality of the sexes.

Article 25:

(1) All people shall have the right to maintain the minimum standards of wholesome and cultured living.

(2) In all spheres of life, the State shall use its endeavors for the promotion and extension of social welfare and security, and of public health.

Article 26:

(1) All people shall have the right to receive an equal education correspondent to their ability, as provided for by law.

(2) All people shall be obligated to have all boys and girls under their protection receive ordinary education as provided for by law. Such compulsory education shall be free.

Article 27:

(1) All people shall have the right and the obligation to work.

(2) Standards for wages, hours, rest and other working conditions shall be fixed by law.

(3) Children shall not be exploited.

Article 28:

The right of workers to organize and to bargain and act collectively is guaranteed.

Article 29:

(1) The right to own or to hold property is inviolable.

(2) Property rights shall be defined by law, in conformity with the public welfare.

(3) Private property may be taken for public use upon just compensation therefor.

Article 30:

The people shall be liable to taxation as provided for by law.

Article 31:

No person shall be deprived of life or liberty, nor shall any other criminal penalty be imposed, except according to procedure established by law.

Article 32:

No person shall be denied the right of access to the courts.

Article 33:

No person shall be apprehended except upon warrant issued by a competent judicial officer which specifies the offense with which the person is charged, unless he is apprehended, the offense being committed.

Article 34:

No person shall be arrested or detained without being at once informed of the charges against him or without the immediate privilege of counsel; nor shall he be detained without adequate cause; and upon demand of any person such cause must be immediately shown in open court in his presence and the presence of his counsel.

Article 35:

(1) The right of all persons to be secure in their homes, papers and effects against entries, searches and seizures shall not be impaired except upon warrant

issued for adequate cause and particularly describing the place to be searched and things to be seized, or except as provided by Article 33.

(2) Each search or seizure shall be made upon separate warrant issued by a competent judicial officer.

Article 36:

The infliction of torture by any public officer and cruel punishments are absolutely forbidden.

Article 37:

(1) In all criminal cases the accused shall enjoy the right to a speedy and public trial by an impartial tribunal.

(2) He shall be permitted full opportunity to examine all witnesses, and he shall have the right of compulsory process for obtaining witnesses on his behalf at public expense.

(3) At all times the accused shall have the assistance of competent counsel who shall, if the accused is unable to secure the same by his own efforts, be assigned to his use by the State.

Article 38:

(1) No person shall be compelled to testify against himself.

(2) Confession made under compulsion, torture or threat, or after prolonged arrest or detention shall not be admitted in evidence.

(3) No person shall be convicted or punished in cases where the only proof against him is his own confession.

Article 39:

No person shall be held criminally liable for an act which was lawful at the time it was committed, or of which he had been acquitted, nor shall he be placed in double jeopardy.

Article 40:

Any person may, in case he is acquitted after he has been arrested or detained, sue the State for redress as provided for by law.

Chapter IV: The Diet

Article 41:

The Diet shall be the highest organ of the state power, and shall be the sole law-making organ of the State.

Article 42:

The Diet shall consist of two Houses, namely the House of Representatives and the House of Councillors.

Article 43:

(1) Both Houses shall consist of elected members, representative of all the people.

(2) The number of the members of each House shall be fixed by law.

Article 44:

The qualifications of members of both Houses and their electors shall be fixed by law. However, there shall be no discrimination because of race, creed, sex, social status, family origin, education, property or income.

Article 45:

The term of office of members of the House of Representatives shall be four years. However, the term shall be terminated before the full term is up in case the House of Representatives is dissolved.

Article 46:

The term of office of members of the House of Councillors shall be six years, and election for half the members shall take place every three years.

Article 47:

Electoral districts, method of voting and other matters pertaining to the method of election of members of both Houses shall be fixed by law.

Article 48:

No person shall be permitted to be a member of both Houses simultaneously.

Article 49:

Members of both Houses shall receive appropriate annual payment from the national treasury in accordance with law.

Article 50:

Except in cases as provided for by law, members of both Houses shall be exempt from apprehension while the Diet is in session, and any members apprehended before the opening of the session shall be freed during the term of the session upon demand of the House.

Article 51:

Members of both Houses shall not be held liable outside the House for speeches, debates or votes cast inside the House.

Article 52:

An ordinary session of the Diet shall be convoked once per year.

Article 53:

The Cabinet may determine to convoke extraordinary sessions of the Diet. When a quarter or more of the total members of either House makes the demand, the Cabinet must determine on such convocation.

Article 54:

(1) When the House of Representatives is dissolved, there must be a general election of members of the House of Representatives within forty (40) days from the date of dissolution, and the Diet must be convoked within thirty (30) days from the date of the election.

(2) When the House of Representatives is dissolved, the House of Councillors is closed at the same time. However, the Cabinet may, in time of national emergency, convoke the House of Councillors in emergency session.

(3) Measures taken at such session as mentioned in the proviso of the preceding paragraph shall be provisional and shall become null and void unless agreed to by the House of Representatives within a period of ten (10) days after the opening of the next session of the Diet.

Article 55:

Each House shall judge disputes related to qualifications of its members. However, in order to deny a seat to any member, it is necessary to pass a resolution by a majority of two-thirds or more of the members present.

Article 56:

(1) Business cannot be transacted in either House unless one-third or more of total membership is present.

(2) All matters shall be decided, in each House, by a majority of those present, except as elsewhere provided for in the Constitution, and in case of a tie, the presiding officer shall decide the issue.

Article 57:

(1) Deliberation in each House shall be public. However, a secret meeting may be held where a majority of two-thirds or more of those members present passes a resolution therefor.

(2) Each House shall keep a record of proceedings. This record shall be published and given general circulation, excepting such parts of proceedings of secret session as may be deemed to require secrecy.

(3) Upon demand of one-fifth or more of the members present, votes of the members on any matter shall be recorded in the minutes.

Article 58:

(1) Each House shall select its own president and other officials.

(2) Each House shall establish its rules pertaining to meetings, proceedings and internal discipline, and may punish members for disorderly conduct. However, in order to expel a member, a majority of two-thirds or more of those members present must pass a resolution thereon.

Article 59:

(1) A bill becomes a law on passage by both Houses, except as otherwise provided for by the Constitution.

(2) A bill, which is passed by the House of Representatives, and upon which the House of Councillors makes a decision different from that of the House of Representatives, becomes a law when passed a second time by the House of Representatives by a majority of two-thirds or more of the members present.

(3) The provision of the preceding paragraph does not preclude the House of Representatives from calling for the meeting of a joint committee of both Houses, provided for by law.

(4) Failure by the House of Councillors to take final action within sixty (60) days after receipt of a bill passed by the House of Representatives, time in recess excepted, may be determined by the House of Representatives to constitute a rejection of the said bill by the House of Councillors.

Article 60:

(1) The budget must first be submitted to the House of Representatives.

(2) Upon consideration of the budget, when the House of Councillors makes a decision different from that of the House of Representatives, and when no agreement can be reached even through a joint committee of both Houses, provided for by law, or in the case of failure by the House of Councillors to take final action within thirty (30) days, the period of recess excluded, after the receipt of the budget passed by the House of Representatives, the decision of the House of Representatives shall be the decision of the Diet.

Article 61:

The second paragraph of the preceding Article applies also to the Diet approval required for the conclusion of treaties.

Article 62:

Each House may conduct investigations in relation to government, and may demand the presence and testimony of witnesses, and the production of records.

Article 63:

The Prime Minister and other Ministers of State may, at any time, appear in either House for the purpose of speaking on bills, regardless of whether they are members of the House or not. They must appear when their presence is required in order to give answers or explanations.

Article 64:

(1) The Diet shall set up an impeachment court from among the members of both Houses for the purposes of trying those judges against whom removal proceedings have been instituted.

(2) Matters relating to impeachment shall be provided for by law.

Chapter V: The Cabinet

Article 65:

Executive power shall be vested in the Cabinet.

Article 66:

(1) The Cabinet shall consist of the Prime Minister, who shall be its head, and other Ministers of State, as provided for by law.

(2) The Prime Minister and other Ministers of State must be civilians.

(3) The Cabinet shall, in the exercise of executive power, be collectively responsible to the Diet.

Article 67:

(1) The Prime Minister shall be designated from among the members of the Diet by a resolution of the Diet. This designation shall precede all other business.

(2) If the House of Representatives and the House of Councillors disagree and if no agreement can be reached even through a joint committee of both Houses, provided for by law, or the House of Councillors fails to make designation within ten (10) days, exclusive of the period of recess, after the House of Representatives has made designation, the decision of the House of Representatives shall be the decision of the Diet.

Article 68:

(1) The Prime Minister shall appoint the Ministers of State. However, a majority of their number must be chosen from among the members of the Diet.

(2) The Prime Minister may remove the Ministers of State as he chooses.

Article 69:

If the House of Representatives passes a non-confidence resolution, or rejects a confidence resolution, the Cabinet shall resign en masse, unless the House of Representatives is dissolved within ten (10) days.

Article 70:

When there is a vacancy in the post of Prime Minister, or upon the first convocation of the Diet after a general election of members of the House of Representatives, the Cabinet shall resign en masse.

Article 71:

In the cases mentioned in the two preceding Articles, the Cabinet shall continue its functions until the time when a new Prime Minister is appointed.

Article 72:

The Prime Minister, representing the Cabinet, submits bills, reports on general national affairs and foreign relations to the Diet and exercises control and supervision over various administrative branches.

Article 73:

The Cabinet shall, in addition to other general administrative functions, perform the following functions:

(1) Administer the law faithfully; conduct affairs of state.

(2) Manage foreign affairs.

(3) Conclude treaties. However, it shall obtain prior or, depending on circumstances, subsequent approval of the Diet.

(4) Administer the civil service, in accordance with standards established by law.

(5) Prepare the budget, and present it to the Diet.

(6) Enact cabinet orders in order to execute the provisions of this Constitution and of the law.

(7) However, it cannot include penal provisions in such cabinet orders unless authorized by such law.

(8) Decide on general amnesty, special amnesty, commutation of punishment, reprieve, and restoration of rights.

Article 74:

All laws and cabinet orders shall be signed by the competent Minister of State and countersigned by the Prime Minister.

Article 75:

The Ministers of State shall not, during their tenure of office, be subject to legal action without the consent of the Prime Minister. However, the right to take that action is not impaired hereby.

Chapter VI: Judiciary

Article 76:

(1) The whole judicial power is vested in a Supreme Court and in such inferior courts as are established by law.

(2) No extraordinary tribunal shall be established, nor shall any organ or agency of the Executive be given final judicial power.

(3) All judges shall be independent in the exercise of their conscience and shall be bound only by this Constitution and the laws.

Article 77:

(1) The Supreme Court is vested with the rule-making power under which it determines the rules of procedure and of practice, and of matters relating to attorneys, the internal discipline of the courts and the administration of judicial affairs.

(2) Public procurators shall be subject to the rule-making power of the Supreme Court.

(3) The Supreme Court may delegate the power to make rules for inferior courts to such courts.

Article 78:

Judges shall not be removed except by public impeachment unless judicially declared mentally or physically incompetent to perform official duties. No disciplinary action against judges shall be administered by any executive organ or agency.

Article 79:

(1) The Supreme Court shall consist of a Chief Judge and such number of judges as may be determined by law; all such judges excepting the Chief Judge shall be appointed by the Cabinet.

(2) The appointment of the judges of the Supreme Court shall be reviewed by the people at the first general election of members of the House of Representatives following their appointment, and shall be reviewed again at the first general election of members of the House of Representatives after a lapse of ten (10) years, and in the same manner thereafter.

(3) In cases mentioned in the foregoing paragraph, when the majority of the voters favors the dismissal of a judge, he shall be dismissed.

(4) Matters pertaining to review shall be prescribed by law.

(5) The judges of the Supreme Court shall be retired upon the attainment of the age as fixed by law.

(6) All such judges shall receive, at regular stated intervals, adequate compensation which shall not be decreased during their terms of office.

Article 80:

(1) The judges of the inferior courts shall be appointed by the Cabinet from a list of persons nominated by the Supreme Court. All such judges shall hold office for a term of ten (10) years with privilege of reappointment, provided that they shall be retired upon the attainment of the age as fixed by law.

(2) The judges of the inferior courts shall receive, at regular stated intervals, adequate compensation which shall not be decreased during their terms of office.

Article 81:

The Supreme Court is the court of last resort with power to determine the constitutionality of any law, order, regulation or official act.

Article 82:

(1) Trials shall be conducted and judgment declared publicly. Where a court unanimously determines publicity to be dangerous to public order or morals, a trial may be conducted privately, but trials of political offenses, offenses involving the press or cases wherein the rights of people as guaranteed in Chapter III of this Constitution are in question shall always be conducted publicly.

Chapter VII: Finance

Article 83:

The power to administer national finances shall be exercised as the Diet shall determine.

Article 84:

No new taxes shall be imposed or existing ones modified except by law or under such conditions as law may prescribe.

Article 85:

No money shall be expended, nor shall the State obligate itself, except as authorized by the Diet.

Article 86:

The Cabinet shall prepare and submit to the Diet for its consideration and decision a budget for each fiscal year.

Article 87:

In order to provide for unforeseen deficiencies in the budget, a reserve fund may be authorized by the Diet to be expended upon the responsibility of the Cabinet. The Cabinet must get subsequent approval of the Diet for all payments from the reserve fund.

Article 88:

All property of the Imperial Household shall belong to the State. All expenses of the Imperial Household shall be appropriated by the Diet in the budget.

Article 89:

No public money or other property shall be expended or appropriated for the use, benefit or maintenance of any religious institution or association, or for any charitable, educational or benevolent enterprises not under the control of public authority.

Article 90:

(1) Final accounts of the expenditures and revenues of the State shall be audited annually by a Board of Audit and submitted by the Diet, together with the statement of audit, during the fiscal year immediately following the period covered.

(2) The organization and competency of the Board of Audit shall be determined by law.

Article 91:

At regular intervals and at least annually the Cabinet shall report to the Diet and the people on the state of national finances.

Chapter VIII: Local Self-Government

Article 92:

Regulations concerning organization and operations of local public entities shall be fixed by law in accordance with the principle of local autonomy.

Article 93:

(1) The local public entities shall establish assemblies as their deliberative organs, in accordance with law.

(2) The chief executive officers of all local public entities, the members of their assemblies, and such other local officials as may be determined by law shall be elected by direct popular vote within their several communities.

Article 94:

Local public entities shall have the right to manage their property, affairs and administration and to enact their own regulations within law.

Article 95:

A special law, applicable only to one local public entity, cannot be enacted by the Diet without the consent of the majority of the voters of the local public entity concerned, obtained in accordance with law.

Chapter IX: Amendments

Article 96:

(1) Amendments to this Constitution shall be initiated by the Diet, through a concurring vote of two-thirds or more of all the members of each House and shall thereupon be submitted to the people for ratification, which shall require the affirmative vote of a majority of all votes cast thereon, at a special referendum or at such election as the Diet shall specify.

(2) Amendments when so ratified shall immediately be promulgated by the Emperor in the name of the people, as an integral part of this Constitution.

Chapter X: Supreme Law

Article 97:

The fundamental human rights by this Constitution guaranteed to the people of Japan are fruits of the age-old struggle of man to be free; they have survived the many exacting tests for durability and are conferred upon this and future generations in trust, to be held for all time inviolate.

Article 98:

(1) This Constitution shall be the supreme law of the nation and no law, ordinance, imperial rescript or other act of government, or part thereof, contrary to the provisions hereof, shall have legal force or validity.

(2) The treaties concluded by Japan and established laws of nations shall be faithfully observed.

Article 99:

The Emperor or the Regent as well as Ministers of State, members of the

Diet, judges, and all other public officials have the obligation to respect and uphold this Constitution.

Chapter XI: Supplementary Provisions

Article 100:
(1) This Constitution shall be enforced as from the day when the period of six months will have elapsed counting from the day of its promulgation.
(2) The enactment of laws necessary for the enforcement of this Constitution, the election of members of the House of Councillors and the procedure for the convocation of the Diet and other preparatory procedures necessary for the enforcement of this Constitution may be executed before the day prescribed in the preceding paragraph.

Article 101:
If the House of Councillors is not constituted before the effective date of this Constitution, the House of Representatives shall function as the Diet until such time as the House of Councillors shall be constituted.

Article 102:
The term of office for half the members of the House of Councillors serving in the first term under this Constitution shall be three years. Members falling under this category shall be determined in accordance with law.

Article 103:
The Ministers of State, members of the House of Representatives, and judges in office on the effective date of this Constitution, and all other public officials who occupy positions corresponding to such positions as are recognized by this Constitution shall not forfeit their positions automatically on account of the enforcement of this Constitution unless otherwise specified by law. When, however, successors are elected or appointed under the provisions of this Constitution, they shall forfeit their positions as a matter of course.

Date of promulgation: 3 November 1946
Date of enforcement: 3 May 1947

THE CONSTITUTION OF JAPAN (November 3, 1946)

I rejoice that the foundation for the construction of a new Japan has been laid according to the will of the Japanese people, and hereby sanction and promulgate the amendments of the Imperial Japanese Constitution effected following the consultation with the Privy Council and the decision of the Imperial Diet made in accordance with Article 73 of the said Constitution.

Signed:

HIROHITO, Seal of the Emperor, This third day of the eleventh month of the twenty-first year of Showa (November 3, 1946).

Countersigned:

Prime Minister and concurrently
Minister for Foreign Affairs
YOSHIDA Shigeru,

Minister of State
Baron SHIDEHARA Kijuro,

Minister of Justice
KIMURA Tokutaro,

Minister for Home Affairs
OMURA Seiichi,

Minister of Education
TANAKA Kotaro,

Minister of Agriculture and Forestry
WADA Hiroo,

Minister of State
SAITO Takao,

Minister of Communication
HITOTSUMATSU Sadayoshi,

Minister of Commerce and Industry
HOSHIJIMA Jiro,

Minister of Welfare
KAWAI Yoshinari,

Minister of State
UEHARA Etsujiro,

Minister of Transportation
HIRATSUKA Tsunejiro,

Minister of Finance
ISHIBASHI Tanzan,

Minister of State
KANAMORI Tokujiro,

Minister of State
ZEN Keinosuke

Appendix B
Parlimentary Election Results

The National Diet

Under Japan's postwar constitution, the National Diet of Japan replaced
the Imperial Diet that was founded under the Meiji and first met in 1890.
The National Diet is a bicameral legislature with an upper house, the
House of Councillors (HC), and a lower house, the House of Representatives (HR). Over the years there have been changes in the electoral
laws for both houses, as reflected in the sectioning of the table (see pp.
310–311).

Major Parties

The Liberal Democratic Party **(LDP)**. Until 1955, the seats listed for the
LDP in the first section of the table represent the combined strength
of different conservative parties, particularly the Liberal Party and the
Democratic Party.

The Japan Socialist Party **(JSP)**. In 1952, 1953, and 1955, the party
was divided into left and right wings, which ran candidates separately.
The Democratic Socialist Party **(DSP)** (1960–1996) split from the JSP.
In 1996 the party renamed itself the Social Democratic Party **(SDP)**.

Kōmeitō (1964–1998), the "Clean Government Party," since 1998 New
Kōmeitō, grew out of the Kōmeitō Political Assembly (1961–1964).

In the late 1990s several anti-LDP opposition parties combined to form
the Democratic Party of Japan **(DPJ)**.

Parliamentary Election Results, 1946–1980

Election	House	LDP	JSP	DSP	Kōmeitō	NLC	JCP	Other
4-10-46	HR	140	92				5	119
4-20-47	HC	14	17				3	63
4-25-47	HR	252	143				4	38
1-23-49	HR	333	48				35	29
6-4-50	HC	19	15				2	19
10-1-52	HR	240	111				0	26
4-19-53	HR	199	138				1	13
4-24-53	HC	19	11				0	13
2-27-55	HR	297	156				2	33
7-8-56	HC	61	49				2	15
5-22-58	HR	287	166				1	13
6-2-59	HC	71	38				1	17
11-20-60	HR	296	145	17			3	6
7-1-62	HC	69	37	4	9		3	5
11-21-63	HR	283	144	23			5	12
7-4-65	HC	71	36	3	11		3	3
1-1-67	HR	277	140	30	25		5	9
7-7-68	HC	69	28	7	13		4	5
12-27-69	HR	288	90	31	47		14	16
6-27-71	HC	62	39	6	10		6	2
10-12-72	HR	271	118	19	29		38	16
7-7-74	HC	62	28	5	14		13	8
12-5-76	HR	249	123	29	55	17	17	21
7-10-77	HC	63	27	6	14	3	5	7
10-7-79	HR	248	107	35	57	4	39	21
6-22-80	HR	284	107	32	33	12	29	14
6-22-80	HC	69	22	5	12		7	10

LDP = Liberal Democratic Party; JSP = Japan Socialist Party; DSP = Democratic Socialist Party; NLC = New Liberal Club; JCP = Japan Communist Party

Parliamentary Election Results, 1983–1993

Election	House	LDP	JSP	DSP	Kōmeitō	NLC	JCP	JNP	RP	NH	Other
6-26-83	HC	68	22	6	14	2					7
12-18-83	HR	250	112	38	58	8	26				19
7-6-86	HR	300	85	26	56	6	26				13
7-6-86	HC	72	20	5	10	1	9				-9
7-23-89	HC	36	46	3	10		5				26
2-18-90	HR	275	136	14	45		16				
7-26-92	HC	69	22	4	14		4				
7-18-93	HR	223	70	15	51		15	35	55	13	34

LDP = Liberal Democratic Party; JSP = Japan Socialist Party; DSP = Democratic Socialist Party; NLC = New Liberal Club; JCP = Japan Communist Party; JNP = Japan New Party; RP = Renewal Party; NH = New Harbinger Party

Parliamentary Election Results, 1995–2007

Election	House	LDP	SDP	JCP	NFP	DPJ	Ind.	NCP	Liberal	New Kōmeitō	Other
7-23-1995	HC	110	38	14	56		12				22
10-20-1996	HR	239	15	26	156	52	9				3
6-12-1998	HC	44	5	15		27	20		6	9	0
6-25-2000	HR	223	19	20		127	3	7	22	31	21
7-29-2001	HC	64	3	5		26	5	1	6	13	0
11-9-2003	HR	237	6	9		177		4		34	13
7-11-2004	HC	49	2	4		50	18			11	0
9-11-2005	HR	296	7	9		113				31	2
7-29-2007	HC	37	2	3		60	7			9	3

LDP = Liberal Democratic Party; SDP = Social Democratic Party (new name of JSP from 1996); JCP = Japan Communist Party; NFP = New Frontier Party; DPJ = Democratic Party of Japan; NCP = New Conservative Party

Appendix C
Prime Ministers of Japan

Name	Terms	Political Party
Shigeru Yoshida	May 1946–May 1947	Liberal
Tetsu Katayama	May 1947–March 1948	Socialist
Hitoshi Ashida	March 1948–October 1948	Democratic
Shigeru Yoshida	October 1948–February 1949	Liberal
	February 1949–October 1952	Liberal
	October 1952–May 1953	Liberal
	May 1953–December 1954	Liberal
Ichirō Hatoyama	December 1954–March 1955	Democratic
	March 1955–November 1955	Democratic
	November 1955–December 1956	Liberal Democratic (LDP)
Tanzan Ishibashi	December 1956–February 1957	LDP
Nobusuke Kishi	February 1957–June 1958	LDP
	June 1958–July 1960	LDP
Hayato Ikeda	July 1960–December 1960	LDP
	December 1960–December 1963	LDP
	December 1963–November 1964	LDP
Eisaku Satō	November 1964–February 1967	LDP
	February 1967–January 1970	LDP
	January 1970–July 1972	LDP
Kakuei Tanaka	July 1972–December 1972	LDP
	December 1972–December 1974	LDP
Takeo Miki	December 1974–December 1976	LDP
Takeo Fukuda	December 1976–December 1978	LDP
Masayoshi Ohira	December 1978–November 1979	LDP
	November 1979–June 1980	LDP
Zenkō Suzuki	July 1980–November 1982	LDP
Yasuhiro Nakasone	November 1982–December 1983	LDP
	December 1983–July 1986	LDP
	July 1986–November 1987	LDP
Noboru Takeshita	November 1987–June 1989	LDP
Sūsuke Uno	June 1989–August 1989	LDP
Toshiki Kaifu	August 1989–February 1990	LDP
	February 1990–November 1991	LDP
Kiichi Miyazawa	November 1991–August 1993	LDP
Morihiro Hosokawa	August 1993–April 1994	Japan New

Tsutomu Hata	April 1994–June 1994	Renewal
Tomiichi Murayama	June 1994–January 1996	Socialist
Ryūtarō Hashimoto	January 1996–November 1996	LDP
	November 1996–July 1998	LDP
Keizō Obuchi	July 1998–April 2000	LDP
Yoshirō Mori	April 2000–July 2000	LDP
	July 2000–April 2001	LDP
Junichirō Koizumi	April 2001–November 2003	LDP
	November 2003–September 2005	LDP
	September 2005–September 2006	LDP
Shinzō Abe	September 2006–September 2007	LDP
Yasuo Fukuda	September 2007–September 2008	LDP
Taro Aso	September 2008–	LDP

Notes

Introduction

1. It has not always been that way. "At the beginning of the Tokugawa age, Japan was one of the largest exporters of precious metals in the Old World" (Morris-Suzuki, *The Technological Transformation of Japan*, 43).
2. Yoshikazu, "The Dying Japanese Village."
3. Fujiwara and Carvell, *Japanese Women in Turmoil*, 19.
4. Dale, *The Myth of Japanese Uniqueness*.
5. Scheiner, "The Japanese Village: Imagined, Real, Contested," in Vlastos, *Mirror of Modernity*, 67.
6. *The Economist*, December 12, 1985, 4.
7. Tsuneishi, *Japanese Political Style*, 21.
8. Morris, *Nationalism and the Right Wing in Japan*, 146.
9. Kyogoku, *The Political Dynamics of Japan*, 185–186.
10. Ike, *Japanese Politics*, 16–17.
11. Richardson and Flanagan, *Politics in Japan*, 146.
12. Reischauer, *The Japanese*, 213–224.

1. General History

1. Webb, *The Japanese Imperial Institution in the Tokugawa Period*, 9.
2. Wakabayashi, *Anti-Foreignism and Western Learning in Early Modern Japan*, 22.
3. Webb, *The Japanese Imperial Institution in the Tokugawa Period*, 162.
4. Jansen, "The Ruling Class," in Jansen and Rozman, *Japan in Transition*, 71. For a discussion of the legitimation of the shogun, see Toby, *State and Diplomacy in Early Modern Japan*, 109.
5. Webb, *The Japanese Imperial Institution in the Tokugawa Period*, 129.
6. Fujita, *Japan's Encounter with Christianity*, 3.
7. Berry, *Hideyoshi*, 111–131.
8. Webb, *The Japanese Imperial Institution in the Tokugawa Period*, 73.
9. Berry, *Hideyoshi*, 104.
10. Ibid.
11. Umegaki, *After the Restoration*, 22.
12. Fujita, *Japan's Encounter with Christianity*, 9.
13. Calman, *The Nature and Origins of Japanese Imperialism*, 313–314.
14. Toby, *State and Diplomacy in Early Modern Japan*, 5–11.
15. See Arnason, "Paths to Modernity: The Peculiarities of Japanese Feudalism," in McCormack and Sugimoto, *The Japanese Trajectory: Modernization and Beyond*, 235–263.

16. Barnhart, *Japan and the World Since 1868*, 7.

17. Wakabayashi, *Anti-Foreignism and Western Learning in Early Modern Japan*, 90.

18. Fujita, *Japan's Encounter with Christianity*, 257–265.

19. Totman, *The Collapse of the Tokugawa Bakafu, 1862–1868*, 430–443.

20. Ruoff, *The People's Emperor*, 20.

21. Gluck, *Japan's Modern Myths*, 78.

22. Itoh and Beer, *The Constitutional Case Law in Japan*, 4.

23. Umegaki, *After the Restoration*, 54.

24. Hane, *Modern Japan*, 93.

25. Harry D. Harootunian, "The Economic Rehabilitation of the Samurai in the Early Meiji Period," 433–435.

26. Prestowitz, *Trading Places*, 107.

27. Gluck, *Japan's Modern Myths*, 159.

28. D. Eleanor Westney, "The Military," in Jansen and Rozman, *Japan in Transition*, 169, 192.

29. Hane, *Modern Japan*, 118–126.

30. Barnhart, *Japan and the World Since 1868*, 22.

31. Gluck, *Japan's Modern Myths*, 102.

32. Fukutake, *Japan's Social Structure: Its Evolution in the Modern Century*, 16.

33. Mitchell, *Thought Control in Prewar Japan*, 20–21.

34. Gluck, *Japan's Modern Myths*, 3.

35. Tipton, *The Japanese Police State*, 17.

36. Ibid., 59.

37. Beer, *Freedom of Expression in Japan*, 56.

38. Ibid., 70.

39. Pempel, "Uneasy Towards Autonomy: Parliament and Parliamentarians in Japan," in Suleiman, *Parliaments and Parliamentarians in Democratic Politics*, 118.

40. Tipton, *Japanese Police State*, 18; Beer, *Freedom of Expression*, 68.

41. Mitchell, *Thought Control in Prewar Japan*, 23–25. This special political role of the police originated in France at the time of Napoleon (Tipton, *Japanese Police State*, 45).

42. Tipton, *Japanese Police State*, 22.

43. Ibid., 62.

44. Young, *Imperial Japan*, 203–205.

45. Mitchell, *Political Bribery in Japan*, 41.

46. Theodore McNelly, "The Japanese Constitution," 195.

47. Reischauer and Craig, *Japan*, 245.

48. Interestingly, this authoritarian rule was achieved without the mass application of terror that usually attends such processes. Widespread arrests, executions, and forced labor in concentration camps were not visited on the Japanese citizenry (Mitchell, *Thought Control in Prewar Japan*, 191).

49. Morris, *Nationalism and the Right Wing in Japan*, 115–135.

50. Hsu, *The Rise of Modern China*, 494; Young, *Imperial Japan*, 203–205.

51. Barnhart, *Japan Prepares for War*, 115–135.

52. The most notorious example of this racial bias occurred during World War II, when Japanese Americans were interned because they were considered a security threat. Americans of German or Italian descent did not suffer a similar fate.

53. Young, *Imperial Japan,* 179ff.

54. Barnhart, *Japan Prepares for War,* 83.

55. Young, *Imperial Japan,* 201.

56. Mitchell, *Political Bribery in Japan,* 58.

57. Toland, *The Rising Sun,* 1–22.

58. Fukutake, *Japan's Social Structure,* 73.

59. Barnhart, *Japan and the World Since 1968,* 99.

60. Barnhart, *Japan Prepares for War,* 56.

61. Pyle, *The Making of Modern Japan,* 147.

62. Bouissou, *Japan: The Burden of Success,* 34–38.

63. Some Japanese see the period of militarism in their history as an aberration, inconsistent with the "true" Japan. This fascist-militarist interlude is attributed to communist subversion (Dower, *Empire and Aftermath,* 135).

64. Emperor Akihito has attempted to make the emperor less distant from the people by, for example, having his motorcade stop at traffic lights.

65. For example, the mayor of Nagasaki was shot by an ultranationalist in January 1990 for suggesting that Emperor Hirohito bore some responsibility for World War II (*New York Times,* January 19, 1990, A8).

2. The Occupation

1. Fearey, *The Occupation of Japan,* 7. The eleven members of the Far Eastern Commission were the United States, Great Britain, the Soviet Union, China, France, the Netherlands, Canada, Australia, New Zealand, India, and the Philippines.

2. Manchester, *The American Caesar.*

3. Hane, *Modern Japan,* 344.

4. McNelly, "The Japanese Constitution," 176–195.

5. Moore and Robinson, *Partners for Democracy,* 147.

6. "General MacArthur, quintessential American that he was, easily became a stock figure in the political pageantry of Japan: the new sovereign, the blue-eyed shogun, the paternalistic military dictator, the grandiloquent but excruciatingly sincere Kabuki hero. MacArthur played this role with consummate care" (Dower, *Embracing Defeat,* 203).

7. Ward, "Conclusion," in Ward and Yoshikazu, *Democratizing Japan,* 396.

8. "Using threats and promises, SCAP's GS compelled the cabinet to adopt MacArthur's line that the draft was a Japanese government product, approved by the emperor in accordance with the existing constitution. He then tried to convince the FEC (and the world) that it was a Japanese draft, months in the making, supported by the 'freely expressed will of the Japanese people.' Whitney and his staff intimidated Japanese officials in secret negotiations, forcing them to accept most of the SCAP draft as a Japanese product, then offered the FEC fictitious 'evidence' of Japanese authorship. When the suspicious allies demanded more information, MacArthur stonewalled" (Moore and Robinson, *Partners for Democracy,* 331).

9. See Spector, *Eagle Against the Sun.*

10. This amateur quality continues to be a fixture of U.S. foreign policy. Mideast policy and especially the invasion of Iraq were crafted and executed by people with only the barest understanding of the region.

11. Moore and Robinson, *Partners for Democracy*, 23.

12. Reischauer and Craig, *Japan*, 278.

13. Fearey, *The Occupation of Japan*, 182.

14. Robert E. Ward, "Presurrender Planning: Treatment of the Emperor and Constitutional Changes," in Ward and Yoshikazu, *Democratizing Japan*, 36.

15. Dower, *Empire and Aftermath*, 294.

16. Yoshida, *The Yoshida Memoirs*, 53.

17. Aldous, *Police in Occupation Japan*, 65.

18. Dower, *Embracing Defeat*, 300.

19. Hane, *Modern Japan*, 335.

20. Fearey, *The Occupation of Japan*, 15.

21. Weinstein, *Japan's Postwar Defense Policy*, 32.

22. Sakakibara, "Japanese Politico-Economic System and the Public Sector," in Kernell, *Parallel Politics*, 55.

23. Susan J. Pharr, "The Politics of Women's Rights," in Ward and Yoshikazu, *Democratizing Japan*, 223; Dower, *Embracing Defeat*, 365–366.

24. Dower, *Embracing Defeat*, 211.

25. One aspect of the occupation and a common aspect of official American foreign activities was to exclude from important positions those individuals with language or other expertise regarding Japan. Rather the occupation was guided by professionals such as lawyers and economists who knew next to nothing about Japan (Dower, *Embracing Defeat*, 224).

26. Morris, *Nationalism and the Right Wing in Japan*, 42.

27. Hardacre, *Shinto and the State*, 136.

28. On decentralization efforts, see Steiner, *Local Government in Japan*, 90–98.

29. Hane, *Modern Japan*, 345–346; Dower, *Embracing Defeat*, 447.

30. Fearey, *The Occupation of Japan*, 27.

31. Hirohito was an active player in politics before the war and continued to be so afterward (Ruoff, *The People's Emperor*, 106).

32. Dower, *Empire and Aftermath*, 112.

33. Bouissou, *Japan*, 43–44.

34. Ward, "Presurrender Planning," in Ward and Yoshikazu, *Democratizing Japan*, 15.

35. Koh, *Japan's Administrative Elite*, 66.

36. Aldous, *Police in Occupation Japan*, 49.

37. Ibid., 144–145.

38. Schaler, *The American Occupation of Japan*, 77–97.

39. Yoshida, *The Yoshida Memoirs*, 163.

40. Dower, *Empire and Aftermath*, 369.

41. Among other things, Yoshida favored suppression of revolutionary tendencies, restoration of the traditional political elite, and revival of prewar economic institutions such as the zaibatsu (ibid., 277).

42. Schaler, *The American Occupation of Japan*, 110.

43. Ibid., 145–146.

44. Martin, *The Allied Occupation of Japan*, 32.

45. Cohen, *Japan's Economy in War and Reconstruction*, 436–442.

46. Fearey, *The Occupation of Japan*, 82–84.

47. Schoppa, *Educational Reform in Japan*, 39.

48. Schaler, *The American Occupation of Japan*, 44.

49. Dower, *Embracing Defeat*, 272.

50. Hane, *Modern Japan*, 347.

51. Dore, *Land Reform in Japan*, 147–148.

52. Hane, *Modern Japan*, 347–348.

53. Fearey, *The Occupation of Japan*, 89.

54. Dore, *Land Reform in Japan*, 175–182.

55. Fearey, *The Occupation of Japan*, 33–35.

56. Yoshida, *The Yoshida Memoirs*, 169.

57. Thurston, *Teachers and Politics in Japan*, 23.

58. Duke, *Japan's Militant Teachers*, 26. Education had been perhaps the most important institution in promoting the emperor-state ideology that guided Japan from the 1890s to World War II (Horio, *Education Thought and Ideology in Modern Japan*, 65–105).

59. Rohlen, *Japan's High Schools*, 68–69.

60. Yoshida, *The Yoshida Memoirs*, 171.

61. Pempel, *Patterns of Japanese Policymaking*, 41.

62. Hane, *Modern Japan*, 349.

63. Schaler, *The American Occupation of Japan*, 32–34.

64. Cohen, *Japan's Economy in War and Reconstruction*, 419–420.

65. Fearey, *The Occupation of Japan*, 70–71.

66. Forsberg, *America and the Japanese Miracle*, 63.

67. Prestowitz, *Trading Places*, 157.

68. Kades, "The American Role in Revising Japan's Imperial Constitution."

69. Tanaka Hideo, "The Conflict Between Two Legal Traditions in Making the Constitution of Japan," in Ward and Yoshikazu, *Democratizing Japan*, 112.

70. Inoue, *MacArthur's Japanese Constitution*, 69. The Americans finessed the issue of the "official" version of the constitution, claiming the document finally produced was an exact and official translation of the original Japanese version. The official version was, of course, in English and translated into Japanese, often raising some serious linguistic problems (Moore and Robinson, *Partners for Democracy*, 141).

71. Moore and Robinson, *Partners for Democracy*, 98.

72. Colbert, *The Left-Wing in Japanese Politics*, 113ff; Scalapino, *The Japanese Communist Movement*, 52.

73. Inoue, *MacArthur's Japanese Constitution*, 173–220.

74. Hideo, "The Conflict Between Two Legal Traditions in Making the Constitution of Japan," in Ward and Yoshikazu, *Democratizing Japan*, 126.

75. Moore and Robinson, *Partners for Democracy*, 121.

76. Sissons, "The Pacifist Clause in the Japanese Constitution: Legal and Political Problems of Rearmament," 46–47.

77. Moore and Robinson, *Partners for Democracy*, 27.

78. Inoue, *MacArthur's Japanese Constitution*, 221–265.

79. Itoh and Beer, *The Constitutional Case Law in Japan*, 8.

80. Moore and Robinson, *Partners for Democracy*, 85.

81. Hideo, "The Conflict Between Two Legal Traditions in Making the Constitution of Japan," in Ward and Yoshikazu, *Democratizing Japan*, 117.

82. Yoshida, *The Yoshida Memoirs*, 60.

83. Aldous has a less sanguine view: "Thus, defeat and Occupation represented a moment of great potential, an opportunity, some felt, to implant democracy in Japan. This study contends that the moment passed without significant incident, that the op-

portunity to unlock Japan's democratic potential was wasted" (*Police in Occupation Japan*, 208).

3. The Structure of Government

1. The doctrine of the Mandate of Heaven in imperial China comes to mind.

2. Kan Ori, "The Diet and the Japanese Political System," in Valeo and Morrison, *The Japanese Diet and the U.S. Congress*, 22.

3. Baerwald, *Japan's Parliament*, 124.

4. Reischauer, *The Japanese*, 252.

5. Shoichi Izumi, "Diet Members," in Valeo and Morrison, *The Japanese Diet and the U.S. Congress*, 70.

6. *Time*, February 19, 1990, 46.

7. Ishibashi and Reed, "Second Generation Diet Members and Democracy in Japan."

8. Stockwin, *Japan*, 103.

9. *Far Eastern Economic Review*, June 19, 1986.

10. Koichi Kishimoto, "Diet Structure, Organization and Procedures," in Valeo and Morrison, *The Japanese Diet and the U.S. Congress*, 48–49.

11. Baerwald, *Japan's Parliament*, 90.

12. Ori, "The Diet and the Japanese Political System," 18.

13. Pempel, "Uneasy Toward Autonomy," 138–139; Reischauer, *The Japanese*, 254.

14. Baerwald, *Japan's Parliament*, 134.

15. Pempel, "Uneasy Toward Autonomy," in Suleiman, *Parliaments and Parliamentarians in Democratic Politics*, 120.

16. Izumi, "Diet Members," 74.

17. Baerwald, *Party Politics in Japan*, 91.

18. Muramatsu and Mabuchi, "Introducing a New Tax in Japan," in Kernell, *Parallel Politics*, 184–186.

19. Pempel, "The Dilemma of Parliamentary Opposition in Japan," 69–70.

20. Nagaharu, "Tax Revision for Better or for Worse," 124–129.

21. *Japan Times Weekly Overseas Edition*, January 7, 1989.

22. Izumi, "Diet Members," 63.

23. Campbell, *Contemporary Japanese Budget Politics*, 121–128.

24. Cheng, "Japanese Interest Group Politics: An Institutional Approach," 256.

25. Schoppa, *Education Reform in Japan*, 11.

26. Sakakibara, "The Japanese Politico-Economic System and the Public Sector," in Kernell, *Parallel Politics*, 76.

27. Kishimoto, "Diet Structure, Organization and Procedure," in Valeo and Morrison, *The Japanese Diet and the U.S. Congress*, 50.

28. Stockwin, "Parties, Politicians, and the Political System," in Stockwin et al. *Dynamic and Immobilist Politics in Japan*, 42.

29. Campbell, *Contemporary Japanese Budget Politics*, 151. The average term of a minister is 278 days (Koji Kakizawa, "The Diet and the Bureaucracy: The Budget," in Valeo and Morrison, *The Japanese Diet and the U.S. Congress*, 80).

30. Hayao, *The Japanese Prime Minister and Public Policy*.

31. Fukui, "Japan's Takeshita Takes the Helm," 174–175; Thayer, *How the Conservatives Rule Japan*, 195.

32. Stockwin, "Parties, Politicians, and the Political System," 40.

33. Fukui, "Japan's Takeshita Takes the Helm," 185.

34. Ike, *Japanese Politics*, 26.

35. "Japan, in its fairly long history, has produced few, if any, dictatorial or charismatic leaders of the caliber of Napoleon, Hitler or Peter the Great. Japanese groupism does not permit any individual to shine or stand out" (Haitani, "The Paradox of Japan's Groupism, 241).

36. Wolferen, *The Enigma of Japanese Politics*, 146.

37. Kyogoku, *The Political Dynamics of Japan*, 69.

38. Reischauer, *The Japanese*, 297.

39. Campbell, *Contemporary Japanese Budget Politics,* 21.

40. Haley, "Governance by Negotiation," 343–357.

41. Woronoff, *Politics: The Japanese Way*, 122. "Japan has a clearly discernable ruling class. Its members—mainly bureaucrats, top businessmen and one section of the LDP—are all administrators; there is no room among them for the aspiring statesman" (van Wolferen, *The Enigma of Japanese Politics*, 109).

42. For a contrast between the bureaucracy as dominant view vs. the party as dominant view, see Koh, *Japan's Administrative Elite*, 204–218.

43. Pempel, *Patterns of Japanese Policymaking*, 82–87.

44. Johnson, *MITI and the Japanese Miracle*, 154.

45. Ramseyer and Rosenbluth, *Japan's Political Marketplace*, 120.

46. T.J. Pempel, "The Tar Baby Target: 'Reform' of the Japanese Bureaucracy," in Ward and Yoshikazu, *Democratizing Japan*, 159.

47. Koh, *Japan's Administrative Elite*, 71.

48. Koh, "The Recruitment of Higher Civil Servants in Japan," 293–295.

49. Koh, *Japan's Administrative Elite*, 102–103.

50. Koh, "The Recruitment of Higher Civil Servants in Japan," 300; Reischauer, *The Japanese*, 297.

51. Kim, *Japan's Civil Service System*, 30.

52. Ibid., 43–44.

53. Kubota, *Higher Civil Servants in Postwar Japan*, 129.

54. Campbell, *Contemporary Japanese Budget Politics,* 49–50.

55. Kubota, *Higher Civil Servants in Postwar Japan,* 129.

56. There is also the practice, called "side slip," where a retiree takes a job with another government entity. Those who do this more than once are called "migratory birds" (Koh, *Japan's Administrative Elite*, 234–244).

57. Blumenthal, "The Practice of *Amakudari* Within the Japanese Employment System."

58. Woodall, *Japan Under Construction,* 70.

59. Yasunori, "Interest Groups and the Process of Political Decision-Making in Japan," in Sugimoto and Mouer *Constructs for Understanding Japan*, 271.

60. Kim, *Japan's Civil Service*, 9.

61. Ibid., 76–77.

62. Tsuji, *Public Administration in Japan*, 58–62.

63. Hrebenar, *Japan's New Party System*, 29, 47.

64. Kim, *Japan's Civil Service*, 29, 47.

65. On numbers of civil servants, see Koh, *Japan's Administrative Elite*, 70–71.

66. Steiner, *Local Government in Japan*, 64–113.

67. Ibid., 262–299; Bingman, *Japanese Government Leadership and Management*, 67–75.

68. Tani Satomi, "Japan Socialist Party in Creating Single Party Democracy," in Kataoka, *Creating Single-Party Democracy*, 91.

69. Masayasu, "The Prospects for Promoting Local Autonomy," 13.

70. Reed, *Japanese Prefectures and Policymaking*, 163–164, 168.

71. Reed, "Is Japanese Government Really Centralized?"

72. Reed, *Japanese Prefectures and Policymaking*, 54.

73. Bingman, *Japanese Government Leadership and Management*, 59.

74. Itoh, *The Japanese Supreme Court*, 4, 9.

75. Ibid., 155.

76. Ibid., 10.

77. Beer, *Freedom of Expression in Japan*, 133.

78. Itoh, *The Japanese Supreme Court*, 27.

79. Beer, *Freedom of Expression in Japan*, 135.

80. Itoh, *The Japanese Supreme Court*, 33.

81. Itoh and Beer, *The Constitutional Case Law in Japan*, 10; Itoh, *The Japanese Supreme Court*, 77.

82. Itoh, *The Japanese Supreme Court*, 82–83.

83. Ibid., 224.

84. Ibid., 103.

85. Ibid., 88.

86. Ibid., 31.

87. Clifford, *Crime Control in Japan*, 65.

88. Itoh, *The Japanese Supreme Court*, 186–193.

89. Ramseyer and Rosenbluth, *Japan's Political Marketplace*, 162.

90. Takeyoshi Kawashima, "Dispute Resolution in Contemporary Japan," in von Mehren, *Law in Japan*, 50–52.

91. Smith, *Japanese Society*, 44.

92. Parker, *The Japanese Police System Today: An American Perspective*, 23–24.

93. *Japan Times Online*, March 18, 2008; Haley, "Sheathing the Sword of Justice in Japan," 274.

94. Hakaru Abe, "Education of the Legal Profession in Japan," in von Mehren, *Law in Japan*, 153–199; Beer, *Freedom of Expression in Japan*, 131.

95. Beer, *Freedom of Expression in Japan*, 133.

96. Itoh, *The Japanese Supreme Court*, 28.

97. Ibid., 159–220.

98. Van Wolferen, *The Enigma of Japanese Politics*, 217.

99. Ramseyer and Rosenbluth, *Japan's Political Marketplace*, 82.

100. Beer, *Freedom of Expression in Japan*, 140.

101. For a critique of Japanese democracy, see Woronoff, *Politics: The Japanese Way*.

4. Political Parties—I

1. The term "political party" is used here in the liberal democratic sense of an organization the purpose of which is to win elections in order to control or at least influence the machinery of government. Totalitarian parties such as communists and fascists are a product of the twentieth century and are mechanisms of state control over society rather than instruments of democratic politics. See LaPalombara and Weiner, eds., *Political Parties and Political Development*, 6.

2. Reischauer, *Japan,* 4th ed., 212–214.

3. See Duverger, *Political Parties.*

4. Foster, "Ghost Hunting," 845.

5. Reed, "Japan: Haltingly Towards a Two-Party System," 284.

6. Ibid., 286.

7. Scalapino and Masumi, *Parties and Politics in Contemporary Japan,* 147; Curtis, *The Japanese Way of Politics,* 200.

8. "With the LDP paying off faithful support groups through the provision of the usual rewards associated with pork barreling—subsidies, public works, contracts, procurements, allocations from the General Accounts Budget, tax breaks, protection against foreign competition, administrative guidance (for example, concerning the stabilization of prices), and favorable legislation—LDP support groups in the labor intensive sectors—farmers, fishermen, local construction firms, real estate interests, distributors, small retailers, and others—reaped the benefits of continual redistribution of income as Japan's industrial economy expanded" (Okimoto, *Between MITI and the Market,* 187–88).

9. Flanagan, "The Japanese Party System in Transition," 223.

10. Flanagan, "Voting Behavior in Japan," 400–401.

11. Thomas R. Rochon, "Electoral Systems and the Basis of the Vote: The Case of Japan," in Campbell, *Parties, Candidates, and Voters in Japan,* 11.

12. Curtis, *The Logic of Japanese Politics,* 223.

13. Flanagan and Richardson, *Japanese Electoral Behavior,* 38.

14. Ibid., 50–51.

15. Christensen, *Ending the LDP Hegemony,* 195.

16. Bowen quips with good reason that the LDP "is neither liberal, nor democratic nor a party" (*Japan's Dysfunctional Democracy,* 45).

17. Uchida, "The Disintegration of Japan's Party System of 1955 and After," 6.

18. Forsberg, *America and Japan's Miracle,* 48.

19. Masumi Junnosuke, "The 1955 System: Origin and Transformation," in Tetsuya, *Creating Single-Party Democracy,* 35.

20. Johnson, *MITI and the Japanese Miracle,* 50. In 1955, 21 percent of the LDP candidates elected to the HR were from the higher civil service (Okimoto, *Between MITI and the Market,* 216).

21. Campbell, *Contemporary Japanese Budget Politics,* 117.

22. Toyozo, "When the Political Wind Shifts," 372. Tetsuya Kataoka notes that despite the importance of factions, the party itself is significant for at least one reason: "The LDP exists to maintain the U.S.-Japan security tie by containing the JSP. On this issue, all factions always come out together" (*Creating Single-Party Democracy,* 166).

23. Kohno, "Rational Foundations for the Organization of the Liberal Democratic Party of Japan," 371.

24. Ibid., 373; Junnosuke, "The 1955 System," in Tetsuya, *Creating Single-Party Democracy,* 48.

25. Ibid., 49.

26. Curtis, *The Logic of Japanese Politics,* 226.

27. Feldman and Kawakami, "Leaders and Leadership in Japanese Politics," 284.

28. Thayer, *How the Conservatives Rule Japan,* 17.

29. Curtis, *The Japanese Way of Politics,* 88.

30. Campbell, *Contemporary Japanese Budget Politics,* 134.

31. Thayer, *How the Conservatives Rule Japan,* 315; Totten and Kawakami, "The Functions of Factionalism in Japanese Politics," 113.

32. Fukui, "Japan's Takeshita Takes the Helm," 185.

33. Baerwald, *Party Politics in Japan,* 23.

34. See Leiserson, "Political Opposition and Development in Japan," in Dahl, *Regimes and Opposition,* 372–394.

35. Reed, "Japan: Haltingly Towards a Two-Party System," 288.

36. Bowen, *Japan's Dysfunctional Democracy,* 101. "Over time, a lower house seat had come to be viewed as a family heirloom, the supportive constituency as a family-owned business, and control of each as something that an incumbent can transfer to a designated successor (Woodall, *Japan Under Construction,* 87).

37. Ramseyer and Rosenbluth, *Japan's Political Marketplace,* 84.

38. *New York Times,* May 12, 1974.

39. Tsurutani, "The LDP in Transition? Mass Membership Participation in Party Leadership Selection."

40. Curtis, *The Japanese Way of Politics,* 103.

41. The primary approach was subsequently abandoned and the choice of party president returned to party leader's control.

42. *New York Times,* December 7, 1978.

43. *New York Times,* December 13, 1983.

44. Pempel, "Uneasy Towards Autonomy," in Suleiman, *Parliament and Parliamentarians in Democratic Politics,* 128.

45. *New York Times,* March 5, 1985.

46. Masumi, "Nakasone's Bid to Stay in Power," 127.

47. *Far Eastern Economic Review,* June 5, 1986.

48. Akihiro, "Reform of the Red Ink Railroad," 25–30.

49. *Far Eastern Economic Review,* March 27, 1986. "A close look reveals that Japan is exporting arms, albeit on a very small scale, and the character of new weapons are bound to lead to an increase in these exports and eventually to the abandonment of the 1967 ban on arms exports" (Drifte, *Arms Production in Japan,* 73).

50. *Time,* July 21, 1986.

51. Yashushi, "The High Noon of Pragmatic Conservatism" 351–352.

52. Keddell, *The Politics of Defense in Japan,* 184.

53. *Far Eastern Economic Review,* July 24, 1986, 14.

54. See Takashi, "The Legacy of a Weathercock Prime Minister."

55. Takeshi, "Farewell to the Peace-Loving State?" 22.

56. Pharr, "Japan in 1985," 55–56.

57. See Muramatsu, "In Search of National Identity."

58. *New York Times,* June 24, 1976.

59. *New York Times,* July 5, 1989.

60. *Japan Times Weekly Overseas Edition,* July 1, 1988, 2.

61. *New York Times,* July 4, 1989.

62. *New York Times,* July 24, 1989, A1, A4.

63. Hrebenar, *Japan's New Party System,* 150–152.

64. Reed, "Who Won the 1996 Election," in Reed, *Japanese Electoral Politics,* 146.

65. Hrebenar, *Japan's New Party System,* 153–157.

66. Ibid., 2.

67. Reed, "Realignment Between the 1983 and 1996 Elections," in Reed, *Japanese Electoral Politics*, 31.

68. Hrebenar, *Japan's New Party System*, 142.

69. Bowen, *Japan's Dysfunctional Democracy*, 21.

5. Political Parties—II

1. Curtis, *The Japanese Way of Politics*, 5.

2. In February 1991, the Japan Socialist Party formally changed its English name to the Social Democratic Party of Japan to call attention to its shift toward social democracy. Bowing to pressure from the party's left wing, however, the Japanese name—Nihon Shakaitō—remained the same.

3. Thayer, *How the Conservatives Rule Japan*, 8.

4. Curtis, *The Japanese Way of Politics*, 8.

5. Takamae Eiji, "Early Postwar Reform Parties," in Ward and Yoshikazu, *Democratizing Japan*, 351.

6. Tani Satomi, "The Japan Socialist Party Before the Mid-1960s: An Analysis of Its Stagnation," in Kataoka, *Creating Single-Party Democracy*, 82.

7. Scalapino and Masumi, *Parties and Politics in Contemporary Japan*, 38.

8. Stockwin, *Japan: Divided Politics in a Growth Economy*, 174.

9. Satomi, "The Japan Socialist Party," in Kataoka, *Creating Single-Party Democracy*, 84.

10. Thurston, *Teachers and Politics in Japan*, 75.

11. van Wolferen, *The Enigma of Japanese Power*, 77.

12. Thurston, *Teachers and Politics in Japan*, 78; Duke, *Japan's Militant Teachers*, 150.

13. Masumi, "The JSP Under New Leadership," 79–81.

14. Richard J. Samuels, "Local Politics in Japan: The Changing of the Guard," *Asian Survey* 22 (July 1982): 631.

15. Ibid., 632–635.

16. Curtis, *The Japanese Way of Politics*, 29.

17. *Japan Times Weekly International Edition*, April 16–22, 1990, 1.

18. Michitoshi, "The Local Elections of 1975," 119.

19. *Far Eastern Economic Review*, February 20, 1986, 38.

20. Masumi, "The Socialists' Belated Image Change," 369–373.

21. *New York Times*, February 20, 1990, A1.

22. Colbert, *The Left Wing in Japanese Politics*, 142.

23. Ibid., 198–199.

24. Reischauer, *The Japanese*, 319ff.

25. Ibid., 300, 304, 320.

26. Koichiro, "Political Parties in the Next Decade," 145.

27. Masashi, "The Road to Unarmed Neutrality," 142–144.

28. Stockwin, *The Japanese Socialist Reality and Neutralism*, 31.

29. Brannen, *Soka Gakkai*, 75–76.

30. Palmer, *Buddhist Politics*, 32.

31. Helton, "Political Prospects of Soka Gakkai," 232–233.

32. White, *The Sōkkagakkai and Mass Society*, 137.

33. Ibid., 200–201; Dator, *Soka Gakkai, Builders of the Third Civilization*, 105.

34. Hrebenar, *The Japanese Party System*, 152.

35. White, *The Sōkkagakkai and Mass Society,* 126.
36. Dator, *Soka Gakkai,* 9–15.
37. White, *The Sōkkagakkai and Mass Society,* 203–204.
38. Ibid., 138.
39, Helton, "Political Prospects of *Soka Gakkai,*" 234.
40. Johnson, *Opposition Politics in Japan,* 11.
41. *Japan Times Weekly Overseas Edition,* December 10–16, 1990, 1.
42. Ibid.
43. Scalapino, *The Japanese Communist Movement, 1920–1966,* 19.
44. Chapman, *Inventing Japan,* 11.
45. Scalapino, *Japanese Communist Movement,* 49.
46. Berton, "Japanese Eurocommunists: Running in Place," 21.
47. Colbert, *The Left Wing in Japanese Politics,* 107.
48. Berton, "Japanese Eurocommunists," 6.
49. *Japan Times Online,* June 22, 2003.
50. Curtis, *The Logic of Japanese Politics,* 136.
51. Thus, Hosokawa came to power as head of a motley coalition of reformers, political opportunists, socialists, pacifists, internationalists, and others. The potential for conflict within the coalition was obvious from the beginning (ibid., 114).
52. Fukui and Fukui, "Japan in 1996," 27–28.
53. Curtis, *The Logic of Japanese Politics,* 26.
54. Thayer, *How the Conservatives Rule Japan,* 13; see also Toyozo, "When the Political Wind Shifts," 359.
55. See White, *The Sōkagakkai and Mass Society,* 276.
56. Van Wolferen, *The Enigma of Japanese Power,* 73.
57. Johnson, *Opposition Politics in Japan,* 179.
58. Christensen, *Ending the LDP Hegemony,* 155.
59. Johnson, *Opposition Politics in Japan,* 180.
60. Masayasu, "The Prospects for Promoting Local Autonomy," 17.

6. Political Corruption and Political Reform

1. Mitchell, *Political Bribery in Japan,* 39.
2. Chapman, *Inventing Japan,* 155.
3. Bowen, *Japan's Dysfunctional Democracy,* 56.
4. Political corruption, as the term suggests, is normally viewed as a pathological or at least morally objectionable phenomenon. "While there is a consensus that corrupt behavior involves misuse of public authority for private gain, debate exists over the criteria used to determine when authority has been misused" (Gillespie and Okruhlik, "The Political Dimensions of Corruption Cleanups," 77).
5. Mikuni and Murphy, *Japan's Policy Trap,* 243.
6. Given the propensity for financial irregularities and mild public hostility toward it, regarding the flow of money in the political process as corruption may not be entirely accurate. "A corrupt exchange in and of itself may not be particularly noteworthy. However, the perception of and response to the corrupt activity among sizable or powerful groups can transform corruption into a politically salient issue" (Gillespie and Okruhlik, "The Political Dimensions of Corruption Cleanups," 80).
7. *New York Times,* March 5, 1985.
8. *Japan Times Weekly Overseas Edition,* May 6, 1989, 1.

9. Chapman, *Inventing Japan*, 164.

10. *Japan Times Weekly Overseas Edition*, July 1, 1988, 3.

11. Ibid., 2.

12. *New York Times*, July 4, 1989. The Japan Socialist Party changed its name to the Social Democratic Party of Japan in February 1991.

13. *New York Times*, July 24, 1989.

14. Ibid., February 8, 1989.

15. Ibid., July 20, 1989.

16. Ibid., October 13, 1989.

17. Bridges, *Japan and Korea*, 125.

18. *The New York Times*, 25 July 1989, p. 1.

19. Ibid., March 5, 1989, p. C1.

20. Ibid., February 20, 1990, p. A9.

21. Ibid., February 28, 1990, A7.

22. *The Japan Times*, March 9.

23. Ibid., October 24, 1992.

24. *The Japan Times,* March 14, 1993.

25. *The Japan Times Online,* May 21, July 17, 2003.

26. *The Japan Times Online,* November 10, 2007.

27. Estimates of LDP candidate expenditures range as high as $10 million or more each at the current rate of exchange (105 yen to the U.S. dollar) (Cox and Rosenbluth, "The Electoral Fortunes of Legislative Factions in Japan," 580.

28. *The Japan Times*, December 29, 1992, p. 1.

29. Curtis, *The Logic of Japanese Politics*, 80.

30. Toyozo, "Breakup of the Tanaka Faction: End of an Era," 372.

31. "The Japanese voter will typically forego a distant, marginal tie to a more powerful politician for a closer tie to a less influential candidate. As a result, the ruling party can field two to four candidates in the lower house two-to-six-member elections districts without a great deal of concern that one of their stronger and more popular candidates will attract all the conservative votes and cause defeat of the party's other candidates" (Flanagan et al., *The Japanese Voter*, 196).

32. Kyogoku, *The Political Dynamics of Japan*, 191.

33. The importance of faction bosses in fund raising has declined while that of individual members has grown. See Cox and Rosenbluth, "The Electoral Fortunes of Legislative Factions in Japan," 577. Among other things, this weakens the power base of faction leadership.

34. Thayer, *How the Conservatives Rule Japan*, 17.

35. The LDP members of parliament who share common policy interests form groups called *zoku* or "tribes."

36. See Leiserson, "Political Opposition and Development in Japan," in Dahl, *Regimes and Opposition*, 372–394.

37. Fukui, "Japan's Takeshita Takes the Helm," 185.

38. Baerwald, *Party Politics in Japan*, 23.

39. Calder, *Crisis and Compensation*, 194–195.

40. On the subject of money in politics see Taro, "The Recruit Scandal," 107–112.

41. *Japan Times*, March 10, 1993.

42. Chapman, *Inventing Japan*, 165.

43. Mikuni and Murphy, *Japan's Policy Trap,* 54.

44. Woodall, *Japan Under Construction,* 38.

45. Ibid., 2.

46. "Most Japanese politicians perceive their primary responsibility to be prying spending out of the bureaucracy for favored constituents. Many Japanese voters thus regard politics as a joke; they do not vote, or they vote as they are asked by their employers and local patrons" (Mikuni and Murphy, *Japan's Policy Trap*, 247).

47. The most votes received by a winning candidate in the 1993 House of Representatives election were 231,720. The fewest votes received by a winning candidate were 34,784. The most votes received by a losing candidate were 125,643.

48. Wolfe, "Japan's LDP Considers Electoral Reform," 777.

49. *Japan Times*, March 3, 1993, 3; March 5, 1993, 1.

50. Ibid., September 18, 1993, 1.

51. Shuichi, "The Electoral System and Political Reform," in Hideo, *How Electoral Reform Boomeranged*, 175.

52. Otake Hideo, "Overview," in ibid., xi–xxxi.

53. Bouissou, *Japan: The Burden of Success*, 252.

7. Political Participation

1. Not everyone thinks Japan is democratic. See van Wolferen, *The Enigma of Japanese Power*.

2. Scalapino and Masumi, *Parties and Politics in Contemporary Japan*, 79.

3. J.A.A. Stockwin, "Parties, Politicians and the Political System," in Stockwin et al., *Dynamic and Immobilist Politics in Japan*, 30–37.

4. Factionalism is characteristic of all parties except the Communist and Kōmeitō.

5. Lijphart, Lopez Pintor, and Sone, "The Limited Vote and the Single Nontransferable Vote: Lessons from the Japanese and Spanish Examples," in Grofman and Lijphart, *Electoral Laws and the Political Consequences,* 159.

6. Hrebenar, *The Japanese Party System*, 37.

7. Reed, *Japanese Prefectures and Policymaking*, 169.

8. Tsurutani, "The LDP in Transition?," 853.

9. Ibid.

10. Stockwin, *Japan*, 85.

11. Beer, *Freedom of Expression in Japan*, 372–378.

12. Thayer, *How the Conservatives Rule Japan*, 122; Craft, "The High-Decibel Election."

13. Thurston, *Teachers and Politics in Japan*, 223.

14. Curtis, *The Japanese Way of Politics*, 168.

15. Richardson, *Japanese Democracy*, 29.

16. Reed, *Japanese Prefectures and Policymaking,* 281.

17. Woodall, *Japan Under Construction*, 95.

18. Hrebenar, *Japan's New Party System,* 66.

19. Reischauer, *The Japanese*, 274.

20. Michisada, "Glitter and Expense in LDP Factional Politics," 150.

21. Curtis, *The Japanese Way of Politics,* 179–180.

22. *Japan Times Weekly Overseas Edition*, July 29, 1988, 5.

23. Michisada, "Glitter and Expense in LDP Factional Politics," 150. Richardson observes the close relationship between the LDP and business may be

overstated. In fact, the relationship may be rather contentious (*Japanese Democracy*, 184).

24. *New York Times,* January 29, 1990, 1.

25. Curtis, *The Japanese Way of Politics,* 175.

26. Reed, *Japanese Prefectures and Policymaking,* 386.

27. Curtis, *The Japanese Way of Politics,* 160–162.

28. Curtis, *The Logic of Japanese Politics,* 63.

29. Curtis, *The Japanese Way of Politics,* 169.

30. Ibid., 176.

31. Tasker, "Media: Directing the Deluge," in *The Japanese: A Major Exploration of Modern Japan,* 127.

32. Ikuo and Broadbent, "Referent Pluralism: Mass Media and Politics in Japan."

33. Lee, *Political Character of the Japanese Press*, 74. Foreign journalists generally find themselves excluded from the clubby environment of the Japanese press.

34. Tasker, "Media: Directing the Deluge," in *The Japanese: A Major Exploration of Modern Japan,* 118.

35. See Taketoshi, "The Press Clubs in Japan."

36. Johnson, *MITI and the Japanese Miracle,* 68.

37. Patricia G. Steinhoff, "Protest and Democracy," in Ishida and Krauss, *Democracy in Japan,* 172.

38. Ibid., 177.

39. Van Wolferen, *The Enigma of Japanese Politics,* 337.

40. Farrell, *Blood and Rage.*

41. Masayuki, "Missiles from the Radical Left"

42. Cole, *Japanese Blue Collar,* 173.

43. *New York Times,* March 22, 1995, A6.

44. Steinhoff, "Protest and Democracy,"177.

45. Irokawa Daikichi, "Popular Movements in Modern Japanese History," in McCormack Sugimoto, *The Japanese Trajectory*, 69–75.

46. Reed, "Environmental Politics: Some Reflections on the Japanese Case," 261.

47. Fukutake, *The Japanese Social Structure,* 192.

48. Pempel, *Policymaking in Contemporary Japan,* 221.

49. Setsuo, "Environmental Pollution," 402.

50. Pempel, *Policymaking in Contemporary Japan,* 223.

51. Setsuo, "Environmental Pollution," 403–404.

52. Ibid., 401.

53. Ui Jun, "A Citizens' Forum."

54. Masumi Junnosuke, "The 1955 System: Origin and Transformation," in Kataoka, *Creating Single-Party Democracy,* 45.

55. Mouer and Sugimoto, *Images of Japanese Society,* 69–71.

56. Junnosuke, "The 1955 System," 45.

57. Pempel, *Policymaking in Contemporary Japan,* 229.

58. Reed, "Environmental Politics," 260.

59. Reed, *Japanese Prefectures and Policymaking,* 46.

60. Johnson, *MITI and the Japanese Miracle,* 284.

61. Upham, *Law and Social Change in Postwar Japan,* 56, 58.

62. Woronoff, *Politics,* 266–267.

63. Reed, *Japanese Prefectures and Policymaking,* 69, 81.

64. Upham, *Law and Social Change in Postwar Japan,* 54–55.

65. *Kodansha Encyclopedia of Japan,* 224.

66. Upham, *Law and Social Change in Postwar Japan,* 59–61.

67. Beverly Smith, "Democracy Derailed: Citizens' Movements in Historical Perspective," in McCormack and Sugimoto, *Democracy in Contemporary Japan,* 157–72.

68. Upham, *Law and Social Change in Postwar Japan,* 62.

69. Susan Pharr, "Conclusion: Targeting by an Activist State: Japan as Civil Society Model," in Schwartz and Pharr, *The State of Civil Society in Japan,* 316.

70. Cheng, "Japanese Interest Group Politics," 252.

71. Ibid., 260.

72. Curtis, *The Logic of Japanese Politics,* 51.

73. Ken, "Enter Keidanren''s Young Leaders," 368–369. On pressure groups in general see Aurelia George, "Japanese Interest Group Behavior: An Institutional Approach," in Stockwin, *Dynamic and Immobilist Politics in Japan,* 106–140.

74. *New York Times,* May 24, 1974.

75. Calder, *Crisis and Compensation,* 185.

76. Hyoe and Hirschmeier, *Politics and Economics in Contemporary Japan,* 67–75; Richardson and Flanagan, *Politics in Japan,* 292.

77. George, "The Japanese Farm Lobby and Agricultural Policy-Making," 414.

78. George, "The Politics of Interest Representation in the Japanese Diet," 509.

79. In mid-1988, the Japanese agreed to a phase-out of restrictions on beef and citrus imports.

80. *New York Times,* July 14, 1989; Curtis, *Japanese Way of Politics,* 53–61.

81. George, "The Politics of Interest Representation in the Japanese Diet," 513, 527.

82. Colbert, *The Left-Wing in Japanese Politics,* 5; Koshiro Kazutoshi, "Japan's Labor Unions: The Meeting of Blue and White Collar," in Hyoe and Hirschmeier, *Politics and Economics in Contemporary Japan,* 144.

83. Richardson and Flanagan, *Politics in Japan,* 73.

84. It is consistent among groups to affiliate with one party rather than seeking to bargain with several (Ellis S. Krauss, "Politics and the Policymaking Process," in Ishida and Krauss, *Democracy in Japan,* 59).

85. *Japan Times Weekly Overseas Edition,* December 9, 1989, 4.

86. Ibid.

87. *Wall Street Journal,* February 23, 1988; *Japan Times Weekly Overseas Edition,* December 9, 1989, 4.

88. Patricia L. MacLachlan, "The Struggle for an Independent Consumer Society: Consumer Activism and the State's Response in Postwar Japan," in Schwartz and Pharr, *The State of Civil Society in Japan,* 232.

89. Chalmers, *Industrial Relations in Japan,* 174.

90. Ibid., 234.

91. Kawanishi Hirosuke, "The Reality of Enterprise Unionism," in McCormack and Sugimoto, *Democracy in Contemporary Japan,* 156.

92. See Christena Turner, "Democratic Consciousness in Japanese Unions," in Ishida and Krauss, *Democracy in Japan,* 299–323.

93. Solomon B. Levine, "Japanese Industrial Relations: An External Perspective," in Sugimoto and Mouer, *Constructs for Understanding Japan,* 310.

94. Cole, *Japanese Blue Collar,* 226, 229.

95. Thurston, *Teachers and Politics in Japan,* 177.

96. Ibid., 39.

97. Duke, *Japan's Militant Teachers*, 97, 101.

98. Ibid., 189.

99. Thurston, *Teachers and Politics in Japan,* 257.

100. Rohlen, *Japan's High Schools,* 221–229; Schoppa, *Education Reform in Japan,* 150–167.

101. Curtis, *The Logic of Japanese Politics,* 46.

102. Bouissou, *Japan: The Burden of Success,* 89.

103. Pempel, *Patterns of Japanese Policymaking,* 190.

104. Takashi and Ikuo, "The Status Quo Student Elite."

8. The Social Order

1. Flanagan and Richardson, *Japanese Electoral Behavior,* 18. "Neither Shinto-ism nor Buddhism provides the contemporary Japanese with anything approaching political principles, a view of life or even moral standards" (van Wolferen, *The Enigma of Japanese Power,* 274).

2. The Internet, among its other influences, is weakened group solidarity and promoting individualism (Parker, *The Japanese Police System Today: A Comparative Study,* 238).

3. See for example, Vogel, *Japan's New Middle Class,* 147–156; Langdon, *Japan,* 72; Beer, *Freedom of Expression in Japan,* 100–110. For a different perspective, see David W. Plath, "Arc, Circle and Sphere: Schedules for Selfhood," in Sugimoto and Mouer, *Constructs for Understanding Japan,* 67–93.

4. See Dale, *The Myth of Japanese Uniqueness.*

5. Yoshio Sugimoto, "The Manipulative Bases of 'Consensus' in Japan," in Mc-Cormack and Sugimoto, *Democracy in Contemporary Japan,* 65–75.

6. Smith, *Japanese Society,* 68–105; Haitani, "The Paradox of Japanese Groupism."

7. Hendry, *Understanding Japanese Society,* 70–85; Ross Mouer and Yoshio Sugimoto, "A Multi-Dimensional View of Stratification: A Framework for Comparative Analysis," in Sugimoto and Mouer, *Constructs for Understanding Japan,* 157–201; Haitani, "The Paradox of Japanese Groupism."

8. In government ministries, especially Finance, most top executives are trained in law followed at a distant second by persons trained in economics (Campbell, *Contemporary Japanese Budget Politics,* 44).

9. White, *The Japanese Educational Challenge: A Commitment to Children,* 175.

10. Mannari, *The Japanese Business Leaders,* 31.

11. Abegglen and Stack, *Kaisha,* 283.

12. Mannari, *Japanese Business Leaders,* 31.

13. Ibid., 108.

14. Wood, *The End of Japan Inc.,* 163.

15. See Mouer and Sugimoto, *Images of Japanese Society,* especially chap. 5.

16. Susan J. Pharr, "Resolving Social Conflicts: A Comparative View of Interpersonal and Inter-Group Relations in Japan," in ibid., 228–258.

17. Beer, "Group Rights and Individual Rights in Japan," 442.

18. Van Wolferen, *The Enigma of Japanese Power,* 329–332.

19. Frost, *For Richer, For Poorer*, 67–69.

20. On the family see Hendry, *Understanding Japanese Society,* 21–36.

21. Thayer, *How the Conservatives Rule Japan,* 221.

22. Christopher, *The Japanese Mind,* 186. On the perplexities and frustrations confronting non-Japanese trying to adapt to life in Japan see Shapiro, *In the Land of the Heartbroken.*

23. *The Guardian*, October 14, 1990, 10.

24. Mitchell, *The Korean Minority in Japan*, 75.

25. Ibid., 160; Kim, "The Korean Minority in Japan," 117.

26. Eighty-five percent of the second- and third-generation Koreans living in Japan know *only* Japanese (ibid., 115).

27. Bridges, *Japan and Korea.*

28. Mitchell, *The Korean Minority in Japan,* 132; Buckley, *Japan Today*, 99. "Blatant discrimination is widely practiced among Japanese employers against Koreans" (Kim, "The Korean Minority in Japan," 121).

29. Ryu, "Why Koreans Oppose the Fingerprint Law."

30. *New York Times,* November 1, 1991, A3.

31. Yung-Hwan Jo, "Japan," in Sigler, *International Handbook on Race and Race Relations,* 137.

32. For a detailed discussion of this point, see Lee and De Vos, *Koreans in Japan,* 21–30.

33. Mitchell, *Korean Minority in Japan,* 68.

34. Ibid., 115.

35. Jo, "Japan," 143–146.

36. *New York Times,* September 26, 1986. Despite cultural barriers, the lure of employment in Japan is strong. In 1989, some Chinese tried to gain admission to Japan masquerading as Vietnamese refugees. Since they could not claim political refugee status themselves, they acquired Vietnamese papers and tried to enter Japan with a group of Vietnamese boat people.

37. Ibid., October 24, 1989, p. A3.

38. Ibid., December 20, 1989.

39. Ibid., December 11, 1974.

40. Pharr, *Losing Face*, 78.

41. Takaaki, "Ainu, The Invisible Minority," 145; Reischauer, *The Japanese*, 34–35.

42. Coleman, *Family Planning in Japanese Society*, 149–55; Sandra Buckley and Vera Mackie, "Women in the New Japanese State," in McCormack and Yoshio Sugimoto, *Democracy in Contemporary Japan,* 173–185.

43. Upham, *Law and Social Change in Postwar Japan*, 144.

44. Ueno Chizuko, "The Japanese Women's Movement," in McCormack and Sugimoto, *The Japanese Trajectory,* 181.

45. Smith, "Gender Inequality in Contemporary Japan," 9.

46. *Japan Times Online*, September 18, 2003.

47. Katsutoshi, "Divorce, Japanese Style."

48. Norgren, *Abortion Before Birth Control*, 3.

49. Ibid., 50, 112.

50. Buckley and Mackie, "Women in the New Japanese State," in McCormack and Yoshio Sugimoto, 179.

51. Norgren, *Abortion Before Birth Control,* 132.

52. Pharr, "Women in Japan Today," 174, 176.

53. *International Higher Education,* no. 40 (Summer 2005).

54. Pempel, *Patterns of Japanese Policymaking,* 46.

55. Ahl, "Women's Rights? Not in Japan," 62; Hane, *Modern Japan,* 392.

56. Lois Dilatush, "Women in the Professions," in Lebra, *Women in Changing Japan,* 191.

57. James McClendon, "The Office: Way Station or Blind Alley?" in Plath, *Work and Life Course in Japan,* 164.

58. Rose Carter and Lois Dilatush, "Office Ladies," in Lebra, *Women in Changing Japan,* 78.

59. Reischauer, *The Japanese,* 211.

60. Pharr, *Losing Face,* 63.

61. Elizabeth Knipe Mouer, "Women in Teaching," in Lebra, *Women in Changing Japan,* 157.

62. Upham, *Law and Social Change in Postwar Japan,* 125.

63. Ibid., 140.

64. Women candidates did well in upper house elections during 1989 following revelations of financial and sexual misconduct by LDP politicians.

65. Hendry, *Understanding Japanese Society,* 103–117.

66. See the discussion on values in Kyogoku, *The Political Dynamics of Japan,* 153–174.

67. Shinto has its origins in prehistory. It crystallized into a coherent religious system beginning in the eighth century. It is a syncretistic religion consisting of a complex system of beliefs and rituals and has been heavily influenced by Buddhism. Shinto differs from Western religions in that there are no gods as such but multitudes of divinities (*Kami*) which include everything from natural forces to people (the emperor.) Pre-1945 state Shinto was essentially patriotic ritual.

68. Helen Hardacre, "After Aum: Religion and Civil Society in Japan," in Schwartz and Pharr, *The State of Civil Society in Japan,* 135.

69. White, *The Sōkagakkai and Mass Society,* 57, 59.

70. *Japan Times Online,* May 30, 2003.

71. "In the aftermath of Aum Shinrikyō's attacks, religion has come under intense scrutiny, and its position in civil society has been significantly undermined, with any capacity it had to restrain the state effectively nullified" (Hardacre, "After Aum," 153).

72. Metraux, "Religious Terrorism in Japan."

73. Morris, *Nationalism and the Right Wing in Japan,* 136.

74. Ibid., 100–101.

75. McIntosh, *Japan Re-Armed,* 137–139.

9. The Economy

1. "Japanese companies seem to have enjoyed extraordinary latitude in their technical relationship with western companies, largely, no doubt, because Europeans and Americans were still quite unable to conceive of Japan as a serious competitor in technologically advanced industries" (Morris-Suzuki, *The Technological Transformation of Japan,* 112).

2. Courdy, *The Japanese,* 226.

3. Brands, Jr., "The United States and the Reemergence of Independent Japan," 400.

4. Harootunian, "The Progress of Japan and the Samurai Class," 266.

5. See Osamu Saito, "The Rural Economy: Commercial, Agricultural, By-Employment, and Wage Work," in Jansen and Rozman, *Japan in Transition*, 400–420.

6. Cohen, *Japan's Economy in War and Reconstruction*, 417.

7. Chapman, *Inventing Japan*, 96.

8. Johnson, *MITI and the Japanese Miracle*, 239.

9. Mikuni and Murphy, *Japan's Policy Trap*, 3.

10. Friedman, *The Misunderstood Miracle*, 126–176.

11. Chalmers, *Industrial Relations in Japan*, 47.

12. Buckley, *Japan Today*, 45.

13. Belassa and Noland, *Japan in the World Economy*, 54.

14. Katz, *Japan*, 202.

15. Burks, *Japan: A Postindustrial Power*, 157.

16. Ibid., 190.

17. Okimoto, *Between MITI and the Market*, 8.

18. "But to the Japanese elite, competition carries with it the deadly whiff of disorder and loss of control. Asking Japan's governing elite to embrace competition is like asking the Pentagon to embrace radical pacifism" (Mikuni and Murphy, *Japan's Policy Trap*, 245).

19. Tilton, *Restrained Trade*, 21.

20. Forsberg, *American and Japan's Miracle*, 190.

21. This pattern is changing slightly. See Okimoto, *Between MITI and the Market*, 136.

22. Lincoln, *Arthritic Japan*, 84.

23. Ballon, *Doing Business in Japan*, 118; Lincoln, *Japan: Facing Economic Maturity*, 132–135.

24. Abegglen and Stark, *Kaisha*, 185.

25. Hatch and Yamamura, *Asia in Japan's Embrace*, 68.

26. Mikuni and Murphy, *Japan's Policy Trap*, 72.

27. James Horne, "The Economy and the Political System," in Stockwin et al., *Dynamic and Immobilist Politics in Japan*, 146–159.

28. Banks and corporations "play their respective roles in the Japanese economy, ensconced in an all-enveloping system of mutual protection, with their viability the ultimate responsibility of the bureaucracy" (Mikuni and Murphy, *Japan's Policy Trap*, 31).

29. Abegglen and Stark, *Kaisha*, 23–30.

30. Okimoto, Between *MITI and the Market*, 21.

31. See Samuels, "The Industrial Destructuring of the Japanese Aluminum Industry."

32. Tilton, *Restrained Trade*, 50.

33. See, for example, Vogel, *Japan as Number One*, especially chap. 5.

34. Chapman, *Inventing Japan*, 107.

35. Cole, *Japanese Blue Collar*, 171.

36. Ishida and Krauss, eds., *Democracy in Japan*, 264.

37. Johnson, *MITI and the Japanese Miracle*, 81.

38. Ibid., 239.

39. Ken'ichi, "The Competition Principle in Japanese Companies and Labor Unions," 25.

40. Johnson, *MITI and the Japanese Miracle*, 16.

41. Hamada, "Corporation, Culture and Environment," 1222.

42. Katz, *Japan*, 276.

43. Lincoln, *Japan's New Global Role.*

44. Lincoln, *Japan*, 48.

45. Ibid., 49.

46. Ibid.

47. Friedman, *The Misunderstood Miracle*, 2, 20.

48. Okimoto, *Between MITI and the Market*, 125.

49. *New York Times*, April 11, 1990, A1.

50. Vogel, "Pax Nipponica?" 753.

51. Ibid., 754.

52. Drifte, *Arms Production in Japan*, 66.

53. "Unlimited low-cost financing served as an essential ingredient in industrial Japan's ability to wrest global market leadership from Western companies in a succession of industries" (Mikuni and Murphy, *Japan's Policy Trap*, 76).

54. Prestowitz, *Trading Places*, 171.

55. Wood, *The End of Japan Inc.*, 140.

56. Frost, *For Richer, For Poorer*, 46.

57. Vogel, "Pax Nipponica?" 754.

58. Drifte, *Japan's Foreign Policy*, 66.

59. Haruo Shimada, "Structural Policies in Japan," in Kernell, *Parallel Politics; Economic Policymaking in the United States and Japan*, 288.

60. "Japan's notorious high prices are a disguised income transfer mechanism as well as a vehicle for disguised unemployment." (Katz, *Japan*, 105).

61. Shimada, "Structural Politcs in Japan," in Kernell, *Parallel Politics*, 287.

62. Ibid., 285–288.

63. Hall, "Japanese Spirit, Western Economics," in Helleiner and Pickel, *Economic Nationalism in a Globalizing World*, 136.

64. Hamada, "Corporation, Culture and Environment," 1214–1228.

65. Chalmers, *Industrial Relations in Japan*, 54.

66. Jones, "The Economic Implications of Japan's Aging Population," 962.

67. Lincoln, *Japan*, 11.

68. Wan, *The Political Economy of East Asia: Striving for Wealth and Power,* 29.

69. Recent trends suggest that for increasing numbers of women, marriage and childbearing do not bring an end to employment (Karen C. Holden, "Changing Employment Patterns of Women," in Plath, *Work and Life Course in Japan*, 34).

70. Cole, *Japanese Blue Collar*, 165, 169–170.

71. Vogel, *Japan's New Middle Class*, 7.

72. Cole, *Japanese Blue Collar*, 73.

73. Lincoln, *Japan*, 97. There is little tradition of social welfare policy in Japan. Up to 1945, public intervention in welfare matters was inhibited by the Confucian teaching that family and community are the proper agencies to relieve individual and collective distress. During the Tokoguwa period, the government intervened in social welfare matters only in times of disaster. Laissez-faire economic attitudes were dominant under which intervention was regarded as bad (Martin Collick, "Social

Policy: Pressures and Responses," in Stockwin, *Dynamic and Immobilist Politics in Japan*, 205).

74. Allen, *A Short Economic History of Modern Japan*, 220.

75. Cole, *Japanese Blue Collar*, 178.

76. Vogel, *Japan's New Middle Class*, 22.

77. Sato, "Japanese-American Economic Relations in Crisis," 436.

78. Lincoln, *Japan*, 73.

79. Katz, *Japan*, 334.

80. There has been a significant increase in karōshi (death from overwork) among "salarymen."

81. *Wall Street Journal*, February 23, 1988.

82. Fukui, "Japan in 1988: At the End of an Era," 2.

83. The Japanese seek to avoid what they consider the mistakes of others on the matter of immigration. "Let's learn from the German lesson" refers to the cultural conflicts that developed when Turkish and other nationalities entered Germany as "guest workers" to overcome a labor shortage (*Japan Times Weekly Overseas Edition*, July 1, 1988, 4).

84. Ibid., June 4, 1989, 4.

85. Japanese workers are inclined to work rather than pursue leisure not because of inherent characteristics of the labor population, but because of structural restraints in society. See Linhart, "From Industrial to Postindustrial Society," 307.

86. *New York Times*, May 14, 1974. The demand for professional babysitters, however, is increasing (*Japan Times Weekly Overseas Edition*, August 13, 1989, 6).

87. See Ouchi, *Theory Z*; Prestowitz, *Trading Places*, 71.

88. Muto Ichiyo, "Class Struggle in Postwar Japan," in McCormack and Sugimoto, *Democracy in Contemporary Japan*, 125.

89. Japan Institute for Social and Economic Affairs, *Japan 1988*, 71. Figures for most Western countries vary considerably from year to year as multiyear labor agreements expire and frequently lead to strikes.

90. Among industrialized countries, Japan ranks at the top in terms of the equitable distribution of income (Okimoto, *Between MITI and the Market*, 180).

91. Frost, *For Richer, For Poorer*, 41.

92. The average price for residential real estate went up 56.1 percent in Osaka in 1989 (*Japan Times Weekly International Edition*, April 2–8, 1990, 6).

93. Fukutake, *Man and Society in Japan*, 147.

94. The same approach is employed in public organizations. "Most Japanese governments hold to the opinion that a ministry, like a family, depends on an established structure, and that appointing a new public employee is like accepting a new family member. The important thing here is that human relationships within the governmental organization—or household group—are considered to have priority over all other relationships. Consequently, the Japanese public recruitment system aims at finding the person who will maintain harmonious relations with the others, and who will be able to work as a member of the team" (Kim, *The Japanese Civil Service System*, 33).

95. Ozaki, "The Humanistic Enterprise System in Japan," 833; Prestowitz, *Trading Places*, 156.

96. In September 1999, U.S. auto workers won a contract containing a lifetime employment provision.

97. Vogel, *Japan's New Middle Class*, 33.

98. Solomon B. Levine, "Careers and Mobility in Japan's Labor Market," in Plath, *Work and Life Course in Japan*, 27.

99. *New York Times*, May 14, 1974.

100. Wan, Political Economy of East Asia, 29.

101. Wood, *The End of Japan Inc,* 75.

102. Holden, "Changing Employment Patterns of Women, "in Plath, *Work and Life Course in Japan*, 45.

103. Frost, *For Richer, For Poorer,* 108.

104. Mikuni and Murphy, *Japan's Policy Trap,* 27.

105. Akira, "The Nature of the Japanese Corporation."

106. Okimoto, *Between MITI and the Market,* 42–43.

107. Abegglen and Stark, *Kaisha,* 208.

108. Hane, *Modern Japan,* 380.

109. Mikuni and Murphy, *Japan's Policy Trap,* 5.

110. "By holding its reserves in dollars, Japan has more or less encouraged the United States to spend and import more" (ibid., 28).

111. Hamada, "Winds of Change: Economic Realism and Japanese Labor Management," 406.

112. Drucker, "Japan's Choices," 923.

113. Okimoto, *Between MITI and the Market,* 105.

114. Ibid., 93.

115. The French retaliated with their own procedure targeted against Japanese VCRs. Called the Poitiers effect, the French required all imported Japanese VCRs clear customs at a single customs post 200 miles from the coast. The process, needless to say, was slow.

116. One approach is the public corporation that is not only a channel for public subsidy but also a mechanism for encouraging private efficiency. See Anchordoguy, "The Public Corporation."

117. Belassa and Noland, *Japan in the World Economy,* 215–237.

118. Okimoto, *Between MITI and the Market,* 36; *New York Times,* November 12, 1990, A1. The number of small shops declined about 10 percent from 1982 to 1988. The number of larger retailers (more than 500 square feet of floor space) rose slightly during the same period (*Japan Times Weekly International Edition,* April 2–8, 1990, 7).

119. Mark C. Tilton, "Regulatory Reform and Market Opening in Japan," in Carlile and Tilton, *Is Japan Really Changing Its Ways?* 168.

120. Ibid., 167.

121. Ibid., 189.

122. Lonny E. Carlile and Mark C. Tilton, "Is Japan Really Changing?" in Carlile and Tilton, *Is Japan Really Changing Its Ways?* 200.

123. Tilton, *Restrained Trade*, 82. "The trade associations that run cartels do not function primarily as lobbying groups outside the government but are seen as administrative organs that assist the government" (ibid., 205).

124. *Far Eastern Economic Review,* August 28, 1986.

125. Resistance to rice imports is based to a large degree on the argument that rice is the cultural foundation of Japanese society. Stephen Vlastos argues that the elevation of rice to the level of cultural icon has been a fairly recent development ("Agrarianism Without Tradition: The Radical Critique of Prewar Japanese Modernity," in Vlastos, *Mirror of Modernity*, 79–80).

126. George, "The Japanese Farm Lobby and Agricultural Policy-Making," 423.

127. Ibid., 425.

128. Katz, *Japan,* 65.

129. Maswood, *Japan in Crisis*, 68.

130. Katz, *Japan*, 88–89.

131. Okimoto, *Between MITI and the Market*, 49.

132. *New York Times*, February 18, 1988. Recent trends suggest that for increasing numbers of women, marriage and childbearing do not bring an end to employment (Holden, "Changing Employment Patterns of Women," in Plath, *Work and Life Course in Japan*, 34).

133. Katz, *Japan*, 274.

134. Tilton, *Restrained Trade*, 12. "In 1997, Japan produced almost all the aluminum it consumed. Sixteen years later in 1983, it was producing virtually none. However, 80 percent of the lost output was replaced by imports from Japanese-owned plants overseas" (Katz, *Japan*, 190).

135. Drucker, "Japan's Choices," 930–933.

136. *New York Times*, February 21, 1990, 1, C4.

137. Ibid., November 24, 1989, 1.

138. Drifte, *Japanese Foreign Policy*, 24–26.

139. Lincoln, *Arthritic Japan*, 62.

140. Ibid., 66.

141. Ibid.

142. Pempel, *Regime Shift*, 143.

143. Katz, *Japan*, 35.

144. "Public construction spending likewise is used to allocate money and income to favored construction firms and their owners, who do not actually do much work but put the funds they receive on deposit" (Mikuni and Murphy, *Japan's Policy Trap*, 54).

145. Wood, *End of Japan Inc.*, 134.

146. Bouissou, *Japan*, 250.

147. *Japan Times Online*, May 30, 2003.

148. Wood, *End of Japan Inc.*, 137.

149. Maswood, *Japan in Crisis*, 27.

150. Ibid., 56.

151. Asher, "What Became of the Japanese 'Miracle'?" 225.

152. Katz, *Japan*, 4.

153. Ibid.

154. Land values had reached unsustainable levels. Theoretically, the value of the land upon which the Imperial Palace grounds were situated exceeded that of the whole of Canada (Mikuni and Murphy, *Japan's Policy Trap*, 171).

155. *Japan Times Online*, September 19; October 1, 2003.

10. Education and Health Care

1. Fukutake, *The Japanese Social Structure*, 156–157. The Japanese government reports that only 0.2 percent consider themselves upper class and 8.6 percent lower class (Japan Institute for Social and Economic Affairs, *Japan in 1988*, 87).

2. Yoneyama, *Japanese High School*, 12.

3. Rohlen, *Japan's High Schools*, 87.

4. Yoneyama, *Japanese High School*, 139.

5. Rohlen, *Japan's High Schools*, 84–85.

6. On vocational education, see Dore and Sako, *How the Japanese Learn to Work*.

7. *Far Eastern Economic Review*, April 10, 1986.

8. Horio, *Educational Thought and Ideology in Modern Japan*, 173.

9. Nomi, "Inequality and Japanese Education: Urgent Choices."

10. White, *The Japanese Educational Challenge*, 20.

11. Duke, *Japanese School*, 63.

12. White, *The Japanese Educational Challenge*, 121.

13. Vogel, *Japan's New Middle Class*, 40.

14. See White, *The Japanese Educational Challenge*, 23ff.

15. Ibid., 73.

16. Hendry, *Understanding Japanese Society*, 91.

17. White, *The Japanese Educational Challenge*, 142.

18. Rohlen, *Japan's High Schools*, 77–110.

19. The role of fathers in the education of their children is distinctly secondary. In fact, many Japanese men have little contact with their children, especially younger ones. Father may leave for work before the children arise and return home after they have gone to bed (Vogel, *Japan's New Middle Class*, 22; Lebra, *Japanese Women*, 197, 199).

20. Richardson and Flanagan, *Politics in Japan*, 153.

21. Vogel, *Japan's New Middle Class*, 46, 211–215.

22. Edward Beauchamp, "Education," in Ishida and Krauss, *Democracy in Japan*, 236.

23. "Mothers are made the accomplices in all the children's acts, both positive and negative" (Mariko, "It's All Mother's Fault," 91).

24. Duke, *Japanese School*, 90–96.

25. Vogel, *Japan's New Middle Class*, 46.

26. Lebra, *Japanese Women*, 202–203.

27. Ibid., 197; Vogel, *Japan's New Middle Class*, 55–57.

28. Horio, *Educational Thought and Ideology in Modern Japan*, 15.

29. Lee, "Task Persistence of Young Children in Japan and the U.S."

30. Lebra, *Japanese Women*, 205–206.

31. "Japanese *ijime* distinctly differs from bullying in other societies, however, in that it is *always* collective bullying" (Yoneyama, *Japanese High School*, 164).

32. McVeigh, *Japanese Higher Education as Myth*, 4.

33. Students do not seek admission to a university as such. Rather they must apply for admission to a specific faculty or department and thus take the exam designed by that faculty. In turn, admission decisions are made by faculty.

34. Universities have high schools affiliated with them. The top 10 percent of the graduates of such high schools are admitted to the affiliated university without all the examinations required of others. Of course, they may prefer to go elsewhere.

35. Parker, *The Japanese Police System Today: An American Perspective*, 149; Rohlen, *Japan's High Schools*, 330; Buckley, *Japan Today*, 90.

36. Buckley, *Japan Today*, 90.

37. Woronoff, *Japan: The Coming Social Crisis*, 120.

38. In short order, students learn of these practices. There are compilations of courses prepared by students describing the approach taken by the professor and the kind of work expected. Some professors take attendance once a month or so and students upon learning these procedures, adjust their attendance schedules accordingly.

39. The graduation rate is lower for engineering students than for those in the arts.

40. Dore, *The Diploma Disease*, 48–49.

41. Koh, *Japan's Administrative Elite*, 159–170.

42. Fukutake, *Japan's Social Structure*, 210.

43. Mason, *A History of Japan*, 126.

44. Hane, *Modern Japan*, 398.

45. Belassa and Noland, *Japan in the World Economy*, 44–45.

46. Michio, "Developments in Postwar Japan," 16–17.

47. Tatsuno, *Created in Japan*, 224–232.

48. Professors hold a regular faculty position in one university and are part-time instructors at others.

49. The government does not encourage donations. Companies giving money to universities incur a 60 percent tax. McIntosh, *Arms Across the Pacific*, 20.

50. Pempel, *Patterns of Japanese Policymaking*, 149. Private universities receive 60 percent of their funds from tuition (*Japan Times Weekly Overseas Edition*, January 14, 1989, 3).

51. *Japan Times Weekly Online*, April 14, 2006.

52. Ibid., October 29, 2004.

53. McVeigh, *The Nature of the Japanese State,* 27.

54. Ibid., 136.

55. Rohlen, *Japan's High Schools*, 294–301.

56. Yoshiya, "Changing Patterns of Juvenile Aggression."

57. Vogel, *Japan's New Middle Class*, 143.

58. Dore, *Diploma Disease*, 50.

59. Ohnuke-Tierney, *Illness and Culture in Contemporary Japan*, 33.

60. Campbell and Ikegami, *The Art of Balance in Health Policy*, 45.

61. Ikegami and Campbell, "Japan's Health Care System," 30.

62. Campbell and Ikegami, *The Art of Balance in Health Care Policy,* 146.

63. Ibid., 161.

64. Neary, *The State and Politics in Japan* (Cambridge, UK: Polity Press, 2002), 194.

65. Ibid., 192.

66. Web site of the Ministry of Health, Labor and Welfare.

67. Campbell and Ikegami, *The Art of Balance in Health Care Policy*, 17.

68. Ibid., 177.

69. Ibid., 68.

70. Ibid., 166.

71. Ibid., 179.

72. Nomura and Nakayama, "The Japanese Health Care System," 348–349.

73. Ikegami and Campbell, "Japan's Health Care System," 33.

74. Campbell and Ikegami, *The Art of Balance in Health Care Policy,* 35.

11. Public Safety

1. Westermann and Burfeind, *Crime and Justice in Two Societies*, 74.

2. Yoshida, *The Yoshida Memoirs*, 176.

3. Haley, "Sheathing the Sword of Justice in Japan," 265.

4. Ambaras, *Bad Youth*, 195.

5. *Japan Times Online,* February 5, 2005.

6. Ibid., January 30, 2007.

7. Ibid., November 6, 2004.

8. Web site of the UN Office of Drugs and Crime.

9. Seventh United Nations Survey of Crime Trends and Operations of Criminal Justice Systems, 1998–2000 (United Nations Office on Drugs and Crime, Centre for International Crime Prevention).

10. *Japan Times Online,* December 12, 2003.

11. *Japan Times Weekly Overseas Edition,* January 13, 1990, 2.

12. *Japan Times Online,* December 12, 2003.

13. Westermann and Burfeind, *Crime and Justice in Two Societies,* 47–48, 151.

14. Clifford, *Crime Control in Japan,* 8.

15. Haley, "Sheathing the Sword of Justice in Japan," 269.

16. Parker, *The Japanese Police System: A Comparative Study,* 149.

17. Clifford, *Crime Control in Japan,* 10.

18. Hiroshi, "Some Cultural Assumptions Among the Japanese," 372–373.

19. Westermann and Burfeind, *Crime and Justice in Two Societies,* 37–41.

20. Johnson, *The Japanese Way of Justice,* 26.

21. Ibid., 219; Parker, *The Japanese Police System Today: An American Perspective,* 107.

22. Johnson, *Japanese Way of Justice,* 37.

23. Ibid., 46.

24. Ibid., 246.

25. Ryuichi Hirano, "The Accused and Society: Some Aspects of Japanese Criminal Law," in von Mehren, *Law in Japan,* 298–304.

26. Tokyo, Ministry of Justice, *Criminal Justice in Japan,* 10.

27. Clifford, *Crime Control in Japan,* 67.

28. Parker, *The Japanese Police System Today: An American Perspective,* 108. Westermann and Burfeind say the opposite: "Imprisonment is a fairly common outcome for criminal offenses, with 43% of criminal convictions in 1987 resulting in imprisonment" (Westermann and Burfeind, *Crime and Justice in Two Societies,* 117).

29. Japan's prison population has increased 30 percent since 2005. Still the number is comparatively low. Japan has 62 persons per 100,000 population incarcerated, while the United States has 738 per 100,000. The United States has the world's largest prison population, 2.9 million (*Japan Times Online,* January 30, 2007).

30. Haley, "Sheathing the Sword of Justice in Japan," 273; Westermann and Burfeind, *Crime and Justice in Two Societies,* 117.

31. *Japan Times Online,* January 30, 2007; *New York Times,* September 20, 1988.

32. Johnson, *Japanese Way of Justice,* 199; *Japan Times Online,* September 13, 2003. From 1976 to 2007, there were 1,095 executions in the United States.

33. *New York Times,* September 20, 1988.

34. Johnson, *Japanese Way of Justice,* 114.

35. While in jail, prisoners are not allowed to smoke, chew gum, eat candy or even talk unless authorized to do so (Beer, *Freedom of Expression in Japan,* 362).

36. Westermann and Burfeind, *Crime and Justice in Two Societies,* 139.

37. *Japan Times Online,* May 21, 2003.

38. There are only about 150,000 guns in Japan compared to 150 million in the United States (Westermann and Burfeind, *Crime and Justice in Two Societies,* 89).

39. Parker, *The Japanese Police System Today: An American Perspective,* 59–60.

40. Ibid., 197.

41. Government of Japan, National Police Agency, *White Paper on Police 1996* (Excerpt) (Tokyo: Japan Times, 1996), 54–61.

42. Katzenstein, *Cultural Norms and National Security*, 67.

43. Ibid.

44. Kaplan and Dubro, *Yakuza*, 14.

45. Ibid., 116.

46. Parker, *The Japanese Police System Today: An American Perspective*, 142.

47. Miyazawa, *Policing in Japan*, 22.

48. Katzenstein, *Cultural Norms and National Security*, 63.

49. Japan Public Opinion Location Library, Roper Center for Public Opinion Research, University of Connecticut.

50. Clifford, *Crime Control in Japan*, 73.

51. Johnson, "Above the Law."

52. Parker, *The Japanese Police System Today: An American Perspective*, 156–163.

53. Ibid., 58.

54. Ibid.

55. There are no academic programs in the areas of criminology or criminal justice in Japan. So once on the force, learning opportunities in the field are limited. See Parker, *The Japanese Police System Today: A Comparative Study*, 34.

56. Ibid., 52.

57. Miyazawa, *Policing in Japan*, 12–13.

58. Bayley, *Forces of Order*, 42–43, 55–60; Ames, *Police and Community in Japan*, 198.

59. For details see Ames, *Police and Community in Japan*, 151–179.

60. See Parker, *The Japanese Police System Today: An American Perspective*, 128–129.

61. *New York Times*, November 5, 1984.

62. *Japan Times Weekly Overseas Edition*, February 18, 1989.

63. Johnson, *The Japanese Way of Justice*, 58.

64. Schreiber, *Shocking Crimes of Postwar Japan*, 19–27.

65. Westermann and Burfeind, *Crime and Justice in Two Societies*, 153.

66. Clifford,*Crime Control in Japan*, 81.

67. *New York Times*, October 12, 1983.

68. Johnson, "Crime and Punishment in Contemporary Japan."

69. Clifford, *Crime Control in Japan*, 167.

12. Foreign Relations

1. Smith, *Japanese Society*, 109.

2. Klein, *Rethinking Japan's Identity and International Role*, 5.

3. Seizaburo Sato, "The Foundations of Modern Japanese Foreign Policy," in Scalapino, *The Foreign Policy of Modern Japan*, 375.

4. Soon Cho, "A Korean View on Korea-Japan Economic Relations," in Chung et al., *Korea and Japan in World Affairs*, 133.

5. Buzan, "Japan's Future," 571.

6. As World War II recedes further into the past, the Japanese see themselves more as victims of it than its cause. "Many young people are amazed when told that neighboring countries suffered also, possibly more, at the hands of the Japanese" (van Wolferen, *The Enigma of Japanese Power*, 426).

7. Buzan, "Japan's Future," 559.

8. Fukui, "Japan in 1988," 2.

9. Suspicion is not limited to Japan's neighbors. France's Minister of Euro-

pean Affairs was quoted as saying: "Japan is an adversary that does not play the game and has an absolute desire to conquer the world (*New York Times,* January 17, 1990, A6).

10. Roy, "North Korea's Relations with Japan."

11. Ducke, *Status Power,* 59.

12. Johnson, "The Patterns of Japanese Relations with China, 1952–1982," 419–425.

13. Ducke, *Status Power,* 35. In May 1990 during a visit to Japan by the president of South Korea, Emperor Akihito expressed "deep regret" for Japan's actions while governing Korea. This fell short of the complete apology demanded by the Koreans.

14. Woronoff, *Japan's Commercial Empire*, 266–274.

15. *New York Times,* January 21, 1974.

16. Hoong, "Malaysia-Japan Relations in the 1980s," 1100.

17. See, for example, Zhao, "The Making of Public Policy in Japan."

18. Masao, "The 'Japan as Number One' Syndrome," 48. See also Christopher, *The Japanese Mind.*

19. Fukutake, *The Japanese Social Structure*, 218.

20. Kim and Nanto, "Emerging Patterns of Sino-Japanese Economic Cooperation," 29–39.

21. *New York Times,* July 7, 1990, A2.

22. Garrett and Glaser, "Chinese Apprehensions About Revitalization of the U.S.-Japan Alliance," 395–397.

23. *New York Times,* October 31, 1990, A5.

24. Kim, "Japan and China in the 1980's," 426ff.

25. Rozman, *Japan's Response to the Gorbachev Era, 1985–1991*, 82. This interpretation of Soviet actions contributes to the widely held view that Japan was the victim in World War II (ibid., 83).

26. Hellmann, *Japanese Foreign Policy and Domestic Politics*, 29–40.

27. For the Japanese view see, Shigeo, "Japan's Northern Territories."

28. Njorge, "The Japan-Soviet Union Territorial Dispute," 499.

29. Mack and O'Hare, "Moscow-Tokyo and the Northern Territories Dispute," 381–384.

30. See Martin, *The Allied Occupation of Japan*, 36.

31. Tow, "Sino-Japanese Security Cooperation," 59. With the Soviet empire coming unraveled, giving up captured territory becomes more difficult. See Mack and O'Hare, "Moscow-Tokyo and the Northern Territories Dispute," 386; Menon and Abele, "Security Dimensions of Soviet Territorial Disputes with China and Japan," 3–19.

32. Rees, "Soviet Border Problems: China and Japan," 22–25.

33. *Japan Times Weekly Overseas Edition,* January 7, 1989.

34. *New York Times,* September 8, 1990, A1.

35. Mack and O'Hare, "Moscow-Tokyo and the Northern Territories Dispute," 380.

36. *New York Times,* May 19, 1988; Rozman, *Japan's Response to the Gorbachev Era,* 115. Some Japanese are skeptical that there is much opportunity for profit in an expanded economic link with Russia (ibid., 29).

37. *New York Times,* July 7, 1990, 2.

38. Packard, "The Coming U.S.-Japan Crisis," 348; Prestowitz, *Trading Places*, 218.

39. Johnson, "Japanese-Soviet Relations in the Early Gorbachev Era."

40. Zagoria, "Soviet Policy in East Asia," 20; Mochizuki, "Japan's Foreign Policy," 404. See also Satoshi, "The Soviet Union Smiles at Japan."

41. *Far Eastern Economic Review,* August 4, 1988, 24–25.

42. Pan, *The United Nations in Japan's Foreign and Security Policymaking, 1945–1992,* 115.

43. *New York Times,* January 10, 1990, 8, A6.

44. Pan, *United Nations in Japan's Foreign and Security Policymaking,* 99–109.

45. Osaki and Arnold, *Japan's Foreign Relations,* 157.

46. *New York Times,* January 4, 1990, A6; *Japan Times Weekly Overseas Edition,* July 22, 1988.

47. *Japan Times Weekly Overseas Edition,* February 25, 1989, 10.

48. Ogata, "Japan's United Nations Policy in the 1980's."

49. *New York Times,* November 13, 1984.

50. Mansfield, "The U.S. and Japan," 15.

51. Forsberg, *America and the Japanese Miracle,* 9.

52. Ibid., 11.

53. Except for Reagan and Nakasone, U.S. presidents and Japanese prime ministers have not had close personal relationships.

54. *New York Times,* February 23, 1990, A6.

55. *South* (February 1986).

56. The disintegration of this empire makes it less likely the Japanese public would support efforts to expand militarily.

57. Cf. Westwood, "Japan and Soviet Power in the Pacific."

58. Orr, "The AID Factor in U.S.–Japan Relations," 748.

59. Brooks and Orr, "Japan's Foreign Economic Assistance," 323.

60. Organization for Economic Co-operation and Development. *Development Co-operation Directorate (DCD-DAC)*

61. Orr, "The AID Factor in U.S.-Japan Relations," 744.

62. See Koppel and Plummer, "Japan's Ascendancy as a Foreign Aid Power."

63. *Japan Times Weekly Overseas Edition,* June 24, 1989, 4.

64. Prestowitz sees the FSX deal as another example of the United States giving away its technology and getting little in return (*Trading Places,* 5–58).

65. McIntosh, *Japan Re-Armed.*

66. Packard, "The Coming U.S.-Japan Crisis," 356.

67. *Japan Times Weekly Overseas Edition,* December 17, 1988, 4.

68. See Prestowitz, *Trading Places,* 5–58.

69. *New York Times,* November 26, 1990, A7.

70. Ibid., March 28, 1990, A1, A4.

71. Frost, *For Richer, For Poorer,* 124.

72. In early 1990, a poll revealed that the percentage of Americans with "generally friendly feelings toward Japan" had declined from 74 percent in June 1989 to 67 percent (*New York Times,* February 6, 1990, A16).

73. Ibid., February 22, 1990, C6.

74. Ibid., January 18, 1990, C1.

75. Lester, "U.S.-Japanese Nuclear Relations."

76. *New York Times,* January 3, 1988.

77. Ibid., February 2, 1990, C1.

78. Ibid., February 11, 1991, A3; February 12, 1991, A3.

79. See Nemetz et al., "Japan's Energy Strategy at the Crossroads."

80. *New York Times,* January 17, 1975.

81. Ibid., November 17, 1973.

82. Ibid., November 18, 1974.

83. Katz, *Japan,* 55–56.

84. Ibid., 175.

85. Sato, "Japanese-American Economic Relations in Crisis," 407–408.

86. Katz, *Japan,* 199.

87. Tsuneo, "What Japan Can't Do About Trade Friction," 255.

88. Belassa and Noland, *Japan in the World Economy* 183.

89. *Far Eastern Economic Review,* January 16, 1986, 94.

90. Ibid., December 7, 1985, 79.

91. Kosuke Oyama, "The Policymaking Process Behind Petroleum Industry Reform," in Carlile and Tilton, *Is Japan Really Changing Its Ways?* 144.

92. Upham, *Law and Social Change in Postwar Japan,* 192–198.

93. *Far Eastern Economic Review,* September 26, 1985.

94. Prestowitz, *Trading Places,* 210.

95. *Far Eastern Economic Review,* January 16, 1986, 90, 95.

96. *New York Times,* March 31, 1990.

97. *Far Eastern Economic Review,* September 29, 1988, 97.

98. Charges of dumping are not always valid. Japanese efficiency allows them to sell at prices that appear to be below production costs. See, for example, Kawahito, "The Steel Dumping Issue in Recent U.S.-Japanese Relations."

99. *Newsweek,* April 6, 1987.

100. Van Wolferen, *The Enigma of Japanese Power,* 422.

101. Frost, *For Richer, For Poorer,* 17–22.

102. While belaboring the Japanese for restricting imports of beef and citrus products, the United States maintains price supports for domestically produced sugar and quotas restricting cheaper imports. The practice reportedly costs the American consumer billions of dollars.

103. Masataka Kosaka, "The International Economic Policy of Japan," in Scalapino, *The Foreign Policy of Modern Japan,* 216–217.

104. *Far Eastern Economic Review,* August 16, 1990, 16.

105. Masaru, "U.S. Protectionists—Still Fighting Yesterday's War," 355.

106. Mikuni and Murphy, *Japan's Policy Trap,* 241.

107. Frost, *For Richer, For Poorer,* 150.

108. A poll commissioned by Japan revealed that 64 percent of Americans view Japanese investment in the United States as more of a threat than a benefit (*Japan Times Weekly Overseas Edition,* March 18, 1989, 11).

109. Frost, *For Richer, For Poorer,* 7–10.

13. Defense

1. Buck, *The Modern Japanese Military System.*

2. Yoshida, *The Yoshida Memoirs,* 185.

3. Ibid., 189.

4. Weinstein, *Japan's Postwar Defense Policy,* 59.

5. Drifte, *Arms Production in Japan,* 9.

6. Forsberg, *America and the Japanese Miracle,* 234.

7. Gher, "Status of Forces Agreements," 239.

8. The United States guaranteed Japan's security when the treaty was revised in 1960 (Aurelia George, "Japan and the United States: Dependent Ally or Equal Partner," in Stockwin, *Dynamic and Immobilist Politics in Japan,* 246).

9. Weinstein, *Japan's Postwar Defense Policy,* 62.

10. Quoted in Drifte, *Arms Production in Japan,* 14–16.

11. Holland, *Managing Defense*, xii.

12. Gher, "Status of Forces Agreements," 240.

13. O'Hanlon, "A New Japan-U.S. Security Bargain," 12.

14. Kim, "Prospects for US-Japan Security Cooperation," 189–190.

15. Due to the increased value of the yen against the dollar, Japan's ranking in terms of expenditures on the military rose considerably.

16. Kim, *The Japanese Civil Service System*, 104.

17. Drifte, *Japan's Foreign Policy*, 35–36.

18. "The Defense of Japan: Should the Rising Sun Rise Again?"; *Far Eastern Economic Review,* July 14, 1988, 32.

19. *Far Eastern Economic Review,* August 18, 1988.

20. McIntosh, *Japan Re-Armed*, 44–49.

21. Akaha, "Japan's Nonnuclear Response," 863–74.

22. Cf. Woods, "Japan's Defense Policies: The Winds of Change."

23. See George, "Japan and the United States," 260–264.

24. *New York Times,* August 5, 1991, C8.

25. See Akaha, "Japan's Response to the Threats of Shipping Disruptions in Southeast Asia and the Middle East."

26. Tow, "Sino-Japanese Security Cooperation," 61.

27. See Donald C. Hellman, "Japanese Security and Postwar Japanese Foreign Policy," in Scalapino, *The Foreign Policy of Modern Japan,* 332.

28. Holland, *Managing Defense, xiii.*

29. *Japan Times Weekly Overseas Edition,* February 11, 1989.

30. *New York Times,* October 10, 1989, 8, A9.

31. Drifte, *Arms Production in Japan,* 73.

32. *Far Eastern Economic Review,* November 20, 1989, 25–26.

33. Ducke, *Status Power,* 139.

34. Calder, "Japan in 1991: Uncertain Quest for a Global Role," 33.

35. *Japan Times Online,* December 12, 2003.

36. Akio Watanabe, "Japanese Public Opinion and Foreign Affairs: 1964–73," in Scalapino, ed., *The Foreign Policy of Modern Japan,* 114–115.

37. Weinstein, *Japan's Postwar Foreign Policy,* 125.

38. McIntosh, *Japan Re-Armed,* 36.

39. van Wolferen, *The Enigma of Japanese Power*, 319.

40. Langdon, "The Security Debate in Japan," 404–405.

41. Watanabe, "Japanese Public Opinion and Foreign Affairs," 139–143.

42. See Sissons, "The Pacifist Clause in the Japanese Constitution," 55–59.

43. *New York Times,* September 8, 1973.

44. *Japan Times Online,* May 23, 2003, and September 14, 2003.

45. *Far Eastern Economic Review,* September 26, 1985.

46. *Japan Times Weekly Overseas Edition,* February 4, 1989.

47. Ibid., February 11, 1989, 4.

48. Holland, *Managing Defense*, 92–93.

49. Donald C. Hellmann, "Japanese Security and Postwar Japanese Foreign Policy," in Frank, *The Japanese Economy in International Perspective*, 22.

50. Gavan McCormack, "Beyond Economism: Japan in a State of Transition," in McCormack and Sugimoto, *Democracy in Contemporary Japan,* 44.

51. Watanabe, "Japanese Public Opinion and Foreign Affairs,"117.

52. Masumi, "A State Visit to the Yasukuni Shrine," 21; see also Toland, *The Rising Sun*, 819.

53. Domestic opposition to the Yasakuni shrine as a state symbol comes from the political left and from new religious groups such as the Sōka Gakkai. They view Yasakuni as a symbol of oppression and religious persecution (Hardacre, *Shinto and the State*, 41).

54. *Christian Science Monitor,* October 4, 1988; *New York Times,* October 14, 1988.

55. This missile was replaced by the more powerful SS-25.

56. McIntosh, *Japan Re-Armed,* 77.

57. The Soviet presence in Southeast Asia declined and the Vietnamese government suggested perhaps the United States might resume use of the port facility at Cam Ranh Bay.

58. Olsen, "Evolving U.S.-ROK Security Relations: 167.

59. Mochizuki, "Japan's Foreign Policy," 402–403.

60. Langdon, "The Security Debate in Japan," 404–405.

61. Hughes, *Japan's Security Agenda,* 202.

62. Ibid., 204.

14. Problems and Prospects

1. Bowen describes Japan as a dysfunctional democracy. "Japan's democracy is real, but it suffers from personalism, graft, cronyism, favoritism, bribery, money politics, factionalism, and collusion—all elements of what the Japanese refer to as 'structural corruption'" (*Japan's Dysfunctional Democracy,* 3).

2. The most complete statement of this view is van Wolferen, *The Enigma of Japanese Power*.

3. Christopher, *The Japanese Mind,* 321.

4. Tsurutani, *Political Change in Japan,* 2–16.

5. Belassa and Noland, *Japan in the World Economy,* 21.

6. Lee and De Vos, *Koreans in Japan,* 356.

7. Fukutake, *The Japanese Social Structure,* 136.

8. At the national level, women have yet to make a significant impression. In 1989, 1.4 percent of the members of the House of Representatives were women. The situation is better in the House of Councillors, where women held 13 percent of the seats (*Japan Times Weekly Overseas Edition,* October 14, 1989, 5).

9. Richardson and Flanagan, *Politics in Japan,* 218–229.

10. "Japan's Choices," 934–939.

11. *The Economist,* December 7, 1985, 25.

12. White, *The Japanese Educational Challenge,* 15.

13. Masakazu, "Signs of a New Individualism."

14. *Japan Times Weekly Overseas Edition,* August 12, 1989, 1.

15. Ibid., July 8, 1989, 8.

16. *New York Times,* November 20, 1989.

17. Kosaka, "The International Economic Policy of Japan," in Scalapino, *The Foreign Policy of Modern Japan,* 223.

18. Ibid., 225.

19. Fukui, "Japan in 1988," 8.

20. Reischauer, *The Japanese,* 193–194.

Bibliography

General Works

Banno, Junji. *Democracy in Pre-war Japan: Concepts of Government, 1871–1937: Collected Essays.* New York: Routledge, 2001.

Beauchamp, Edward R., ed. *Japanese Society Since 1945.* New York: Garland, 1998.

Bouissou, Jean-Marie. *Japan: The Burden of Success.* Boulder, CO: Lynne Rienner, 2002.

Breen, John, ed. *Yasukuni, the War Dead and the Struggle for Japan's Past.* New York: Hurst; Columbia University Press, 2008.

Calder, Kent. *Crisis and Compensation: Public Policy and Political Stability in Japan 1949–86.* Princeton: Princeton University Press, 1988.

Chapman, William. *Inventing Japan: The Making of a Postwar Civilization.* Englewood Cliffs, NJ: Prentice-Hall, 1991.

Christopher, Robert C. *The Japanese Mind: The Goliath Explained.* New York: Simon and Schuster, 1983.

Curtis, Gerald L. *The Logic of Japanese Politics: Leaders, Institutions and the Limits of Change.* New York: Columbia University Press, 1999.

Dale, Peter N. *The Myth of Japanese Uniqueness.* New York: St. Martin's Press, 1986.

Friedman, David. *The Misunderstood Miracle: Industrial Development and Political Change in Japan.* Ithaca: Cornell University Press, 1988.

Goodman, Roger, and Kirsten Refsing, eds. *Ideology and Practice in Modern Japan.* London: Routledge, 1992.

Kataoka, Tetsuya, ed. *Creating Single-Party Democracy: Japan's Postwar Political System.* Stanford, CA: Hoover Institution Press, 1992.

———. *The Price of a Constitution: The Origin of Japan's Postwar Politics.* New York: Crane Russak, 1991.

Kyogoku, Jun'ichi. *The Political Dynamics of Japan.* Tokyo: University of Tokyo Press, 1987.

Langdon, Frank C. *Japan.* Boston: Little, Brown, 1967.

———. *The Japanese Trajectory: Modernization and Beyond.* Cambridge: Cambridge University Press, 1988.

McVeigh, Brian J. *The Nature of the Japanese State.* London: Routledge, 1998.

Masakazu, Yamasaki. "Signs of a New Individualism." *Japan Echo* 11 (Spring 1984): 8–18.

Masao, Kunihiro. "The 'Japan as Number One' Syndrome." *Japan Echo* 11 (Autumn 1984).

Masumi, Fukatsu. "A State Visit to the Yasukuni Shrine." *Japan Quarterly* (June–April 1986).

Masumi, Junnosuke. *Contemporary Politics in Japan,* trans. Lonny E. Carlile. Berkeley: University of California Press, 1995.

———. *Postwar Politics in Japan. 1945–1955.* Berkeley: University of California Press, 1985.

Morris, I.I. *Nationalism and the Right Wing in Japan: A Study of Post-War Trends.* Westport, CT: Greenwood Press, 1974.

Morris-Suzuki, Tessa. *The Technological Transformation of Japan: From the Seventeenth to the Twenty-first Centuries.* Cambridge: Cambridge University Press, 1994.

Murakami, Hyoe, and Johannes Hirschmeier. *Politics and Economics in Contemporary Japan.* Tokyo: Kodansha, 1983.

Reed, Steven R. "Environmental Politics: Some Reflections on the Japanese Case." *Comparative Politics* 13 (April 1981).

Reischauer, Edwin O. *Japan, the Story of a Nation.* New York: Alfred A. Knopf, 1974.

———. *Japan: The Story of a Nation,* 4th ed. New York: McGraw-Hill, 1990.

———. *The Japanese.* Cambridge: Harvard University Press, 1984.

Richardson, Bradley M. *The Political Culture of Japan.* Berkeley: University of California Press, 1974.

Richardson, Bradley M., and Scott C. Flanagan, *Politics in Japan.* Boston: Little, Brown, 1984.

Ruoff, Kenneth J. *The People's Emperor: Democracy and the Japanese Monarchy, 1945–1995.* Cambridge: Harvard University Press, 2001.

Scheiner, Irwin. "The Japanese Village: Imagined, Real, Contested." In *Mirror of Modernity: Invented Traditions of Modern Japan,* ed. Stephen Vlastos. Berkeley: University of California Press, 1998.

Stockwin, J.A.A. *Japan: Divided Politics in a Growth Economy.* New York: W.W. Norton, 1982.

———. "Parties, Politicians and the Political System." In *Dynamic and Immobilist Politics in Japan,* ed. Stockwin et al. Honolulu: University of Hawaii Press, 1988.

Tasker, Peter. "Media: Directing the Deluge." In *The Japanese: A Major Exploration of Modern Japan.* New York: E.P. Dutton, 1988.

Tatsuno, Sheridan M. *Created in Japan: From Imitators to World-Class Innovators.* New York: Harper and Row, 1990.

Tsuneishi, Warren M. *Japanese Political Style: An Introduction to the Government and Politics of Modern Japan.* New York: Harper and Row, 1966.

Tsurutani, Taketsugu. *Political Change in Japan: Response to Postindustrial Challenge.* New York: David McKay, 1977.

van Wolferen, Karel. *The Enigma of Japanese Power: People and Politics in a Stateless Nation.* New York: Alfred A. Knopf, 1989.

Varley, Paul H. *Japanese Culture,* 3d ed. Honolulu: University of Hawaii Press, 1984.

Vogel, Ezra F. *Japan as Number One: Lessons for America.* Cambridge: Harvard University Press, 1979.

White, James W., Michio Umegaki, and Thomas Havens. *The Ambivalence of Nationalism.* New York: University Press of America, 1990.

Woronoff, Jon. *Politics: The Japanese Way.* New York: St. Martin's Press, 1986.

Yasunori, Sone. "Interest Groups and the Process of Political Decision-Making in

Japan." In *Constructs for Understanding Japan*, ed. Yoshio Sugimoto and Ross E. Mouer. London: Kegan Paul International, 1989.

History

Allen, G.C. *A Short Economic History of Modern Japan*, 2d ed. New York: St. Martin's Press, 1981.

Anchordoguy, Marie. "The Public Corporation: A Potent Japanese Policy Weapon." *Political Science Quarterly* 103 (Winter 1988–89): 707–724.

Arnason, Johann. "Paths to Modernity: The Peculiarities of Japanese Feudalism." In *The Japanese Trajectory: Modernization and Beyond*, ed. Gavan McCormack and Yoshio Sugimoto. Cambridge: Cambridge University Press, 1988.

Banno, Junji. *Democracy in Pre-War Japan: Concepts of Government, 1871–1937: Collected Essays*. New York: Routledge, 2001.

Barnhart, Michael A. *Japan and the World Since 1868*. London: Edward Arnold, 1995.

———. *Japan Prepares for War: The Search for Economic Security, 1919–41*. Ithaca: Cornell University Press, 1987.

Beasley, William G. *The Meiji Restoration*. Stanford: Stanford University Press, 1972.

Berry, Mary Elizabeth. *Hideyoshi*. Cambridge: Harvard University Press, 1982.

Bouissou, Jean-Marie. *Japan: The Burden of Success*. Boulder, CO: Lynne Rienner, 2002.

Calman, Donald. *The Nature and Origins of Japanese Imperialism: A Reinterpretation of the Great Crisis of 1873*. London: Routledge, 1992.

Coble, Parks M. *Facing Japan: Chinese Politics and Japanese Imperialism 1931–37*. Cambridge: Harvard University Press, 1991.

Cooper, Michael, ed. *They Came to Japan: An Anthology of European Reports on Japan, 1543–1640*. Berkeley: University of California Press, 1965.

Dower, John W. *Embracing Defeat: Japan in the Wake of World War II*. New York: Diane, 2003.

———. *Empire and Aftermath*. Cambridge, MA: Harvard University, Council on East Asian Studies, 1979.

Farrell, William. *Blood and Rage: The Story of the Japanese Red Army*. Lexington, MA: Lexington Books, 1990.

Fogel, Joshua A., ed. *Late Qing China and Meiji Japan: Political and Cultural Aspects*. Norwalk, CT: Eastbridge, 2004.

Fraser, Andrew, R.H.P. Mason, and Philip Mitchell. *Japan's Early Parliaments 1890–1905: Structures, Issues, Trends*. London: Routledge, 1995.

Fujita, Neil S. *Japan's Encounter with Christianity: The Catholic Mission in Pre-Modern Japan*. New York: Paulist Press, 1991.

Gluck, Carol. *Japan's Modern Myths: Ideology in the Late Meiji Period*. Princeton: Princeton University Press, 1985.

Hane, Mikiso. *Modern Japan: A Historical Survey*. Boulder, CO: Westview Press, 1986.

Hardacre, Helen. *Shinto and the State, 1868–1988*. Princeton: Princeton University Press, 1989.

Harootunian, Harry D. "The Economic Rehabilitation of the Samurai in the Early Meiji Period." *Journal of Asian Studies* 19 (August 1960): 433–444.

———. "The Progress of Japan and the Samurai Class, 1868–1882." *Pacific Historical Review* 28 (August 1959): 255–266.

———. *Toward Restoration: The Growth of Political Consciousness in Tokugawa Japan.* Berkeley: University of California Press, 1970.

Hiroshi, Wagatsuma. "Some Cultural Assumptions Among the Japanese." *Japan Quarterly* 31 (October–December 1984).

Jansen, Marius B., and Gilbert Rozman. *Japan in Transition: From Tokugawa to Meiji.* Princeton: Princeton University Press, 1986.

Keene, Donald. *Emperor of Japan: Meiji and His World, 1852–1912.* New York: Columbia University Press, 2002.

Large, Stephen S. *Emperor Hirohito and Showa Japan.* London: Routledge, 1992.

Masayuki, Takagi. "Missiles from the Radical Left." *Japan Quarterly* 33 (October–December 1986): 391–394.

Mason, R.H. *A History of Japan.* New York: Free Press, 1972.

Massarella, Derek. *A World Elsewhere: Europe's Encounter with Japan in the Sixteenth and Seventeenth Centuries.* New Haven: Yale University Press, 1990.

Michio, Nagi. "Developments in Postwar Japan." *Japan Quarterly* 32 (January–March 1985).

Mitchell, Richard H. *Janus-Faced Justice: Political Criminals in Imperial Japan.* Honolulu: University of Hawaii Press, 1992.

———. *Thought Control in Prewar Japan.* Ithaca: Cornell University Press, 1976.

Montgomery, Michael. *Imperialist Japan.* London: Christopher Helm, 1987.

Morley, James W., and Kuo Ting-yee. *Sino-Japanese Relations 1862–1927.* New York: Columbia University Press, 1965.

Nish, Ian. *Alliance in Decline: A Study in Anglo-Japanese Relations 1908–23.* London: Athlone Press, 1972.

———. *Japanese Foreign Policy in the Interwar Period.* Westport, CT: Praeger, 2002.

Pyle, Kenneth B. *The Making of Modern Japan.* Lexington, MA: Heath, 1978.

Reischauer, Edwin O. *Japan, the Story of a Nation.* New York: Alfred A. Knopf, 1974.

Reischauer, Edwin O., and Albert M. Craig. *Japan: Tradition and Transformation.* Boston: Houghton Mifflin, 1978.

Sato, Hideo. "Japanese-American Economic Relations in Crisis." *Current History* (December 1985).

Silberman, Bernard S., and Harry D. Harootunian. *Japan in Crisis: Essays on Taishō Democracy.* Princeton: Princeton University Press, 1970.

Tipton, Elise K. *The Japanese Police State: The Tokko in Interwar Japan.* Honolulu: University of Hawaii Press, 1990.

———. *Modern Japan: A Social and Political History.* 2d ed. London: Routledge, 2008.

Toby, Ronald P. *State and Diplomacy in Early Modern Japan.* Princeton: Princeton University Press, 1984.

Toland, John. *The Rising Sun: The Decline and Fall of the Japanese Empire.* New York: Bantam Books, 1971.

Totman, Conrad. *The Collapse of the Tokugawa Bakufu, 1862–1868.* Honolulu: University of Hawaii Press, 1980.

Umegaki, Michio. *After the Restoration: The Beginning of Japan's Modern State.* New York: New York University Press, 1988.

Wakabayashi, Bob Tadashi. *Anti-Foreignism and Western Learning in Early Modern Japan: The New Theses of 1825.* Cambridge: Harvard University Press, 1986.
Webb, Herschel. *The Japanese Imperial Institution in the Tokugawa Period.* New York: Columbia University Press, 1968.
Young, A. Morgan. *Imperial Japan.* Westport, CT: Greenwood Press, 1938.

The Occupation

Aldous, Christopher. *The Police in Occupation Japan: Control, Corruption and Resistance to Reform.* London: Routledge, 1997.
Buckley, Roger. *Occupation Diplomacy: Britain, the United States and Japan, 1945–52.* Cambridge: Cambridge University Press, 1982.
Fearey, Robert A. *The Occupation of Japan: Second Phase, 1948–50.* New York: Macmillan, 1950.
Harries, Meirion, and Susan Harries. *Sheathing the Sword: The Demilitarization of Japan.* London: Hamish and Hamilton, 1987.
Inoue, Kyoko. *MacArthur's Japanese Constitution: A Linguistic and Cultural Study of Its Making.* Chicago: University of Chicago Press, 1991.
Kades, Charles L. "The American Role in Revising Japan's Imperial Constitution." *Political Science Quarterly* 104 (Summer 1989): 215–248.
Kataoka, Tetsuya. *The Price of a Constitution: The Origin of Japan's Postwar Politics.* New York: Crane Russak, 1991.
Kersten, Rikki. *Democracy in Post-war Japan: Maruyama and Masao and the Search for Autonomy.* London: Routledge, 1995.
McNelly, Theodore. "The Japanese Constitution: Child of the Cold War." *Political Science Quarterly* 74 (June 1959): 176–195.
Manchester, William. *The American Caesar: Douglas MacArthur.* Boston: Little, Brown, 1978.
Martin, Edwin M. *The Allied Occupation of Japan.* New York: Institute of Pacific Relations, 1948.
Masumi, Junnosuke. *Postwar Politics in Japan. 1945–1955.* Berkeley: University of California Press, 1985.
Moore, Ray A., and Donald L. Robinson. *Partners for Democracy: Crafting a New Japanese State Under MacArthur.* New York: Oxford University Press, 2002.
Oppler, Alfred C. *Legal Reform in Occupied Japan.* Princeton, NJ: Princeton University Press, 1976.
Schaler, Michael. *The American Occupation of Japan.* London: Oxford University Press, 1985.
Spector, Ronald H. *Eagle Against the Sun: The American War with Japan.* New York: Free Press, 1985.
Tsutsui, William M. *Banking Policy in Japan: American Efforts at Reform During the Occupation.* London: Routledge, 1998.
Ward, Robert E., and Sakamote Yoshikazu, ed. *Democratizing Japan: The Allied Occupation.* Honolulu: University of Hawaii Press, 1987.
Yoshida, Shigeru. *The Yoshida Memoirs: The Story of Japan in Crisis.* Boston: Houghton Mifflin, 1962.

Structure of Government

Baerwald, Hans. *Japan's Parliament: An Introduction*. London: Cambridge University Press, 1974.

Beer, Lawrence W. *Freedom of Expression in Japan: A Study in Comparative Law, Politics, and Society*. Tokyo: Kodansha International, 1984.

Bingman, Charles F. *Japanese Government Leadership and Management*. New York: St. Martin's Press, 1989.

Blumenthal, Tuvia. "The Practice of *Amakudari* Within the Japanese Employment System." *Asian Survey* 25 (March 1985): 310–321.

Craft, Lucille. "The High-Decibel Election." *Japan Quarterly* 33 (October–December 1986): 365–377.

Fukui, Haruhiro. "Japan's Takeshita Takes the Helm." *Current History* 87 (April 1988).

———. "Japan in 1988: At the End of an Era." *Asian Survey* 24 (January 1989).

Fukui, Haruhiro, and Shigeko N. Fukui. "Japan in 1996: Between Hope and Uncertainty." *Asian Survey* 37 (January 1977).

Haley, John O. "Governance by Negotiation: A Reappraisal of Bureaucratic Power in Japan." *Journal of Japanese Studies* 13 (Summer 1987).

Hayao, Kenji. *The Japanese Prime Minister and Public Policy*. Pittsburgh: University of Pittsburgh Press, 1993.

Ike, Nobutaka. *Japanese Politics: Patron-Client Democracy*, 2d ed. New York: Alfred A. Knopf, 1972.

Ishida, Takeshi, and Ellis S. Krauss, eds. *Democracy in Japan*. Pittsburgh: University of Pittsburgh Press, 1989.

Itoh, Hiroshi. *The Japanese Supreme Court: Constitutional Policies*. New York: Markus Weiner, 1989.

Itoh, Hiroshi, and Lawrence Ward Beer. *The Constitutional Case Law in Japan: Selected Supreme Court Decisions, 1961–70*. Seattle: University of Washington Press, 1978.

Johnson, Chalmers. *MITI and the Japanese Miracle: The Growth of Industrial Policy, 1925–75*. Stanford: Stanford University Press, 1985.

Kim, John S. *Japan's Civil Service System: Its Structure, Personnel, and Politics*. New York: Greenwood Press, 1988.

Kim, Paul S. *The Japanese Civil Service System: Its Structure, Personnel, and Politics*. Westport, CT: Greenwood Press, 1988.

Koh, B.C. *Japan's Administrative Elite*. Berkeley: University of California Press, 1989.

———. "The Recruitment of Higher Civil Servants in Japan: A Comparative Perspective." *Asian Survey* 25 (March 1985).

Kohno, Masaru. "Rational Foundations for the Organization of the Liberal Democratic Party of Japan." *World Politics* 44 (April 1992).

Kubota, Akira. *Higher Civil Servants in Postwar Japan*. Princeton: Princeton University Press, 1969.

Kyogoku, Jun'ichi. *Political Dynamics of Japan*. Tokyo: University of Tokyo Press, 1987.

McCormack, Gavan, and Yoshio Sugimoto, eds. *Democracy in Contemporary Japan*. Armonk, NY: M.E. Sharpe, 1986.

McNelly, Theodore. "The Japanese Constitution: Child of the Cold War." *Political Science Quarterly* 74 (June 1959): 176–195.

Masayasu, Namuri. "The Prospects for Promoting Local Autonomy." *Japan Quarterly* 34 (January–March 1987): 13–18.

Masayasu, Narumi, ed. *Policymaking in Contemporary Japan.* Ithaca: Cornell University Press, 1977.

Masumi, Ishikawa. "Nakasone's Bid to Stay in Power." *Japan Quarterly* 33 (January–April 1986).

Neary, Ian. *The State and Politics in Japan.* Cambridge, UK: Polity, 2002.

Nomura, Hideki, and Takeo Nakayama. "The Japanese Health Care System: The Issue Is to Solve the 'Tragedy of the Commons' Without Making Another." *BMJ* 331 (September 24, 2005).

Pempel, T.J. "Uneasy Towards Autonomy: Parliament and Parliamentarians in Japan." In *Parliaments and Parliamentarians in Democratic Politics,* ed. Ezra N. Suleiman. New York: Holmes and Meier, 1986.

Ramseyer, J. Mark, and Frances McCall Rosenbluth. *Japan's Political Marketplace.* Cambridge: Harvard University Press, 1997.

Richardson, Bradley. *Japanese Democracy: Power, Coordination, and Performance.* New Haven: Yale University Press, 1997.

Setsuo, Kobayashi. "Environmental Pollution." *Japan Quarterly* 17 (October–December 1970).

Steiner, Kurt. *Local Government in Japan.* Stanford: Stanford University Press, 1965.

Thayer, Nathaniel B. *How the Conservatives Rule Japan.* Princeton: Princeton University Press, 1969.

Toyozo, Tanaka. "When the Political Wind Shifts." *Japan Quarterly* 33 (October–December 1986).

———. "Breakup of the Tanaka Faction: End of an Era." *Japan Quarterly* 34 (October 1987).

Tsuji, Kiyoaki. *Public Administration in Japan.* Tokyo: University of Tokyo Press, 1984.

Ui Jun. "A Citizens' Forum: 15 Years Against Pollution." *Japan Quarterly* 32 (July 1885): 271–276.

Upham, Frank K. *Law and Social Change in Postwar Japan.* Cambridge: Harvard University Press, 1987.

Valeo, Francis R., and Charles E. Morrison. *The Japanese Diet and the U.S. Congress.* Boulder, CO: Westview Press, 1983.

Political Parties

Baerwald, Hans. *Party Politics in Japan.* Boston: Allen and Levinson, 1986.

Berger, Gordon. *Parties Out of Power in Japan: 1931–1941.* Princeton: Princeton University Press, 1977.

Berton, Peter A. "Japanese Eurocommunists: Running in Place." *Problems of Communism* (July–August 1986): 21.

Bowen, Roger. *Japan's Dysfunctional Democracy: The Liberal Democratic Party and Structural Corruption.* Armonk, NY: M.E. Sharpe, 2003.

Brannen, Noah. *Soka Gakkai: Japan's Militant Buddhists.* Richmond, VA: John Knox Press, 1968.

Campbell, John Creighton, ed. *Parties, Candidates, and Voters in Japan: Six Quantitative Studies*. Michigan Papers in Japanese Studies no. 2. Ann Arbor: University of Michigan Press, 1981.

Carlile, Lonny E. "Party Politics and the Japanese Labor Movement: Rengo's 'New Political Force.'" *Asian Survey* 34 (July 1994): 606–620.

Colbert, Evelyn S. *The Left Wing in Japanese Politics*. New York: Institute of Pacific Relations, 1952.

Cole, Alan Burnett. *Socialist Parties in Postwar Japan*. New Haven: Yale University Press, 1966.

Dator, James Allen. *Soka Gakkai, Builders of the Third Civilization: American and Japanese Members*. Seattle: University of Washington Press, 1969.

Duverger, Maurice. *Political Parties: Their Organization and Activity in the Modern State*. New York: John Wiley, 1963.

Flanagan, Scott C., and Bradley M. Richardson. *Japanese Electoral Behavior: Social Cleavages, Social Networks and Partisanship*. London: Sage, 1977.

Foster, James J. "Ghost Hunting: Local Party Organization in Japan." *Asian Survey* 22 (September 1982).

Gillespie, Kate, and Gwenn Okruhlik. "The Political Dimensions of Corruption Cleanups: A Framework for Analysis." *Comparative Politics* 24 (October 1991).

Helton, William R. "Political Prospects of Soka Gakkai." *Pacific Affairs* 37 (Fall and Winter, 1965–66): 231–244.

Hrebenar, Ronald J. *The Japanese Party System: From One-Party Rule to Coalition Government*. Boulder, CO: Westview Press, 1986.

———. *Japan's New Party System: The Post-1993 System*. Boulder, CO: Westview Press, 2000.

Johnson, Stephen. *Opposition Politics in Japan: Strategies Under a One-Party Dominant Regime*. London: Routledge, 2000.

Koichiro, Kuwata. "Political Parties in the Next Decade." *Japan Quarterly* 17 (April–June 1970).

LaPalombara, Joseph, and Myron Weiner, eds. *Political Parties and Political Development*. Princeton: Princeton University Press, 1966.

Leiserson, Michael. "Political Opposition and Development in Japan." In *Regimes and Opposition*, ed. Robert A. Dahl. New Haven: Yale University Press, 1973.

Lijphart, Arend, Raphael Lopez Pintor, and Yasunori Sone. "The Limited Vote and the Single Nontransferable Vote: Lessons from the Japanese and Spanish Examples." In *Electoral Laws and the Political Consequences*, ed. Bernard Grofman and Arend Lijphart. New York: Agathon Press, 1986.

Masumi, Fukatsu. "The Socialists' Belated Image Change." *Japan Quarterly* 32 (October–December 1985): 369–374.

Masumi, Ishikawa. "The JSP Under New Leadership." *Japan Quarterly* 31 (January–March 1984): 79–82.

Metraux, Daniel A. "Religious Terrorism in Japan: The Fatal Appeal of *Aum Shinrikyo*." *Asian Survey* 35 (December 1995): 1140–1154.

Mulgan, Aurelia George. *Japan's Failed Revolution: Koizumi and the Politics of Economic Reform*. Canberra: Asia Pacific Press, 2002.

Muramatsu, Michio. "In Search of National Identity: The Politics and Policies of the Nakasone Administration." *Journal of Japanese Studies* 13 (Summer 1987): 307–342.

Palmer, Arvin. *Buddhist Politics: Japan's Clean Government Party*. The Hague: Martinus Nijhoff, 1971.

Scalapino, Robert A. *The Japanese Communist Movement, 1920–1966.* Berkeley: University of California Press, 1967.

Stockwin, J.A.A. *The Japanese Socialist Reality and Neutralism: A Study of a Political Party and Its Foreign Policy.* London: Cambridge University Press, 1968.

Takashi, Inoguchi. "The Legacy of a Weathercock Prime Minister." *Japan Quarterly* 34 (October–December 1987): 363–370.

Takeshi, Igarashi. "Farewell to the Peace-Loving State?" *Japan Echo,* no. 2 (1983).

Totten, George O., and Tamio Kawakami. "The Functions of Factionalism in Japanese Politics." *Pacific Affairs* 37 (Summer 1965): 109–122.

Tsurutani, Taketsugu. "The LDP in Transition? Mass Membership Participation in Party Leadership Selection." *Asian Survey* 20 (August 1980): 844–859.

Uchida, Mitsuru. "The Disintegration of Japan's Party System of 1955 and After." *Waseda Political Studies* (March 1988).

White, James W. *The Sōkkagakkai and Mass Society.* Stanford: Stanford University Press, 1970.

Yu, Lydia N. "The Japan Communist Party." *Japan Quarterly* 21 (July–September 1974): 265–272.

Corruption

Bowen, Roger W. *Japan's Dysfunctional Democracy: The Liberal Democratic Party and Structural Corruption.* Armonk, NY: M.E. Sharpe, 2003.

Christensen, Raymond V. *Ending the LDP Hegemony: Party Cooperation in Japan.* Honolulu: University of Hawaii Press, 2000.

Johnson, Chalmers. "Tanaka Kakuei, Structural Corruption, and the Advent of Machine Politics in Japan." *Journal of Japanese Studies* 12 (Winter 1986): 1–28.

Mitchell, Richard H. *Political Bribery in Japan.* Honolulu: University of Hawaii Press, 1996.

Pharr, Susan J. *Losing Face: Status Politics in Japan.* Berkeley: University of California Press, 1990.

———. "Japan in 1985: The Nakasone Era Peaks." *Asian Survey* 25 (Winter 1986).

Shuichi, Wade. "The Electoral System and Political Reform." In *How Electoral Reform Boomeranged,* ed. Otake Hideo. Tokyo: Japan Center for International Exchange, 1998.

Taro, Yayama. "The Recruit Scandal: Learning from the Causes of Corruption." *Journal of Japanese Studies* 16 (Winter 1990): 93–114.

Woodall, Brian. *Japan Under Construction: Corruption, Politics, and Public Works.* Berkeley: University of California Press, 1996.

Political Participation

Ayusawa, Iwao. *A History of Labor in Modern Japan.* Honolulu: East-West Center Press, 1966.

Broadbent, Jeffrey. *Environmental Politics in Japan: Networks of Power and Protest.* Cambridge: Cambridge University Press, 1998.

Cheng, Peter P. "Japanese Interest Group Politics: An Institutional Approach." *Asian Survey* 30 (March 1990).

Christensen, Raymond V. "Electoral Reform in Japan: How It Was Enacted and Changes It May Bring." *Asian Survey* 34 (July 1994): 589–605.

Cole, Robert E. *Japanese Blue Collar: The Changing Tradition.* Berkeley: University of California Press, 1971.

Cox, Gary W., and Frances Rosenbluth. "The Electoral Fortunes of Legislative Factions in Japan." *American Political Science Review* 87 (September 1993).

Curtis, Gerald. *Election Campaigning Japanese Style.* New York: Columbia University Press, 1971.

———. *The Japanese Way of Politics.* New York: Columbia University Press, 1988.

Farley, Miriam. *Labor in Japan.* New York: Institute of Pacific Relations, 1949.

Feldman, Ofer, and Kazuhisa Kawakami. "Leaders and Leadership in Japanese Politics: Images During a Campaign Period." *Comparative Political Studies* 22 (October 1989).

Flanagan, Scott C. "The Japanese Party System in Transition." *Comparative Politics* 3 (January 1971).

———. "Voting Behavior in Japan: The Persistence of Traditional Patterns." *Comparative Political Studies* 1 (October 1968).

Flanagan, Scott C., and Bradley M. Richardson. *Japanese Electoral Behavior: Social Cleavages, Social Networks and Partisanship.* London: Sage, 1977.

Flanagan, Scott C., et al. *The Japanese Voter.* New Haven: Yale University Press, 1991.

Garon, Sheldon. *The State of Labor in Modern Japan.* Berkeley: University of California Press, 1987.

George, Aurelia D. "The Japanese Farm Lobby and Agricultural Policy-Making." *Pacific Affairs* 54 (Fall 1981): 409–430.

———. "The Politics of Interest Representation in the Japanese Diet: The Case of Agriculture." *Pacific Affairs* 64 (Winter 1991–92).

Gresser, Julian, Koichiro Fujikura, and Akio Morishima. *Environmental Law in Japan.* Cambridge, MA: MIT Press, 1981.

Hamada, Tomoko. "Corporation, Culture and Environment: The Japanese Model." *Asian Survey* 25 (December 1985): 1214–1228.

———. "Winds of Change: Economic Realism and Japanese Labor Management." *Asian Survey* (April 1980).

Helton, William R. "Political Prospects of Soka Gakkai." *Pacific Affairs* 37 (Fall/Winter, 1965–66): 231–244.

Ikuo, Kabashima, and Jeffrey Broadbent. "Referent Pluralism: Mass Media and Politics in Japan." *Journal of Japanese Studies* 12 (Summer 1986): 329–361.

Ishibashi, Michihiro, and Steven R. Reed. "Second Generation Diet Members and Democracy in Japan." *Asian Survey* 32 (April 1992): 366–379.

Ken, Otani. "Enter Keidanren's Young Leaders." *Japan Quarterly* 33 (October–December 1986).

Ken'ichi, Odawara "The Competition Principle in Japanese Companies and Labor Unions." *Japan Quarterly* (January–March 1984): 25–28.

Krauss, Ellis S. *Japanese Radicals Revisited: Student Protest in Postwar Japan.* Berkeley: University of California Press, 1974.

Krauss, Ellis S., Thomas P. Rohlen, and Patricia G. Steinhoff. *Conflict in Japan.* Honolulu: University of Hawaii Press, 1984.

Lee, Jung Bock. *The Political Character of the Japanese Press.* Honolulu: University of Hawaii Press, 1987.

Maclachlan, Patricia L. *Consumer Politics in Postwar Japan: The Institutional Boundaries of Citizen Participation.* New York: Columbia University Press, 2002.

Marsland, Stephen E. *The Birth of the Japanese Labor Movement: Takano Fusataro and the Rodo Kumiai Kiseikai.* Honolulu: University of Hawaii Press, 1989.

Michisada, Hirose. "Glitter and Expense in LDP Factional Politics." *Japan Quarterly* 33 (April–June 1986).

Michitoshi, Takabatake. "The Local Elections of 1975." *Japan Quarterly* 22 (July–September 1975).

Mitchell, Richard H. *Political Bribery in Japan.* Honolulu: University of Hawaii Press, 1996.

Mouer, Ross, and Yoshio Sugimoto. *Images of Japanese Society: A Study in the Social Construction of Reality.* London: Kegan Paul International, 1986.

Packard, George R., III. *Protest in Tokyo: The Security Crisis of 1960.* Princeton: Princeton University Press, 1966.

Plath, David. *Work and Life Course in Japan.* Albany: State University of New York Press, 1983.

Reed, Steven R. *Japanese Prefectures and Policymaking.* Pittsburgh: University of Pittsburgh Press, 1986.

———. "Is Japanese Government Really Centralized?" *Journal of Japanese Studies* 8 (Winter 1982): 133–164.

———. "Japan: Haltingly Towards a Two-Party System." *Politics of Electoral Systems,* September 15, 2005.

Reed, Steven R., ed. *Japanese Electoral Politics: Creating a New Party System* London: Routledge Curzon, 2003.

Samuels, Richard J. "Local Politics in Japan: The Changing of the Guard." *Asian Survey* 22 (July 1982).

Scalapino, Robert A., and Junnosuke Masumi. *Parties and Politics in Contemporary Japan.* Berkeley: University of California Press, 1962.

Schwartz, Frank J., and Susan J. Pharr, ed. *The State of Civil Society in Japan.* London: Cambridge University Press, 2003.

Taketoshi, Yamamoto. "The Press Clubs in Japan." *Journal of Japanese Studies* 15 (Summer 1989): 371–388.

Vogel, Ezra F. *Japan's New Middle Class: The Salary Man and His Family in a Tokyo Suburb.* Berkeley: University of California Press, 1963.

Wolfe, Eugene L. "Japan's LDP Considers Electoral Reform: A Neglected Political Debt." *Asian Survey* 32 (September 1992).

The Social Order

Ahl, David H. "Women's Rights? Not in Japan." *Creative Computing* (August 1984).

Austin, Lewis. *Saints and Samurai: The Political Culture of the American and Japanese Elites.* New Haven: Yale University Press, 1975.

Beer, Lawrence W. "Group Rights and Individual Rights in Japan." *Asian Survey* 21 (April 1981): 437–453.

Benedict, Ruth. *The Chrysanthemum and the Sword: Patterns of Japanese Culture.* New York: World, 1967.

Bernstein, Gail L. *Haruko's World: A Japanese Farm Woman and Her Community.* Stanford: Stanford University Press, 1983.

Brands, H.W., Jr. "The United States and the Reemergence of Independent Japan." *Pacific Affairs* 59 (Fall 1986).

Buruma, Ian. *Behind the Mask.* New York: Pantheon, 1984.

Christopher, Robert C. *The Japanese Mind: The Goliath Explained.* New York: Simon and Schuster, 1983.

Coleman, Samuel. *Family Planning in Japanese Society: Traditional Birth Control in a Modern Urban Culture.* Princeton: Princeton University Press, 1983.

Courdy, Jean-Claude. *The Japanese: Everyday Life in the Empire of the Rising Sun,* trans. Raymond Rosenthal. New York: Harper and Row, 1984.

Dale, Peter N. *The Myth of Japanese Uniqueness.* New York: St. Martin's Press, 1986.

De Vos, George, and Hiroshi Wagatsuma. *Japan's Invisible Race: Caste in Culture and Personality.* Berkeley: University of California Press, 1966.

Doi, Takeo. *Anatomy of Dependence.* Tokyo: Kodansha, 1971.

———. *The Anatomy of Self: The Individual Versus Society.* Tokyo: Kodansha International, 1985.

Dore, Ronald P., ed. *Aspects of Social Change in Modern Japan.* Princeton: Princeton University Press, 1967.

———. *City Life in Japan.* Berkeley: University of California Press, 1963.

Dore, Ronald, and Mari Sako. *How the Japanese Learn to Work.* London: Routledge, 1989.

Earhart, H. Byron. *Religions of Japan: Many Traditions Within One Sacred Way.* San Francisco: Harper and Row, 1984.

Fujiwara, Mariko, and Kermit Carvell. *Japanese Women in Turmoil.* Tokyo: Hakuhodo Institute of Life and Living, 1984.

Fukutake, Tadashi. *Japan's Social Structure: Its Evolution in the Modern Century.* Tokyo: Tokyo University Press, 1962.

———. *Man and Society in Japan.* Tokyo: Tokyo University Press, 1962.

Gelb, Joyce. *Gender Policies in Japan and the United States: Comparing Women's Movements, Rights, and Politics.* New York: Palgrave-Macmillan, 2003.

Haitani, Kanji. "The Paradox of Japan's Groupism: Threat to Future Competitiveness?" *Asian Survey* 30 (March 1990): 237–250.

Hendry, Joy. *Understanding Japanese Society.* London: Routledge, 1989.

Imamura, Anne E. *Urban Japanese Housewives: At Home and in the Community.* Honolulu: University of Hawaii Press, 1987.Jones, Randall S. "The Economic Implications of Japan's Aging Population." *Asian Survey* 28 (September 1988): 958–969.

Jun, Eto. "Japanese Youth: Their Fears and Anxieties." *Japan Quarterly* 21 (April–June 1974): 152–159.

Katsutoshi, Yamashita. "Divorce, Japanese Style." *Japan Quarterly* 33 (October–December 1986): 416–421.

Kim, Hong Nack. "The Korean Minority in Japan." *Korea and World Affairs* 12 (Spring 1990): 111–136.

———. "Japan and China in the 1980's." *Current History* (December 1985).

Klein, Susanne. *Rethinking Japan's Identity and International Role: An Intercultural Perspective.* New York: Routledge, 2002.

Koyama, Takashi. *The Changing Social Position of Women in Japan.* Paris: United Nations Educational, Scientific, and Cultural Organization, 1961.

Lebra, Joyce, et al. *Women in Changing Japan.* Boulder, CO: Westview Press, 1976.

Lebra, Takie Sugiyama. *Japanese Women: Commitment and Fulfillment.* Honolulu: University of Hawaii Press, 1984.

Lee, Changsoo, and George De Vos. *Koreans in Japan: Ethnic Conflict and Accommodation*. Berkeley: University of California Press, 1981.

Linhart, Sepp. "From Industrial to Postindustrial Society: Changes in Japanese Leisure-Related Values and Behavior." *Journal of Japanese Studies* 14 (Summer 1988): 271–307.

Mannari, Hiroshi. *The Japanese Business Leaders*. Tokyo: University of Tokyo Press, 1974

Mitchell, Richard H. *The Korean Minority in Japan*. Berkeley: University of California Press, 1967.

Mouer, Ross, and Yoshio Sugimoto. *Images of Japanese Society: A Study in the Social Construction of Reality*. London: Kegan Paul International, 1986.

Norgren, Tiana. *Abortion Before Birth Control: The Politics of Reproduction in Postwar Japan*. Princeton: Princeton University Press, 2001.

Ogawa, Naohiro. "Economic Implications of Japan's Aging Population." *International Labor Review* 121 (January–February 1982).

Ohnuke-Tierney, Emiko. *Illness and Culture in Contemporary Japan: Anthropological View*. Cambridge: Cambridge University Press, 1984.

Pharr, Susan J. "Women in Japan Today." *Current History* (April 1975): 171–176.

Plath, David. *Adult Episodes in Japan*. Leiden: E.J. Brill, 1975.

———. *The After Hours: Modern Japan and the Search for Enjoyment*. Berkeley: University of California Press, 1969.

Raz, Jacob. *Aspects of Otherness in Japanese Culture*. Tokyo: Institute for the Study of Languages and Cultures of Asia and Africa, 1992.

Rob, Steven. *Classes in Contemporary Japan*. Cambridge: Cambridge University Press, 1983.

Robertson, Jennifer. *Native and Newcomer: Making and Remaking a Japanese City*. Berkeley: University of California Press, 1991.

Robins-Mowry, Dorothy. *The Hidden Sun: Women of Modern Japan*. Boulder, CO: Westview Press, 1983.

Rosenberger, Nancy R. *Gambling with Virtue: Japanese Women and the Search for Self in a Changing Nation*. Honolulu: University of Hawaii Press, 2001.

Rosenberger, Nancy R., ed. *Japanese Sense of Self*. Cambridge: Cambridge University Press, 1992.

Rozman, Gilbert. *Japan's Response to the Gorbachev Era, 1985–1991: A Rising Superpower Views a Declining One*. Princeton: Princeton University Press, 1992.

Ryu, Sanghee. "Why Koreans Oppose the Fingerprint Law." *Japan Quarterly* 32 (July–September 1985): 308–312.

Saisho, Yuriko. *Women Executives in Japan*. Tokyo: Yuri International, 1981.

Sato, Barbara. *The New Japanese Woman: Modernity, Media, and Women in Interwar Japan*. Durham: Duke University Press, 2003.

Shapiro, Michael. *In the Land of the Heartbroken*. New York: Henry Holt, 1989.

Sigler, Jay A., ed. *International Handbook on Race and Race Relations*. New York: Greenwood Press, 1987.

Smith, Herbert W. *The Myth of Japanese Homogeneity: Social-Ecological Diversity in Education and Socialization*. Commack, NY: Nova Science, 1994.

Smith, Robert J. *Japanese Society: Tradition, Self, and Social Order*. Cambridge: Cambridge University Press, 1983.

———. "Gender Inequality in Contemporary Japan." *Journal of Japanese Studies* 13 (Winter 1987): 1–26.

Steslicke, William E., et al. "Medical Care for the Elderly in Japan." *Pacific Affairs* 57 (Spring 1984): 45–89.

Stevens, Carolyn S. *On the Margins of Japanese Society: Volunteer Work with the Urban Underclass.* London: Routledge, 1997.

Takaaki, Mizuno. "Ainu, the Invisible Minority." *Japan Quarterly* 34 (April–June 1987): 143–148.

Tobin, Joseph J., ed. *Re-made in Japan: Everyday Life and Consumer Taste in a Changing Society.* New Haven: Yale University Press, 1992.

Williams, Noel. *The Right to Life in Japan.* London: Routledge, 1997.

Woronoff, Jon. *Japan: The Coming Social Crisis.* Tokyo: Lotus Press, 1980.

Yashushi, Yamaguchi. "The High Noon of Pragmatic Conservatism." *Japan Quarterly* 33 (October–December 1986).

Yoshikazu, Hiraike. "The Dying Japanese Village." *Japan Quarterly* 32 (July–September 1985): 316–320.

The Economy

Abegglen, James C., and George Stark, Jr. *Kaisha: The Japanese Corporation.* New York: Basic Books, 1985.

Akihiro, Kamitsuka. "Reform of the Red Ink Railroad." *Japan Quarterly* 33 (January–April 1986).

Akira, Esaka. "The Nature of the Japanese Corporation." *Japan Echo* 11 (Autumn 1984): 35–43.

Allen, G.C. *A Short Economic History of Modern Japan,* 2d ed. New York: St. Martin's Press, 1981.

Asher, David L. "What Became of the Japanese 'Miracle'?" *Orbis* (Spring 1996): 215–234.

Ballon, Robert J., ed. *Doing Business in Japan.* Rev. ed. Rutland, VT: Charles E. Tuttle, 1968.

Belassa, Bela, and Marcus Noland. *Japan in the World Economy.* Washington, DC: Institute for International Economics, 1988.

Buckley, Roger. *Japan Today.* Cambridge: Cambridge University Press, 1985.

Burks, Ardath W. *Japan: A Postindustrial Power,* 2d ed. Boulder, CO: Westview Press, 1984.

Campbell, John C. *Contemporary Japanese Budget Politics.* Berkeley: University of California Press, 1977.

Campbell, John Creighton, and Naoki Ikegami. *The Art of Balance in Health Policy: Maintaining Japan's Low Cost, Egalitarian System.* Cambridge: Cambridge University Press, 1998.

Carlile, Lonny E., and Mark C. Tilton, eds. *Is Japan Really Changing Its Ways? Regulatory Reform and the Japanese Economy.* Washington, DC: Brookings Institution Press, 1998.

Chalmers, Norma. *Industrial Relations in Japan: The Peripheral Workforce.* London: Routledge, 1989.

Cohen, Jerome B. *Japan's Economy in War and Reconstruction.* Minneapolis: University of Minnesota Press, 1949.

Denison, Edward Fulton. *How Japan's Economy Grew So Fast: The Sources of Postwar Expansion.* Washington, DC: Brookings Institution Press, 1976.

Dore, Ronald P. *Flexible Rigidities: Industrial Policy and Structural Adjustment in the Japanese Economy 1970–1980.* Stanford: Stanford University Press, 1986.

———. *Land Reform in Japan.* London: Oxford University Press, 1959.

Frank, Isaiah, ed. *The Japanese Economy in International Perspective.* Baltimore: Johns Hopkins University Press, 1975.

Gordon, Andrew. *The Wages of Affluence: Labor and Management in Postwar Japan.* Cambridge: Harvard University Press, 1998.

Hatch, Walter, and Kozo Yamamura. *Asia in Japan's Embrace: Building a Regional Production Alliance.* Cambridge: Cambridge University Press, 1996.

Ikegami, Naoki, and John Creighton Campbell. "Japan's Health Care System: Containing Costs and Attempting Reform." *Health Affairs* 23, no. 3 (May–June 2004).

Katz, Richard. *Japan: The System That Soured.* Armonk, NY: M.E. Sharpe, 1998.

———. *Japanese Phoenix: The Long Road to Economic Revival.* Armonk, NY: M.E. Sharpe, 2003.

Lincoln, Edward J. *Arthritic Japan: The Slow Pace of Economic Reform.* Washington, DC: Brookings Institution Press, 2001.

———. *Japan's New Global Role.* Washington, DC: Brookings Institution Press, 1993.

———. *Japan: Facing Economic Maturity.* Washington, DC: Brookings Institution Press, 1988.

Maswood, S. Javed. *Japan in Crisis.* New York: Palgrave, 2002.

Mikuni, Akio, and R. Taggart Murphy. *Japan's Policy Trap: Dollars, Deflation, and the Crisis of Japanese Finance.* Washington, DC: Brookings Institution Press, 2002.

Morris-Suzuki, Tessa. *A History of Japanese Economic Thought.* London: Routledge, 1991.

Muramatsu, Michio, and Masaru Mabuchi. "Introducing a New Tax in Japan." In *Parallel Politics: Economic Policymaking in the United States and Japan,* ed. Samuel Kernell. Washington, DC: Brookings Institution Press, 1991.

Nagaharu, Hayabusa. "Tax Revision for Better or for Worse." *Japan Quarterly* 34 (April–June 1987).

Nemetz, P.N., et al. "Japan's Energy Strategy at the Crossroads." *Pacific Affairs* 57 (Winter 1984–85): 553–574.

Okimoto, Daniel I. *Between MITI and the Market: Japanese Industrial Policy for High Technology.* Stanford: Stanford University Press, 1989.

Ouchi, William. *Theory Z: How American Business Can Meet the Japanese Challenge.* New York: Avon, 1981.

Ozaki, Robert S. "The Humanistic Enterprise System in Japan." *Asian Survey* 28 (August 1988): 830–848.

Peck, Merton J., Richard C. Levin, and Akira Goto. "Picking Losers: Public Policy Toward Declining Industries in Japan." *Journal of Japanese Studies* 13 (Winter 1987): 79–123.

Pempel, T.J. *Regime Shift: Comparative Dynamics of the Japanese Political Economy.* Ithaca: Cornell University Press, 1998.

———. "The Dilemma of Parliamentary Opposition in Japan." *Polity* 8 (Fall 1975).

Roberts, John G. *Mitsui: Three Centuries of Japanese Business.* New York: Weatherhill, 1973.

Sakakibara, Eisuke. *Structural Reform in Japan: Breaking the Iron Triangle.* Washington, DC: Brookings Institution Press, 2003.

————. "Japanese Politico-Economic System and the Public Sector." In *Parallel Politics: Economic Policymaking in the United States and Japan,* ed. Samuel Kernell. Washington, DC: Brookings Institution Press, 1991.

Samuels, Richard J. "The Industrial Destructuring of the Japanese Aluminum Industry." *Pacific Affairs* (Fall 1983): 495–509.

Shimada, Haruo. "Structural Policies in Japan." In *Parallel Politics: Economic Policymaking in the United States and Japan*, ed. Samuel Kernell. Washington, DC: Brookings Institution Press, 1991.

Tatsuno, Sheridan M. *Created in Japan: From Imitators to World-Class Innovators.* New York: Harper and Row, 1990.

Tilton, Mark C. *Restrained Trade: Cartels in Japan's Basic Materials Industries.* Ithaca: Cornell University Press, 1996.

Tsuneo, Iida. "What Japan Can't Do About Trade Friction." *Japan Quarterly* 33 (July–September 1986).

Wan, Ming. *The Political Economy of East Asia: Striving for Wealth and Power.* Washington, DC: CQ Press, 2008.

Wood, Christopher. *The End of Japan Inc.: And How the New Japan Will Look*. New York: Simon and Schuster, 1994.

Education

Beauchamp, Edward R. *Learning to Be Japanese: Selected Writing on Japanese Society and Education.* Hamden, CT: Linnet Books, 1978.

Blumenthal, Tuvia. "Japan's *Juken* Industry." *Asian Survey* 32 (May 1992): 448–460.

Buckley, Roger. *Japan Today*. Cambridge: Cambridge University Press, 1985.

Cummings, W.K. *Education and Equality in Japan*. Princeton: Princeton University Press, 1980.

Dore, Ronald D. *The Diploma Disease: Education, Qualification and Development.* Berkeley: University of California Press, 1976.

Duke, Benjamin C. *Japan's Militant Teachers: A History of the Left-Wing Teachers' Movement.* Honolulu: University Press of Hawaii, 1973.

————. *The Japanese School: Lessons for Industrial America*. Westport, CT: Praeger, 1986.

Fujita, Mariko. "'It's All Mother's Fault': Childcare and the Socialization of Working Mothers in Japan." *Journal of Japanese Studies* 15 (Winter 1989): 67–91.

Goodman, Roger and David Phillips. *Can the Japanese Change Their Education System?* Oxford: Symposium Books, 2003.

Hood, Christopher P. *Japanese Educational Reform: Nakasone's Legacy.* London: Routledge, 2001.

Horio, Teruhisa. *Educational Thought and Ideology in Modern Japan: State Authority and Intellectual Freedom.* Tokyo: University of Tokyo Press, 1988.

Lee, Beverly. "Task Persistence of Young Children in Japan and the US: A Comparative Study." Paper presented at the Western Conference of the Association for Asian Studies, Seattle, October 21–22, 1988.

McVeigh, Brian J. *Japanese Higher Education as Myth.* Armonk, NY: M.E. Sharpe, 2002.

Nomi, Tomoaki. "Inequality and Japanese Education: Urgent Choices." *Japan Focus,* February 11, 2006.

Patience, Allan. "A Comparison of Japanese and Australian University Systems." *Japan Quarterly* 31 (April–June 1984): 206–214.

Pempel, T.J. *Patterns of Japanese Policymaking: Experiences from Higher Education.* Boulder, CT: Westview Press, 1978.

Rohlen, Thomas P. *Japan's High Schools.* Berkeley: University of California Press, 1983.

Schoppa, Leonard J. *Education Reform in Japan: A Case of Immobilist Politics.* London: Routledge, 1991.

Takashi, Inoguchi, and Kabashima Ikuo. "The Status Quo Student Elite." *Japan Echo* 11 (Spring 1984): 27–34.

Thurston, Donald R. *Teachers and Politics in Japan.* Princeton: Princeton University Press, 1973.

Tsuchimochi, Gary. *Education Reform in Postwar Japan: The 1946 Mission.* Tokyo: University of Tokyo Press, 1993.

White, Merry. *The Japanese Educational Challenge: A Commitment to Children.* New York: Free Press, 1987.

Yoneyama, Shoko. *The Japanese High School: Silence and Resistance.* London: Routledge, 1999.

Health Care

Campbell, John Creighton, and Naoki Ikegami. *The Art of Balance in Health Policy: Maintaining Japan's Low Cost, Egalitarian System.* Cambridge: Cambridge University Press, 1998.

Ikegami, Naoki, and John Creighton Campbell. "Japan's Health Care System: Containing Costs and Attempting Reform." *Health Affairs* 23, no. 3 (May–June 2004).

Nomura, Hideki, and Takeo Nakayama. "The Japanese Health Care System: The Issue Is to Solve the 'Tragedy of the Commons' Without Making Another." *BMJ* 331 (September 24, 2005).

Steslicke, William E., et al. "Medical Care for the Elderly in Japan." *Pacific Affairs* 57 (Spring 1984): 45–89.

Public Safety

Aldous, Christopher. *Police in Occupation Japan: Control, Corruption, and Resistance to Reform.* London: Routledge, 1997.

Ambaras, David R. *Bad Youth: Juvenile Delinquency and the Politics of Everyday Life in Modern Japan.* Berkeley: University of California Press, 2006.

Ames, Walter L. *Police and Community in Japan.* Berkeley: University of California Press, 1981.

Bayley, David H. *Forces of Order: Police Behavior in Japan and the United States.* Berkeley: University of California Press, 1976.

Beer, Lawrence W. *Freedom of Expression in Japan: A Study in Comparative Law, Politics, and Society.* Tokyo: Kodansha International, 1984.

Clifford, William. *Crime Control in Japan.* Lexington, MA: D.C. Heath, 1976.

Haley, John O. "Sheathing the Sword of Justice in Japan: An Essay on Law Without Sanctions." *Journal of Japanese Studies* 8 (Summer 1982).

Johnson, David T. "Above the Law: Police Integrity in Japan." *Social Science Japan Journal* 6, no. 1 (2003): 19–37.

————. "Crime and Punishment in Contemporary Japan." *Crime and Justice* 36 (2007): 1–35.

————. *The Japanese Way of Justice: Prosecuting Crime in Japan.* Oxford: Oxford University Press, 2002.

Kaplan, David E., and Alec Dubro. *Yakuza: The Explosive Account of Japan's Criminal Underground.* Reading, MA: Addison-Wesley, 1986.

Katzenstein, Peter J. *Cultural Norms and National Security: Police and Military in Postwar Japan.* Ithaca: Cornell University Press, 1996.

Krauss, Ellis S. *Japanese Radicals Revisited: Student Protest in Postwar Japan.* Berkeley: University of California Press, 1974.

Krauss, Ellis S., Thomas P. Rohlen, and Patricia G. Steinhoff. *Conflict in Japan.* Honolulu: University of Hawaii Press, 1984.

Miyazawa, Setsuo. *Policing in Japan: A Study on Making Crime.* Albany: State University of New York Press, 1992.

National Police Agency, Government of Japan. *White Paper on Police, 1986.* Tokyo: Japan Times, 1986.

Packard, George R., III. *Protest in Tokyo: The Security Crisis of 1960.* Princeton: Princeton University Press, 1966.

Parker, L. Craig, Jr. *The Japanese Police System Today: A Comparative Study.* Armonk, NY: M.E. Sharpe, 2001.

————. *The Japanese Police System Today: An American Perspective.* Tokyo: Kodansha International, 1984.

Ramseyer, J. Mark, and Eric B. Rasmussen. *Measuring Judicial Independence: The Political Economy of Judging in Japan.* Chicago: University of Chicago Press, 2003.

Saga, Junichi. *The Gambler's Tale: A Life in Japan's Underground,* trans. John Bester. Tokyo: Kodansha International, 1991.

Schreiber, Mark. *Shocking Crimes of Postwar Japan.* Tokyo: Yen Books, 1996.

Von Mehren, Arthur T., ed. *Law in Japan: The Legal Order in a Changing Society.* Cambridge: Harvard University Press, 1963.

West, Mark Davis. "The Japanese Legal System: Why Many Americans Fail." *Journal of Northeast Asia Studies* 8 (Spring 1989): 20–38.

Westermann, Ted D., and James W. Burfeind. *Crime and Justice in Two Societies: Japan and the United States.* Pacific Grove, CA: Brooks/Cole, 1991.

Yoshiya, Soeda. "Changing Patterns of Juvenile Aggression." *Japan Echo* 10 (Autumn 1983): 9–17.

Foreign Relations

Bridges, Brian. "Japan and Europe: Rebalancing a Relationship." *Asian Survey* 32 (March 1992): 230–245.

————. *Japan and Korea: From Antagonism to Adjustment.* Brookfield, VT: Edward Elgar, 1993.

Brooks, William L., and Robert M. Orr, Jr. "Japan's Foreign Economic Assistance." *Asian Survey* 25 (March 1985).

Buzan, Barry. "Japan's Future: Old History Versus New Roles." *International Affairs* 64 (Autumn 1988): 557–574.

Calder, A. Kent. "Japan in 1991: Uncertain Quest for a Global Role." *Asian Survey* (January 1992): 32–41.

Cho, Soon. "A Korean View on Korea-Japan Economic Relations." In *Korea and*

Japan in World Affairs, ed. Chin-Wee Chung et al. Seoul: Korea Association for International Relations, 1985.

Curtis, Gerald L., ed. *New Perspectives on U.S.-Japan Relations.* Tokyo: Japan Center for International Exchange, 2000.

"The Defense of Japan: Should the Rising Sun Rise Again?" *Defense Monitor* 13.

Dore, Ronald. *Japan, Internationalism and the UN.* London: Routledge, 1997.

Drifte, Reinhard. *Japan's Foreign Policy.* New York: Royal Institute of International Affairs, 1990.

Drucker, Peter F. "Japan's Choices." *Foreign Affairs* 65 (Summer 1987).

Ducke, Isa. *Status Power: Japanese Foreign Policy Making Toward Korea.* New York: Routledge, 2002.

Duus, Peter. *The Abacus and the Sword: The Japanese Penetration of Korea, 1895–1910.* Berkeley: University of California Press, 1995.

Forsberg, Aaron. *America and the Japanese Miracle: The Cold War Context of Japan's Postwar Economic Revival, 1950–1960.* Chapel Hill: University of North Carolina Press, 2000.

Frost, Ellen L. *For Richer, For Poorer: The New U.S.-Japan Relationship.* New York: Council on Foreign Relations, 1987.

Garrett, Banning, and Bonnie Glaser. "Chinese Apprehensions About Revitalization of the U.S.-Japan Alliance." *Asian Survey* 37 (April 1997).

Hall, Derek. "Japanese Spirit, Western Economics." In *Economic Nationalism in a Globalizing World,* ed. Eric Helleiner and Andreas Pickel. Ithaca: Cornell University Press, 2005.

Hara, Kimie. *Japanese-Soviet/Russian Relations Since 1945: Difficult Peace.* London: Routledge, 1998.

Hellmann, Donald C. *Japanese Foreign Policy and Domestic Politics: The Peace Agreement with the Soviet Union.* Berkeley: University of California Press, 1969.

Hoong, Khong Kim. "Malaysia-Japan Relations in the 1980s." *Asian Survey* 28 (October 1987): 1095–1108.

Hughes, Christopher W. *Japan's Security Agenda: Military, Economic, and Environmental Dimensions.* Boulder, CO: Lynne Rienner, 2004.

Johnson, Chalmers. "The Patterns of Japanese Relations with China, 1952–1982." *Pacific Affairs* 59 (Fall 1986).

Kim, Hong N., and Richard K. Nanto. "Emerging Patterns of Sino-Japanese Economic Cooperation." *Journal of Northeast Asian Studies* 4 (Fall 1988): 29–47.

Koppel, Bruce, and Michael Plummer. "Japan's Ascendancy as a Foreign Aid Power." *Asian Survey* 30 (November 1989): 1043–1056.

Lee, Chong-Sik. *Japan and Korea: The Political Dimension.* Stanford, CA: Hoover Institution Press, 1985.

Mack, Andrew, and Martin O'Hare. "Moscow-Tokyo and the Northern Territories Dispute." *Asian Survey* 30 (April 1990): 380–394.

Mansfield, Mike. "The U.S. and Japan: Sharing Our Destinies." *Foreign Affairs* 68 (Spring 1968).

Mochizuki, Mike. "Japan's Foreign Policy." *Current History* (December 1985): 401–404.

Nester, William R. *The Foundation of Japanese Power: Continuities, Changes, and Challenges.* Armonk, NY: M.E. Sharpe, 1990.

———. *Power Across the Pacific: A Diplomatic History of American Relations with Japan.* Basingstoke, UK: Macmillan, 1996.

Nish, Ian. *Alliance in Decline: A Study in Anglo-Japanese Relations, 1908–23*. London: Athlone Press, 1972.

Njorge, Lawrence M. "The Japan-Soviet Union Territorial Dispute." *Asian Survey* 25 (May 1985).

Ogata, Sadako. "Japan's United Nations Policy in the 1980's." *Asian Survey* 27 (September 1987): 957–972.

Olsen, Edward A. "Evolving U.S.-ROK Security Relations: The Basis for a Korean Maritime Strategy." *Korean Journal of Defense Analysis* 11 (Summer 1990): 161–178.

Orr, Robert M., Jr. "The AID Factor in U.S.–Japan Relations." *Asian Survey* 28 (July 1989): 740–756.

Osaki, Robert S., and Walter Arnold, ed. *Japan's Foreign Relations: A Global Search for Economic Community*. Boulder, CO: Westview Press, 1985.

Pan, Liang. *The United Nations in Japan's Foreign and Security Policymaking, 1945–1992*. Cambridge: Harvard University Press, 2005.

Prestowitz, Clyde, Jr. *Trading Places: How We Are Giving Our Future to Japan and How to Reclaim It*. New York: Basic Books, 1988.

Roy, Denny. "North Korea's Relations with Japan: The Legacy of War." *Asian Survey* 28 (December 1988): 1280–1293.

Saito, Shiro. *Japan at the Summit: Japan's Role in the Western Alliance and Asian Pacific Co-operation*. London: Routledge, 1990.

Satoshi, Takayama. "The Soviet Union Smiles at Japan." *Japan Quarterly* 33 (April 1986): 129–137.

Scalapino, Robert A. *The Foreign Policy of Modern Japan*. Berkeley: University of California Press, 1977.

Shigeo, Omori. "Japan's Northern Territories." *Japan Quarterly* 17 (January–March 1970): 18–26.

Teow, Heng *Japanese Cultural Policy Toward China, 1918–1931: A Comparative Perspective*. Cambridge: Harvard University Press, 1999.

Toby, Ronald P. *State and Diplomacy in Early Modern Japan*. Princeton: Princeton University Press, 1984.

Vogel, Ezra F. "Pax Nipponica?" *Foreign Affairs* (Spring 1986).

Westwood, James T. "Japan and Soviet Power in the Pacific." *Strategic Review* (Fall 1983): 27–35.

Woronoff, Jon. *Japan's Commercial Empire*. Armonk, NY: M.E. Sharpe, 1984.

Zhao, John Quansheng. "The Making of Public Policy in Japan: Protectionism in Raw Silk Importation." *Asian Survey* 28 (September 1988): 926–944.

Defense

Akaha, Tsuneo. "Japan's Nonnuclear Response." *Asian Survey* 24 (August 1984): 852–877.

———. "Japan's Response to the Threats of Shipping Disruptions in Southeast Asia and the Middle East." *Pacific Affairs* 59 (Summer 1986): 255–277.

Buck, James H., ed. *The Modern Japanese Military System*. Beverly Hills, CA: Sage, 1975.

Chapman, J.W.M. *Japan's Quest for Comprehensive Security: Defense, Diplomacy, and Dependency*. New York: St. Martin's Press, 1983.

DiFilippo, Anthony. *The Challenges of the U.S.-Japan Military Arrangement: Com-

peting Security Transitions in a Changing International Environment. Armonk, NY: M.E. Sharpe, 2002.

Drifte, Reinhard. *Arms Production in Japan: The Military Applications of Civilian Technology.* Boulder, CO: Westview Press, 1986.

Gher, Jaime M. "Status of Forces Agreements: Tools to Further Effective Foreign Policy and Lessons to Be Learned from the United States–Japan Agreement." *University of San Francisco Law Review* 37 (Fall 2002).

Harries, Meirion, and Susan Harries. *Sheathing the Sword: The Demilitarization of Japan.* London: Hamish and Hamilton, 1987.

Holland, Harrison M. *Managing Defense: Japan's Dilemma.* Lanham, MD: University Press of America, 1988.

Johnson, Chalmers. "Japanese-Soviet Relations in the Early Gorbachev Era." *Asian Survey* 27 (November 1987): 1145–1160.

Kawahito, Kiyoshi. "The Steel Dumping Issue in Recent U.S.-Japanese Relations." *Asian Survey* 20 (October 1980): 1038–1047.

Keddell, Joseph P., Jr. *The Politics of Defense in Japan: Managing Internal and External Pressures.* Armonk, NY: M.E. Sharpe, 1993.

Kim, Young-sun. "Prospects for US-Japan Security Cooperation." *Asian Survey* 35 (December 1995).

Langdon, Frank C. "The Security Debate in Japan." *Pacific Affairs* 58 (Fall 1985): 397–410.

Lester, Richard K. "U.S.-Japanese Nuclear Relations: Structural Change and Political Strain." *Asian Survey* 22 (May 1982): 417–433.

McIntosh, Malcolm. *Arms Across the Pacific.* New York: St. Martin's Press, 1988.

———. *Japan Re-Armed.* New York: St. Martin's Press, 1986.

Masaru, Yoshitomi. "U.S. Protectionists—Still Fighting Yesterday's War." *Japan Quarterly* 34 (October–December 1987).

Masashi, Ishibashi. "The Road to Unarmed Neutrality." *Japan Quarterly* 31 (April–June 1984): 142–146.

Menon, Rajan, and Daniel Abele. "Security Dimensions of Soviet Territorial Disputes with China and Japan." *Journal of Northeast Asian Studies* 8 (Spring 1989).

O'Hanlon, Michael. "A New Japan-U.S. Security Bargain." *Japan Quarterly* (October–November 1997).

Packard, George R. "The Coming U.S.-Japan Crisis." *Foreign Affairs* 66 (Winter 1987/88).

Purrington, Courtney, and "A.K." "Tokyo's Policy Responses During the Gulf Crisis." *Asian Survey* 31 (April 1991): 307–323.

Rees, David. *Soviet Border Problems: China and Japan.* Conflict Studies, no. 139. London: Institute for the Study of Conflict, 1982.

Sissons, D.C.S. "The Pacifist Clause in the Japanese Constitution: Legal and Political Problems of Rearmament." *International Affairs* 37 (January 1961): 45–59.

Tow, William T. "Sino-Japanese Security Cooperation: Evaluation and Prospects." *Pacific Affairs* 56 (Spring 1983): 51–83.

Weinstein, Martin E. *Japan's Postwar Defense Policy: 1947–1968.* New York: Columbia University Press, 1971.

Woods, J. "Japan's Defense Policies: The Winds of Change." *Defense Force Journal* (September/October 1984).

Zagoria, Donald. "Soviet Policy in East Asia: The Quest for Constructive Engagement." *Korean Journal of Defense Analysis* 11 (Summer).

Index

Louis D. Hayes is a professor of political science at the University of Montana, where he teaches courses on Asian politics, comparative politics, and international relations. He has taught and conducted research in Nepal, Pakistan, Afghanistan, and Japan under Fulbright-Hays and other grants. His previously published books include *The Struggle for Legitimacy in Pakistan, The Crisis of Education in Pakistan*, and *Japan and the Security of Asia.*